STARDOM

What makes a star? Why do we have stars? Do we want or need them?

Newspapers, magazines, TV chat shows, record sleeves – all display a proliferation of film star images. In the past, we have tended to see stars as cogs in a mass entertainment industry selling desires and ideologies. But since the 1970s, new approaches have explored the active role of the star in producing meanings, pleasures and identities for a diversity of audiences. *Stardom* brings together some of the best recent writing which represents these new approaches. Drawn from film history, sociology, textual analysis, audience research, psychoanalysis and cultural politics, the essays raise important questions for the politics of representation, the impact of stars on society and the cultural limitations and possibilities of stars.

STARDOM

Industry of Desire

Edited by
Christine Gledhill

London and New York

First published 1991
by Routledge
11 New Fetter Lane, London EC4P 4EE

Simultaneously published in the USA and Canada
by Routledge
a division of Routledge, Chapman and Hall, Inc.
29 West 35th Street, New York, NY 10001

Phototypeset in 10/12pt Garamond by
Intype, London
Printed and bound in Great Britain by
T J Press (Padstow) Ltd, Padstow, Cornwall

British Library Cataloguing in Publication Data
Stardom: Industry of desire
1. Cinema films. Acting. Stars, history
I. Gledhill, Christine
791.430280922

Library of Congress Cataloging in Publication Data
Stardom: Industry of desire
p. cm.
Includes bibliographical references and index.
1. Motion picture industry – United States – History. 2. Motion
picture actors and actresses – United States. 3. Motion picture
studios – United States. 4. Public relations – Motion picture
industry. I. Gledhill, Christine.
PN1995.62.G85 1991
791.43'028'092273–dc20 91–33813 CIP

ISBN 0 415 05217 3
0 415 05218 1 (pbk)

CONTENTS

Notes on contributors   viii
Acknowledgements   xii

Introduction   xiii
Christine Gledhill

Part I: The system

1 Seeing stars   3
   Janet Staiger

2 The emergence of the star system in America   17
   Richard deCordova

3 The Carole Lombard in Macy's window   30
   Charles Eckert

4 The building of popular images:
   Grace Kelly and Marilyn Monroe   40
   Thomas Harris

5 Fatal beauties: Black women in Hollywood   45
   Karen Alexander

Part II: Stars and society

6 Charisma   57
   Richard Dyer

7 Shirley Temple and the house of Rockefeller   60
   Charles Eckert

8 'Puffed sleeves before tea-time':
   Joan Crawford, Adrian and women audiences   74
   Charlotte Cornelia Herzog and Jane Marie Gaines

v

CONTENTS

9 The return of Jimmy Stewart:
The publicity photograph as text   92
Charles Wolfe

10 Three Indian film stars   107
Behroze Gandhy and Rosie Thomas

11 *A Star is Born* and the construction
of authenticity   132
Richard Dyer

12 Feminine fascinations: Forms of
identification in star–audience relations   141
Jackie Stacey

Part III: Performers and signs

13 Articulating stardom   167
Barry King

14 Screen acting and the commutation test   183
John O. Thompson

15 Stars and genre   198
Andrew Britton

16 Signs of melodrama   207
Christine Gledhill

Part IV: Desire, meaning and politics

17 In defence of violence   233
Michel Mourlet

18 The politics of 'Jane Fonda'   237
Tessa Perkins

19 The glut of the personality   251
David Lusted

20 Pleasure, ambivalence, identification:
Valentino and female spectatorship   259
Miriam Hansen

21 A queer feeling when I look at you:
Hollywood stars and lesbian spectatorship in the 1930s 283
Andrea Weiss

CONTENTS

22 Monster metaphors – Notes on Michael
   Jackson's *Thriller*   300
   Kobena Mercer

   Select bibliography   317
   Index   332

NOTES ON CONTRIBUTORS

Karen Alexander has taught film and video at St Martin's School of Art and works extensively in the field of black people and representation. She is currently writing a fiction film for Channel 4's *TV with a Difference*.

Andrew Britton has lectured at Warwick and Essex Universities and has published widely in film, including articles in *Movie* and *CineAction!* and two monographs, *Cary Grant: Comedy and Male Desire* (Tyneside Cinema, 1983) and *Katharine Hepburn: The Thirties and After* (Tyneside Cinema, 1984).

Richard deCordova teaches film and television studies at DePaul University. His book, *Picture Personalities: The Emergence of the Star System in America*, was recently published by University of Illinois Press.

Richard Dyer teaches film studies at the University of Warwick and is the author of *Stars, Heavenly Bodies* and *Now You See It: Studies on Lesbian and Gay Film*. He is currently working on collections of articles on entertainment, representation and (with Ginette Vincendeau) popular European cinema, before beginning a study of the representation of white identity in film.

Charles Eckert (1927–76), taught at the University of Indiana, Bloomington and at the time of his death was working on a book about Hollywood in the 1930s. 'The Anatomy of a Proletarian Film: Warners' *Marked Women*' appeared in *Film Quarterly*, 27, 2, Winter 1973/4.

Jane Gaines and **Charlotte Herzog** have written several articles together on motion picture costume and co-edited the recent *Fabrications: Costume and the Female Body* (Routledge–American Film Institute, 1990). Herzog, Associate Professor of Art at William Rainey Harper College in Chicago, is currently working on nineteenth-century women illustrators and television as interior decoration; Gaines has just published *Contested Culture:*

The Image, the Voice, and the Law (University of North Carolina Press, 1991) and is Assistant Professor of English at Duke University in Durham, North Carolina.

Behroze Gandhy is an independent television and film producer, most recently for the Channel Four series *On the Other Hand* and Kumar Shahani's *A Ship Aground*. She also works part-time as a film and video examiner for the British Board of Film Classification. She has had articles published in *Screen*, *Framework* and *Movie*, has organised a number of seasons of Indian films at the NFT, ICA and the Pesaro Film Festival, and has lectured in film studies for the University of London.

Christine Gledhill works in the Research Division of the British Film Institute, is a freelance writer and lecturer, and mother of two sons. Her publications include contributions to *Re-Vision, Essays in Feminist Film Criticism* (American Film Institute, 1984), *Female Spectators: Looking at Film and Television* (Verso, 1988) and an edited anthology on melodrama and the woman's film, *Home is Where the Heart Is* (British Film Institute, 1987).

Miriam Hansen is Professor of English at the University of Chicago. Her most recent book is *Babel and Babylon: Spectatorship in American Silent Film* (Harvard University Press, 1991). She is co-editor of *New German Critique* and is currently working on a study of the film theory of the Frankfurt School from Kracauer through Kluge.

Thomas Harris published 'The building of popular images: Grace Kelly and Marilyn Monroe' in *Studies in Public Communication*, 1 (1957).

Barry King currently lectures in media and cultural studies at Widener University, Chester, Pennsylvania. He is a member of the Editorial Advisory Board of *Screen* and the author of a number of articles on acting and the semiotics of performance. He also worked as a consultant for British Actors' Equity on a survey of employment conditions in the UK. This research is continuing in the USA. He is currently completing a text on stardom for Polity Press.

David Lusted is a freelance media educationist and runs The Media Education Agency. Writing includes *Raymond Williams: Film, TV, Culture* (BFI, 1989) and *The Media Studies Book* (Routledge, 1991) as editor. He is cultural consultant to theatre productions and an occasional actor. Currently, he is teaching part-time in the University of Reading sub-department of Film and Drama.

Kobena Mercer has written widely on the cultural politics of race and sexuality in visual representation and currently teaches in the art history department at the University of California, Santa Cruz.

Michel Mourlet is a noted contributor to *Cahiers du Cinema*, a novelist and author of a book on cinema, *Sur un art ignore* (Paris, La Table Ronde, 1965).

Tessa Perkins trained and worked as a stage manager, worked as a secretary, read sociology as a mature student at Essex in the sixties, raised (and is raising) children, taught sociology, researched women's part-time employment and wrote about it, wrote about stereotypes, and Doris Day, and other matters, and is now senior lecturer in communication studies at Sheffield City Polytechnic teaching popular culture, television fictions, feminist film theory, media studies and cultural theory.

Jackie Stacey teaches media studies and women's studies at Lancaster University. She is co-editor of the forthcoming collection *Off-Centre: Feminism and Cultural Studies* (eds Sarah Franklin, Celia Lurey and Jackie Stacey, Unwin Hyman, 1991), and has published articles on feminist theory, representation and sexuality in *Screen*, *Feminist Review* and *Media, Culture and Society*.

Janet Staiger is an associate professor teaching critical and cultural studies of film and television at the University of Texas at Austin. Her most recent book is *Interpreting Film: Studies in the Historical Reception of American Cinema*, forthcoming from Princeton University Press.

Rosie Thomas is a senior lecturer in film theory at Harrow College of the Polytechnic of Central London and is course leader of the BA Hons in Photography, Film and Video. She also works as an independent television producer for Channel Four. She has published and lectured widely on Indian cinema.

John O. Thompson is a lecturer in the School of Politics and Communication Studies, University of Liverpool. He is co-author (with Ann Thompson) of *Shakespeare, Metaphor and Meaning* (1987) and co-editor (with Manuel Alvarado) of *The Media Reader* (1990).

Andrea Weiss is a New York-based writer and filmmaker, whose films include *International Sweethearts of Rhythm* and *Tiny & Ruby, Hell Divin' Women*. She won an Emmy for her research on *Before Stonewall: the Making of a Gay and Lesbian Community*, and co-authored a book by the same title (Naiad Press, 1988). Currently she is completing a book on lesbian representation in the cinema.

Charles Wolfe is Associate Professor of Film Studies at the University of California, Santa Barbara. He is the author of *Frank Capra: A Guide to References and Resources* (G. K. Hall, 1987) and editor of *Meet John Doe* (Rutgers University Press, 1989).

ACKNOWLEDGEMENTS

I would like to thank the Routledge readers of the initial proposal for this anthology, many of whose helpful suggestions it incorporates. Also Jane Armstrong, Helena Reckitt and Penny Wheeler for their encouragement and patience.

INTRODUCTION

This anthology offers a guide to studying the stars and the phenomenon of stardom. Its concern is not individual stars but the cultural and theoretical issues stars raise, although particular stars feature as examples. These are largely American because Hollywood has established the dominant paradigm of both mainstream cinema and stardom. However, Behroze Gandhy and Rosie Thomas' work on Indian stars highlights both the separate identity of other world cinemas and the national specificity of Hollywood.

The hegemony of Hollywood is also a reason for the almost exclusive focus on *film* stars. Yet stardom arose in the theatre before burgeoning in the cinema, a relation discussed in a number of these essays. Latterly, with the break up of the studio system and the emergence of the star as independent producer, freer to choose roles and focus on acting rather than image, the production of the bezazz and gossip of stardom appears to have passed from the cinema to the music industry or sports world. However, as Kobena Mercer's closing analysis of Michael Jackson's pop video, *Thriller*, suggests, while other entertainment industries may manufacture stars, cinema still provides the ultimate confirmation of stardom. So it is argued, the very different forms of television produce personalities not stars; to achieve stardom means breaking out of the medium. Nevertheless, as David Lusted shows, television circulates and elaborates star personae who originate in other entertainment fields.[1]

The star challenges analysis in the way it crosses disciplinary boundaries: a product of mass culture, but retaining theatrical concerns with acting, performance and art; an industrial marketing device, but a signifying element in films; a social sign, carrying cultural meanings and ideological values, which expresses the intimacies of individual personality, inviting desire and identification; an emblem of national celebrity, founded on the body, fashion and personal style; a product of capitalism and the ideology of individualism, yet a site of contest by marginalised groups; a figure consumed for his or her personal life, who competes for allegiance with statesmen and politicians. Not all these facets can be equally represented in an anthology of necessity limited as to length and cost. The major emphasis of this selection is the role of stars in the production, circulation and negotiation of meanings, identities, desires, and ideologies. Other areas of interest such as theatrical stardom, fashion, national stars, performance and kinesics, television personality – which receive limited attention here – may be followed up through the bibliography.

A decade has passed since the publication of Richard Dyer's *Stars* which laid the groundwork for star analysis within film studies.[2] Till then, work on stars had been largely the province of fandom on the one hand or of sociology on the other. While the one focused on personal biographies, the other took stars as industrial marketing devices or social role models – a means of creating and organising audiences and disseminating stereotypes. Film criticism acknowledged the role of the star in films only rarely, generally in connection with genre (the western and John Wayne) or with a director (John Ford and John Wayne). Richard Dyer's approach, combining semiotics and sociology, introduced the notion of the *star text*. He analyses the star image as an intertextual construct produced across a range of media and cultural practices, capable of intervening in the working of particular films, but also demanding analysis as a text in its own right. While semiotics provides methods for analysing such 'texts', sociology asks how they function in society. Thus study of stars becomes an issue in the social production and circulation of meaning, linking industry and text, films and society.

Such issues were consolidated in the seventies under the rubric of cultural studies which responded to and fed an increasing awareness within subordinated cultures of the political significance of representation. In this perspective, stars personalise social meanings and ideologies. Actors become stars when their off-screen life-styles and personalities equal or surpass acting ability in importance. Stardom enacts the power and material success of individual lives. Thus stars are implicated in the critique of individualism, consumerism, and social stereotyping; they become an object of cultural politics.

Such a politics, however, cannot neglect the meanings and pleasures that stars hold out to their audiences. Richard Dyer's work offered two routes into the cultural complexity of stars. If star images relate to social meanings and values, this relation is not one of simple reflection or reproduction. Textual analysis shows how star images reconcile, mask, or expose ideological contradictions. However, the premiss that such images are intertextual and contradictory opens up the possibility for divergent or oppositional readings by different audiences.

Dyer's work on stars coincided with a period of growing interest in psychoanalytic approaches to the cinema, which produced quite a different conception of stars and of their textual and ideological effects. Cinepsychoanalysis is concerned with the source of cinema's fascination for

xiv

audiences, and in particular with the interrelation of psychic and cinematic mechanisms of identification. In this respect, it introduced into star analysis the fundamental issue of desire and pleasure, attempting to answer the question ignored by traditional economic analyses as to *why* stars have the power to sell goods and films. Drawing on Lacanian psychoanalysis, it propounded a homology between the construction of the gendered human subject in language and the 'ideal' spectator of narrative film. Both processes involve identification with human figures – parents and stars. Both, through mechanisms of fetishism and voyeurism, produce apparently coherent, complete and fixed identities through the denial of *difference* – that 'otherness' which femininity, ethnicity or divergent sexualities enact for white, patriarchal society. Such identificatory figures also deny the fact of *process,* whereby meanings and identities are never fixed but in constant flux. In this analogy a film's 'ideal spectator' is a masculine construct, offering identification with the male star as a narrative position of illusory mastery; the female star, as object of the cinematic gaze, is reduced to a male fetish.[3]

For cinepsychoanalysis the culturalist argument that stars become stars because they *mean* something to their audiences sidesteps their ideological nature as mechanisms of identification and neglects the complex subjective processes involved in the production of meaning. From this perspective, the fragmentary, extra-cinematic circulation of the star image acts as an inducement to the consumption of films for their promise to the viewer of completion both of star image and self image through the structure of identification offered by classic narrative. Thus the differences between stars which interest the cultural analyst of social meanings are, as in earlier critiques of mass culture, conceived as marketing devices, enticing audiences to return to the same old scenario of patriarchal subjecthood and bourgeois consumption.[4]

The cultural politics which arose with the various liberation movements of the sixties and onward has been ambivalent about the political effectivity of stars. Some feminists, for example, have found that by virtue of their public prominence and economic power women stars, particularly in the thirties and forties, appeared to offer positive figures of identification. Feminist critics like Molly Haskell argued that such strong, independent female images overrode repressive narrative resolutions and debates arose over the degree to which star figures could be reappropriated to serve politicised imaginations.[5] On the other hand, the female star who inevitably becomes a focus of visual pleasure for an apparently masculine spectator appears the epitomy of the male fetish.

However, against the rejection of the star as a patriarchal construct, groups hardly yet represented – gays and blacks, for example – demand images that recognise marginalised social existences and that offer affirmative identities and fantasies. Moreover, as Jackie Stacey points out, feminists confront a dilemma when considering the popular female audience whose pleasurable identifications with a female star theorised as fetish or voyeuristic object must be counted either narcissistic or masochistic.

By the end of the seventies an impasse appeared to have arisen between a culturalist approach concerned with the social circulation of meanings and identities as 'social facts', analysable for their contradictory ideological effects, and a psychoanalytic concern with the unconscious yet formative processes which underlie such meanings and identities, determining their subjective effects.[6]

This collection, while anthologising a few exemplary pieces from earlier debates, largely represents later developments. These suggest that the impasse of the early 1980s is in the process of breaking up as sociological, semiotic and psychoanalytic approaches begin to inform each other, recasting the object of study and the terms of analysis. Major developments in film history, audience research, and the theorisation of feminine subjectivity have contributed to this rapprochement.

The anthology is organised in four parts: *The system; Stars and society; Performers and signs;* and *Desire, meaning and politics.* These headings represent emphases in approach and focus, not rigid demarcations. The increasing impossibility of separating industry and text, economics and aesthetics, sociology and semiotics, cultural politics and psychoanalysis and all these from history is demonstrated in the overlaps between issues raised across sections. Articles within sections are organised so as to point towards succeeding issues.

The focus of *Part I: The system* is the economic and institutional base of Hollywood stardom. However, the opening essays on the origins of the star system by Janet Staiger and Richard de Cordova raise questions of historiography and cultural context. Whereas traditional film histories stress cinematic specificity and innovation, Staiger and de Cordova consider the complex interaction of economic motives and existing cultural practices in the formation of the star system, in particular its relation to theatrical stardom, the acting profession and the middle-class audiences cinema sought to win.

Exploitation and fabrication are the key themes in Charles Eckert's and Thomas Harris's accounts of respectively the use of stars in tie-ups between film studios and consumer industries and the publicity machines used by the studios to manufacture star images. Karen Alexander situates such industrial processes within the wider context of representation and ideology. Recording the exclusion of black actors from stardom and the severe restriction of their roles in conformity to racist assumptions and arguments, she suggests how 'the system' has material effects in the sphere of subjectivity and identity.

Part II: Stars and society develops this issue, focusing on the cultural role of the star system. Richard Dyer adapts Weber's concept of charisma to suggest that certain performers become stars rather than others because their images embody central but threatened values within a given social conjuncture. Charles Eckert and Charles Wolfe, using respectively neo-Marxist/Freudian structuralism and semiotics, develop sophisticated inter-textual readings of star images as they circulate in society through filmic, political and journalistic discourses. All three writers use textual analysis to interpret the ideological work star images perform in a given society.

Charles Eckert concludes his dissection of the political content of the 'Shirley Temple' text with an ironic acknowledgement of the power of the fantasy she embodies. Charlotte Herzog and Jane Gaines challenge textual interpretation with questions of audience. Drawing on ethnographic approaches, they treat fantasy as practice rather than image, examining the extra-cinematic circulation of Joan Crawford within the discourses of fashion and related social practices of women who remake dresses worn by the stars. Read in relation to Eckert's work, this research suggests a struggle in the arena of fantasy between the exploitative aims of the producer and the appropriations practised by specific groups of consumers.

Behroze Gandhy and Rosie Thomas, writing on three stars who span the history of Indian cinema, raise issues of national cultural context. While under British imperialism, Indian cinema adapts the Hollywood model, producing in different historical moments three distinctive and exemplary female stars. Negotiation is a key term in their analysis of the cultural productivity of these stars, recalling Richard Dyer's work on the relations between star images and ideological contradiction.[7] In the case of Fearless Nadia, Nargis Dutt and Smita Patil, a major contradiction emerges between modernity and tradition. In their images, changing values of motherhood, sexuality, and gender meet with the deeply mythological embedding of the female image in Indian culture. Gandhy and Thomas suggest the powerful resonances produced in the negotiations between such contradictory forces, endowing these stars with a political potency and national status that appear to exceed anything attained by comparable women stars in the West.

Stars and Society concludes by shifting from the functioning of stars within larger social structures and practices to the operation of the social within personal reception. Richard Dyer addresses the ideological con-struct at the heart of Western stardom – the individual person. The star promises what mass society and the human sciences – sociology, Marxism, psychoanalysis – throw into question: intimate access to the authentic self. In this respect, stars offer their audiences not only consumable images or ideological values but personal relationships. This raises the issue of identification with which Jackie Stacey closes this section. In the written responses of self-confessed fans she finds a range of identificatory modes and practices in which, contrary to early cinepsychoanalytic formulations, difference from the star is equally important as recognised similarity.

xvii

In these sections stars are discussed mainly as industrial, ideological and cultural products. *Part III: Performers and signs* focuses on stars as the products of film aesthetics, considering issues of performance, text, genre and mode. Barry King's conception of stardom as the actor's professional adaptation to institutional and filmic conditions of production brings the interdependence of economics and aesthetic forms to bear on star perform-ance. John O. Thompson, drawing on semiotic approaches to textual meaning, suggests how the contribution of particular star images to film texts can be analysed, while Andrew Britton teases out the interrelation between star images and generic conventions. Finally, my own piece con-siders stars as symbolic figures within the broader aesthetic tradition of melodrama, suggesting that stardom with its intense focus on the moral drama of personal identity offers evidence of the continuing activity of the melodramatic imagination in popular culture.

Each section closes on questions of identity and desire which are central to the effectivity of stars. *Part IV: Desire, meaning and politics* applies institutional, semiotic, cultural, and psychoanalytic approaches to ques-tions of desire, audiences, readings, pleasures, meanings and politics. What emerges from these essays written from their different perspectives is a new conception of identity as multiple, ambivalent, contradictory, always in process of construction, but rarely dispensible. Work on feminine sub-jectivity suggests that the construction of the patriarchal, bourgeois subject is a hegemonic project rather than an achieved dominance, needing con-stant reassertion, contested by groups who cannot develop within it, and open to transformation.[8] Stars as objects of desire, 'social hieroglyphs', and role models provide a vital link between personal identity and politics.

Michel Mourlet's opening pean to Charlton Heston defends the violence entailed in the spectacle of masculinity, identifying the energy of desire with male machismo, in an eloquent exemplification of masculine spec-tatorship, at once engaging and disturbing. Miriam Hansen looks at another male star, Rudolph Valentino, renowned as an erotic cult figure for a huge female audience. Reworking cinepsychoanalytic models, she explores the vexing question of female spectatorship, examining those constructions of narrative, camera and the look which anticipate a female audience. Feminine spectatorship is characterised by sexual ambivalence, oscillation, multivalent looking; the construction of the male image for this 'undomesticated female gaze' unsettles the fixity and mastery of mas-culinity, animating the feminine and ethnic 'otherness' of the Valentino persona in an oscillation between passivity and activity, sadism and maso-chism, which offers the female audience a fantasy of 'erotic reciprocity'.

Andrea Weiss focuses on the relation of female audiences to female stars. Given the dearth of representation for lesbian viewers, she asks how oppressed, oppositional identities emerge, looking at the way dominant discourses and cultural practices can be re-read within subcultural lesbian discourses. In the thirties and forties, the Hollywood star system supported strong female stars, often in women's genres, who under pressure of censorship were denied explicit heterosexual expression. The resulting sexually ambiguous, androgynous figures filled a gap in the public imagery available for lesbian audiences, while the circulation of subsidiary texts detailing the off-screen lives of stars was paralleled by a lesbian network of 'gossip' and rumour; consequently lesbian audiences drew on different knowledges from heterosexual audiences. Looking at the films of Dietrich, Garbo and Hepburn, Andrea Weiss suggests the textual strategies which enable alternative sexual identities to be 'read-in' against those preferred in heterosexual discourse.

In that she has been popularly taken to represent the new, 'politicised' woman of the sixties and seventies – feminism's answer to 'what do women want?' – desire and politics meet overtly in Jane Fonda. The issue is whether and how the star as a product of a mass entertainment industry and a singular individual can be used for oppositional politics. Tessa Perkins takes up the question, what and who does 'Jane Fonda' represent? In examining the attempts of the press to contain by belittling the radical claims of her image, the ambivalent responses of many feminists, and the frequent contradiction between image and film roles, Tessa Perkins effectively recasts this question, shifting from the quest for conclusive meaning or political judgement to the proposition that ambivalence itself is part of Jane Fonda's significance. The intense negotiations which her image provokes clarify issues at stake in the public contest around women and politics. Thus stars offer not fixed meanings nor role models but a focus in the continuous production and struggle to define and redefine desires, meanings and identities.

David Lusted's essay on Tommy Cooper, Diana Dors and Eric Morecombe, stars of British variety and cinema who found an alternative existence as television personalities, develops the issue of subcultural contestation in relation to the institution of television, working-class audiences and, implicitly, British culture. While these stars are not overtly political, they represent their audiences through the subcultural readings they make possible. The emphasis here is less on image than on the institutional and generic practices of different television programme formats which they exploit or subvert. Against the individualism of the star system, David Lusted stresses the *social* dimension of the meanings and pleasures offered to working-class audiences by these stars. Their work in other entertainment traditions calls up 'a rich repertoire of reference in popular cultural memory' and through their refusal of television's protocols and their manipulation of its codes, they both represent and collude with working-class experience.

Finally, the different strands of this anthology meet in Kobena Mercer's analysis of the convergence of different media industries, music, performance, the horror film, stardom, sex, race, masculinity and cinema in the transformations of Michael Jackson's face alluded to or performed in the pop-video, *Thriller*. The racial and sexual ambiguity of Jackson's androgynous, Peter Panish, Europeanised black looks, the eroticism of the Afro-American soul singer's voice, and *Thriller's* play with the conventions of the horror film all, in Kobena Mercer's analysis, combine to question prevailing stereotypes of black masculinity. Beyond this, Mercer implies, Jackson's success in popularising black music in white markets is linked to his revitalisation of stardom itself. *Thriller* in its parodic play with show bizz and film genre conventions celebrates both the desire and the horror involved in the metamorphosis which produces the 'star-as-image'. Kobena Mercer's account of Jackson's resonant intertextual image demonstrates that despite the retraction of the Hollywood studio system, stars continue to be produced across the media. More importantly, his analysis shows how a particular star contributes to the arena of cultural contestation when pleasure and politics intersect.

NOTES

1 See D. Kehr, 'A star is made', *Film Comment*, 1986, vol. 15, no. 1, which contrasts the careers of Henry Winkler and John Travolta; J. Langer, 'Television's "personality system"', *Media, Culture and Society*, 1981, vol. 3, no. 1, October, and J. Ellis, 'Stars as a cinematic phenomenon', in *Visible Fictions: Cinema, Television, Video*, London, Routledge & Kegan Paul, 1982.
2 R. Dyer, *Stars*, London, British Film Institute, 1979.
3 See C. Johnston, 'Women's cinema as counter-cinema', in C. Johnson (ed.) *Notes on Women's Cinema*, London, Society for Education in Film and Television, 1973, and L. Mulvey, 'Visual pleasure and narrative cinema', *Screen*, 1975, vol. 16, no. 3, Autumn.
4 See A. Friedberg, 'Identification and the star: A refusal of difference', in C. Gledhill (ed.) *Star Signs: Papers from a Weekend Workshop*, London, British Film Institute Education Department, 1982; P. Cook, 'Star Signs', *Screen*, 1979/80, vol. 20, nos. 3/4, Winter; and John Ellis, 'Stars as a cinematic phenomenon', in *Visible Fictions*, London, Routledge & Kegan Paul, 1982.
5 M. Haskell, *From Reverence to Rape*, New York, Holt, Rinehart & Winston, 1974 and Harmondsworth, Penguin, 1974.
6 See C. Gledhill, 'Introduction' and P. Cook, 'Stars and politics' in C. Gledhill (ed.) *Star Signs: Papers from a Weekend Workshop*, op. cit.
7 For discussion of the concept of negotiation see C. Gledhill, 'Pleasurable negotiations' in D. Pribram (ed.) *Female Spectators*, London, Verso, 1988.
8 See L. Williams, 'When the woman looks' in M. A. Doane, P. Mellencamp and L. Williams (eds) *Revision: Essays in Feminist Film Criticism*, Los Angeles, American Film Institute, 1984 and '"Something else besides a mother": *Stella Dallas* and the Maternal Melodrama' in C. Gledhill (ed.) *Home is Where the Heart Is*, London, British Film Institute, 1987; J. Walker, 'Psychoanalysis and feminist film theory: The problem of sexual difference and identity', *Wide Angle*, 1984, vol. 6, no. 3; D. Pribram, *Female Spectators*, op. cit.

Part I
THE SYSTEM

1

SEEING STARS

Janet Staiger

Having studied film history for little more than five years, my first tendency, like so many youth in any field, is to presume that the older histories are wrong. Revisionist history has, I am sure, as much to do with the Oedipal complex as it has to do with changing ideological conditions which position those of us in more recent times to see facts in new ways. Of interest, then, to me is that the more I study US film history, the more I realise that the older histories are less wrong than I used to believe they were. Often, the problems I have with them are not so much in *fact* but in *emphasis*, or more precisely, in the theoretical assumptions that have determined their choice and arrangement of those facts.

Much work on film historiography has been done recently.[1] What I would like to contribute here is a gesture towards our new histories of film. I am interested in reasserting the value of background study, of study of adjacent facts in understanding events in the area upon which we are focusing. I am concerned that related histories become requisites in any study of film. I also find of interest the effect that a detailed chronology with careful dating of events can have on the representation of the events and their significance. Take, for instance, the standard representation of the appearance of the star system in the US film industry. Both a fuller set of dates and facts and an analysis of the concurrent theatrical scene can significantly alter our version of its appearance and development.

David A. Cook in the most recent extensive history of film repeats the story that in 1910 Carl Laemmle's promotion of Florence Lawrence led to the star system.[2] The reputed reason was Laemmle's competitive move as an independent to take business away from the Patents Trust. Cook is relying on Lewis Jacobs' and Benjamin B. Hampton's histories. Jacobs' version is the more descriptive. Mentioning the movie audiences' attraction to some of the players, Jacobs posits that the Trust manufacturers 'diligently kept [the player's identities] secret, reasoning that any public recognition actors received would inspire demands for bigger salaries'. Laemmle, however, lured Lawrence from Biograph to IMP through an increased salary and promises of publicity. IMP's advertisement in the *Moving*

We Nail a Lie

The blackest and at the same time the silliest lie yet circulated by enemies of the "Imp" was the story foisted on the public of St. Louis last week to the effect that Miss Lawrence (the "Imp" girl, formerly known as the "Biograph" girl) had been killed by a street car. It was a black lie because so cowardly. It was a silly lie because so easily disproved. Miss Lawrence was not even in a street car accident, is in the best of health, will continue to appear in "Imp" films, and very shortly some of the best work in her career is to be released. We now announce our next films:

"The Broken Bath"
(Released March 14th. Length 950 feet.)

A powerful melodrama dealing with a young chap, his sweetheart and a secret society. There's action from the first foot of film and it keeps you five million miles up in the air until the happy finale. This is the kind of film dozens of our customers have been begging us to produce. Watch for it.

"The Time-Lock Safe"
(Released March 17th. Length 960 feet.)

A drama that suddenly and unexpectedly turns into a farce. It is a story of a safe locked on a safe and a wit paid a professional safe cracker a lot of money to get him out, and then found the lock easily... opened the bank, towel bucket and set on the safe at all would you be the ready's reckon for once. Imagine what a corking good picture this would keep in the plot.

We also guarantee another day's pay on July 3rd. Matinee Love Lord Victor Jacobs. It's something disappointed!

Independent Moving Pictures Co. of America
102 West 113th Street, New York City

She's an "Imp"

She's an "Imp"

"Little Mary's" First Appearance in Imp Films!

WILL TAKE PLACE ON MONDAY, JANUARY 9th

Figure 1.2 Moving Picture World

Picture World of 12 March 1910, that an earlier story of Lawrence's death was a lie marked a clever publicity gimmick launching her name and film career as a star. Jacobs then comments that other independents began promoting their players by name while the licensed firms held back. While Jacobs notes that 'Vitagraph, Lubin and Kalem were the first of the licensed groups to adopt the star policy' (withholding the dates of their move to this), he writes that Biograph finally 'was forced into line' in April 1913. Jacobs notes the methods of publicising the new stars: trade photographs, slides, posters in lobbies, 'star post cards' and fan magazines. The latter began with Vitagraph: J. Stuart Blackton financed the *Motion Picture Magazine*. (Again, Jacobs supplies no clear date except to note that in October 1912 one writer requested stories about independent players as well as Trust ones.[3])

Hampton's account, although less dramatic, is similar – except that he sees Mary Pickford as the pivotal personality. Declaring 'Little Mary' as probably 'the first player ever to register deeply and generally in the minds of the screen patrons', Hampton argues that the independents had 'more faith in the box-office appeal of individual players' than a skilled presentation of a story such as D. W. Griffith's work for Biograph. In his account, Hampton stresses IMP's hiring of Pickford at double her Biograph wages and 'movie patrons soon learned that "Mary Pickford" was the name of the actress they had enjoyed so much in Biograph films'. (Again, no dates.) While Hampton notes that the 'star system had operated on the stage for more than a century', he asserts that a great distance existed between legitimate theatre and the movies. Because of the exceptional profitability from low-cost film exhibition, the use of personalities had not previously been part of the 'calculation of possible larger revenues'. Furthermore, the film industry exploited its perceived link with the masses: audiences knew film stars by their first names rather than the more austere Mrs Fiskes of the stage. Hampton discredits the assertion that the independents had better business acumen than the Trust manufacturers; he writes that everyone in the business was surprised by the 'almost hysterical acceptance of personality exploitation'.[4]

One other history of the star system's appearance is worth reviewing before we analyse these accounts. Anthony Slide has meticulously combed through early trade material to determine 'the first film actor to be recognised by the trade press'. He finds a story about Ben Turpin in the 3 April 1909 issue of *Moving Picture World*, an article on Pearl White in 3 December 1910 and a full page on Pickford three weeks later. Slide's interest is in part in whether the actors and actresses might have wanted their identities kept secret because of the stigma of working in the lowly movies. Slide refers to Robert Grau's allegation that most of the film players were not of the upper ranks of legitimate theatre but from 'provincial stock companies'. In addition, Slide dates Kalem's and Vitagraph's publicising of their players' identities. In January 1910, Kalem innovated 'a new method of lobby advertising': the company was making available to exhibitors posters with stills of the players and their names. Vitagraph exploited their players through public appearances, with Florence Turner live on a Brooklyn stage in April 1910.[5]

Several observations can be made about these histories. For one thing, both Jacobs' and Hampton's discussions are parts of larger arguments. In the case of Jacobs, he is attempting to explain the eventual demise of the Patents Trust. His explanation hinges on a neo-classical economic model: the independents were better competitors, innovating product differences which won out over more conservative business practices. Hampton is generally in the same model although he tends to credit the independents with more direct contact with their consumers' desires. Hence, they were better able to gauge public preferences. For both historians, it is in the interest of the larger arguments to credit the independents with the innovation of personality exploitation. Slide is also constructing an argument but not one which revolves around the Independent-Trust competition. He wishes to disabuse us of the conception that either faction prohibited name recognition. His implicit intervention seems to be against Jacobs' assertion that the Trust held back on the promotion of its players.

Figure 1.3 Moving Picture World, 15 January 1910

7

Besides the clear garnering of particular facts to support a larger position, these histories are notorious in their failure to compare dates (and sometimes even to give them). Such an 'unspoken', as Pierre Macherey would note, is symptomatic: dating and comparing dates might become problematic to the arguments.

Furthermore, less symptomatic but rather a practical factor in any writing of large histories is these histories' gaps regarding the background both Hampton and Slide allude to but do not explore – the theatrical star system. Failure to discuss this impairs our comprehension of this important change in the US film industry. The questions then are, what do we learn when we review the events in the related field of the stage? And what happens when we start dating events and comparing them with the ones supplied?

Alfred L. Bernheim's economic history of the legitimate theatre can be a start in supplying the background information we need. Writing in 1929, Bernheim sets out four phases of the US theatre's economic structure through the 1920s. In the earliest years, a 'stock system' typified the theatre. Numerous permanent groups of players were attached to specific theatres where they played most of the season. Leads often changed with the rotation of the play repertoire of the company. About 1820, the 'star system' started. Here a theatre advertised a particular player more than the plays. Moreover, the stars, at first famous foreign actors and actresses, travelled across the country for limited special engagements. A result of the star system was devaluing the local stock players to supporting roles and diminishing the stock players' salaries to provide funds for the stars. Stock companies further declined when the stars began travelling with their own companies. Bernheim dates this 'combination system' as securing economic dominance in the mid-1870s. The stock system almost vanished.[6]

The last phase was the 'syndication' of the theatre business. As combination companies ruled the theatrical stages in the US, efficient booking and distribution between engagements became essential for profit-making. Circuits of theatres developed along which companies regularly travelled. Taking advantage of this, booking agencies supplied the contacts between individual circuits and the attractions. In August 1896, three agencies (Klaw & Erlanger, Hayman & Frohman and Nixon & Zimmerman) formed the Theatrical Syndicate. It asserted a monopoly control through contracts demanding exclusive use of its services by both the entertainers and the theatres. Similar to the upcoming battle between the Patents Trust and the independents in the film industry, not all members of the theatre industry were willing to submit to the Syndicate's terms. The Shuberts (another agency) joined forces with notable independents such as David Belasco and the Fiskes.[7]

Through the 1920s, various battles and truces typified the relations between the two alliances. Occasionally one or the other sought to improve its share of the market, and after a flurry of acquisitions or losses, the two leaders settled into a suspension of hostilities. One period of intense competition occurred between spring 1909 and 1913. While the giants fought, the industry noted a resurgence of stock companies formed by those frozen out of the two alliances. In 1908, trade papers reported over 100 active stock theatres in various cities.[8]

Bernheim notes that the problems of the star system, syndication and the reappearance of the stock company were commonly discussed in the period trade papers. Not an observation by later historians, these difficulties were widely known by the participants.[9]

With this background, let me add a few more facts and set what is known into a more complete chronology. The Edison Company seems to have been one of the earliest and most aggressive companies to promote their players. In September 1909, Edison's publicity paper to exhibitors announced that while others tried to bring out 'some new press story' about their 'stars' lives', Edison knew that it had secured 'some of the best talent the theatrical profession affords'. In its 'stock company', it had 'under contract actors from the best companies in the business, companies such as Charles Frohman, David Belasco, E. S. Sothern, Ada Rehan, Otis Skinner, Julia Marlowe, Mrs Fiske, the late Richard Mansfield'. Subsequently, Edison introduced in its catalogues its stock players with individual lengthy descriptions of their prior experiences and stage successes.[10]

A couple of points can be noted about Edison's publicity move. For one thing, the film industry was barely fourteen years old. It was just experiencing its first real spurt of expansion. The nickelodeon boom, which Robert C. Allen dates as developing about 1906–7,[11] had only recently supplied enough capital growth to support widespread investment in large, permanent staffs. Individual cameramen shooting scenics, topicals and set vaudeville acts had typified the industry up to about 1907. Although companies shot narratives, these were generally chase films and were short: five to fifteen minutes. While some firms such as Vitagraph and Edison had used actors, player employment seems to have been temporary and occasional. Better stage players from the legitimate syndicates or provincial stock companies could hardly have found film work as desirable as their more long-term arrangements. Vitagraph was early in hiring a permanent theatrical director in 1904. Film firms moved to the director system of production only after mass production of narratives increased around 1906–7.[12] Furthermore, investment in theatrical workers was handicapped by the tenuous nature of the business. Only in early 1908 after the courts validated one of Edison's camera patents and Edison licensed most of the manufacturers, allying into the Film Service Association, did the industry witness the necessary stability to turn investment away from patent litigation and into product development. If theatrical workers hesitated to work in motion pictures, it may well have been from

9

the movies' earlier lack of financial remuneration. With the cessation of hostilities, however, Trust members began hiring these professionals.

For another thing, Edison makes this announcement at the beginning of a period (spring 1909–13) of intense warfare between the two theatrical alliances. As noted, the Theatrical Syndicate attempted to secure its monopoly through exclusive-service contracts. A December 1909 *Denver Post* article suggests that the Syndicate forbid its actors and actresses from working on films, reportedly because of the competition by film.[13] Certainly, the Syndicate needed to control its entertainers if it was to maintain its industry position with its allied theatres. Thus, Edison and other film companies (independent as well as Trust) posed a threat to both theatrical alliances. Another factor entered, upsetting the balance. As I will show, other theatrical people agreed to work in films in the next years. Whether or not this was with prearranged consent by their parent alliances or a thrust of independence by the players or a seeking after better salaries and deals needs further investigation. (Probably all the situations occurred.) At any rate, it seems that a Trust manufacturer was one of the earliest to exploit personalities. Furthermore, the timing of that exploitation is related to the current economic conditions in both film and theatre.

In 1910, personality exploitation took off. In February 1910, a *Nickelodeon* writer commented:

> The mere fact that picture theater patrons are demanding of exhibitors a better acquaintance with those they see upon the screen, and that the exhibitors themselves are becoming more and more interested in the personnel of those with whom they have become so familiar in the image, shows that it is an enterprising move on the part of the film maker to gratify that natural desire. The development of the art has produced actors in the silent drama second to none on the legitimate stage, and they richly deserve the public recognition which is even now awaiting them.[14]

In the same issue, Edison had secured space for a picture of its stock company with paragraph biographies of each of the players. Laemmle's ploy with Lawrence in March 1910 occurs even after Kalem is widely advertising its lobby display cards (January), and Vitagraph's Turner does a personal appearance a month later (April). By August, Edison was promoting the appearance of the famous theatrical pantomimist, Mlle Pilar Morin. And in February 1911 one letter writer suggests a series of films to be called 'The Motion Picture Gallery of Theatrical Stars', a suggestion later exploited most notably by Famous Players.[15]

While exhibitors may have been privy to this publicity, we might also ask whether or not the audiences were also seeing stars. Our post-recognition of Pickford's fame may lead us to overemphasise the appearance of her pictures in papers circulated to exhibitors. Methods of building new stars and of advertising recognised ones to the customer included not only lobby cards and personal appearances, but rapidly spread to other gimmicks directed toward the audiences. In April 1911, manufacturers offered to exhibitors slides of favourite players for between-reel entertainment. By then the distribution system was regular enough to allow the exhibitors to publicise with those slides the dates of the favourites' next screen appearances at the local houses.[16]

The credit system in the films also seems to have been started by Edison. In May 1911, the trade papers remarked as 'notable' Edison's innovation of listing the members of the cast on a brief introductory title card. By 1913, Edison had expanded this strategy by showing an image of a player and an intertitle with both the character's and actor's names at the beginning of a film. (Clearly this was a carry-over from theatre programmes.)[17]

Finally, fan magazines were useful in exploiting both the films and the players. Blackton started the *Motion Picture Story Magazine* in late 1910. In February 1911, he announced its format:

> It is a symposium of film scenarios, as the name implies, but these have been amplified by competent writers into really interesting storiettes of the approved magazine style. The first number of over 100 pages, is sumptuously illustrated with engraved reproductions of scenes in the films.

Exhibitors could order copies for sale in the theatres. Within a year, two other such publications were available: *Moving Picture Tales* (published by the trade paper *Motion Picture News*) and the Sunday edition of the *Chicago Tribune*. Publicity directly emphasising the lives and loves of the players quickly followed the first issue of the *Motion Picture Story Magazine*. The trade papers noted the move in May 1911 by the *Cleveland Leader*, 'one of the first' newspapers to devote space to information about film-making rather than just synopses of the films. *Photoplay* also began in 1911.[18]

General profit-making by both the licensed and independent manufacturers soon allowed the hiring of established theatrical stars, not just supporting players. A major factor in this was the increasing investment in longer and more expensive films. Once multiple-reel films became more common in 1911 and 1912, film companies were able to induce these players into moviemaking. As explained in late 1911:

> Single reel pictures marketed on the system that has been built up in this country could result in only moderate profit for each individual production . . .
>
> The new possibility of making it pay to present a distinguished stage star in motion pictures, as is the case of Miss (Mabel) Taliaferro (and Miss Mildred Holland) comes from the multiple-reel pro-

Figure 1.4 A full-page advertisement for Mildred Holland in *Moving Picture World*, 30 December 1911

Figure 1.5 Double-page spread for Sarah Bernhardt in *Moving Picture World*, 10 February 1912

ductions, only recently becoming popular. With single-reel pictures, the project would have been impracticable unless a series had been resorted to. But with a three-reel film netting almost three times the money of an ordinary release, and with the chance of the picture having a long life with reprint orders in the future, the manufacturer can see profit ahead to warrant the exceptional outlay.[19]

Even then there were fears that the distribution system could not provide sufficient profits, but by 1912 the 'star system' – with legitimate theatrical stars – arrived. Publicity promoted 'all star casts' from the Royal Theatre of Copenhagen, Sarah Bernhardt and the 'All Star' Film Company. Legitimate stars in films of 1912 included Rejane, Goodwin, Mrs Fiske, James K. Hackett and James O'Neill. While many of the eventual movie stars rose through the film ranks, in 1912 'stars' were the leading theatrical players, and audiences were certainly seeing them and knowing they were seeing them.[20]

What does this background information and a more precise chronology do to our understanding of the innovation of the star system into films? We might note, for one thing, that in the theatrical business it was acknowledged at the time that the star system may not have been to its total advantage. The syndication of the industry had not been readily acceded to by all its participants. If the film companies labelled their player groups as 'stock companies', they were in some ways harkening to the contemporary dispute between the star system and the older stock system. Biograph's hesitancy to emphasise players rather than plays may have been a move to keep salaries in line; it may also have been a tactic in keeping with one strand in a debate – a strand which eventually lost out to the more dominant one of stars. Bernheim writes that the theatre business found heartening the 1905 success of *The Lion and The Mouse* in which no established player was featured.[21] Biograph's actions can be more readily understood as perhaps a poor business calculation but not one without some rationale.

In addition, it is evident that neither Trust nor independent manufacturers dominated in the strategy of exploiting stars. While independents may have been more aggressive in employing players that appealed to the audiences even this needs more research before we draw a conclusion about product competition.

Whether Hampton is right that film exploitation of personalities took a different twist than in theatre is worth research. Richard deCordova has made a useful contribution in this direction. He has argued recently that film discourse about the players shifted in the early teens from information about their professional lives to their personal lives. This was due, he believes, to a backlash against the notoriety of the theatrical stars' lives and in an attempt to promote an image of the moral healthiness of cinema.

14

It had, as well, ideological implications for the reception of the films themselves.[22]

Finally, it is important to discover when players actually were advertised as more important than the plays – the visible sign, according to Bernheim, of a move to a star system. Seeing stars, it seems, is much more complex than our earlier histories would have us believe – but important to our revisionist histories of cinema.

NOTES

First published in *The Velvet Light Trap*, 20 (Summer 1983).

1 Several excellent essays are: J. Douglas Gomery, 'The coming of the talkies: invention, innovation, and diffusion', in *The American Film Industry* (ed.) Tino Balio (Madison: University of Wisconsin Press, 1976), 193–211; Geoffrey Nowell-Smith, 'On writing of the history of the cinema: some problems', *Edinburgh '77 Magazine*, 2 (1977), 8–12; Robert C. Allen, 'Contra the chaser theory', *Wide Angle*, 3, 1 (1979), 4–11; Edward Branigan, 'Color and cinema: problems in the writing of history', *Film Reader*, 4 (1979), 16–34; and Kristin Thompson and David Bordwell, 'Linearity, materialism and the study of the early American cinema', *Wide Angle* (forthcoming).

2 David A. Cook, *A History of Narrative Film* (New York: W. W. Norton, 1981), 40. Also see similar accounts in Robert Sklar, *Movie-Made America: A Cultural History of American Movies* (New York: Vintage, 1976), 40, and Gorham Kindem, 'Hollywood's movie star system: a historical overview', in *The American Movie Industry: The Business of Motion Pictures* (ed.) Gorham Kindem (Carbondale: Southern Illinois University Press, 1982), 80–2.

3 Lewis Jacobs, *The Rise of the American Film: A Critical History*, 2nd edn (New York: Teachers College, Columbia University, 1968), 86–9.

4 Benjamin B. Hampton, *History of the American Film Industry: From its Beginnings to 1931* (1931, rpt, New York: Dover, 1970), 85–9.

5 Anthony Slide, 'The evolution of the film star', *Films in Review*, 25 (December 1974), 591–4. One other account of the star system is worth reading: Gerald D. McDonald, 'Origin of the star system', *Films in Review*, 4 (November 1953), 449–58. Although McDonald provides a number of previously unmentioned details, the information is undocumented. In addition, his causal analysis for the change is similar to Jacobs' and Hampton's positions.

6 Alfred L. Bernheim, *The Business of the Theatre: An Economic History of the American Theatre, 1750–1932* (1932, rpt, New York: Benjamin Blom, Inc., 1964), 2–33.

7 Bernheim, *Business*, 34–109.

8 On the revival of the stock company in the first decade of 1900, besides Bernheim, see J. Dennis Rich and Kevin L. Seligman, 'New Theatre of Chicago, 1906–1907', *Educational Theatre Journal*, 26, 1 (March 1974), 53–68. Bernheim also notes as significant the Little Theater, amateur and experimental groups which developed in part from the European movements in theatre starting in 1887 with André Antoine's The Free Theatre. Little Theater is usually dated as emerging in the United States in 1911–12. See Bernheim, *Business*, 101–3, and Oscar G. Brockett, *The Theatre: An Introduction* (New York: Holt, Rinehart and Winston, 1964), 284–6.

9 See, for instance, the discussion on writing plays for specific actors: Jules Eckert

Goodman, 'Concerning the "Star" play', *The New York Dramatic Mirror* (hereafter *NYDM*), 65, 1695 (14 June 1911), 5.

10 'The Edison Stock Company', *The Edison Kinetogram* (hereafter *EK*), 1, 4 (15 September 1909), 13; 'Our Stock Company', *EK*, 1, 5 (1 October 1909), 13–14.

11 Robert C. Allen, *Vaudeville and Film 1895–1915: A Study in Media Interaction* (New York: Arno Press, 1980), 23–92.

12 Janet Staiger, 'The Hollywood mode of production: The construction of divided labor in the film industry' (Unpub. Ph.D. Diss., University of Wisconsin-Madison, 1981), 89–101.

13 'The Essanay Company out west', *The Denver Post*, rpt in *Moving Picture World* (hereafter *MPW*), 5, 23 (4 December 1909), 801–2, rpt in George C. Pratt, *Spellbound in Darkness: A History of the Silent Film*, rev. edn (Greenwich, CT: New York Graphic Society, Ltd, 1973), 127–30.

14 'Moving picture personalities', *The Nickelodeon* (hereafter *NKL*), 3, 3 (1 February 1910), 60.

15 Oliver Kendall, 'Faces we see on the screen', *NKL*, 3, 3 (1 February 1910), 63–5; 'From tyranny to liberty', *EK*, 3, 2 (15 August 1910), 11; 'Letters to "The Spectator"', *NYDM*, 65, 1676 (1 February 1911), 30.

16 'Your favorite player on a slide', *Motion Picture News* (hereafter *MP News*), 4, 15 (15 April 1911); (untitled), *MPW*, 8, 18 (6 May 1911), 999.

17 '"Aida" (Edison)', *MPW*, 8, 20 (20 May 1911), 1140. Also see: Earl Theisen, 'The story of slides and titles', *International Photographer* (hereafter *IP*), 5, 11 (December 1933), 6; Earl Theisen, 'The evolution of the motion picture story, part II', *IP*, 8, 4 (May 1936), 12; J. Berg Esenwein and Arthur Leeds, *Writing the Photoplay* (Springfield, MA: The Home Correspondence School, 1913), 92–3.

18 'The Motion Picture Story Magazine', *MPW*, 8, 5 (4 February 1911), 228; 'Film stories in Sunday papers', *NYDM*, 67, 1725 (10 January 1912), 30; 'Cleveland', *MPW*, 8, 20 (20 May 1911), 1126.

19 'Spectator', '"Spectator's" comments', *NYDM*, 66, 1721 (13 December 1911), 28.

20 'Spectator', '"Spectator's" comments', *NYDM*, 66, 1721 (13 December 1911), 28; 'Will present big productions', *MPW*, 11, 2 (13 January 1912), 109–10; Robert Grau, 'Will vaudeville's salary uplift itself in picturedom', *MP News*, 5, 6 (10 February 1912), 10: 'The independent situation', *MPW*, 12, 11 (15 June 1912), 1016; William Lord Wright, 'William Lord Wright's page', *MP News*, 7, 2 (11 January 1913), 14.

21 Bernheim, *Business*, 26.

22 Richard deCordova, 'The emergence of the star system', Athens, Ohio, 1982 Ohio University Film Conference, 7–10 April 1982.

2

THE EMERGENCE OF THE STAR SYSTEM IN AMERICA

Richard deCordova

In standard histories the forces which put the star system in place are reduced to the play of personal initiative on the one hand and a reified notion of the public desire on the other. The star system is not simply the creation of one person or even one company; nor is the desire for movie stars something that arose unsolicited.

The emergence of the star system can perhaps best be seen as the emergence of a knowledge and analysed in these terms. Before 1909 virtually none of the players' names were known to the public, but by 1912 most of them had been 'discovered'.[1] It is clear from this example that the 'picture personality' was the result of a particular production and circulation of knowledge. Studio publicity departments, films and fan magazines produced and promulgated this knowledge. In this paper I want to examine the rules by which this knowledge was produced and the various transformations these rules underwent.

The emergence of the star system involved a strict regulation of the *type* of knowledge produced about the actor. I will argue that the development of this system was effected through three significant transformations in this regard. These can be listed in the order of their appearance: (1) the discourse on acting, (2) the picture personality and (3) the star.

Before discussing these three stages individually, let me note that the appearance of the second, the picture personality, did not mean the disappearance of the first, the discourse on acting (or for that matter, the third the disappearance of the second). This transformation can best be characterised as a progressive overlaying of discourses and knowledges about a particular site – the actor.

THE DISCOURSE ON ACTING

It is perhaps misleading to say that this site was *the actor* as if this site was constituted in itself. Before 1907 there was no discourse on the film actor. Textual productivity was focused elsewhere, for the most part on the apparatus itself, on its magical abilities and its capacity to reproduce

17

Figure 2.1 Mary Pickford promotion: 'Hulda from Holland', 1916

the real. It was obvious that people were represented on the screen, but the thought that these people were actors was very likely not considered. Acting was a profession of the legitimate stage, quite foreign to the milieu of the cinema's early development. The stage, after all, not only had actors, but also stars. The cinema's complete non-observance of these forms prior to 1907 is a testament to its relatively thoroughgoing disassociation from a theatrical model of representation.

Journalistic discourse of the time focused primarily on the scientific aspects of the apparatus. Eric Smoodin has convincingly demonstrated that this discourse characterised film as a product independent of human labour. This 'reification of the apparatus' is clear in the titles of articles such as 'Moving Pictures and the Machines which Create Them' and 'Revelations of the Camera'.[2]

Around 1907 another discourse began to supersede this discourse on the apparatus, one which included and eventually placed into the foreground the role of human labour in the production of film. This should not be viewed as a demystification of the means of production but rather as the regulated appearance of a certain kind of knowledge. This knowledge entered into a struggle destined to resituate the site of textual productivity for the spectator away from the work of the apparatus itself. A number of potential 'sites of productivity' were involved in this struggle – the manufacturer, the cinematographer (or director) and the photoplaywright – but of course it was the actor/star that finally became central in this regard.

It is in this context that one must view the earliest appearances of the discourse on acting. In 1907 a series of articles appeared in *Moving Picture World* entitled 'The Cinematographer and Some of His Difficulties'. These articles, geared towards describing the work of the cinematographer, offered the following definition of the picture performer.

> Those who make a business of posing for the kinetoscope are called 'picture performers' and many a hard knock they have to take. Practically all of them are professional stage people, and while performing on Broadway at night they pick up a few dollars day times in a moving picture studio. In a variety show, therefore, it sometimes happens that the same tumblers who a moment ago were turning handsprings and somersaults in real life, again appear in such roles as the traditional 'Rube' and the 'green goods man', but only in a phantom form upon the pictured screen.[3]

This article and many which follow it use the verb 'pose' to describe the activity of those who appear in films. Before the discourse on acting this activity was understood largely in terms of a photographic tradition. Even after the discourse on acting emerged we can see a sort of struggle between a photographic and a theatrical conception of the body, between posing and acting. There are important links between this contradictory situation and the changes that were taking place in the industry at the time. Robert C. Allen has noted that 'between 1907–1908 a dramatic change occurred in American Motion Picture Production; in one year narrative forms of cinema (comedy and dramatic) all but eclipsed documentary forms in volume of production'.[4] Even more remarkable is the shift in the percentage of *dramatic* productions from 17 per cent in 1907 to 66 per cent in 1908.[5] There is little doubt that this shift in production supported the contention that people acted in films, but it is not surprising that the suddenness of the documentary's demise left behind powerful vestiges of film's association with a photographic tradition.

The activity of those who appear in films was the subject of a number of stories in this early series of articles. All of these stories followed the same basic pattern. An example can be offered here. It is a story of the filming of a bank robbery scene:

> In the most realistic way, the 'robbers' broke into the bank, held up the cashier, shot a guard 'dead' who attempted to come to the rescue, grabbed up a large bundle of money, and made their escape. Thus far all went well. The thieves were running down the street with the police in pursuit, just as the picture had been planned, when an undertaker, aroused by the racket, looked out of his shop. One glance sufficed to tell him that the time had come at last when he might become a hero. The 'robbers' were heading toward him, and, leaping into the middle of the sidewalk, he aimed a revolver at the foremost fugitive with the threat: 'Stop, thief, or I'll blow your brains out.'[6]

The real undertaker apprehended both of the fictional bandits and refused to release them until he was convinced by the head of the bank that the robbery had been staged.

This story plays upon a confusion between the filmic, the profilmic and the real, but it does so primarily as a way of making distinctions between the three. The possibility of these distinctions was a necessary condition for the emergence of what is called here the 'picture performer'. First of all, this emergence depended upon a knowledge of the performer's existence outside of the narrative of the film itself. By introducing the contingency of the profilmic event into what is otherwise a simple retelling of the planned narrative of the film, such stories differentiate the profilmic from the filmic and ascribe to the former a relatively distinct status. Another narrative is set forth (separable from that of the film) which takes as its subject the performer's part in the production of film.

More obviously perhaps, the story distinguishes the profilmic from the real. A character mistakes the arranged scene for an event in real life. In straightening the two out the character – and the reader – must confront

20

the fictional status of that which is photographed by the camera. This attention to the fact that the scenes enacted in moving pictures were 'not real but feigned' had a direct bearing on the status of those who appeared in films; it worked to establish the filmed body as a site of fictional production.

Structured through a play upon the 'reality' of filmic representation, such stories refer one to the reality *behind* that representation: that is, to the creative labour of those who appear in films. What I want to turn to now is an examination of the way in which this labour was symbolised through a discourse on acting. This symbolisation was somewhat tentative in these early articles. Note, for instance, the use of the term 'performer' in the definition quoted previously. Its connotations of popular entertainment undercut any claim that the art of the legitimate actor could be translated directly to the screen. Such claims would proliferate in the next few years, but in 1907 film acting was patently different from legitimate acting. The following quote, from a later instalment of 'The Cinematographer and Some of His Difficulties', stresses these differences while at the same time valorising the talent of the film actor.

> [In moving pictures] regular actors are engaged and usually first class actors because they must understand how to express an emotion of a happening perfectly with gestures and action. The actor must understand the trick thoroughly, however, or he is no good for this purpose. The actor who is too reposeful on the stage and expresses his meaning and feeling merely by the tones of his voice or in subtle movements is utterly worthless for the moving picture. Sometimes the actor who has risen no higher than to scrub parts or the chores can be made good use of for the moving pictures because of his great proneness to gesture and motion.[7]

Although film acting is identified with stage acting here, it is clear that the film actor's responsibility is to a large extent restricted to his/her function of rendering the action comprehensible. A reviewer of *The Cobbler and the Millionaire* offered one of the earliest assessments of 'good acting' precisely on these criteria. 'The acting in this film is so good that one could follow the story even without a title.'[8] Psychological nuance is not particularly at issue here: the emotion expressed is viewed in broad, unindividuated terms: 'the emotion of a happening'.

This emphasis on plot and action sharply differentiated film from the legitimate stage, both in the type of acting it required, and, more prominently, in the type of film it implied. Early genres such as the chase film relied wholly on action, casting performers only in broad social types (the policeman, the green goods man, etc.). The disjunction between the types of films being produced and the artistic pretensions of the discourse on acting often manifested itself in a rather ironic treatment of film actors.

The words 'actor' and 'artist' usually appear in quotes in these early articles. In 'The Canned Drama' Walter Prichard Eaton parodies the contention that professional actors appear in films by distinguishing between two horses on a movie set – one was a professional actor and the other merely an amateur.⁹

By 1908, a number of films had begun to appear which were used as proof that the art of acting could be translated to the screen. The most important of these, by far, were the French Films d'Art of the Pathé Company. The following quotes point clearly to the importance of these films in so far as the discourse on acting is concerned.

> The greatest improvement at present (and there is still plenty of room for more) is along the line of dramatic structure and significant acting. Does it sound silly to talk thus pedantically, in the language of dramatic criticism, about moving pictures? If you will watch a poor American picture unroll blinkingly, and then a good French one, you will feel that it is not silly after all.¹⁰

> With reference to the Pathé film d'art, 'The Return of Ulysses', to which I referred last week, it is interesting to point out that the story was written by Jules Lemaître, of the Acadamie Française, and the principal characters are taken by Mme Bartet, MM Albert Lambert, Lelauny and Paul Mounet, all of the Comédie Française, Paris. This is equivalent to David Belasco and his Stuyvesant Company doing work for the Edison Company. Again I say, American Manufacturers please note!¹¹

The aesthetic categories engaged by the discourse on acting and supported by these films involved a clear articulation of class difference. References to the art of acting in film worked to legitimise the cinema and dissipate the resistance of those strata of the middle and upper classes that had been left out of the nickelodeon boom. A new site of consumption emerged geared very much towards those with pretensions of refinement and taste.

In 1909 a number of articles began to appear which opposed action and acting across class lines. The following quote is virtually manifesto in this regard.

> The majority of 'our public' insist on action in a picture. . . . There must be somethin' doin' every minute. On the other hand there are a large number who demand good acting, who like 'delicate touches', who want to see the heroine LOOK as if her lover's life was in danger and not as though she were ordering a plate of 'beef and' at Dolan's.¹²

The writer goes on to valorise those films which combine both action and acting, and which therefore appeal to both classes of people. This is significant since it is the creation of a mass audience that is at issue here,

Figure 2.2 Sarah Bernhardt

not the expatriation of any particular segment of it. The discourse on acting was an important part of a larger strategy which asserted the respectability of the cinema and worked to guarantee the expansion of the audience during these years.

The discourse on acting was fundamental to the institutionalisation of the cinema in another sense. I have argued that this discourse superseded the discourse on the apparatus and worked to resituate the site of textual productivity in human labour. This resituation signalled a new form of product individuation more in keeping with an increasingly rationalised production system; the audience's appreciation would no longer be confined to the magic of the machine or to the socio-cultural interest of the

23

move from fascination w/
apparatus → the site
of fascination is human
labour, "acting"

thing photographed but would involve the possibility of discriminating –
at the level of performance – between specific films.

THE PICTURE PERSONALITY

The picture personality was to be the principal site of product individuation throughout this period. By 1909 picture personalities had begun to
appear, either by their own names or by names the public assigned them.
This is usually considered the beginning of the star system. It is indeed
around this time that the star emerges as an economic reality. However,
I have made a distinction between the picture personality and the star,
assigning the emergence of the former to the year 1909 and the latter to
1914. There is a regulation of knowledge specific to the picture personality
which distinguishes it significantly from the star.

Three predominant forms of knowledge emerged to produce the picture
personality. The first pertained to the circulation of the name. Through a
dual movement of concealment and revelation the player's name was
constituted as a site of knowledge. The manufacturers' refusal to reveal
the names of their players is greatly exaggerated. Biograph is the only
company that followed this policy with any consistency. Magazines, newspapers and advertising constantly named names (and obviously with the
co-operation of the manufacturers); in fact, there was an intense proliferation of knowledge about the picture personalities during this time.

What has undoubtedly misled many historians is that this knowledge
emerged in an explicitly secretive context. The 'truth' of the human labour
involved in film was constituted as a secret, one whose discovery would
be all the more pleasurable since it would emerge out of ostensible attempts
to conceal it.[13] One of the major reasons given for the supposed concealment of the players' names, for instance, was that the players were in fact
legitimate actors (perhaps well known) who did not want to risk their
reputations by being discovered in films. Such an explanation hardly
resolves the enigma, however; it only compounds it, doubling its status
as secret. Fans who did not know the name of a particular actor were to
assume, by this logic, that it was because that actor was well known.

Early fan magazines depended to a large extent on the pleasure the
public took in knowing the players' names. Such features as *Motion Picture
Story Magazine*'s 'Popular Player Puzzle' appealed precisely to this. The
following puzzle, for example, was proposed: 'A favorite pet of the
children'. The answer was the actor John Bunny.[14]

The magazine also had a question and answer section. Almost all of the
questions asked who had the lead in a particular picture. These sort of
questions point to the difficulty of separating the circulation of the players'
names and the circulation of the films they were in. What is at stake here
is a type of identification in the most usual sense of the word: the

Figure 2.3 The picture personality as site of product individuation

identification of an actor in a specific film with a name. However, this identification extended well beyond the single film. What the name designated above all was a form of intertextuality, the recognition and identification of an actor from film to film.

This intertextuality emerged as a measure of the increasing regularity and regulation of the cinematic institution – both in its product (the same actors appeared regularly) and more crucially, in terms of its audience, which had to go to the cinema often for this intertextual meaning to arise. This intertextuality can be posited as the second form of knowledge which constituted the picture personality. This knowledge however, was not produced solely in the cinema; journalistic discourse supported it as well. The most important point to make about this intertextuality is that it restricted knowledge about the players to the textuality of the films they were in. The term 'picture personality' is itself evidence of this restriction. The site of interest was to be the personality of the player as it was depicted in film. In one article Frank Lessing explained his success in acting by saying, 'one cannot express more than one really is'.[15] The correct formulation would have been, 'one is no more than one expresses on film', since this defines fairly accurately the tautological existence of the picture personality.

A third type of knowledge that constituted the picture personality pertained to the professional experience of the actor. In so far as this knowledge related to the actor's previous film experience it worked to establish the intertextual space between films discussed earlier. However, this knowledge often referred to the actor's stage experience and can be seen as a continuation of the discourse on acting.

> The great success of Miss Lottie Briscoe is not surprising when it is remembered that she was, for years, with that master of dramatic art, Richard Mansfield. Miss Briscoe has already won a host of admirers in the motion picture world by her clever and her pleasing personality.[16]

I have discussed the way this discourse on acting worked to legitimise film through reference to the acting of the stage. It is important to note that this legitimation was effected entirely at the level of profession. The emergence of the picture personality did not signal any significant shift in this regard. One writer, attempting to explain why people were falling in love with matinee idols, concluded that it proved that the idol's 'acting, as well as their personality must be pretty much the same thing'.[17] Knowledge about the picture personality was restricted to the player's professional existence – either to his/her representation in films or to his/her previous work in film and theatre.

THE STAR

It is along these lines that one can distinguish the star from the picture personality. The star is characterised by a fairly thoroughgoing articulation of the paradigm professional life/private life. With the emergence of the star, the question of the player's existence outside his/her work in films entered discourse.

This question entailed a significant transformation in the regulation of knowledge concerning the player. The manufacturers would no longer be able to restrict knowledge about the players to the textuality of the films they were in. Thus, the absolute control the studios had over the picture personality's image was, in one sense, relinquished, but only so that it could be extended to another sphere. The private lives of the stars emerged as a new site of knowledge and truth.

In 1914 a short story appeared in *Photoplay* entitled 'Loree Starr – Photoplay Idol'.[18] It is most remarkable for its subtitle – 'A Fascinating Serial Story Presenting a New Type of Hero'. This new hero is precisely the star as distinguished from the picture personality. It is around this time that the star becomes the subject of a narrative which is quite separable from his/her work in any particular film.

Here is a quote from 1916 which quite explicitly poses the question of the star: 'And even in these days of the all-seeing camera-eye there are scores of heroic deeds, of patently self-sacrificing acts, performed by the film folk which never reach pictures or print.'[19] It ends by asking – 'Is your REEL hero ever a REAL hero?'

So, private and professional become two autonomous spheres that can be articulated in paradigm. It is important to note however, that these two spheres are constituted in what might be called an analogous or redundant relation. The real hero behaves just like the reel hero. The knowledge which emerged concerning the star was restricted to the parameters of this analogy. The private life of the star was not to be in contradiction with his/her film image – at least not in terms of its moral tenor.[20] The two would rather support each other. The power of the cinema was thus augmented by the extension of its textual and ideological functioning into the discourse on the star.

Two related strategies were effected through the star discourse. The first involved a kind of backlash against the theatre. The private lives of theatrical stars had quite commonly been associated with scandals of all sorts. The star discourse involved a work which disassociated the film star from this aspect of the theatrical tradition. Harry S. Northrup explains his reasons for not returning to the stage:

What? The Stage? Not on your life, not if I know myself . . . Look around you here. What more could a man ask than this? A comfortable, attractive home, fifty-two weeks in the year income. Could the stage give me that? It could not.[21]

The following quote is even more explicit.

Stage life, with its night work, its daytime sleep, its irregular meals, its travelling and close contact, does not make for a natural existence and throws a so-called glamour over many people. Contrast its possibilities with those of the picture studio. In the latter place work is done in regular office hours – daylight work; no glamour of night, of orchestra, of artificial light. A player is located in one neighbourhood and is recognised as a permanent and respectable citizen. Evenings can be spent at home, and the normal healthiness of one's own fireside is an atmosphere conductive to refining influences. Healthy outdoor daytime work and a permanent circle of friends make for a sane and non-precarious existence. The restlessness and loneliness attendant on a life of travel is also eliminated.[22]

What is undoubtedly at stake here is the moral healthiness of the cinema as an institution. The discourse on the star worked to assert that the cinema was, 'at its source', a healthy phenomenon.

This healthiness was proven largely through reference to the stars' families. One of the major differences between the picture personality and the star is that the latter supports a family discourse. In fact, it doubles the family discourse produced in the films of the day.[23] The narrative which emerged to create the star was entrenched in the same forms of representation as the films in which the stars acted.

The redundancy of these two spheres is linked to the specific articulation of power and knowledge which characterises the emergence of the star system. As the private lives of the players became a valorised site of knowledge, a work of regulation was effected which kept this knowledge within certain bounds. In this way, the star system worked to support the same ideological project as the films of the day. A great deal of work needs to be done on the apparent failure of this regulation in the star scandals of the early twenties, and the relation this has to the creation of the Hays Office in 1922.

NOTES

This is a slightly shortened version of an article that first appeared in *Wide Angle*, 6, 4 (1985); this argument is developed more fully in Richard deCordova's *Picture Personalities: The Emergence of the Star System in America*, published by University of Illinois Press in 1990.

1 See Anthony Slide, *Aspects of American Film History Prior to 1920* (Metuchen, NJ: Scarecrow Press, 1978).
2 Eric Smoodin, 'Attitudes of the American printed medium toward the cinema: 1894–1908', Unpublished Paper, University of California at Los Angeles, 1979.
3 'How the cinematographer works and some of his difficulties', *Moving Picture World* (hereafter *MPW*), 1, 14 (8 June 1907), 212.
4 Robert C. Allen, *Vaudeville and Film 1895–1915: A Study in Media Interaction* (New York: Arno, 1980), 212.
5 Ibid., 213.
6 'How the cinematographer works and some of his difficulties', *MPW*, 1, 11 (18 May 1907), 166.
7 *MPW*, 1, 19 (13 July 1907), 298.
8 *MPW*, 5, 9 (28 August 1909), 281.
9 Walter Prichard Eaton, 'The canned drama', *American Magazine*, 68 (September 1909), 493–500.
10 Eaton, 499.
11 Thomas Bedding, 'The modern way in moving picture making', *MPW*, 4, 12 (20 March 1909), 326.
12 *MPW*, 5, 14 (2 October 1909), 443.
13 This situation is similar to that discussed by Foucault regarding 'the secret' of sexuality. See Michel Foucault, *The History of Sexuality*, vol. 1, trans. Robert Hurley (New York: Random House, 1978).
14 *The Motion Picture Magazine*, 5, 6 (July 1913), 127.
15 *MPW*, 8, 5 (4 February 1911), 23.
16 *The Motion Picture Story Magazine*, 1, 1 (February 1911), 23.

17 *MPW*, 6, 12 (26 March 1910), 468.

18 Robert Kerr, 'Loree Starr – Photoplay idol', *Photoplay*, September 1914.

19 *The Motion Picture Classic* (February 1916), 55.

20 Some precision is necessary here. A certain level of contradiction was absolutely essential to the presentation of performance during this period. The force of Mary Pickford's performance in *Stella Maris* (1918), for instance, is dependent upon the discrepancy between Pickford's identity as a wealthy movie star and her appearance in the film (in one of two roles) as a penniless orphan. My argument here is that this field of contradiction did not generally engage moral categories.

21 *Photoplay* (September 1914), 70.

22 *Motion Picture Magazine* (February 1915), 85–8.

23 For an interesting discussion of the family discourse in films of the period see Nick Browne, 'Griffith and Freud: Griffith's family discourse', *Quarterly Review of Film Studies*, 6, 1 (Winter 1981), 76–80.

3

THE CAROLE LOMBARD IN MACY'S WINDOW

Charles Eckert

In the last quarter of the nineteenth century American business was pre-occupied with production. Most of its energy went into expanding its physical plant, increasing efficiency and grinding the face of labour so that greater profits could be extracted and invested in production. In the last five years of the nineteenth century when, coincidentally, motion pictures were invented, American business discovered that it was up to its neck in manufactured goods for which there were no buyers. So it became sales minded. Through the first two decades of the twentieth century, sales techniques were developed so intensely that they produced gross excesses, alienating the public and giving impetus to antibusiness and antimaterialist attitudes among intellectuals. About 1915, fixation upon sales gave way to an obsession with management, to internal re-structuring and systemis-ation. Profits were decisively improved, but the contradiction between production and consumption, between the efficient manufacture and mar-keting of goods and the capacity of wage-poor workers to buy them, was no closer to solution. Therefore, throughout the 1920s business became consumer-minded.

While all of this was going forward, Hollywood had evolved from a nickel and dime business to an entertainment industry funded by the likes of A.T. & T., Hayden Stone, Dillon Reid, RCA, The House of Morgan, A. P. Giannini's Bank of America, The Rockefellers' Chase National Bank, Goldman Sachs, Lohoran Brothers, Halsey Stuart – in short, all the major banks and investment houses and several of the largest corporations in America. With the representatives of those several economic powers sitting on the directorates of the studio, and with the world of business pervaded by the new *zeitgeist* of consumerism, the conditions were right for Holly-wood to assume a role in the phase of capitalism's life history that the emerging philosophy of consumerism was about to give birth to.

All of which brings me to a story, a sort of romance, which I shall begin, as all good storytellers do, in Medias Res.

30

I

Awakened by the brakes of the train, Bette Davis pulled aside a window curtain. Beneath a winter moon the Kansas plains lay grey with late winter snow. The mail clerk glimpsed Bette's face, but was too astounded by the pullman car itself to recognise his favourite star. The pullman was totally covered with gold leaf. The rest of the train was brilliantly silvered. From one car a tall radio aerial emerged mysteriously. Lost in his wonder, the clerk barely noticed that the train was underway again. He would later tell his children about the train with the golden pullman, perhaps fashioned for some Western gold baron, or for a Croesus from a foreign land. But he would never know that the interior of the train held greater wonders still.

As the cars gathered speed, other passengers shifted in their sleep, among them Laura La Plante, Preston Foster and numerous blond women with muscular legs (was one of them the supernal Toby Wing?). In an adjacent lounge car Claire Dodd, Lyle Talbot and Tom Mix were still awake, attending to a reminiscing Leo Carillo. In still another car a scene as surrealistic as a Dali floated through the Kansas night. Glenda Farrell lay in her Jantzen swimsuit upon a miniature Malibu Beach beneath a manufactured California sky made up of banks of GE ultraviolet lamps. The sand on the beach was genuine sand. Everything else was unreal.

The next to last car held no human occupants. The hum, barely discernible above the clack of the rails, emerged from the GE Monitor-top refrigerator positioned next to the GE all-electric range. When one grew accustomed to the dark, one saw that this was merely a demonstration kitchen lifted bodily, it seemed, from Macy's or Gimbels, and compressed into the oblong confines of a railway diner. In the last car was a magnificent white horse. An embroidered saddle blanket draped over a rail beside him bore the name 'King'. The horse was asleep.

The occasion that had gathered this congeries of actresses and appliances, cowboys and miniaturised Malibus, into one passenger train and positioned them in mid-Kansas on a night in February 1933, was the inauguration of Franklin Delano Roosevelt. If the logic of this escapes you, you simply must make the acquaintance of Charles Einfeld, sales manager for Warner Brothers.

Charles Einfeld was a dreamer. But, unlike yours and mine, his dreams always came true. Charles Einfeld dreamed (and it came true) that Warner's new musical, *42nd Street*, would open in New York on the eve of Roosevelt's inauguration, that the stars of the picture (with other contract stars, if possible) would journey to New York on a train to be called the Better Times Special, and that they would then go to Washington for the inauguration itself. The film, after all, was a boost for the New Deal philosophy of pulling together to whip the depression, and its star, Warner

31

Baxter, played a role that was a patent allegory of F.D.R. Einfeld then sought a tie-up with a large concern that would share the expenses of the train in exchange for a quantity of egregious advertising. General Electric, already linked with Warner as a supplier of appliances for movie props, rose to the bait.

The gold and silver train was given a definitive name: The Warner–GE Better Times Special. As it crossed North America from Los Angeles to New York its radio broadcasted Dick Powell's jazz contralto, GE ad-copy, and optimism (GE, as the parent organisation of RCA and NBC, was in a position to facilitate hook-ups with local stations). When the train arrived at a major city, the stars and chorus girls motored to the largest available GE showroom and demonstrated whatever appliances they found themselves thrust up against. In the evenings they appeared at a key theatre for a mini-première. Their *ultima Thule* was, of course, *42nd Street*.

On 9 March bawdy, gaudy 42nd Street looked as spiffy as a drunkard in church: American flags and red, white and blue bunting draped the buildings; the ordinary incandescent bulbs were replaced with scintillant 'golden' GE lamps; a fleet of Chrysler automobiles (a separate tie-up) and GE automotive equipment was readied for a late afternoon parade which would catch those leaving work. In the North River a cruiser stood at anchor to fire a salute – a great organ-boom to cap off a roulade of aerial bombs. As the train approached New York from New Rochelle, a pride of small airplanes accompanied it. Once it arrived, the schedule was as exacting as a coronation: a reception at Grand Central by the Forty-Second Street Property Owners and Merchants Association, the parade, a GE sales meeting at the Sam Harris Theatre, and the grand première at the Strand.

This stunning synthesis of film, electrical, real-estate and transportation exploitation, partisan patrio-politics, and flecked-at-the-mouth starmania did not lurch fully armed from the head of Charles Einfeld, splendid dreamer though he was. It can only be explained in terms of the almost incestuous hegemony that characterised Hollywood's relations with vast reaches of the American economy by the mid-1930s.

The story of Hollywood's plunge into the American marketplace involves two separate histories: that of the showcasing of fashions, furnishings, accessories, cosmetics and other manufactured items, and that of the establishment of 'tie-ups' with brand-name manufacturers, corporations and industries. The two histories are interpenetrating, but they were distinctive enough to give rise to specialists who worked independently within and without the studio.

The scope of the first history can be set forth in a sentence: at the turn of the century Hollywood possessed one clothing manufacturer (of shirts) and none of furniture; by 1937 the Associated Apparel Manufacturers of

Los Angeles listed 130 members, and the Los Angeles Furniture Manufacturers Association listed 150, with an additional 330 exhibitors. Furthermore, 250 of the largest American department stores kept buyers permanently in Los Angeles.

When those intimately associated with this development reminisced about its origins, they spoke first of Cecil B. DeMille. In his autobiography DeMille maintained that the form of cinema he pioneered in the late teens and twenties was a response to pressures he received from the publicity and sales people in New York. They wanted few (preferably no) historical 'costume' dramas, but much 'modern stuff with plenty of clothes, rich sets, and action'. DeMille brought to Paramount's studios talented architects, designers, artists, costumiers and hairdressers who both drew upon the latest styles in fashions and furnishings and created hallmarks of their own. DeMille's 'modern photoplays' – films like *For Better, For Worse* and *Why Change Your Wife?* – guaranteed audiences a display of all that was chic and avant-garde.

While DeMille perfected a film display aimed at the fashion conscious, fan magazines and studio publicity photos helped spread an indigenous Hollywood 'outdoors' style made up of backless bathing suits, pedal-pushers, slacks, toppers and skirts. By the early 1930s these styles had penetrated the smallest of American small towns and had revolutionised recreational and sport dress.

The years 1927 through 1929 saw an explosive expansion of fashion manufacture and wholesaling in Los Angeles. Some of DeMille's designers opened shops which catered to a well-heeled public. The Country Club Manufacturing Company inaugurated copyrighted styles modelled by individual stars and employing their names. It was followed by 'Miss Hollywood Junior' which attached to each garment a label bearing the star's name and picture. This line was sold exclusively to one store in each major city, with the proviso that a special floor space be set aside for display. Soon, twelve cloak and suit manufacturers banded together to form Hollywood Fashion Associates. In addition, the Associated Apparel Manufacturers began to co-ordinate and give national promotion to dozens of style lines. The latter association took the lead in a form of publicity that became commonplace through the 1930s: it shot thousands of photographs of stars serving as mannequins in such news-editor pleasing locales as the Santa Anita race track, the Rose Bowl, Hollywood swimming pools and formal film receptions. The photos were distributed free, with appropriate text, to thousands of newspapers and magazines. In a more absurd vein, the Association organised bus and airplane style shows, which ferried stars, designers and buyers to resorts and famous restaurants amid flashbulbs and a contrived sense of occasion.

If one walked into New York's largest department stores toward the end of 1929 one could find abundant evidence of the penetration of

Hollywood fashions, as well as a virulent form of moviemania. One store employed uniformed Roxy ushers as its floor managers. Another advertised for sales girls that looked like Janet Gaynor and information clerks that looked like Buddy Rogers. At Saks, Mrs Pemberton would inform you that she was receiving five orders a day for pyjamas identical to the pair that Miriam Hopkins wore in *Camel Thru a Needle's Eye*. She also had received orders for gowns and suits worn by Pauline Lord, Lynne Fontaine, Frieda Innescourt, Sylvia Fields and Murial Kirkland.

The New York scene became organised, however, only with the advent in 1930 of Bernard Waldman and his Modern Merchandising Bureau. Waldman's concern soon played the role of fashion middle-man for all the major studios except Warner Brothers (Warners, always a loner, established its own Studio Styles in 1934). By the mid-1930s Waldman's system generally operated as follows: sketches and/or photographs of styles to be worn by specific actresses in specific films were sent from the studios to the Bureau (often a year in advance of the film's release). The staff first evaluated these styles and calculated new trends. They then contracted with manufacturers to have the styles produced in time for the film's release. They next secured advertising photos and other materials which would be sent to retail shops. This advertising material mentioned the film, stars and studio as well as the theatres where the film would appear. Waldman's cut of the profits was 5 per cent. The studios at first asked for 1 per cent, but before 1937 provided their designs free in exchange for abundant advertising.

Waldman's concern also established the best-known chain of fashion shops, Cinema Fashions. Macy's contracted for the first of these shops in 1930 and remained a leader in the Hollywood fashion field. By 1934 there were 298 official Cinema Fashions shops (only one permitted in each city). By 1937 there were 400, with about 1,400 other shops willing to handle some of the dozens of the Bureau's star-endorsed style lines. Cinema Fashions catered only to women capable of spending 30 dollars and more for a gown. It agreed with the studios that cheaper fashions, even though they would be eagerly received, would destroy the aura of exclusivity that surrounded a Norma Shearer or Loretta Young style. Cheaper lines might also cheapen the stars themselves, imperilling both box-office receipts and the Hollywood fashion industry.

Inevitably, competitors and cheaper lines did appear. Copyrighted styles that had had their run in the Waldman-affiliated shops were passed on to mass production (though seldom if the style was associated with a currently major star). By the later 1930s Waldman had added a line of Cinema shops that sold informal styles at popular prices. The sale of these fashions was tremendously aided by the release of photos to newspapers (they saturated Sunday supplements), major magazines and the dozens of fan magazines – *Hollywood, Picture Play, Photoplay, Shadowplay, Silver*

Screen, Screenbook, Movieland, Movie Story, Movie Stories, Modern Movies, Modern Screen, Motion Pictures and the rest. In monthly issues of each of these magazines, millions of readers saw Bette Davis, Joan Crawford, Claudette Colbert and Norma Shearer in a series of roles unique to this period: as mannequins modelling clothes, furs, hats and accessories that they would wear in forthcoming films. The intent behind these thousands of style photos is epitomised in a 1934 *Shadowplay* caption for a dress modelled by Anita Louise: 'You will see the dress in action in Warner's *First Lady*'. Occasionally one was informed that the fashions were 'on display in leading department and ready-to-wear stores this month'. The names of the leading studio designers, Adrian of MGM, Orry-Kelly of Warners, Royer of 20th Century-Fox, Edward Stevenson of RKO, Edith Head of Paramount, Walter Plunkett of Selznick, became as familiar to readers as the stars themselves.

To all this we must add Hollywood's influence upon the cosmetics industry. In a field dominated by Eastern houses like Helena Rubinstein, Elizabeth Arden and Richard Hudnut, Hollywood's Max Factor and Perc Westmore were merely two large concerns. But Hollywood seemed to dominate the cosmetics industry because its stars appeared in the hundreds of thousands of ads that saturated the media. In the mid-1930s cosmetics ranked only second to food products in amount spent on advertising. The cycle of influence made up of films, fashion articles, 'beauty hints', columns featuring stars, ads which dutifully mentioned the star's current film and tie-in advertising in stores, made cosmetics synonymous with Hollywood. The same was true for many brands of soap, deodorants, toothpastes, hair preparations and other toiletries. No more potent endorsements were possible than those of the women who manifestly possessed the most 'radiant' and 'scintillant' eyes, teeth, complexions and hair.

Almost as significant for films as the scope of this merchandising revolution was the conception of the consumer that underpinned it. As one reads the captions beneath the style photos, the columns of beauty advice and the articles on the co-ordination of wardrobes and furnishings, one senses that those who bought these things were not varied as to age, marital status, ethnicity or any other characteristics. Out there, working as a clerk in a store and living in an apartment with a friend, was *one girl* – single, nineteen years old, Anglo-Saxon, somewhat favouring Janet Gaynor. The thousands of Hollywood-associated designers, publicity men, sales heads, beauty consultants and merchandisers had internalised her so long ago that her psychic life had become their psychic life. They empathised with her shyness, her social awkwardness, her fear of offending. They understood her slight weight problem and her chagrin at being a trifle too tall. They could tell you what sort of man she hoped to marry and how she spent her leisure time.

35

Now for our second history, that of the tie-up. In the 1930s, the two most powerful studios, Warners and MGM, evolved a form of tie-up that revolutionised sales and publicity – and permanently affected the character of films. The keystone of the method was a contractual agreement with a large established manufacturer. If the product would seem blatantly displayed if shown in a film – a bottle of Coca-Cola, for instance – the contract provided merely for a magazine and newspaper campaign that would employ pictures and endorsements of stars, and notice of recent studio releases. MGM signed a $500,000 contract with Coca-Cola in March 1933, providing that company with the vaunted 'star-power' of the most star-laden studio.

There were other products, however, that could be prominently displayed in films without arousing criticism, except from the most knowledgeable. Warner's tie-up with General Electric and General Motors provided both for the use of Warner's stars in magazine ads and for the display of appliances and autos in films. Anyone familiar with the GE Monitor-top refrigerator will recognise it in a number of Warner films of this period. A tie-up with Buick (GM) provided for the display of autos in films and for a national advertising campaign that tied Buick to ten Warner films, among them *Gold Diggers of 1935*, *Go Into Your Dance*, *The Goose and the Gander*, *A Night at the Ritz* and *In Caliente*.

At the end of the campaign, in May 1935, *Variety* reported, 'Automobile manufacturers have gone daffy over picture names following the campaign just completed by Buick and Warners: Latter company has tied up to stars on the last 10 pictures with Buick buggies.'

While Warners probably secured more major tie-ups than any other studio, MGM ran it a close race. We can illustrate its exploitational technique by examining the pressbook for *Dinner at Eight*, the studio's most ambitiously promoted film of 1934. A page of photos of department store displays arranged in many cities was captioned, 'The merchandising value of Jean Harlow's name was never better demonstrated than by the dozens of *Dinner at Eight* fashion and shoe windows.' The next page was headed, 'Tie Ups A Million Dollars Worth of Promotion' and included this text: '250,000 Coca-Cola dealers will exploit *Dinner at Eight*.'

Through the rest of the thirties, all of the major studios adopted and helped to perfect this system. In its classic – or perhaps Hellenistic – form, the head of exploitation supervised an effort that co-ordinated the creation of the script (tie-ups were often formative influences), the breakdown of the script into categories of products and services and the search for sponsors. Wilma Freeman of Warners told *Nation's Business* in 1940 that she asked firms to design 'a product that conforms with the picture'. In return Ms Freeman offered the sponsor 12,000 theatres and audiences of 80,000,000 each week. When the product came through, a star was posed with it and the pressbook was made up. The formula, as a mathematician would say, had achieved elegance.

Before moving on to some conclusions about how all this affected films, there remains another complicity, that of the studio tie-ins with radio, to be discussed. Prior to 1932 the two major networks, CBS and NBC, did not have studio facilities in Hollywood. Warner Brothers, however, had acquired their own local station in emulation of Paramount which owned a half interest in CBS and used its nation-wide facilities to advertise films and to build up stars. Over 700 hours of Hollywood programming issued from both networks in 1937. The studios had done all in their power to woo the major networks to Hollywood, offering them their rosters of stars, their copyrighted music and advertisers eager to connect their products with star names. The following list suggests the range of programmes and sponsors that came to be associated with Hollywood between 1932 and 1937: Rinso Talkie Time, Hollywood Nights (Kissproof), Hollywood Show (Sterling Drugs), Madame Sylvia (Ralston), Hollywood Hotel (Campbell Soups), Lux Radio Theatre, Mary Pickford Dramas (Royal Gelatin), Gigantic Pictures (Tastyeast), Irene Rich Dramas (Welch Juice), Sally of the Talkies (Luxor), Jimmie Fidler (Tangee), Helen Hayes Theatre (Sanka Coffee), Leslie Howard Theatre (Hinds Cream), the Fred Astaire Programme (Packard Motors) and Ethel Barrymore Theatre (Bayer Aspirin).

The largest advertisers were, however, associated with the largest names. By 1937 CBS paired Al Jolson and Rinso, Eddie Cantor and Texaco, Jeanette McDonald and Vicks, Jack Oakie and Camels and Edward G. Robinson and Kraft. NBC followed suit with Rudy Vallee and Royal Gelatin, Bing Crosby and Kraft, Amos and Andy and Pepsodent and Jack Benny and Jello. This very potent fusion of products and performing stars aroused jealousy in the fields of recording, music publishing and journalism. Newspapers, in particular, felt that the coalition of Hollywood and radio was drying up their advertising revenue. But the most vocal critics were theatre owners. In their trade journals they protested the use of the stars they relied upon for their profits by a medium that gave its product away free. They connected declines in box-office revenue with the increased use of stars by radio, and they saw the studio sales and publicity men as madmen who had created a devouring monster in the foolish belief that they were helping the film industry. The shrewdest critics realised, however, that the tie-ups with radio advertisers gave the studios more than free advertising. Obviously lucrative contracts were involved, similar to those entered into for product tie-ups with films. By 1937 it was, in fact, common knowledge that MGM had a major contract with Maxwell House and that all requests for radio appearances and endorsements of its stars were reviewed in consultation with this company. From about 1934 on, more and more films employed radio personalities, used radio studios as locales and imitated the variety-show format. Hollywood was not so much aiding the growth of a rival medium as it was attempting to co-opt it.

The result, at least through the mid-1930s, was a kind of symbiosis which blurred the outlines of both media. Fred Astaire became as much a radio personality who performed songs from his pictures and acted out abbreviated versions of film plots over your table model Zenith as he was a dancer and performer upon the screen. The products associated with stars in films and radio became subliminally attached to their names and their radio voices. By the late 1930s the power of film and radio as advertising mediums seemed unlimited. The Hollywood studios, with their rosters of contracted stars, had come to occupy a privileged position in the advertising industry.

We can gain considerable insight into Hollywood's role in the evolution of consumerism, and into many of the characteristics of films of the 1930s and later, by combining this history with all the elements we have so far discussed in isolation. First we have an economy suddenly aware of the importance of the consumer and of the dominant role of women in the purchasing of most consumer items. (Consumer statistics widely disseminated in the late 1920s and early 1930s show that women made 80 to 90 per cent of all purchases for family use. They bought 48 per cent of drugs, 96 per cent of dry goods, 87 per cent of raw products, 98 per cent of automobiles.) Second we have a film industry committed to schemes for product display and tie-ins, schemes that brought some direct revenue to the studios but more importantly reduced prop and art department and advertising overheads. Add to all this a star system dominated by women – at MGM Shearer, Loy, Harlow, Garbo, Russell, Crawford, Goddard, Lombard, Turner, Lamarr; at Warners Davis, Francis, Stanwyck, Young, Chatterton and so on – hundreds of women stars and starlets available to the studio publicity, sales tie-in departments as – to use the favoured phrase – merchandising assets.

On one, more local, level, the combination of all these factors had some obvious and immediate effects on the kinds of films that were made. There appeared a steady output of films dominated by starlets – those hundreds of 'women's films', which are of such interest to feminist critics like Haskell and Rosen. In addition, Hollywood developed a preference for 'modern films', because of the opportunities they offered for product display and tie-ins. In many instances storylines were reshaped, to provide more shooting in locales suitable for tie-ins. Movies were made in fashion salons, department stores, beauty parlours, middle and upper-class homes with modern kitchens and bathrooms, large living rooms and so forth.

On another level, the studio tie-ins became important far beyond the influence they exerted on the kinds of films made. It is to this more comprehensive level that I would move as I draw back from the cluttered summary I have led you through, to make some larger suggestions, not just about merchandising's contribution to Hollywood but about Hollywood's contributions to the form and character of consumerism itself. By the early 1930s market analyses were talking about the sovereignty of the consumer, the importance of women as purchasers and the necessity of learning more about their tastes and predilections. By the early 1940s market research had been invented, with its studies of the hidden needs and desires of consumers and its discovery that many products were bought for their images, their associations or the psychological gratifications they provided. Between these two movements Hollywood had co-operated in a massive effort to sell products employing a sales method that was essentially covert, associational and linked to the deeply gratifying and habituating experiences that films provided. Furthermore, the many fine sensibilities of Hollywood's designers, artists, cameramen, lighting men, directors and composers had lent themselves, even if coincidentally, to the establishment of powerful bonds between the emotional fantasy-generating substance of films and the material objects those films contained.

One can argue only from inference that Hollywood gave consumerism a distinctive bent, but what a massive base this inference can claim. Tens of millions of Americans provided the captive audience for the unique experiments in consumer manipulation that the showcasing of products in films and through star endorsements constituted. And this audience reacted so predictably that every large manufacturer in America would have bought its own small MGM had this been possible. Instead they were forced to await the advent of television with its socially acceptable juxtaposition of commercials and entertainment. The form television commercials have taken, their fusion of images augmented by editing and camera techniques, with music, lyrics and charismatic personalities, is obviously an extension of the techniques pioneered by Hollywood.

But is it equally obvious, as market researchers have claimed, that consumerism is grounded in psychological universals? What should we ascribe to the potent acculturation provided by Hollywood for several decades? Were we, as consumers, such skilled and habituated perceivers of libidinal cues, such receptive audiences for associational complexes, such romanticisers of homes, stores and highways before Hollywood gave us *Dinner at Eight*, *The Big Store* and *The Speed that Kills*? I would suggest that we were not, that Hollywood, drawing upon the resources of literature, art and music, did as much or more than any other force in capitalist culture to smooth the operation of the production–consumption cycle by fetishising products and putting the libido in libidinally invested advertising.

This is an abridged version of an article which first appeared in *Quarterly Review of Film Studies*, 3, 1 (1978), © Harwood Academic Publishers.

4

THE BUILDING OF POPULAR IMAGES
Grace Kelly and Marilyn Monroe

Thomas Harris

With Americans allocating an increasing share of their leisure time to the mass media of communication it is not surprising that their choice of public heroes and heroines is, to a large degree, determined by perpetual exposure to the media. The shift of interest from heroes of production – the captains of industry, for example – to heroes of consumption has been pointed out by Leo Lowenthal in his study of magazine biographies. Today's heroes and heroines, reaching the attention of the public through motion pictures, radio or television, become more clearly drawn in the mass mind through the reinforcement of other media.

Modern publicity methods decree that the screen star be known to his or her potential audience not only through film roles but also through fan magazines, national magazines, radio, television and the newspapers. The totality of this publicity build-up is calculated to make the personality better known to a public which will respond by attending the screen hero's starring films.

In building a public personality the motion picture industry has perfected the device of stereotyping its stars. The star system is based on the premise that a star is accepted by the public in terms of a certain set of personality traits which permeate all of his or her film roles. The successful stars have been those whose appeal can be catalogued into a series of such traits, associations and mannerisms.

In the stereotyping process Hollywood publicists have worked with the studio policy makers to assure that their efforts will be consistent with the screen image. If an actress has achieved recognition through 'the-girl-next-door' roles it is important that her publicity reinforce this image. (Many people feel that the birth of an illegitimate child to Ingrid Bergman so undermined her saintly 'Joan of Arc' image, built up by the studio, that the public reacted with bewilderment and rejection.) The star becomes a symbol to an unseen mass audience whose only contact with him/her is through the indirect means of the media.

The trifold publicity apparatus of the studios provides the channels for communicating these symbolic images to the public. Under a director of publicity are three major sub-departments: publicity, advertising and exploitation.

The studio's own image of itself has great influence over its publicity. MGM for example, thinks itself too dignified to engage in stunts and gimmicks of the sort that Paramount unabashedly promotes. Regardless of such discrepancies the channels utilised by principal studios are basically the same. They include a preliminary publicity build-up starting months or even years before the star is seen on the screen. Frequent devices used in such a build-up are a 'discovery' usually concocted by studio publicists, a series of glamour pictures sent to all the print media, a rumoured romance with another star already well known to the public or a rumoured starring role in a major film. This publicity finds a primary outlet in syndicated Hollywood gossip columns and movie fan magazines. When the actor or actress is actually cast in a film, the studio assigns a 'unit man' to 'plant' items about the personality in these places as well as national magazines and Sunday newspaper supplements. A network television appearance is also a highly coveted plum in the studio 'pre-sale' campaign for both the picture and the personality. Prior to and during the filming of a picture all publicity emanates from Hollywood. The New York publicity offices of the studio then take over the film and continue to handle publicity through the distribution-exhibition phase. New York is also charged with the development of national advertising and the creation of stunts and merchandise tie-ins to exploit the picture. Especially important in this total process is the perpetuation of the star stereotype. It is the publicist's job to interpret the new film role in terms of the pre-established stereotypes and to communicate the image through the variety of means at his disposal.

The writer has analysed the Hollywood-created build-up of two female superstars in an effort to reconstruct the image-making process. The method used was to view all the films of Grace Kelly and Marilyn Monroe and to compile magazine features, reviews and studio publicity to reconstruct the thematic content of their individual roles. Studio pressbooks which outline the advertising, publicity and exploitation campaigns for each film were carefully scrutinised. Personal interviews were conducted with key studio publicity personnel in New York and Chicago. Within this framework an analysis was made of all feature material appearing in national magazines during the period from September 1951 to June 1956.

Throughout the publicity campaigns of both stars certain thematic associations were preserved. In the early phases of the build-up of both the Monroe and Kelly images use of the truth as raw material was exploited with phenomenal effectiveness. Actual biographical material was employed in both cases to an extraordinary degree. Major themes repeated in the periodicals closely paralleled the official biographies of each.

Preoccupation of the publicists with family background lends an additional dimension to the screen image and thus further facilitates vicarious audience identification. For example, the carefully disseminated 'lady' image of Grace Kelly is firmly grounded in her actual family background. As a product of wealth, genteel breeding and close family ties she became widely accepted as representative of man's ideal longings within the family structure. Although the Grace Kelly appeal was principally directed at a male audience – as is the case with all female stars – the image is utterly consistent with the concept of respectability fostered by women's magazines. Feature material about Miss Kelly was 'planted' at least once each in such publications as *Cosmopolitan*, *Vogue*, *McCall's*, *Woman's Home Companion*, *Mademoiselle*, *Good Housekeeping* and *The Ladies Home Journal*. Typical of her acceptance by these magazines is this comment from *Vogue*, 1 October 1954: 'There's Grace Kelly, whose gentle, fine-bred prettiness is rapidly reversing Hollywood's ideas of what's box office.'

The two techniques most frequently used to enhance the Kelly image were (1) an emphasis on her family's adherence to the good life, particularly the drama of her father's achievements in sport and business, and (2) the use of quotes from her co-stars about her off-screen lady-like qualities. Both of these techniques served to reinforce the stereotype communicated by the consistent nature of her screen roles. The entire body of magazine feature material on Grace Kelly is distinguished by a dearth of comment from the star herself as if it would be beneath her dignity to discuss topics which made Marilyn Monroe a household name. Yet a careful balance was maintained lest the impression be conveyed that Miss Kelly was aloof from her fellows. Thus there was repeated emphasis on her making her way in the entertainment world 'on her own', spurning family connections. Her wealth, it was always noted, was the result of hard work and determination – qualities admired by Americans who could never tolerate inherited wealth. Terms like 'cool', 'lady', 'genteel', 'elegant', 'reserved', 'patrician' are as frequent in the features and reviews of her film roles as they are in her personal publicity.

If the film makers, with publicity support, typed Grace Kelly as the ideal mate, they accomplished with equal effectiveness the establishment of Marilyn Monroe as the ideal 'playmate'. It was the playmate image which, nourished by the acceptance of her pictures, skyrocketed her to an almost allegoric position as the symbolic object of illicit male sexual desire.

The nature of the image was a natural outgrowth of Miss Monroe's pre-movie experience as a model and cover girl of 'girlie' magazines. Twentieth Century-Fox released a series of pinup type photos which displayed her anatomical properties to the best advantage. She was then publicised by means of a series of suggestive honorary titles inspired by the studio. Prior to her achieving feature billing in a film, Marilyn Monroe was featured by *Esquire* and *Coronet* as well as a host of lesser magazines with a decidedly male slant. As *Vogue* heralded the arrival of Grace Kelly, *Coronet* found its prototype in Marilyn Monroe. In October 1952, writer Grady Johnson said of her:

> Prodded by protectors of public morals, Hollywood for twenty years has been telling the world, with some traces of truth, that its residents were home-loving church-going folks. Belaboring the point, its publicity made glamour girls out as drudges with housemaid's knee, whipping up an angel food cake quicker than you could say censorship-is-ruining-the-movies. Then along came Marilyn Monroe.

While Miss Monroe was still in the starlet stage, studio publicists managed to plan a Monroe feature in *Collier's*. It is interesting to note that in this initial piece, the principal thematic associations later integral to the popular image all appear. As the circumstances of her birth, her youthful trials and her early marriage were revealed, Marilyn Monroe became all the more provocative as a sexual symbol. It was as if the absence of family had rendered her attainable, while the Kellys of Philadelphia were inculcating their Grace with the tenets of propriety and respectability. Publicists concentrated on her breathy voice, her 'horizontal walk', her revealing dress, her half-closed eyes and half-opened mouth. The off-stage image was also perpetuated through the device of her quotes and quips, known to the trade as 'Monroeisms'. Utilisation of this matter-of-fact, humorous approach to sex is consistent with her screen stereotype. It is in keeping with the standard studio practice of having Monroe undress, shower, say and sing suggestive things in her film roles. The impression of detachment so important to the 'cool' Kelly image would be as out of character transposed to Monroe, as would such a comment as Miss Monroe's, 'I do not suntan because I like to feel blonde all over', if attributed to Miss Kelly.

It should be noted that the initial studio publicity efforts and the films of the two stars were so successful in communicating a comprehensible image that both became national celebrities worthy of treatment in newspapers and news magazine departments other than those dealing with the cinema. Thus such events as the marriage of Marilyn Monroe and Joe DiMaggio, their Korean tour, their divorce, and the engagement and marriage of Grace Kelly to Prince Ranier, the birth of their daughter, Marilyn Monroe's controversy with her studio, her marriage to Arthur Miller and her audience with Queen Elizabeth II were treated as national and international news. Both stars were considered to be newsworthy enough to merit a *Time* cover feature.

As both Monroe and Kelly have been so consistently type-cast as to arouse certain expectations from their publics, it is problematical if either or both of them can successfully assume their new changes of status and still maintain the popularity with a public which elevated them to a position that made such changes possible. Can the audience which accepted Marilyn Monroe as a good-natured sex symbol tolerate her association with the intellectuals and her marriage to one of their number? Can the public of Grace Kelly, so infatuated with elements of the American dream embodied in her accomplishments and those of her family, accept her as an expatriot married to the monarch of a European gambling principality?

Whether or not these role modifications can be readily absorbed into the images which have established Marilyn Monroe and Grace Kelly as national heroines is a matter of conjecture which only the passage of time can answer.

First published in *Studies in Public Communication*, 1 (1957).

5

FATAL BEAUTIES
Black women in Hollywood

Karen Alexander

First they said I was too light
Then they said I was too dark
Then they said I was too different
Then they said I was too much the same
Then they said I was too young
Then they said I was too old
Then they said I was too interracial ... [1]

As we approach the 1990s in Britain, black faces have never been more visible. Black women now appear on mainstream magazine covers, they are seen in magazine advertisements, on billboards in the street and even on television, something unheard of even a few years ago. In many ways this may be viewed as a progression from days when black women were heard but not seen, but appearances can be deceiving. We can hardly speak of progress when the most publicised recent use of black skin in advertising – the notorious 'United Colours' Benetton campaign – is not only offensively iconic, using a suspect idea of what blackness stands for, but also fetishistic, using only parts of the black body – a hand (in handcuffs), a breast (breast feeding) – to represent that idea. Moreover it is an idea that exists mainly in the minds of white people. As a black woman, born in Britain and brought up here in the sixties and seventies, my own idea was to find an image of the complete black woman to identify with, someone I could hope, however naively, to be: young, gifted and beautiful. In my search I thumbed through out-of-date, grubby issues of *Ebony* magazine, reading a little and looking a lot, soaking up all I could. Time and again I would read about black achievers – mainly men – and see advertisements that featured exclusively black people – mainly women. These were beautiful women; what they were selling was unimportant, what mattered was the hair styles, the dresses and the make-up. My younger relatives elevated these images into images of stars by sticking them on the ceiling above their beds, alongside their posters of The Jackson Five and Diana Ross.

In such a frame of mind my discovery of a woman who was not only

Figure 5.1 Carmen Jones (1954)

black and beautiful but came complete with a character, a life, a history,
was understandably overwhelming. Seeing Dorothy Dandridge in *Carmen
Jones* for the first time I was astonished and excited; I had never before
seen an all-black movie – genuinely surprising my mother who, brought
up in the thirties and forties in Guyana, had probably seen all of Hollywood's black output; it was also the first time I had seen a black woman
and a black man (Dorothy and Harry Belafonte), represented romantically
on the screen. But my greatest delight was in discovering Dorothy
Dandridge herself. I was hooked; I asked myself where she had come

from? What other films had she made? Was she still alive, was she married, did she have children etc? My enthusiasm for Dorothy was not based on an objective appraisal of the film I had seen, or of her performance, and I do not intend to argue points about its quality here. At the time it was thought good enough by white judges to earn her a Best Actress Oscar nomination, making her the first black person to be considered for the principal dramatic award. For a black actress in 1955 a nomination was as close as she could hope to get to it, and to date no black woman has yet won that particular accolade. Not everyone agreed with the white critics who showered her performance with praise. The film was attacked in the black community: at a time when there was high expectation of change in America's clichéed images of black people, many found that Dandridge in *Carmen Jones* still embodied a stereotype of the dusky, exotic, sexually loose woman. James Baldwin's pointed criticism was that the adaptation of Bizet's opera for an all-black cast and setting depended on 'a certain quaintness, a certain lack of inhibition taken to be typical of Negroes'. He added that *Carmen Jones* was 'far and away the most self-conscious wedding of sex and colour which Hollywood has yet turned out. (It will certainly not be the last.)'[2] For me, however, a heroine-hungry viewer in the seventies, for whom James Baldwin himself had not yet become a hero, Dandridge being there on my television screen was enough. In fact, her role as a lustful, sexy woman, in an all-black society, seducing a black man – stereotype or no stereotype – represented everything I had wanted to see and had never seen in a film. From then on Dorothy joined Rita, Ava, Marilyn and Liz Taylor in the roll-call of my screen heroines.

Like all stars, Dorothy was more than just an image. Behind the public persona, a classically tragic private life was more or less well hidden. In my pursuit of the Complete Black Woman, I wanted to know all about this life. I devoured the primary source materials, her own moving auto-biography, *Everything and Nothing*, and *A Portrait in Black*, the biography written by her manager, Earl Mills, but I discovered only a tale of complete failure. The life of 'America's first sex goddess of colour', as she had been hailed, ended in an overdose of barbiturates that many suggested and others strongly denied was suicide, but which either way meant the death of a sad and broken woman. It seemed the price she had to pay as a black woman for stardom was too high. True, it is just one more Hollywood cliché that female stars yearn desperately for a normal family life and usually fail to achieve it. Dorothy's marriage to the dancer Harold Nicholas represented one attempt to realise that ideal: it began badly, Nicholas proving immediately unfaithful, but when, three months into the marriage, she became pregnant she could expect some consolation. As it turned out her daughter Harolyn suffered brain damage at birth and was mentally retarded. No amount of psychiatric help could console Dorothy or rid her of the deep-seated guilt that it was her fault. She describes in her autobiography how failure as a wife and mother strengthened her resolve to succeed as a performer. Coached by composer and arranger Phil Moore – who had played a formative role in Lena Horne's singing career – she began to build a reputation as a nightclub singer. Her combination of acceptably light-skinned good looks and an acceptable crossover repertoire ensured a prompt rise to stardom. *Life* magazine called her 'the most beautiful Negro singer since Lena Horne', and bore witness to it by making her the first black woman to appear on their front cover. It was a short step to gaining the part in *Carmen Jones* and receiving the nomination. From then on her career should have blossomed uninterrupted, but Hollywood proved unable to accommodate its rising black star. No part she was offered did anything more than reinforce stereotypes that Dorothy strongly despised. A chance came to repeat the success of *Carmen Jones* when she was cast as Bess by Otto Preminger, her lover at the time, in his film of *Porgy and Bess*. Again this all-black 'wedding of sex and colour' was criticised in the black community, and Dorothy herself cites in her autobiography some of the hostile mail she received: 'Why do you always have to play a prostitute role when you are supposed to be holding up negro womanhood with dignity?'[3] Her roles in mixed-race films reproduced similar stereotypes, and if *Island in the Sun* made history by featuring Hollywood's first interracial embraces on screen, between Dorothy and James Mason, and between Harry Belafonte and Joan Fontaine, Dorothy was very much aware of the inherent racism in such depictions. She describes in detail the censorious interruption of her torrid embrace with Trevor Howard in *Malaga*, in which she was cast as a Spanish temptress: 'Another instant and there would have been a bit of motion-picture history, a white man kissing a negro woman on the screen for the first time. Suddenly the director's voice rang out, "Cut!"' (op. cit., p. 191) What enabled these interracial relationships to become visible, however partially, was the repeatedly demeaning nature of the black woman's characterisation. Even *Tamango*, a film made beyond the confines of Hollywood, in France with the blacklisted director John Berry, did no more than reproduce in extreme form a familiar Hollywood role for actresses like Dorothy: the sexually available slave. Columbia's press release for the film coyly illustrates a contradiction between Dorothy's public persona and the parts she was playing: 'It is ironic that, although she is one of the most elegantly groomed women in show business, almost all her film roles have called for a drab and tattered wardrobe. No exception is her latest part of a slave girl.'[4] For Dorothy, however, the conflict between images had far less to do with dress codes and much more to do with skin colour. Expected to fulfil black expectations as a ground-breaking achiever, her private attempts to achieve happiness were publicly reviled, reproducing in her life the hostility her screen images encountered. This is how she concludes her account of the unfulfilled kiss with Trevor Howard: 'These situations are very similar to the events in my private life. My social relations with white men are also barred by protocol and law at certain points.' A large part of the tragedy of Dorothy Dandridge's life stems from her own awareness of the factors in her failure. Conscious of the burden she carried as the strongest image of Black Woman yet projected by Hollywood, she was no less conscious of Hollywood's inability to sustain her within the star-system. She was left contemplating the inadequacy of her image: 'What was I? . . . I was too light to satisfy negroes, not light enough to secure the screen work, the roles, the marriage-status available to white women.' (op. cit., pp. 154–5) She retreated into the disasters of her publicly exposed private life. An unhappy marriage to Jack Denison, a white restaurateur, ended in divorce in 1963, after he had left her morally destroyed and financially bankrupt. She returned to singing in an attempt to revive her career, and had successfully negotiated a return to the screen only four days before she was found dead, on 8 September 1965, in a hotel room in Hollywood.

Was Dorothy Dandridge's failure inevitable? The answer would depend on constructing the alternative, a black female star working consistently, with a marketable public persona and an appeal unlimited by racial difference. Did Hollywood want such a star in the first place? That would depend on her value on the market. The cinema is an industry. Its primary concern is to make profits from investments. Stars are invested in by studios, and then represent an important investment in a film production, being the basis on which films get financed, part of the labour that produces the film and the means whereby the film as a commodity is sold in the market-place. Selling the commodity is a question of exhibition, and in the light of the frequent claims that Hollywood studios depended on exhibition in the racist South for their profits, it was difficult to imagine a black female star performing well enough in that market-place to bring a return on the studio's initial investment. The hostility of Southern censors to the dignified portrayal of blacks is well documented; 'Censor Chairman Lloyd T. Binford, for example, was noted for his use of the shears on any scenes involving Negroes which do not degrade them.'[5] One studio producer saw compliance with Southern standards as 'painful pragmatism . . . Even today, sales take precedence over manufacturing.' (Haskins, op. cit., p. 100) Thomas Cripps has exposed this as 'the myth of the Southern box office', and identified it as yet another tool used to justify and explain away the inherent racism in Hollywood's representations of blacks. According to Cripps, box office in the South was notoriously low, and anyway, increased black patronage would have offset any falling off of the Southern white audience opposed to films treating blacks fairly.[6] Instead the studios continued in the vein opened by films such as *Birth of a Nation*, resisting attempts by the National Association for the

Advancement of Colored People (NAACP) and by other black groups to get them banned.

For black entertainers in Hollywood at the height of the studio system, from the late twenties onwards, the work available was extremely limited. An image of black people in films had been firmly set before the eyes of its audiences, black and white. The first crude stereotypes, derived from white minstrel caricatures of blacks in travelling shows, were supplemented by blacks shown as unwilling or unable to help themselves, as mammies or house niggers who were born to serve or as the equivalent of the village idiot, to be laughed at or chastised but never taken seriously. The archetypes of these images were the roles repeatedly played by Stepin Fetchit and Hattie MacDaniels in films of the thirties and early forties, reaching their peak in the performance as the comically servile maid in *Gone with the Wind* that won Hattie MacDaniels the Oscar for Best Supporting Actress.

The only alternative to these negative images was provided by the black musicals that Hollywood turned out, the consequence mainly of pressure from groups such as the NAACP that had resulted in directives issued from Washington to the heads of MGM and Twentieth Century-Fox to improve their record on the employment of black entertainers. The result was a handful of all-black films were produced, including *Hearts in Dixie*, *Hallelujah*, *Stormy Weather* and *Cabin in the Sky*. They all contained a minimum of drama and featured the cream of black performing talent. *Stormy Weather* and *Cabin in the Sky*, in particular, offered the black serviceman's pin-up girl Lena Horne a chance to develop her acting skills. However, for some of her scenes Horne, in a manner that typified Hollywood's expectations of black performers, was asked to do little more than reproduce her stage act on celluloid. None the less, these films served as the springboard for some sort of a career. Lena represented the acceptable face of black beauty, a tanned skin with Caucasian features, yet even she found it difficult to land roles of any kind. She was contracted to MGM and paid $40,000 a year, but with the need to provide entertainment for black servicemen no longer felt and general changes in the social climate after the war, the studios' sense of obligation to black performers lifted, and no more all-black films were produced. MGM preferred to lose out on their investment, and the more Lena spoke out against the studio's treatment of her the less likely they were to provide her with the means to become an established screen star. She was an active member of the NAACP, and she spoke out also about her treatment as a second-class citizen in Hollywood. She commented herself, in the late 1940s: 'I am in Hollywood, but not of Hollywood because I am a Negro. I'd like to do a good serious role in a mixed-cast movie instead of being confined to cafe singer parts.' (Haskins, op. cit., p. 115) The old argument disguising racism as economic pragmatism was used to deny Lena the part of the

Figure 5.2 Cabin in the Sky (1943)

mulatto Julie in *Showboat*, on the grounds that audiences in the South could not stomach a black person in a leading role; the part went to Ava Gardner, who was none the less encouraged to play it just as Lena would, and was even rendered suitably dark for the role by application of the make-up Max Factor had developed especially for Lena, known as Light Egyptian. Lena herself fell back on singing and personal appearances to sustain her public persona, and it is as a singer who found success away from Hollywood, finally, that Lena Horne is known today.

I have gone some way beyond finding the simple object for identification that I was pursuing when I first encountered Dorothy Dandridge. The narrative of a failure such as hers offers no positive images, only negative lessons. If she had succeeded, would I have then been satisfied? In some sense I do not think so. At a certain point my desire for an image to emulate has been replaced by the need simply to know why such images were not readily available to me when I needed them, to understand how they are constructed, and why they are sometimes not constructed.

Knowledge supersedes desire. To this end Dorothy's failure within the star-system is a more valuable lesson than, say, Lena Horne's success in opting out of it. Applying the lessons drawn from the life and career of 'Hollywood's first love goddess of colour', it has become easier to read the images of black woman being produced today in Hollywood. The depressing first impression is that not much has changed. It is the same story of non or mis-representation. Without counting the all-pervasive bit-parts for black women as hookers, the roles given to rising stars like Lisa Bonet or Cathy Tyson, if more dramatic than those offered to Dandridge in the fifties, none the less say more or less the same thing about black women. To date Tyson has played a prostitute in *Mona Lisa*, a victim of sexual harassment in *Business as Usual* and, in *The Serpent and the Rainbow*, a voodoo-practising psychiatrist, a part that for all its bizarreness remains bound within the exoticising and victimising norms of Hollywood. She herself is somewhat resigned to these dictates of the system: 'Woman equals bed-scene equals nakedness equals beaten up equals raped or whatever. It's so exploitative within the framework of the business. You just get used to reading things like this.'[7] Similarly Lisa Bonet, a star with a relatively virginal role in *The Cosby Show*, on the big screen portrayed a young mother involved in an incestuous relationship with her father, played by Mickey Rourke. In a closing scene of *Angel Heart* he is shown literally fucking her to death. Diana Ross, another star with a reputation established outside of the cinema, fared better in Hollywood in gaining an Oscar nomination for her role as Billie Holiday in *Lady Sings the Blues*. In this film, however, 'a travesty of the life and career of a great artist' in James Baldwin's assessment, Ross was primarily a singer delivering a performance, and no actress. Her other films, *The Wiz* and *Mahogany*, confirm this impression.

One black woman in Hollywood today who does seem to be overcoming the star-system's strictures is Whoopi Goldberg. She is perhaps the first black female star to be so consistently in work, and certainly the first to wear her hair in locks. Although her path into films has been the typical one for black women, taken also by Dorothy Dandridge and Lena Horne, she has graduated from the status of mere 'entertainer' (a comedienne, specifically), if not to be taken seriously as an actress, to become, after a wide range of roles, an actress of considerable force. She departs from the Hollywood stereotype of the Bronze Venus, and the acceptability of her dark skin and negroid features, and of course of that hair, is to some degree due to concentration on comic roles, though this evokes in the process another and equally suspect stereotype, the 'certain quaintness' of negroes in film condemned by James Baldwin. Perhaps the now widespread image of the serious and dramatic Tracy Chapman – of similar dark skin and similar locks – will make it easier for Whoopi Goldberg to renounce the donning of blond wigs for comic effect, and will bring her more serious, dramatic roles. To quote *Black Film Review*: 'Goldberg has proved that she can carry a film. If she can keep working and draw significant crowds at the box-office, she may happen on a decent script, worthy of her talents.'[8] When this comes along the classic 'problems' that Hollywood has constructed for itself will surface again. Already in the comedy *Jumping Jack Flash*, where the plot turns on the fact that the couple in the film communicate only via computer terminals and the audience do not see Whoopi's white 'lover' until the end, the problem of representing an interracial relationship is neatly avoided. More problematically, as the star of *Fatal Beauty*, the love scene with her co-star Sam Elliott was included as a matter of course, only to be cut after audiences at previews expressed disgust at the sight of black and white flesh in coitus. Whoopi, whose husband is white, cogently commented afterwards that if Elliott had put some money on the bedside table the next morning, the scene would have been acceptable. Times may have changed, interracial relationships are no longer against the law, and in other media races seem to mix more freely, but in Hollywood the true interracial movie has yet to be delivered. As with all representation, this failure to deliver says more about the inadequacies of the image makers than about the images they make, or choose not to make.

Testing the limits of popular cinema's willingness or ability to shift its limited range of representations regarding black women has proved difficult, not least because of the meagre resources at my disposal – the paucity of actual stars to explore, people who themselves worked within those limits and suffered directly from them. For this reason above all Dorothy Dandridge is important. I believe she is the only genuine black female star Hollywood produced, if by star is meant that combination of an immediately seductive image with the larger-than-life projection of a persona, the combination that also produced Marilyn Monroe. That Marilyn's tragedy, like Dorothy's, was not of her making should not, however, obscure the difference between the two. Dorothy knew intensely that she was entirely alone, the only black woman in her position, and she knew that she was in so untenable a position because she was a black woman, at a time when Hollywood had no means of dealing with what she represented. The situation today of Dorothy's heiresses, Lisa Bonet, Cathy Tyson and Whoopi Goldberg, if it seems different, strongly evokes the same reluctance on the part of a system to abandon stereotypes when, after all, selling stereotypes has for so long been its business. Success for an actress seems to entail accommodating and adapting to the incapacities of that system, and though the initiative may be passing into the hands of the independently minded, perhaps the price of stardom in Hollywood for the black female is still too high, even for Hollywood itself to meet. The judge will be the image-hungry black teenager in the year 2000 who looks back upon the last decade and the work done by black women actresses.

What will she see in *Angel Heart, The Serpent and the Rainbow* or *Fatal Beauty*? Perhaps she will find something to make use of in Whoopi Goldberg's struggle to diversify, but I suspect her gaze will turn away from images produced by Hollywood, focusing instead on the strategies of black women today who have turned their backs on mainstream cinema. She might see that today the struggle of black women is at the point reached by the women's struggle in the seventies, as described by Molly Haskell: 'The closer women come to claiming their rights and achieving independence in real life, the more loudly and stridently films tell us it's a man's world.'[9] Cinema may, as Truffaut believed, involve no more than finding a beautiful woman and putting her in front of the camera, but that is not a formula for the production of stars, and cinema is no longer a privileged site for the construction of powerful images. For the black woman on the screen her colour has become a kind of blankness which spectators use for their own projections. The result is a reduction of the image's potency. Seeking that power elsewhere, the Strong Black Woman has found a place in media over which she can win greater control: in music, in writing, in television even. The women of this decade who will attract the gaze of my retrospective teenager constitute a different kind of star; they are the strong and vital icons of consciousness, Tracy Chapman, Alice Walker, Oprah Winfrey and their sisters. They are not just film stars. The work of black actresses in the cinema of the eighties will not have added much to the iconography of black culture because black people, however hungry they might be for cultural reflections, necessarily know there is more to their lives than is shown in the images this iconically impotent cinema has offered them. If there is to be again the possibility of a black female star in the cinema, she will be a star of this different kind, beautiful no doubt, but self-determining and in full control of the representations she constructs. She will probably be a director. In fact, she will probably be Euzhan Palcy.

NOTES

1 J. Jordan, *Passion, New Poems 1977–1980* (Boston: Beacon Press, 1980), 78.
2 J. Baldwin, *Carmen Jones: The Dark is Light Enough*, in *Collected Non-Fiction 1948–1985* (London: Michael Joseph, 1986), 109–10.
3 D. Dandridge and E. Conrad, *Everything and Nothing. The Dorothy Dandridge Tragedy* (New York: Abelard & Schuman, 1970), 188 (hereinafter cited in text).
4 *Columbia Campaign Book (UK) for Tamango* (London: 1959), 2.
5 J. Haskins with K. Benson, *Lena. A Personal and Professional Biography of Lena Horne* (New York: Day & Stein, 1984), 101 (hereinafter cited in text).
6 Cited in D. J. Leab, *From Sambo to Superspade. The Black Experience in Motion Pictures* (London: Secker & Warburg, 1975), 41–2.
7 A. Lipman, 'Interview with Cathy Tyson', *City Limits*, 310 (1987), 10.
8 A. J. Johnson, 'Trying Times', *Black Film Review*, 4, 1 (Winter 1987–8), 22.
9 Cited in C. Brunson, *Films for Women* (London: BFI, 1986), 131.

Part II
STARS AND SOCIETY

6

CHARISMA

Richard Dyer

I'd like to discuss the notion of 'charisma' as developed by Max Weber in the field of political theory and its relevance to the star phenomenon. In a suitably modified form, the notion of charisma (in the Weberian sense, not just meaning 'magic', etc.) combines concepts of social function with an understanding of ideology.

Weber was interested in accounting for how political order is legitimated (other than by sheer force), and suggested three alternatives: tradition (doing what we've always done), bureaucracy (doing things according to agreed, but alterable, supposedly rational rules) and charisma (doing things because the leader suggests it). Charisma is defined as: 'a certain quality of an individual personality by virtue of which he [sic] is set apart from ordinary men and treated as endowed with supernatural, superhuman or at least superficially exceptional qualities'.[1] There are certain problems about transferring the notion of charisma from political to film theory. As Alberoni has pointed out, the star's status depends upon her/his not having any institutional political power.[2] Yet there is clearly some correspondence between political and star charisma, in particular the question of how or why a given person comes to have 'charisma' attributed to her or him.

E. A. Shils in 'Charisma, Order and Status' suggests that:

> The charismatic quality of an individual as perceived by others, or himself [sic] lies in what is thought to be his connection with (including possession by or embedment in) some *very central* feature of man's existence and the cosmos in which he lives. The centrality, coupled with intensity, makes it extraordinary.[3]

One does not have to think in terms of 'man's existence' and 'the cosmos', somewhat suspect eternal universals, to accept the general validity of this statement, especially as it is probably very often the case that what is culturally and historically specific about the charismatic person's relationship to her/his society may none the less present itself, or be read, as being an eternal universal relationship.

S. N. Eisenstadt in his introduction to Weber's *Charisma and Institution Building* has taken this one stage further by suggesting, on the basis of a survey of communications research, that charismatic appeal is effective especially when the social order is uncertain, unstable and ambiguous and when the charismatic figure or group offers a value, order or stability to counterpoise this. Linking a star with the whole of a society may not get us very far in these terms, unless one takes twentieth-century western society to have been in constant instability. Rather, one needs to think in terms of the relationships (of the various kinds outlined above) between stars and specific instabilities, ambiguities and contradictions in the culture (which are reproduced in the actual practice of making films and film stars).

This model underlines one of the earliest attempts to analyse a star image, Alistair Cooke's *Douglas Fairbanks, the Making of a Screen Character*, published in 1940. Cooke accounts for Fairbanks' stardom in terms of the appropriateness of his 'Americanness' to the contemporary situation of America:

> At a difficult time in American history, when the United States was keeping a precarious neutrality in the European war, Douglas Fairbanks appeared to know all the answers and knew them without pretending to be anything more than 'an all-round chap, just a regular American' (*The American*). The attraction of this flattering transfer of identity to the audience did not have to be obvious to be enjoyed. The movie fan's pleasure in Fairbanks might have been expressed in the simple sentence of a later French critic: 'Douglas Fairbanks is a tonic. He laughs and you feel relieved.' In this period of his earliest films it was no accident that his best-liked films should have been *His Picture in the Papers*, *Reggie Mixes In*, *Manhattan Madness*, and *American Aristocracy*. These were respectively about the American mania for publicity; about a society playboy who was not above finding his girl in a downtown cabaret and fighting a gangster or two to keep her; about a westerner appalled at the effete manners of the east, and about a Southerner of good family who married into 'bean-can' nobility, and was healthily oblivious of any implied snobbery. Here already was the kernel of a public hero close enough, in a manner and get-up, to contemporary America to leave his admirers with the feeling that they were manfully facing the times rather than escaping from them.[4]

Marilyn Monroe provides another example. Her image has to be situated in the flux of ideas about morality and sexuality that characterised the fifties in America and can here be indicated by such instances as the spread of Freudian ideas in postwar America (registered particularly in the Hollywood melodrama), the Kinsey report, Betty Friedan's *The Feminine*

Mystique, rebel stars such as Marlon Brando, James Dean and Elvis Presley, the relaxation of cinema censorship in the face of competition from television etc. (In turn, these instances need to be situated in relation to other levels of the social formation, e.g. actual social and sexual relations, the relative economic situations of men and women etc.) Monroe's combination of sexuality and innocence is part of that flux, but one can also see her 'charisma' as being the apparent condensation of all that within her. Thus she seemed to 'be' the very tensions than ran through the ideological life of fifties America. You could see this as heroically living out the tensions or painfully exposing them.

Just as star charisma needs to be situated in the specificities of the ideological configurations to which it belongs, so also virtually all sociological theories of stars ignore the *specificities* of another aspect of the phenomenon – the audience. (Assumptions about the audience as a generalised, homogeneous collectivity abound in writings on stars.) The importance of contradictions as they are lived by audience members in considering the star phenomenon is suggested by asides in J. P. Mayer, Andrew Tudor and Edgar Morin to the effect that particularly intense star–audience relationships occur amongst adolescents and women. They point to some empirical evidence for this. I would also point out the absolutely central importance of stars in gay ghetto culture.[5] These groups all share a peculiarly intense degree of role/identity conflict and pressure, and an (albeit partial) exclusion from the dominant articulacy of, respectively, adult, male, heterosexual culture. If these star–audience relationships are only an intensification of the conflicts and exclusions experienced by everyone, it is also significant that, in any discussion of 'subversive' star images, stars embodying adolescent, female and gay images play a crucial role.

NOTES

This extract is from Richard Dyer's *Stars* first published by the British Film Institute.
1   S. N. Eisenstadt (ed.), *Max Weber on Charisma and Institution Building* (Chicago: University of Chicago Press, 1968), 329.
2   F. Alberoni, 'The powerless elite: theory and sociological research on the phenomenon of the stars', translated in McQuail, Denis (ed.), *Sociology of Mass Communications* (London: Penguin, 1972), 75–98.
3   E. A. Shils, 'Charisma, order and status', *American Sociological Review*, 30 (1965), 199–213.
4   (New York: Museum of Modern Art, 1940), 16–17.
5   See 'Judy Garland and gay men', in R. Dyer, *Heavenly Bodies: Film Stars and Society* (London: Macmillan, 1987), 141–94.

7

SHIRLEY TEMPLE AND THE HOUSE OF ROCKEFELLER

Charles Eckert

Through the mid-depression years of 1934 to 1938 Shirley Temple was a phenomenon of the first magnitude: she led in box-office grosses, single-handedly revived Fox and influenced its merger with 20th Century, had more products named after her than any other star and became as intimately experienced at home and abroad as President Franklin Roosevelt. Her significance was then, and has been ever since, accounted for by an appeal to universals: to her cuteness, her precocious talents, her appeal to parental love and so forth. But one can no more imagine her having precisely the same effect upon audiences of any other decade of this century than one can imagine Clint Eastwood and William S. Hart exchanging personas.

One would not feel impelled to state so tawdry a truism if it were not for the anticipated resistance to a serious study of Shirley Temple, and especially to a study that regards her, in part, as a kind of artifact thrown up by a unique concatenation of social and economic forces. One anticipates resistance because Shirley was, first of all, a child (and therefore uncomplex, innocent of history) and, secondly, because the sense of the numinous that surrounds her is unlike that which surrounds culture heroes or political leaders, in that it is deeply sentimental and somehow purified. But this very numinosity, this sense of transcendental and irrational significance, if we measure it only by its degree, should alert us to the fact that we are dealing with a highly overdetermined object (in the Freudian sense of an object affected by more than one determinant).

A search for external determinants, however, initially faces a difficult paradox: there is no evidence in any of Shirley's films or in anything contemporaneously written about her that she was touched by the realities of the depression. For instance, in the mid-1930s, when 20 million people were on relief, Shirley awoke in the morning singing a song entitled 'Early Bird'; in the brutally demanding business of filmmaking, she thought everyone was playing games; and as for economics, Shirley thought a nickel was worth more than a dollar.

All of this would be intimidating if it were not that external determinants often cannot be perceived in a finished object, whether that determinant be the repression that produces a pun or the sweated labour that produces a shirt. And Shirley in film and story was as highly finished an object as a Christmas tree ornament. Some contemporary libels against her that depicted her as a thirty-year-old dwarf or as bald-headed, and the irreverencies of critics who called her the moppet with the 'slightly sinister repertoire of tricks' show that the surface was often too perfect to be accepted and that deceit was suspected. But libels are not theories, and everything written about Shirley was ultimately unable to explain her – or to exorcise her.

We might begin to chip at her surface (analytically, not iconoclastically) by noting that the industry she worked in was possibly more exposed to influences emanting from society, and in particular from its economic base, than any other. To the disruption of production, distribution and consumption shared by all industries one must add the intense economically determined ideological pressures that bore upon an industry whose commodities were emotions and ideas. Politicians directly charged Hollywood with the task of 'cheering Americans up'; and such studio ideologues as Jack Warner and Louis B. Mayer gloried in their new roles as shapers of public attitudes.

But far more significant pressures arose out of the grim economic histories of the major studios. By 1936 all of them had come under the financial control of either Morgan or Rockefeller financial interests (see F. D. Klingender and S. Legge, *Money Behind the Screen*, 1937). In addition to rendering films more formulaic and innocuous, this domination drew Hollywood into a relationship of pandering to the most conservative canons of capitalist ideology.

It is not my intention to recount this history, but rather to assess its effects upon the content of Shirley's films and her public persona. To do this systematically I must first survey a portion of the economic history for the period 1930–4 and describe the ideology it gave rise to. At this point my study will move synchronically, from the economic base through the ideology to Shirley Temple (her first feature films were made in 1934). I will then hedge on the synchrony by including films from 1935 and 1936 (on the pretext that Shirley's films conservatively repeated situations and themes).

ECONOMICS AND IDEOLOGY

The most persistent spectre that the depression offered to those who had come through the crash with some or most of their fortunes intact was, as it turned out, not that of Lenin or Mussolini, although articles on communism and fascism filled the magazines, but that of a small child dressed in welfare clothing, looking, as he was usually depicted, like a gaunt Jackie Coogan, but unsmiling, unresponsive, pausing to stare through the windows of cafeterias or grocery stores, his legs noticeably thin and his stomach slightly swollen. This spectre had thousands of incarnations.

> We were practising for a chorus and a little boy about 12 years old was in the front line. He was clean in his overalls, but didn't have very much on under them. He was standing in the line when all at once he pitched forward in a dead faint. This was two o'clock in the afternoon. . . . He had not had anything to eat since the day before.
>
> Five hundred school children, most with haggard faces and in tattered clothes, paraded through Chicago's downtown section . . . to demand that the school system provide them with food.

These children are, of course, symbolic, both in the context of the depression and of this article. What they symbolised was the flashpoint of the millions on relief who showed themselves, early on in the depression, largely immune to acts of revolt and willing to tough out the hard times if their children's minimal needs for food and clothing could be met. In November 1930 Hoover was forced to reply to the observation by the White House Conference on Child Health and Protection that 6 million American children were chronically undernourished. Hoover said:

> But that we not be discouraged, let us bear in mind that there are thirty-five million reasonably normal, cheerful human electrons, radiating joy and mischief and hope and faith. Their faces are turned toward the light – theirs is the life of great adventure. These are the vivid, romping everyday children, our own and our neighbors.

This may have washed with some at this early stage of the depression, but later on the tactics had to be more frontal. 'No One Is Starving', the *New York Times* and *Herald Tribune* announced in front-page headlines on 17 March 1932. This was the substance of telegrams from thirty-nine governors. The issue of starvation was debated, and many cases of death by starvation were adduced by newspapers; but the statement, which begged the issues of chronic malnutrition and near-starvation, was essentially true. And it was vitally important for those in positions of wealth and power that it remain essentially true.

To this end, the most minimal subsistence needs had to be provided. And as the estimate of those needing help rose, reaching about 20 million on the eve of the election in 1932, it became increasingly likely that a federal relief programme would have to be inaugurated. But to the captains of industry and the traditionally wealthy who made up Hoover's official and private entourages, the prospect of massive federal relief was dismaying. All of the initial reactions of Hoover and the class he so steadfastly represented had been self-serving. Tariffs were placed upon foreign imports, absurdly low income taxes upon the wealthy were reduced even further and federal reserves were hoarded in a miserly fashion or loaned at reduced rates to select banks and industries. The remedy for the depression, the country was told, lay in the protection, and where possible the augmentation, of the capital resources of the wealthy, for these resources were the key to renewed economic growth and revived employment.

Such naked opportunism at so desperate an hour had to be dressed in emperor's clothes of the first order. And Hoover and his supporters spent most of their time spinning and sewing. What they fashioned was a formidable ideological garment. The economy of the country was fuelled, not by labour, but by money. Those who possessed money would bring the country out of the depression as their confidence was restored by a protective and solicitous government. If the needy millions were served instead, a double blow would be struck at the nation's strength. First of all, the capital resources of the government and of the wealthy (who would have to be taxed) would be depleted. And, secondly, the moral fibre of those who received relief would be weakened – perhaps beyond repair.

The latter argument, less amenable to mystification because it was not couched in financial terms, needed more than assertion to give it weight. Recourse was therefore made to the deities who dwelled in the deepest recesses of the capitalist ethos. Initiative, Work and Thrift were summoned forth, blinking at the light. An accusing finger was pointed at England where the dole had robbed thousands of any interest in self-help. Hoover's attacks upon the evils of relief were echoed at state and local levels; and it became common to insist that those who received relief, even a single meal, do some work, such as sweeping streets in compensation. This demeaning, utterly alienating 'work' became one of the most common experiences of the depression, and one of its scandals.

The only ones who seemed to be taken in by the argument that relief destroyed character were reactionary governors and grim county relief agents. Clearly some other ideological weapon was needed, one which could effect material changes in conditions rather than merely mask the hardened indifference of the Hoover administration. And one was found, calculatedly developed and financed with some of the cold cash that was anathema to the poor. Declaring that 'no one with a spark of sympathy can contemplate unmoved the possibilities of suffering', Hoover, late in 1931, appointed Walter S. Gifford Director of the President's Organization on Unemployment Relief and Owen D. Young, Chairman of the Committee on Mobilization of Relief Resources. In their official capacities they took out a series of full-page advertisements in major magazines.

Tonight, Say This to Your Wife.
Then Look Into Her Eyes!
'I gave a lot more than we had planned. Are you angry?'

If you should tell her that you merely 'contributed' – that you gave no more than you really felt obliged to – her eyes will tell you nothing. But deep down in her woman's heart she will feel just a little disappointed – a tiny bit ashamed.

But tonight – *confess* to her that you have dug into the very bottom of your pocket – that you gave perhaps a little *more* than you could afford – that you opened not just your purse, but your heart as well.

In her eyes you'll see neither reproach nor anger. *Trust* her to understand. . . .

It is true – the world *respects* the man who lives within his income. But the world *adores* the man who *gives* BEYOND his income.

No – when you tell her that you have given somewhat *more* than you had planned, you will see no censure in her eyes. But *love*!

The President's Organization on Unemployment Relief –
Walter S. Gifford, Director
Committee on Mobilization of Relief Resources –
Owen D. Young, Chairman

The vulgarity of this charade can be appreciated more fully if we know that Gifford was President of AT&T, and Young Chairman of the Board of Directors of General Electric. This attempt to shift the burden of charitable work to the middle class and the poor was, ironically, unnecessary. As a reporter observed at a later date: 'In Philadelphia, as in most other cities, the poor are taking care of the poor.'

The endorsement of charity by those in power made the attacks upon the concept of welfare more consistent. Early in 1932 the Costigan–LaFollette Bill was voted down by both parties. It would have allocated $350 million for aid to local welfare agencies. A critic noted,

The Democrats want to win the next election. . . . They are constantly currying favour with big business and entrenched wealth. They will do nothing to offend Wall Street. . . . In the words of the Washington correspondent of the Federated Press, the Democrats are 'buying the next election with the lives of the children of the unemployed'.

Roosevelt did, of course, act on the issue of unemployment. The National Recovery Administration, Works Progress Administration and Conference of Catholic Charities produced jobs – at rather pathetic wages – for some. But a distinction must be made between the creation of a few hundred thousand jobs and the vast needs of 20 million destitute. When Roosevelt addressed the first CCC men by radio in July 1933, he said, 'You are evidence that we are seeking to get away, as fast as we possibly can, from the dole, from soup kitchens and from free lodging . . .' And when, a few months later, he signed the Federal Emergency Relief Act which allocated a token $500 million for grants to states, he implored citizens to 'voluntarily contribute to the pressing needs of welfare services'. A sense of foreboding gripped at least one reporter: 'Just why this note should have been sounded when it was hoped the federal government was about to initiate a bold, vigorous and constructive policy in relief . . . is not easy to understand.'

As the second year of Roosevelt's administration drew to a close in the winter of 1934, sufficient federal relief was no longer a serious possibility. Commentators noted that the impression that the Democrats would act had utterly demoralised charity efforts. And yet in New York alone there were 354,000 on relief, 77,000 more than a year before. Relief applications were coming in at the rate of 1,500 a day. One reporter passing through Ohio discovered families receiving 1½ cents per person. *The Nation* noted: 'Within the greatest anthill of the Western Hemisphere the machinery has slowed down. One out of six New Yorkers depends on the dole. One out of three of the city's working population is out of work.'

As the days grew shorter and greyer it became obvious that for millions the hardest times were still ahead. Those already mentally and physically stunted by years of malnutrition would know many more years of diminished existence before the economic boom of the Second World War would turn the depression around. And a few parents, broken under the responsibility of caring for hungry, ill and constantly irritable children, would kill one or more of them – and sometimes themselves.

But then, on the other hand, there was Shirley Temple.

SHIRLEY, AND LOVE

Since birth, Shirley had never awakened at night. She had never been ill, although her mother seemed to remember 'a little cold once'. She refused to take a bottle and had to be fed with a spoon at three months. She spoke at six months and walked at thirteen. She arose every morning either singing or reciting the lines she had memorised for her day's work. She was a genius with an IQ of 155. She did not mark her books, scrawl on wallpaper or break her toys. Doctors and dentists wrote to her mother asking for the secrets of her diet and hygiene: her mother responded that there weren't any. Her relations with her parents were totally loving and natural. She had no concern for, or sense of, herself, and was consequently unspoilable.

If her mother were not so straightforward a woman, and if there were not independent corroborators for some of these facts, one would have to presume that Shirley was not real – that she was a rosy image of childhood projected like a dialectical adumbration from the pallid bodies and distressed psyches of millions of depressed children. But she was real.

Her biographies are not, as with most Hollywood stars, cosmeticised myths, but something on the order of fundamentalist 'witnessings'.

> The cameraman tells me that she went through this emotional scene in such a miraculous way that the crew was spellbound, and when she finished they just stared fascinated. 'I wanted to reach out and touch her as she went by,' said Tony Ugrin who makes all her still pictures. 'I could hardly believe she was real.' Or, Adolfe Menjou speaking: 'That Temple kid. She scares me. She's . . . She's. . . .' He finally settled for 'She's an Ethel Barrymore at four.'

Shirley's relation to the depression history I have outlined goes far beyond this dialectical play between her biographies and the real childhoods of many depression children, however. And it is at once easy and difficult to conceptualise. There is a felt resonance between the persona she assumed in her films and the ideology of charity that no one can miss. But to state *why* its exists demands a theory for her studio's conscious or unconscious ideological bias, and the making of distinctions between unintended ideology (propaganda of the Gifford–Young sort), opportunistic seizing upon current ideas and issues (the 'topical' film syndrome) and a more diffuse attunement to the movie audience's moods and concerns. When one takes into account Fox's financial difficulties in 1934, its resurgence with Shirley Temple and its merger with 20th Century under the guidance of Rockefeller banking interests, one feels that the *least* that should be anticipated is a lackeying to the same interests that dominated Hoover and Roosevelt.

But such lackeying need not appear as a message or the espousal of a class view: it can as well operate (and more freely) as a principle of suppression and obfuscation. Shirley's films and her biographies do contain messages of the Gifford–Young sort – one should care for the unfortunate, work is a happy activity – but they seem more remarkable for what they do not contain, or contain only in the form of displaced and distorted contents.

I will assume that this contention is a viable one and rest the case for it upon the analysis which follows. But before beginning, a few biographical facts are needed to place Shirley relative to the history already outlined.

Shirley was born 23 April 1928, six months before the crash. She was discovered at a dance studio in 1933, given bit parts in shorts, then graduated to a musical number in Fox's *Stand Up and Cheer* early in 1934. During the number she pauses for a moment, puckers, leans forward and blows a little marshmallow kiss past the camera. Audiences emerged from the experience disoriented and possessive. After another minor role in *Change of Heart*, Shirley was moved up to feature roles in *Little*

Miss Marker (Paramount), *Baby, Take a Bow* (Fox), *Now and Forever* (Paramount) and *Bright Eyes* (Fox), all produced in 1934. The box-office grosses made both studios incredulous. No star of the 1930s had affected audiences so. Fox tied up its property with major contracts and produced nine more films in the next two years, the period of our concern.

Shirley's most intimate connections with depression history are those found in her films. I will deal opportunistically with the details of these films: what I shall principally omit are Shirley's functions as an entertainer – her many dances, songs, exchanges with other cute children and so forth. In any given film the sheer quantity of sequences in which Shirley entertains may make her other functions seem peripheral. But in the eleven films made between 1934 and 1936 the sequences devoted to plot and the development of a persona predominate.

In these films Shirley is often an orphan or motherless (*Little Miss Marker, Bright Eyes, Curly Top, Dimples, Captain January*) or unwanted (*Our Little Girl*). She is usually identified with a non-working proletariat made up of the dispossessed and the outcast (clearly in *Baby, Take a Bow, Little Miss Marker* and *Dimples*: more covertly in *Our Little Girl, Now and Forever* and *The Poor Little Rich Girl*). And when she is of well-to-do origins (*The Little Colonel, The Poor Little Rich Girl* and *The Littlest Rebel*) she shows affinities for servants, blacks and itinerants.

Her principal functions in virtually all of these films are to soften hard hearts (especially of the wealthy), to intercede on behalf of others, to effect liaisons between members of opposed social classes and occasionally to regenerate.

We can detect some very obvious forms of repression, displacement and condensation at work within this complex. Although proletarian in association, Shirley is seldom the daughter of a worker, much less an unemployed one. In the two films in which her parents are workers (*Little Miss Marker, Bright Eyes*), they are killed before the film begins or during it. Therefore the fact that the proletariat *works* is generally suppressed in the films. What proletarians do to get money is con people, beg or steal. This libellous class portrait is softened by comedy and irony, which function, as they usually do, as displaced attitudes of superiority and prejudice. A comical proletariat is also a lovable one, opening the way to identification, and even to charitable feeling.

Shirley's acts of softening, interceding and the rest are spontaneous ones, originating in her love of others. Not only do they function as condensations of all the mid-depression schemes for the care of the needy, but they repress the concepts of *duty* to give or of a responsibility to *share* (income tax, federal spending). The solution Shirley offers is natural: one opens one's heart, *à la* Gifford and Young, and the most implacable realities alter or disperse. We should also note that Shirley's love is of a special order. It is not, like God's, a universal *mana* flowing through all things, but a love that is elicited by *need*. Shirley turns like a lodestone towards the flintiest characters in her films: the wizened wealthy, the defensive unloved, figures of cold authority like Army officers, and tough criminals. She assaults, penetrates and opens them, making it possible for them to *give* of themselves. All of this returns upon her at times, forcing her into situations where she must decide who *needs* her most. It is her agony, her calvary, and it brings her to her most despairing moments. This confluence of needing, giving, of deciding whose need is greatest also obviously suggests the relief experience.

So strongly overdetermined is Shirley's capacity for love that she virtually exists within it. In Freudian terms she has no id, ego or superego. She is an unstructured reification of the libido, much as Einstein in popular myth reified the capacity for thought. Einstein's brain bulged his forehead, dwarfed his body and stood his hair on end. Shirley's capacity for love drew her into a small, warm ball, curled her hair, dimpled her cheeks and knees and set her in perpetual motion – dancing, strutting, beaming, wheedling, chiding, radiating, kissing. And since her love was indiscriminate, extending to pinched misers or to common hobos, it was a social, even a political, force on a par with the idea of democracy or the Constitution.

That all of this has great ideological potential scarcely needs arguing; but it would be naive to trace Shirley's film persona exclusively to an origin in the policies of the Hoover and Roosevelt administrations. One senses, rather, that Shirley is a locus at which this and other forces intersect, including those of the mitigation of reality through fantasy, the exacerbated emotions relating to insufficiently cared for children, the commonly stated philosophy of pulling together to whip the depression and others. Yet it would seem equally naive to discount the fact that Shirley and her burden of love appeared at a moment when the official ideology of charity had reached a final and unyielding form and when the public sources of charitable support were drying up.

SHIRLEY: HER WORK, HER MONEY

But depression attitudes towards charity, as we saw earlier, rested on forces emanating from the economic base; and I have so far said nothing of Shirley's relation to economics. Here we must move between her films and her biographies. For our purposes all of this material has the same status: it simply tells us all that people knew about Shirley. We have already noted that one of her functions was to pass between needy people – to be orphaned, exchanged, adopted. She always wound up in the possession of the person who needed her most. And he who possessed her owned the unique philosopher's stone of a depressed economy, the stone whose touch transmuted poverty to abundance, harsh reality to effulgent fantasy, sadness to vertiginous joy. All of this works as a displacement of the social uses and the efficacy of money.

If the argument needs strengthening, we do not have to seek far. Shirley's absolute value was a constant subject of speculation. The usual figure quoted was $10 million – in depression dollars an almost inconceivable sum. As a writer in the *Ladies Home Journal* put it in a symptomatic passage: 'When she was born the doctor had no way of knowing that the celestial script called for him to say, not "It's a girl" but "It's a gold mine." ' Her father was a bank clerk at the time of her discovery (1932) but through his fame (which could attract deposits) he soon became manager of a posh branch of the California Bank. This conjunction of a banker and an inestimably valuable property is in itself suggestive, especially for an era when bankers such as J. P. Morgan symbolised the capitalist system.

If we add to all of this Shirley's function as an asset to the Fox studios, her golden locks and the value of her name to the producers of Shirley Temple dolls and other products, the imagery closes in. She is subsumed to that class of objects which symbolise capitalism's false democracy: the Comstock Lode, the Irish Sweepstakes, the legacy from a distant relative. And if we join her inestimable value with her inability to be shared we discover a deep resonance with the depression-era notion of what capital was: a vital force whose efficacy would be destroyed if it was shared.

Even Shirley's capacity for love is rendered economic by our awareness that Fox duplicated the Hoover–Roosevelt tactic of espousing compassion for anterior economic motives (specifically, by making a profit from the spectacle of compassion). And because of the unique nature of the star-centred movie industry of the 1930s, Shirley was a power for monopoly control of film distribution.

This intricate nexus of functions and meanings contains enough material for a major study of how capitalism simultaneously asserts and denies its fetishistic attachment to money and embeds these attitudes in the metaphoric surfaces of the commodities it creates. Shirley, orphaned, often in poor clothes, with nothing to give but her love, was paradoxically specular with the idea of money. And the paradox could as easily be perceived as an oxymoron in which the terms need/abundance were indissolubly fused.

It is Shirley's relation to her work that we must next, and finally, consider, both because it received constant attention in her biographies and because it may lead us to fresh insights into her relations to love and money. The commonplace that most work under capitalism is alienated seems never more valid than during those crisis moments known as depressions. Work during such periods is not only more affected by feelings of personal insecurity, but by a very real harshening of work conditions.

For instance, millions of workers during the early 1930s suffered from one or more of the following conditions: speed-up, reduced work hours, reduced salaries; the firing of high salaried employees and the employing of those willing to work for much less; exposure to deteriorated and dangerous machinery and a general reduction of safety standards; thought and speech control so intense in some plants that workers never spoke except to ask or give instructions; inability to question deductions from paychecks; beatings by strike-breaking Pinkertons and thugs; and compelled acquiescence to the searches of their homes by company men looking for stolen articles.

And there were the ultimate forms of alienated work: street-cleaning, mopping a floor, painting a wall in exchange for a meal, often a bowl of soup and a piece of baker's stale bread. This was the work that saved one from the loss of initiative and character. One cannot read far in the records of any class of workers during the depression without discovering how abrasive and anxiety-ridden most working experiences were.

None of the biographical articles on Shirley failed to describe her attitudes toward her work. I will give just two examples. First, from *Time*:

> Her work entails no effort. She plays at acting as other small girls play at dolls. Her training began so long ago that she now absorbs instruction almost subconsciously. While her director explains how he wants a scene played, Shirley looks at her feet, apparently thinking of more important matters. When the take starts, she not only knows her own function but frequently that of the other actors. . . . She is not sensitive when criticized. . . . In one morning, Shirley Temple's crony and hero, Tap Dancer Bill Robinson . . . taught her a soft-shoe number, a waltz clog and three tap routines. She learned them without looking at him, by listening to his feet.

Second, from an article written by her mother:

> I never urged Shirley to go to the studio with me. She wanted to go then, as she wants to go now. Motion-picture acting is simply part of her play life. It is untinged with worry about tomorrow or fear of failure. A few times when we have left the studio together, she has looked up at me and said, 'Mommy, did I do all right?' Since there is no right or wrong about it, but only Shirley playing, I have replied, noncommittally, 'All right.' That was the end of it. . . . I do not know whether Shirley understands the plays in which she appears. We do not discuss plots or characters, or, indeed, any phase of her motion-picture work. Her playing is really play. She learns her lines rapidly, just as any child learns nursery rhymes or stories. . . . We usually go over the script the first time with enthusiasm. Sometimes, when it is issued, Shirley cannot wait until we get

home to hear her lines read. 'Turn on the dashboard lights,' she said one night, 'and read my lines while you drive.'

And for this work, accomplished with joy and ease, Shirley received $10,000 per week and over 3,500 letters thanking her for the pleasure she gave. The disparity between Shirley's work and the reality of most depression working experiences was ludicrous; and the frequency and consistency of descriptions of the sort just quoted indicates that the disparity was also mesmerising, much like the disclosure in 1932 that J. P. Morgan paid no income taxes.

Shirley's relation to work adds a further counter to the set already made up of her relations to love and to money; but does it also establish interrelationships with them? One is reminded of Marx's acute observation that money, considered in its relation to the work that produces it, has a repressive and censoring role. It shares this role with most commodities, which are designed and finished so as to conceal traces of the labour that has gone into them. To clarify the point by example, the lace produced by child labour in Nottingham in the 1860s was finished under very exacting standards of quality and cleanliness, effectively effacing evidence of the hand-labour that produced it. The well-to-do who bought it could in no palpable way be reminded of work, or of workers, or the exploitative class structure of their society, much less be led to inquire into the circumstances that saw up to twenty children crowded into an airless, fetid, 12-foot-square room, working under the whip of a mistress for from 12 to 16 hours a day, with their shoes removed, even in winter, so the lace would not be soiled.

One might say, then, that Shirley stands in the same relation to work as does a piece of Nottingham lace or a dollar bill: she censors or conceals work. The relation is not exact, for millions knew that she was awakened every morning by a mother who got her to start reciting her lines and kept her at it all the way to the studio. It was just that Shirley's work was self-obliterating – a whole deck of cards vanished in the air, or rather magically transmuted into $10,000 a week worth of prepubescent games.

But there is an exact correspondence to Marx's insight, in the relation between Shirley's films and work. One probably could not find a depression commodity more like a piece of Nottingham lace than a Shirley Temple film. Her directors, writers, cameramen, composers and the rest were never written about, never mentioned, except as witnesses to something Shirley said or did. And the films they produced obliterate all traces of their craft. They are consummate examples of minimal direction, invisible editing, unobtrusive camera-work and musical scoring and characterless dialogue. Every burr or edge was honed away, and the whole buffed to a high finish.

THE MAGICAL POWERS OF SHIRLEY

There are other relations between love, money and work that I do not have space to develop, and in some instances am not certain that I have grasped. Let me, however, attempt to give some rigour to the analysis made so far.

I have argued that the ideology of charity was the creation of a class intent upon motivating others to absorb the economic burdens imposed by the depression. This privileged class regarded itself as possessed of initiative, as self-made through hard work; and it saw in all governmental plans for aid a potential subversion of the doctrine of initiative.

Charity, then, came to be characterised as the bulwark of initiative. Money was a censored topic (for obvious reasons – Nelson Rockefeller today will not allow reporters to question him about his wealth); but there were clear implications that money as a charitable gift was benevolent, whereas money in the form of a dole was destructive. Money, then, was ambivalent and repressed, whereas charity and initiative were univalent and foregrounded.

In Shirley Temple's films and biographies, through a slight but very important displacement, charity appears as love and initiative as work. Both love and work are abstracted from all social and psychological realities. They have no causes; they are unmotivated. They appear in Shirley merely as prodigious innate capacities, something like Merlin's wisdom or Lancelot's strength; and they are magical in their powers – they can transform reality and spontaneously create well-being and happiness.

Money, in keeping with its ambivalent nature, is subjected to two opposing operations. In Shirley's films and the depictions of real life attitudes toward money, it is censored out of existence. It is less than destructive. It is nothing. But in an opposing movement, found largely in Shirley's biographies, money breaks free and induces an inebriated fantasy that a Caliban would embrace, a vision of gold descending from the heavens, a treasure produced from a little girl's joy and curls and laughter. This fantasy is removed from all thought of effort or anxiety; people can simply sit back in their chairs and, like a Lotus-eater, let the drugged vision possess them.

But any attempt to further clarify these relations would probably be wrong-headed since it would argue for coherence where there is often only a muddled interplay of the forces of censorship and obfuscation. It seems more appropriate to let the whole discourse dissolve back into the existential mass of depression history and Shirley and her films.

I will start it on its way by attacking the last point I made. I said that Shirley's films have no creators. This is untrue. The advertising copy for her films tells us that Shirley Temple made them – sometimes, we must presume, between playing with her pet rabbits and eating her favourite dish, canned peaches and ice cream. I also implied that many workers and their children suffered in material ways during the depression. But President Hoover wisely observed that the depression was 'only a state of mind', and Shirley's life and work provide exemplary proof that Hoover was right. And I hinted that cold cash might have been more desirable to a starving man than a child's warm touch. There is a perverse logic to this; but the thought is materialistic and, above all, dehumanising. Shirley's films never get into such Jesuitical quandaries; they keep the only authentic solution constantly before our eyes: the transforming power of love.

And with those props knocked from beneath the specious edifice of my argument, it shatters, expires and sinks beneath the dark tarn of history from which it was fallaciously raised. But at the point where the last bubbles appear, something bobs to the surface. It begins to rise in the air and to glow, assuming the shape of a luminous being. And now, having attained full power, it begins to flash off and on like a theatre marquee, and its feet begin to do little tap dance routines. It is Shirley Temple! Reborn. Released from the rational spell cast upon her by those sorcerers, Freud and Marx. And now we hear her voice announcing that the depression is over, that it never existed, that it is ending endlessly in each and every of her films, that these films are playing at our neighbourhood theatres and that we should come and see them, and that we must learn to love children and to weep for them and open our hearts to them, that we must not hate rich people because most of them are old and unhappy and unloved, that we should learn to sing at our work and dance away our weariness, that anyone can be an old sourpuss about rickets and protein deficiency but only Shirley Temple fans can laugh their pathology away.

And now that we have immersed ourselves in these egregious irrationalities and utterly clogged the process of thought we once again should be in the proper state of mind to see Shirley's films, and perhaps to accept her simply and naively as she accepted her labours in Hollywood's expedient vineyards.

This is an abridged version of an article first published in *Jump Cut*, 2 (July–August 1974).

8

'PUFFED SLEEVES BEFORE TEA-TIME'

Joan Crawford, Adrian and women audiences

Charlotte Cornelia Herzog and Jane Marie Gaines

> Every little girl, all over the country, within two weeks of the release of Joan Crawford's picture, felt she would die if she couldn't have a dress like that. With the results that the country was flooded with little Joan Crawfords.[1]

For *Letty Lynton* (1932), Gilbert Adrian designed Joan Crawford a gown which was to have far more significance than the film in which it was showcased. The white starched chiffon, featuring gigantic puffed and ruffled sleeves, introduced a fashion that lingered until the end of the thirties. Hollywood designers and fashion historians, recalling the period, have continually cited the 'Letty Lynton' dress as the most dramatic evidence of motion picture 'influence' on fashion behaviour.[2]

In the following, we begin to divide this idea of mass culture 'influence' into the theoretically more productive concepts of cultural production and women's subcultural response, which is in keeping with developments in feminist film criticism. Some of the issues raised by this criticism translate into consideration of women's fashion. For instance, ready-to-wear dresses, like motion pictures, are industrial products which carry cultural meanings. These meanings comprise the 'image' a woman assumes in her own dress and demeanour. We will deal here with how star image was articulated by means of costume, and how female fans in the thirties managed to put together similar 'looks'. This raises several questions: Did women actually 'choose' new fashions? Were women free to adorn their bodies in any imaginable way or was their appearance shaped by fashion ideas circulated by the motion picture and ready-to-wear industries? Was star imitation an indication that young women believed that clothes could change their circumstances?

STAR STYLES

> Some fossils may still look to Paris for their fashions ... but you and I know Paris isn't even a stand-in to Hollywood ... that Paris may decree this and Paris may decree that, but when that Crawford girl pops up in puffed sleeves, then it's puffed sleeves for us before tea-time.[3]

In one sense, the Letty Lynton style was a commercial barometer. Its popularity corresponded with Hollywood's eclipse of Paris as 'oracle' of American style, and marked the new co-operation between the motion picture and women's clothing industries. Macy's sales of a half million 'copies' of the now legendary Letty Lynton dress is a reference to the immediate success of star styles more than anything else.[4] When *Letty Lynton* was released in May 1932, Macy's had a Cinema Shop which specialised in gowns and accessories 'worn by the stars'.

Ready-to-wear copies or reproductions of motion picture gowns were modifications made with less fabric, so a woman was never purchasing the exact dress she had seen on the screen. Some Hollywood designers' work was closely followed in these reproductions. Adrian's designs, however, were not copied the way Orry-Kelly's designs for Warner Brothers had been.[5] Adrian, in fact, had a particular fear that he might be imitated. Part of the distinctiveness of his style can be explained as an effort to thwart copying by creating lines which would be difficult or impossible to duplicate.[6] Although the original Letty Lynton dress would never have been exactly duplicated, references to it abounded.

The puffy sleeve was immediately reinterpreted in a variety of ensembles and fabrics. Star fashion leaders were seen wearing the style both in and out of films. For the opening of *Strange Interlude* in 1932, Norma Shearer wore an Adrian-designed version of the voluminous-sleeved dress in organdie and velvet, and Glenda Farrell appeared in *Lady for a Day* wearing a similar effect in pink tulle.[7] Katherine Hepburn, as Cynthia Darrington in *Christopher Strong* (1933) wore still another rendition. In July of that year, Butterick Pattern Company made similar dresses available to ordinary women (Figure 8.1).[8] The style was resilient and persistent and could be seen on Marlene Dietrich in black tulle with rouche effect in 1935, and on Princess Elizabeth, 10 years old, in 1936.[9] The puffy-sleeved dress was a special occasion 'frock' which a young woman might wear for the country club dance, high school graduation or a wedding. In November 1939, Roberta Koppelman wore purple taffeta with mutton sleeves as her sister's bridesmaid in a Chicago wedding (Figure 8.2).[10]

75

Dance Frocks Are Bursting Into Print

5147 Evening frock. Plain or ruffle-edged scarf. Size 36, frock and plain scarf, 6 yards 39-in. novelty sheer silk. Sizes 12 to 20; 30 to 42 inches bust. Price, 50 Cents.

5183

Boa 5084

5183 Chiffon frock with double-tiered cape sleeves. Size 36, 5¾ yds. 39. Sizes 12 to 20; 30 to 40 bust. 50 Cents.

5186 Organdy frock with detachable capelet. Width 3⅜ yds. Size 36, 5 yards 39. Sizes 12 to 20; 30 to 44 bust. 45 Cents.

5186

5147

5184 Satin evening gown. Attached sectional flared skirt with back fulness. Size 36, 4⅝ yds. satin 39. Sizes 12 to 20; 30 to 40 bust. Price, 50 Cents. Organdy Boa 25 Cts.

5184

Figure 8.1 Butterick Pattern Company, 1933

76

Figure 8.2

WOMEN AUDIENCES AND FASHION ON THE SCREEN

As the first thrilling bars of music herald the latest Greta Garbo, Joan Crawford or Norma Shearer production, you will notice, as the presentation unreels, the simple credit – 'Gowns by Adrian.' That is your cue to sit taut in your seat and strain all your faculties for what you and you and you will next be wearing is about to be revealed![11]

Designer Helen Rose, in her book, *Just Make Them Beautiful*, says that women went to Adrian-designed films just to see what the stars wore. It seemed to her that it hardly mattered at that time if the clothes were even appropriate for the scene.[12] Rose's recollection is perhaps a better description of the Crawford than the Garbo and Shearer vehicles designed by Adrian between 1929 and 1941. During the Adrian years at MGM, the display of clothes became conventionalised in Crawford's films. We have identified, for instance, the use of the 'social whirl' montage and the fashion-show-within-the-film as devices for showcasing shoes, purses, hats, furs and lingerie.[13]

Both the sheer number of costumes and the look of expense were important to Crawford's promotion during the 'clothes horse' phase of her career. The extensiveness of her personal wardrobe and the variety of costume changes in each new release were standard publicity topics, as was Adrian's financial extravagance. Crawford would recall that for these fashion plate films more was often spent on wardrobe than on the rights for the script.[14] Critics at the time said that when there was little to remark about in the films, they could always write about the clothes.[15]

Joan Crawford's popularity rise dating from 1929 was coincident with an industry-wide emphasis on star costume which was immediately translated to women audiences in terms of their own clothing needs.[16] In the late twenties and early thirties, studio publicity departments had begun a large-scale effort to use fashion as a means to draw women into movie theatres. Publicists wrote beauty advice and fashion commentary which was sent to studio exchanges along with sets of fashion stills (Figure 8.3).[17] This material filtered out through exchanges to exhibitors who sent photographs and copy to local newspapers for Sunday supplement or women's feature page fashion specials. To the publicist, fashion was an advertising 'handle' or vehicle. It was a way to get a star featured and, hopefully, a motion picture title printed in the news media.[18] In every major studio, one publicist, always a woman, was the fan magazine contact whose job was to ensure that star publicity material was converted to make-up, hair style, wardrobe or figure care articles.[19] The elite fashion magazines, *Vogue* and *Harper's Bazaar*, which had insisted on looking to Paris and ignoring Hollywood during the twenties, began at this time to acknowledge studio designers and to feature the more aristocratic stars as dress models.[20]

Hollywood publicity at this time was taking on the tone and assuming the preoccupations of the high fashion magazine. Part of our concern here is to examine fashion publicity written in this vein as an index of what mattered to women fans and as a key to how they were involved through shopping and sewing in the cultural production of fashionable clothing. The following MGM publicity description of the Letty Lynton dress addresses women's interests and encourages a kind of absorption in the endless detail of dress and decoration:

Figure 8.3 Joan Crawford in *Letty Lynton* (1932)

The predicted mutton sleeves have arrived . . . Combined with ruffles and tucks and flares they have returned to dress the modern girls. One of the prettiest and most becoming of these styles from the past – with modern trimmings – has been created by Adrian for Joan Crawford to wear in her latest Metro-Goldwyn-Mayer picture, *Letty Lynton*. The frock is of white *mouseline de soi* – a starched chiffon, and shows a rounded-neck and peplum-edged sleeves. The skirt beneath is of flaring and circular fullness with a series of three tucks appearing above the three-ruffled border . . . The ruffles of collar, sleeves, peplum, belt buckle and shirt are all accordian pleated.[21]

First of all, this copy, which would have been used for photo captions or as the basis for articles on Crawford's latest Adrian gown, is directed at those women who *follow* fashion developments. Although not all women would watch these occurrences quite as closely as retailers or designers, the American woman who wished to be stylish would know that the designs she saw on the screen constituted the fashion ideals to which her own dress should refer. It is assumed here that this woman would be particularly attuned to fashion cycles and current trends, designer trademarks and the fabric, cut and line of the clothes she saw the stars wear in the movies.

The woman who wanted never to be 'out of style' but always first to wear the new, would want to know that mutton sleeves were 'predicted'. The idea that the Letty Lynton dress is 'one of the prettiest and most becoming of these styles from the past – with modern trimmings' situates the design within the fashion cycle which, a woman would know, explained why she could expect styles to come back again years later. The 'fashion-conscious' woman would also want to see how a sudden style divergence such as the Letty Lynton dress might fit into the general trend of thirties fashion. She would know that at the time the film was released, the contemporary trend was towards an interest in revival styles. The mutton sleeve, puffed at the shoulder and tight from the elbow down, was a throwback to the 1890s. A fashion follower would further note that the lines of this dress moved upwards instead of down, a reversal of the drooping lines seen between 1930 and 1932. Fitted bodices were popular then as was emphasis on the hips achieved through either draped material or tunic tops. The Letty Lynton dress with its fitted bodice and hip emphasis created by a peplum, an apron-like extension of the top, continued this trend. The distinction between day and evening wear, marked by dress length, was also important in the thirties since both day and evening dresses had been short in the previous decade. Finally, the Adrian gown was the sort of evening or 'party' dress worn during summer months or in warm climates, and ideally, or rather, hopefully, as Joan Crawford had worn the dress in the film – on a shipboard cruise.

The contemporary trend was especially important to motion picture designers because they had an additional factor to contend with in their design calculations: a time lag between conception and unveiling added by production schedules. Due to this lag, a designer would have to create costumes six to eight months in advance of a film's release. In order for these designs to be neither out of date nor too *avant-garde*, the designer would compromise with styles that looked contemporary but added a novel twist. For a designer such as Adrian who aimed to affect American dress significantly, there was another frustration: a new touch might appear either too early or too late to affect the 'prevailing silhouette'.[22] The mutton sleeve announced in the fashion copy arrived and stayed, but of the hundreds of costumes motion pictures premiered in this period, few diverted the course of fashion. Fashion publicity tied to the release of motion pictures, however, encouraged expectations of change with continual 'predictions'.

Designer appeal also suggested a way in which women might follow each new release, and MGM clearly used Adrians' personal as well as his artistic flamboyance to direct attention to his design style. Women would know, for instance, that one of Adrian's trademarks was 'emphasis above the table' – detail which was made especially interesting around the neck with tucks, flaps, inserts, beading or unusually shaped collars. Adrian's work was also characterised by lavish use of expensive materials such as lamé, chiffon, crepe, taffeta, satin, voile, fur, sequins and bugle beads.[23] He might, for an unconventional effect, use expensive fabric in a rather functional item, as seen in Crawford's memorable lamé polo coat.[24] In addition, the viewer might expect to see surprises in Adrian's asymmetrical use of contrasting black and white, in sculptural effects such as accordian pleating and in his exaggeration of a single motif, exemplified by the Letty Lynton sleeve.

Letty Lynton fashion copy acknowledges this interest with references to flares, tucks and accordian pleats in addition to the mutton sleeve, rounded neck and peplum. Women would be as interested in the fabric, *mouseline de soi*, or starched chiffon, and would want to know what it could be made to do or how easy it would be to work with. The film then showed another aspect, the dress 'in action'. Seeing the dress on Crawford would help women audiences imagine how it might 'respond' or move.

Studio publicity which revealed intricacies of costume construction assumed the existence of knowledgeable and resourceful female fans who could sew their own clothes. MGM production stills appeared in *Photoplay*, June 1932, illustrating the steps the costume department had taken to create the silver lamé cocktail dress Crawford wore in the poisoning scene from *Letty Lynton*. The description of the process, from sketch to cutting to final fitting, would be valuable information to a woman who

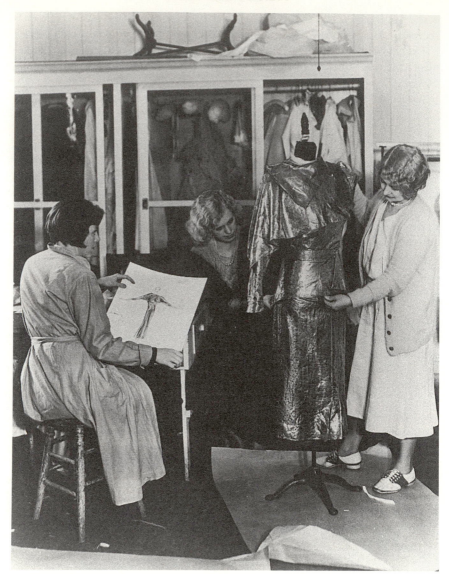

Figure 8.4

knew there were tricks to laying out a pattern in order to save fabric (Figure 8.4).[25] Not only did Butterick add 'Starred Patterns' in response to this interest in sewing glamour outfits, but *Silver Screen* and *Movie Mirror* magazines marketed patterns women could order through the mail.[26] If women were making their own star styles, were they, in fact, recreating Crawford's silver lamé to wear for a 'dinner date'?

During these years, fan magazines interpreted the stars' love affairs and offered dress and grooming as well as romantic advice to those who ostensibly wished they were more like their screen idols. If Joan Crawford's sunburst evening gown seen in *No More Ladies* (1935) used 30 yards of silver tissue at $18 per yard, the reader might modify the dress by using less yardage, *Photoplay* advised.[27] Or, if the reader could not afford silver fox for an evening wrap, she could make the same style in either fabric or less expensive fur.[28] Readers also received advice on how to adapt *one* dress for several different 'looks' or occasions. Seymour, fashion columnist for *Photoplay*, relayed advice from Joan Crawford to her fans on what to take on a trip. He reported that although Joan was taking the boat to Europe in the months after the release of *Letty Lynton* she would not be taking the 'frou frou' organdie dress with her. Instead, she planned to wear several puffed-sleeve blouses in plain organdie, eyelet batiste and dotted Swiss over a deep blue crepe evening gown. 'You could do the same thing for a fall evening costume only not have such summery materials for the blouses', Seymour suggested.[29]

We would make a distinction here, however, between studio glamour information and the modifications of this material which appeared in fan and women's magazines in the thirties. The fan magazines continually recommended that women *adapt* star outfits to fit their own needs, and fashion writers as well as designers suggested that readers carefully select only those styles which suited them. In a 1929 issue of *Photoplay* Adrian advised: 'There are some stars you will do well to copy. Find your prototype on the screen and remember the lines she wears to help you in selecting your wardrobe.'[30] The practicality as much as the frivolity of dress was stressed.

In addition to Adrian, the French designer Elsa Schiaparelli was attributed with statements about appropriate and functional dress and economy in wardrobe planning.[31] Such sources lent validity to the practical approach to fashion.

There are several ways in which this emphasis on practicality can be interpreted. First, women's publications may have recommended caution and practicality as a way of defusing potential criticism of Hollywood values and morals. The motherly tone of advice 'in the best interests of young women' can be seen this way. Second, culture industry manufacturers would know how much money women could afford to spend on clothes, movies and beauty products in the thirties. References to fabric cost per yard and the amount a woman had to 'put aside' each month if, for instance, she wanted a 'good' winter coat or serviceable shoes, all point to this. Would all women, however, have to economise in this manner? This second interpretation requires further breakdown and elaboration. In order to do this, we need to return, briefly, to the history of ready-wear and the question of social class and consumption in the context of the depression.

FASHION AND SOCIAL CLASS

What impulse drove women to exclusive couturiers and bargain basements in their quest for puffed sleeves? Was it the desire to look like Crawford, or the subconscious urge for high romance as usually purveyed by this Grade A Glamour Girl? Did the imitators think that, dressed as Joan Crawford, they, too, might enjoy life as she does – on the screen?[32]

Who were the women who were 'driven' to exclusive couturiers or bargain basements in their search for puffed sleeves? To begin with, the very rich and the wage earners have historically been first to take up new fashions. According to Ingrid Brenninkmeyer in *The Sociology of Fashion*, these two groups have less invested in convention than the middle class.[33] Fashion has had a wedge into the working class through young girls who were free to quickly drop one fashion and pick up another.[34] Can young working-class women account entirely for the success of retail wear star styles, particularly during the depression? Two factors are important here. First, in general, economic depression has historically encouraged mass-produced fashion sales. In both the twenties and thirties, ready-to-wear added customers from the group of more well-to-do women who were no longer able to afford dressmakers.[35] Second, in American society, clothes are relatively affordable commodities and have therefore served to disguise lack. Even during the depression of the thirties, it was possible for Americans to dress as though their circumstances had not changed.[36] Dress was not the indicator of class difference it had been during earlier historical periods. Rather, mass-produced fashion blurred class distinctions and performed an ideological function: it kept up the appearance of equality. The idea that the fashions of the stars were copied by patrons of exclusive couturiers and bargain basements alike went somewhat further. It had the most potency for the latter group, of course. To the woman with less means, the dress and the star held out something more. In order to think how a woman might measure herself against the star, and to fill out our consideration of motion picture 'influence' on fashion behaviour, we need finally to turn to the Crawford star image.

STAR IMAGE

Joan Crawford's life story was one of those star success legends which was often repeated in a way calculated to appeal to fans with similar

Figure 8.5 Joan Crawford in *Letty Lynton* (1932)

economic struggles. Like Lana Turner, Betty Hutton and Dorothy
Lamour, Crawford had lived a hard life before she could relax into the
ease and opulence which sympathetic stories said she had 'earned'. Fans
would know how her father deserted the family and Joan left home in
her teens to sing in clubs and dance in road shows. The Crawford 'hard
luck' stories which were circulated in fan magazines often focused on
clothes as indicators of her changing conditions. In a *Silver Screen* story

about the parallels between her own struggle and the plot of *Dancing Lady* (1933), Joan is quoted as saying that like the aspiring dancer in the film, she too had her first 'chance' when a friend gave her money to buy 'something decent to wear'. With $14 she bought a handbag, gloves, shoes, hat, hose and dress. Recalling that dress, she said, 'I defy Hattie Carnegie to sell me a gown that will make me feel more *chic* than the little four-ninety-eight model I bought that day.'[37] Joan's story repeats the tenets of fashion advice to young women: 'You can be glamorous on "nothing". It is a matter of your own ingenuity and your ability to *wear* budget outfits as though they were Paris couture.'

Crawford's films from the Adrian period further bore this out. In thirteen of the films between 1929 and 1941, she played a character in an elevated social position by birth, such as an heiress or a socialite. In eleven of the Adrian films, she moved from a lower to a higher-class position through marriage. Some of her more memorable lower-class parts were as stenographer (*Grand Hotel*, 1932), factory worker (*Possessed*, 1931; *Mannequin*, 1938), maid (*Sadie McGee*, 1934), sales clerk (*Our Blushing Brides*, 1930; *The Women*, 1939) and cabaret singer (*The Bride Wore Red*, 1937). These films taught finishing school dress and decorum for high-class social occasions and dramatised the penalties of social *faux pas*. The Crawford character was continually lifted out of her social station because she exhibited cultivated tastes and aristocratic manners. She had a fierce aspiration to 'be better', and was often held up to other characters (sometimes other girls and sometimes her own suitors) who were either cynical about success or those who, feeling opportunity had 'evaded them', had 'settled for less'.[38] Joan Crawford, the star who had 'fought' her way to success, held out an idea of social advancement through dedicated work and self-improvement. A woman who read star beauty and fashion advice would know that this rise could be achieved through good grooming, diet, exercise and proper dress.

Although fashion histories report that women avidly copied the dress and imitated the lovemaking of their heroines during the thirties, we have found that there was some disagreement at the time as to whether Holly-wood should offer fans glamour which was beyond their means. This conflict centred at times on the image of the dime store clerk who was thought to idolise Joan Crawford. Reviewers were critical of what they thought were 'unrealistic' representations of shop girls in Adrian gowns.[39] And certainly, even when Crawford played the hoofer, factory worker or maid, she wore silk or silk crepe, cut on the bias with a deep hem. Generally, the answer to this criticism was that fans *wanted* to see stars in silver fox boas and satin negligees no matter what roles they played. Joseph Mankiewicz was said to have explained to Crawford that the shop girl in the audience did not want to see her in a 'housedress with armpit stains'. The shop girl, he said, would prefer to see the star dressed in the Adrian gowns she wished that she could wear.[40]

Designer Edith Head countered this with a concern for the perspective of 'real women' in her interviews during the early years of her career. When a star she was costuming wanted to wear a gold-threaded evening gown to portray a working girl, Head argued that working girls could not be expected to 'wedge silver fox capes and lamé gowns into their clothes budgets'. When the star was not convinced, Head suggested that she listen outside theatres to the 'cynical comments of business girls and housewives concerning the elaborate wardrobes displayed by their screen counterparts'.[41] A third interpretation of the fan and fashion magazine concern for practicality may be that this very emphasis softened the resentment Head described. The debate over copying the stars which arose so frequently should be seen as part of the larger picture in a society which holds out opportunity for all, but withdraws the offer for some.

CONCLUSION

Both the conflict over whether women should copy the stars and the great difference between screen costume and everyday dress have dropped out in the various historical accounts of the 'influence' of motion pictures on fashion behaviour. Also missing is reference to the massive production and promotion effort which poured out fashion fantasies through mass media channels. In 1932, the culture industries were poised to produce both fashionable goods and images of fashionable behaviour which, in effect, created the overnight 'flood' of 'little Joan Crawfords'. Fashion worked to elicit women's participation in star and screen myth-making. Women bought star products and tested star beauty recipes, circulating ideas about star image in their own improvised 'looks'. At some point, then, it seems as though the mania for star fashions 'sprang' directly from women fans.

Following a straight mass culture manipulation theory, one would argue that the function of all motion picture fashion information, whether it appeared in advice columns or advertisements, was to persuade women to buy clothes and cosmetics instead of devising homemade beauty ornaments and treatments. We have found in the material surveyed here, however, a respect for the fashion practices and preferences of ordinary women. What explains this? Women's fan and fashion publications in the thirties could hint at the richness of women's participation in their 'own' cultural activity which involved collecting and making pretty things. At this time, more research is needed on women's sewing and fashioning in the home during the thirties in order to understand how that subcultural production became attached to the culture of the mass-produced fashion.

The publications we have studied make references to colour-coordinat-

ing, mixing and matching separates, shopping for fabric remnants, stretch-
ing a paycheque and selecting accessories that would last for years. We
would argue from this that women were not exactly the 'copy cat' imitators so often described. They did not step into star fashions without
altering or changing something. There would be key differences between
those fashions produced and pictured in magazines and on the screen and
the ones women actually wore. The distance between marks unexplored
cultural space.

AFTERWORD

In the five years since the publication of this article, we have continued
to search for evidence of the existence of the 500,000 'copies' of the Letty
Lynton dress sold in Macy's Cinema Shop coincident with the release
of *Letty Lynton* (1932). One of these dresses did reappear in the 1986
Smithsonian Institute 'Hollywood: Legend and Reality' travelling exhibition. This gave us hope.

But our interviews with publicists and merchandisers, our search
through pressbooks and newspapers and our examination of studio
archives finally revealed something else. The thousands of Letty Lynton
'copies' as well as the hundreds of official Cinema Fashions Shops are
wishful accounts of the tie-up phenomenon. Yes, star styles were a rage
in the 1930s, and loose copies of the flouncy white dress *were* manufactured. But it is unlikely that the ready-wear industry ever produced a run
of 500,000 on a dress of this type. Neither is there evidence that Bernard
Waldman established Cinema Fashions Shops in 400 different US towns
and cities by 1937. One short article on Waldman's Modern Merchandising
Bureau (*Fortune*, 15, 1 (January 1937) appears to be the original source
for the information about the agency. From there, Charles Eckert's
posthumously published unfootnoted classic 'The Carole Lombard in
Macy's Window' (reprinted here in part, ch. 3) ensured the Modern Merchandising Bureau's place in motion picture history.

The myth of the half million copies of the Letty Lynton dress was
spread through fan and fashion magazine articles in the 1930s and has
now passed safely into costume history. The discovery that the Letty
Lynton copies are myth and not fact, however, should not cause us
concern about the state of consumer culture and entertainment history.
Rather, it should lead us to reconsider something else: Why is the publicist's promotional copy *not* valid historical discourse? Should we discount
the skill of the professional publicists whose art lies in passing off promotion as news? The 500,000 dresses should not be treated as incorrect
historical fact. The importance of the Letty Lynton dress is as much
related to the success of a promotional ploy as it is to what women really
wore in 1932.

Finally, the place of the Letty Lynton dress in motion picture and fashion history is even more curious when we consider that the Metro-Goldwyn-Mayer film (in which the dress appeared) has not been publicly exhibited since the year of the film's release. *Letty Lynton* was pulled from distribution because of an important plagiarism case (Sheldon v. Metro-Goldwyn Pictures Corp., 1936). Consequently, the film has become canonised in copyright law rather than film studies texts. The film is an extremely interesting melodrama based on the Marie Belloc-Lowndes 1930 novel (in turn based on the notorious 1857 trial of Scottish heiress Madeleine Smith, accused of murdering her lover). The one existing 35mm print is in the MGM vault in Culver City and is now the property of Lorimar Television. The memory of a film never seen is kept alive by the circulation of the George Hurrell photographs of Joan Crawford looking demure and submissive in the frothy fantasy dress.

NOTES

This is a slightly shortened version of an article which first appeared in *Wide Angle*, 6, 4 (1985) and is published here with a new 'Afterword'.

1 'Does Hollywood create?', *Vogue*, 813 (1 February 1913), 61.
2 'Does Hollywood create?'; David Chierichetti, *Hollywood Costume Design* (New York: Harmony Books, 1976), 17; W. Robert LaVine, *In a Glamorous Fashion* (New York: Charles Scribner's Sons, 1980), 44; Joseph Simms, 'Adrian: American artist and designer', *Costume*, 8 (1974), n.p.; Josephs Simms' biography of Adrian published through the Adrian Archive of Cheltenham Township Senior High School, Wyncote, Pennsylvania for a special Adrian exhibit; Ernestine Carter, *The Changing World of Fashion* (New York: G. P. Putnam's Sons, 1977), 70, 159, with a photograph of Marlene Dietrich wearing a ruched sleeved dress which Carter describes as 'still echoing in 1935 Adrian's Letty Lynton sleeves invented for Joan Crawford in 1932'; Bob Thomas, *Joan Crawford* (New York: Simon and Schuster, 1978), 82, who wrote that 'Edith Head, who has won ten Academy Awards for costume design, has called Letty Lynton the single most important influence on fashion in film history'; and Eleanor Lambert in her article, 'Adrian exhibition to benefit education', *The Oklahoma Journal* (14 March 1971), 5D, who stated that Adrian 'turned Joan Crawford's extrabroad shoulders, large head and large mouth into a fashion identity not only for her, but for the whole late 30s generation'.
3 Wes Colman, 'Fads: Hollywood ideas that spread over the world', *Silver Screen*, 2, 12 (October 1932), 44.
4 Carter, 70; LaVine, 44.
5 Warner Brothers negotiated a separate contract with its designer Orry-Kelly to use his designs in a line of ready-wear clothes called 'Famous Movie Star Creations'. Several letters and interoffice memos dated 9 January 1933, 27 December 1932, 9 March 1941, etc. Orry-Kelly file, Warner Brothers Collection, University of Southern California. Warner Brothers proposed forming a corporation called Famous Star Promotional Corporation, to be in charge of selling franchises to individual manufacturers for the rights to sell designs using stars' names.
6 Lois Winebaum, 'Adrian', *Women's Wear Daily* (14 May 1971), 14.

7 Colman, 44; Marilyn, *Motion Picture*, 46, 2 (September 1933), 85.

8 'Dance frocks are bursting into print', *Butterick Fashion News* (July 1933), 4–5.

9 Carter, 159; *The Tatler*, 1805 (29 January 1936), 208.

10 The photographs referred to in the text are from the collection of Charlotte Koppelman Kopac.

11 Helen Harrison, 'Adrian's fashion secrets', *Hollywood*, 23, 9 (September 1932), 42.

12 Helen Rose, *Just Make Them Beautiful* (Santa Monica, California: Dennis-Landman Publishers, 1976), 147.

13 *Our Blushing Brides* (1930), *Mannequin* (1938) and *The Women* (1939), all include fashion shows within the film; *Chained* (1934), for instance, contains what we would call the 'social whirl' montage in which Crawford as the new wife of the owner of a steamship line is shown at a series of social events: the opera, the ballet, the races.

14 Roy Newquist, *Conversations with Joan Crawford* (New York: Citadel Press, 1980), 57.

15 Newquist, 95, 123.

16 Before this time, fan magazines separated fantasy gowns worn by the stars from practical clothes recommended for readers. The starlet or 'extra girl' modelled these scaled-down glamour outfits. See, for instance, 'Mary Philbin shows the wardrobe of an extra girl', *Screenland*, 17, 5 (September 1928), 38–9.

17 Fashion stills were different from production stills in that they featured both star and costume but did not include 'dramatic ideas'. The difference is made clear for publicists in Victor M. Shapiro's 'Duties of a unit publicity man: "musts" on each production', 1 July 1931, University of California at Los Angeles Special Collections. Also, Whitney Stine, *The Hurrell Style* (New York: John Day, 1976), 12–13, notes that Hurrell, who was employed by Metro-Goldwyn-Mayer at the time *Letty Lynton* was made, took glamour photographs in special sessions in his still gallery that were often reproduced in fan magazines to highlight fashions from a particular film. Other costumes featured in the *Letty Lynton* photo session with Hurrell were a sailor dress and an evening gown in white crepe and black bugle beads with white and black sections tied bandana-style at the neck and around the hips creating an asymmetrical effect. The white organdie, however, received the most photographic attention which suggests that it had been identified by the publicity department as an eye-catcher and was the centrepiece of the promotional campaign for the film.

18 In conversation with John Campbell, publicist, Twentieth Century-Fox, 1938 to 1943, 17 September 1980.

19 'Recollections of C. E. "Teet" Carle', publicist, Paramount Studios, 1927 to 1936, 1940 to 1960, transcript of oral history by Rae Lundquist, 1969, University of California at Los Angeles, 19–21.

20 Adrian, in 'Setting styles through the stars', *Ladies Home Journal*, 50, 2 (February 1933), 10 described how Hollywood was 'becoming the Paris of America', a direct challenge to fashion writers for these magazines who held the opinion that the Hollywood costume was vulgar.

21 Photo caption, Metro-Goldwyn-Mayer publicity still from *Letty Lynton*, MGM Collection, Academy of Motion Picture Arts and Sciences Library.

22 Kathleen Howard, *Photoplay*, 50, 5 (November 1936), 90. Adrian, in an interview with *Photoplay*, speculated about the potential impact of *Camille*, which was not due to be released until Christmas of that year. If the 'crinoline influence' could be seen in the 'prevailing silhouette', then he expected that the

Camille designs could add more new touches, he said. However, it was also possible that they would appear either too early or too late to have any effect at all.

23 The notorious red evening gown (and cape) seen in *The Bride Wore Red* was made entirely of bugle beads.

24 Margaret J. Bailey, *Those Glorious Glamour Years* (Secaucus, New Jersey: Citadel, 1982), 104, identifies this coat as from *I Live My Life* (1935).

25 'How they save Crawford's time', *Photoplay*, 42, 1 (June 1932), 76.

26 'Movie mirror pattern department', *Movie Mirror*, September 1934, 59, and 'Kay Francis selected this dress for Silver Screen's pattern', *Silver Screen*, 4, 12 (October 1934), 54.

27 Marvin Courtenay, 'Mid-summer fashion forecast', *Photoplay*, 48, 2 (July 1935), 101.

28 Ibid.

29 Seymour, 'Little tricks make Hollywood fashions individual', *Photoplay*, 42, 4 (September 1932), 104.

30 Lois Shirley, 'Your clothes come from Hollywood', *Photoplay*, 35, 3 (February 1929), 131.

31 Elsa Schiaparelli, 'How to be chic on a small income', *Photoplay*, August 1936, 60.

32 Dorothy Spensley, 'The most copied girl in the world', *Motion Picture*, 53, 4 (May 1937), 69.

33 Ingrid Brenninkmeyer, *The Sociology of Fashion* (Paris: Librarie du Recueil Sirey, 1963), 72–4.

34 Rene Konig, *The Restless Image* (London: Allen and Unwin, 1973), 213.

35 Brenninkmeyer, 91.

36 Michael Harrington, *The Other America* (New York: Macmillan, 1962), 17.

37 Patricia Keats, 'Our "Dancing Lady" ', *Silver Screen*, 3, 12 (October 1933), 49.

38 The Crawford films illustrated the advantages of social betterment but criticised the ultrawealthy, characterised in the films as decadent, faithless and not serious or hard-working enough to deserve her love. The man who promises to give her everything is sometimes an aimless playboy (*Dancing Lady*, *Our Blushing Brides*), too old or too debauched (*Chained*, *Sadie McGee*). Crawford and her shipping magnate husband (Spencer Tracy) are happiest in *Mannequin* when he goes bankrupt and they have to return to a more modest life.

39 Bob Thomas, *Joan Crawford* (New York: Simon and Schuster, 1978), 107 and Lawrence J. Quirk, *The Films of Joan Crawford* (Secaucus, New Jersey: Citadel, 1968), 20, wrote that one critic of *Reunion in France* (1942) commented that, 'Despite reports of limited yardgoods and costume budgets in Hollywood (it was mid-World War II) Miss Crawford manages to appear in a new gown in virtually every scene.'

40 Thomas, *Joan Crawford*, 107.

41 Beryl Williams, *Fashion Is Our Business* (New York: Lippincott, 1945), 149.

9

THE RETURN OF JIMMY STEWART
The publicity photograph as text
Charles Wolfe

Around the production, distribution and exhibition of films a host of photographic images proliferate: production stills, celebrity photos, photographic poster art, illustrations for pressbooks, programmes, interviews and reviews. They whet our appetite for moving images yet unseen and prolong our pleasure after the act of seeing. They can be held, examined at leisure, collected and catalogued. With time they serve as an archive of images to be drawn from for coffee-table anthologies, journals of history and criticism and monographs of various kinds. They are an important part of the institution of cinema even if we do not at first think of them as related to the film-as-text in a meaningful way.[1] Reproduced and recycled, captured and captioned by authors and editors, these images bear an historical trace, a trace worth pursuing.

The function of these photographs in the first instance is usually publicity; they publicise films, and the stars who help sell films. Within the Hollywood studio system, still photography departments were an important component of the public relations machinery buttressing the star system and the marketing campaigns for individual films. Stills heralded new productions, not only through the direct channel of paid advertising, but also indirectly through the broad coverage given to Hollywood by the expanding national magazine industry from the twenties through the mid-fifties.[2] This publicity function was most naked of course in fan magazines, which sustained a sensational celebrity drama about the lives of the stars. But celebrity photographs were also a staple item of chic, New York based monthlies such as *Vanity Fair* and *Stage*, and middle-class 'women's magazines' such as *Ladies Home Journal* and *McCalls*. From the time of its debut in the fall of 1936, *Life* magazine treated Hollywood movies as privileged cultural territory in its weekly survey of the visible. By 1936, moreover, photographs from Hollywood were a regular item in the two major national news magazines, *Time* and *Newsweek*, where photojournalism was becoming broader and more colourful. A *Time* cover story on Shirley Temple, child star in Hollywood, followed cover stories on Adolf Hitler, man on the move in Europe, and Daniel Webster Hoan, socialist mayor of Milwaukee.[3] Interwoven into the news of the week, publicity photographs acquired a new social dimension, one which makes their history a fertile field for research.

My interest in the historiographic value of these photographs has been prompted by a specific example of news magazine coverage, one I would like to examine here in detail. It is the cover story from *Newsweek* on 30 December 1946, published to coincide with the release of *It's a Wonderful Life*. What first caught my eye in the cover photo was a certain oddity in the pattern of glances among the various figures in the frame (Figure 9.1). What sustained my interest was an ambiguity, signalled by the caption, which could easily be read back into the image itself. Indeed, the image seems to me open to three different 'readings' depending on the contextual frame placed around it. Superimposed, these readings support one another, yet there are also points of resistance; they do not cleanly 'fit'.

From one vantage point, the cover photo functions simply as a *production still*. Anyone who has seen *It's a Wonderful Life* will recognise the passage from the film to which the image refers: the return of George Bailey from the brink of suicide to the embrace of his family on Christmas Eve. The photograph is not an actual frame from the film, nor does it precisely replicate any single shot from the film. Yet I think we have no trouble letting this image represent in some fashion the film's concluding passage, for key graphic and dramatic elements from that conclusion are retained. The grouping of the Bailey family – particularly the central triadic image of George in the middle, Mary on the left and daughter Zuzu on the right – mirrors their reunion in the film. George, back from a terrifying vision in which his family has failed to recognise him, placing into doubt his very existence within their world, clings to his wife and daughter, his mussed hair a sign of his former distress. Mary, solidly anchored in the space of the home in a way her husband has never been, remains calm, unruffled, supporting her husband as much as she is supported by him. Zuzu, echoing the theme of regeneration through her own recovery from a cold, drapes her arm around her father and tugs at his sleeve, secure and relaxed. Furthermore, the prominence given the Christmas tree – the bulbs, light and tinsel – matches the *mise-en-scène* of several of the final images in the film in which decorated branches jut into the frame. And the attention paid to Uncle Billy on the left side of the photograph is partially in keeping with the psychological dynamics of the ending. Having precipitated the final crisis through his negligence at the Bailey Savings and Loan, it is important that Uncle Billy is redeemed as part of the extended family which is reconstituted on Christmas Eve.

On the other hand, elements of this photograph mildly distort the film's narrative. George, Mary and the children, for example, never contemplate Uncle Billy in the intimate and wholly absorbed way this image suggests.

Figure 9.1

In the film Billy ushers in a parade of relatives and neighbours who flood the house, creating an atmosphere of communal euphoria.[4] The original production still from which *Newsweek* struck this image, it should be noted, included four other figures on the right side of the frame: Grand-

Figure 9.2

mother Bailey (George's mother), Grandmother Hatch (Mary's mother), Pete (George and Mary's older son) and an anonymous neighbour (Figure 9.2). All four have been cropped from the photo by the *Newsweek* editor, and the image has been retouched so as to eliminate the profile of the boy's face at Zuzu's sleeve, a profile which otherwise would have fallen within the boundary line of the reframed image. Furthermore, narrow cropping at the bottom of the frame eliminates the money visible in the original, money which Billy has collected from the community and delivered in a basket at the head of the procession into the house. These excisions not only isolate the Bailey reunion from a broader social context, they cut Billy off from the figures he looks at to the right, rendering mysterious, if not peculiar, his distant gaze.

Our awareness of these elements of congruity and incongruity, of course, follows from a familiarity with the narrative of *It's a Wonderful Life*. Without that text as context, this reading makes no sense. For those who have not seen the film, a story could be conjured up from the photograph: the tree, the winter dress of the two men, the nightclothing of the children, all suggest a Christmas Eve setting; the grouping of the

Figure 9.3 Newsweek, December 30, 1946

figures on the right point to a family unit; the figure on the left might well be a relative. Cultural codes work to fill in this scenario, but the clues are vague. The narrative and psychological possibilities of *return* for example, are primarily cued by the caption; at best they remain unclear in the picture. I think if we were asked to find the 'returning' party in this image, we would probably select the figure on the left: he is set apart from the rest graphically (backed by the glitter of the Christmas decor); he is the object of the gaze of all the other figures (save one); and his own gaze seems unfocused, as if perhaps he still is lost in the reverie of another place. Indeed, if glances were the only clue we had to construct a narrative, Billy would probably become the centre of action.

The caption, of course, prevents us from making this mistake. It links the act of returning to a name and face few readers in 1946 would fail to recognise: this is the return of Jimmy Stewart. However tempted we might be to focus upon Thomas Mitchell on the left, surely our attention returns in full measure to Stewart upon reading the caption. The significance of this photograph, we are instructed, has to do with the star of the film. Donna Reed and Thomas Mitchell, Karolyn Grimes and Carol Coomes as the daughters, Jimmy Hawkins as the younger son – these are all supporting actors and actresses and they go unnamed here.

To speak of the image in terms of actors and actresses supporting a central star, instead of characters supporting a fiction, is to read the image in a slightly different way. We are no longer examining a still image from the diegesis of *It's a Wonderful Life*, but a *celebrity photo* which feeds off – and provokes – interest in the career of James Stewart, an interest which, *Newsweek* well knows, sells magazines as well as films. From this perspective, the 'return' has nothing to do with any narrative act within the film. Rather it calls attention to the stage in Stewart's career which the film represents.

In 1946 James Stewart was returning to motion pictures after a five-year absence, during which he had served with distinction as an Air Force pilot. He had enlisted in March 1941, several months before Pearl Harbor, and reportedly worked hard to downplay his status as a movie star while in the military. But his tenure as a bomber pilot and squadron leader in Europe between 1943 and 1945 was highly celebrated, and he returned to civilian life a war hero. The question now remained: could he make the transition back to movie actor? This drama of a star's comeback – part of the fascination of moviegoing, and the calculations of movie marketing, since the days of Florence Lawrence and Carl Laemmle – is fleshed out in detail in the *Newsweek* cover story, as it was in many interviews and reviews at the time of the film's release.[5] The interest in *It's a Wonderful Life* generated in 1946 thus was partly based on the professional test it offered Stewart as a returning star, a concern lost on most viewers of the film today. In alluding to this celebrity drama on the cover, *Newsweek*'s editors select a photograph which superimposes Stewart's celebrity return upon the narrative return within the fiction, trading on the ambivalent status of his presence as actor/character within the space of the shot.

A series of photographs accompanying the feature article inside further illustrates the intricacy of this play between performer and role. Three photographs descend across a double-page layout. The first is a production still from the filibuster sequence in *Mr Smith Goes to Washington* (1939): Jefferson Smith stands upright next to a stack of letters which purportedly oppose his 'lost cause' struggle against political corruption in the nation's capitol. The second is a wartime file photo of Stewart in his officer's uniform: he appears to be seated on a desk or table, his hands folded around an upraised knee. The pose is informal, somewhat awkward, but not without charm, emphasising the actor's characteristic lankiness. The third, like the first, is a production still, this time from *It's a Wonderful Life*: George Bailey, seated low in an ornate chair in Potter's office, puffs on a cigar; one eyebrow is arched. The selection and arrangement of photographs have been done with care to create a sense of logical progression. Stewart's glance is consistently leftward, but as the photographs descend along a rightward diagonal, Stewart is made to 'descend' from a standing to a fully seated position. We have here, in short, a montage effect which reverses the movement of Eisenstein's famous stone lions rising in anger in *Potemkin* (1925). Prewar, Stewart-as-Smith stands in idealistic, even bitter, defiance; postwar, Stewart-as-Bailey flirts with compromise. A running caption helps to stitch the sequence together into a single photographic phrase: 'Stewart: As Mr Smith prewar . . . as an Eighth Air Force colonel . . . and as George Bailey postwar.' The middle term of this sequence is crucial. By virtue of its bracketing by the production stills, the centre photograph appears to represent Stewart in yet another role ('as an Eighth Air Force Colonel') in a different theatre of action – the war. Concomitantly, the two production stills, by virtue of their juxtaposition with the 'real life' Stewart in the centre, illustrate stages in the career of a celebrity, a public hero, under scrutiny.

This seamless interweaving of fictional and non-fictional images is an exceptionally compact example of a more general pattern at work in these magazines. News photos are placed beside pictorial photographs, including decorative advertisements; celebrity portraits and production stills are absorbed into an undifferentiated flow of images across the page. The cover photo in particular becomes a privileged site for displaying the week's most urgent 'story', yet no distinction is made among the various kinds of images which are reprinted there. All reside beneath the banner of '*Newsweek*/The Magazine of News Significance'. All pass as journalistic. The date itself is clearly marked: 30 December 1946.

We might see this then as another kind of image the cover photo represents: the journalistic *news photo*. From this perspective, the film is simply another newsworthy event, part of the viewable world from which an image can be retrieved, reproduced and circulated to the reader. What does the publicity photograph signify in this context?

To answer this, we might look at the photographs *Newsweek* ran on its cover during the Christmas season of the preceding years. December 1941 left little room for nostalgia – cover photos document the outbreak of war in the Pacific. On 28 December 1942, however, *Newsweek* ran a staged shot in which wartime and seasonal sentiments are boldly joined. A woman, clad in a uniform, professional yet somewhat sporty, works beneath the protective canopy of a bomber wing, cheerfully painting the message 'Merry Christmas to Hirohito' on a bomb marked 'Rush' (Figure

Figure 9.4

9.3). The composition is carefully arranged and the colour scheme meticulous; the drabness of the bomber is counterpointed by a bright foreground, and the co-ordination of the woman's rust-coloured Johnny Reb hat, lipstick and nail polish with the similarly coloured Christmas ribbon and

99

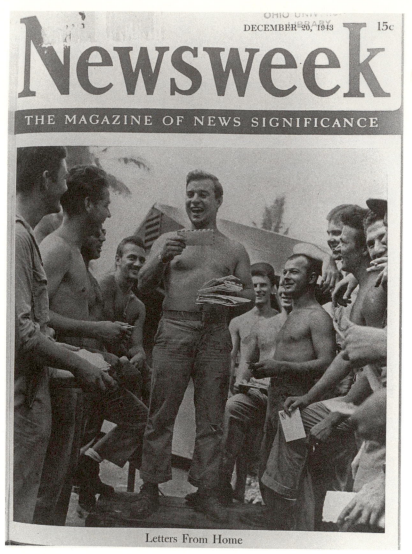

Figure 9.5

table top suggests elements of fashion photography. Moreover, the Christmas convention of gift-giving is deployed here to connote sunny commitment to victory by supportive women on the homefront. A year later, on 20 December 1943, *Newsweek* presented a black-and-white photo from

Figure 9.6

the warfront, captioned 'Letters from Home' (Figure 9.5). Shirtless, the soldiers appear far removed from a more conventional Christmas setting of winter landscapes; the holidays only enter the scene, indirectly, via the mail. The shot, while obviously composed by the photographer to empha-

101

Figure 9.7

sise the smiling, robust soldier in the centre, also has a candid quality to it, coded by the black-and-white, news-photo style. On 25 December 1944, in the aftermath of the invasion of Germany, the receipt of gifts overseas is again the theme in what appears to be a snapshot of an

American soldier, laden with packages, walking alone down the street of a German city (Figure 9.6). There is a certain poignancy to the shot. The recipient of gifts is by himself, and a woman in the background moves away in the opposite direction. But the caption adds a note of aggression: 'He Got His: A Christmas Haul on the German Front' – as if the packages were the spoils of a war which had lasted far too long. Moreover, the soldier, heading away from the cities of Roetgen and Stolberg, seems to be leaving Germany behind.

On 24 December 1945, the reader is brought back home, back to images of women in service as bearers of gifts (Figure 9.7). Here we have a colour photo of a cover girl WAC. The background is indistinct, but appears to blend two signs: stars from the American flag are given a blurry, Christmas tree light effect. This wedding of patriotism and holiday spirit is picked up in the colour scheme of the packages the woman holds in her arms: red, white and blue are the dominant colours of the wrapping paper, matching the stripes of the military patch on her sleeve. We can also assume I think that the packages are not to be mailed, but are to be hand delivered. This sense of transition to domestic life is brought out in the editor's note inside the cover, where we are told that 1945 marks the first, and probably last peacetime Christmas for the Woman's Army Corps, at the time scheduled to be dissolved.

The editor's task in each instance is to forge topical concerns with the ongoing mythology of Christmas, or, perhaps, to recast that mythology in terms of topical concerns. The cover photos are highly emblematic, condensing or distilling a point to be made about the news of the week. This is as true of the candid news photo as it is of the staged cover shot, although the candid photo perhaps needs to be more firmly pinned down with a caption in order to function as efficiently as the more overtly stylised image.

On 30 December 1946, then, with the war concluded on all fronts, we might say that *Newsweek* brings the reader inside the American home. An ideal image of the reconstituted family is presented: the father has returned, the mother appears never to have left. As a news photo, the image no longer appears drawn from a publicity portfolio, but rather from a family album. Indeed, there is an element within the picture which marks the photograph as a kind of *family snapshot*. I am thinking of what is perhaps the most striking glance in the image (although at first we may perceive it only on the periphery of our vision), that of the boy at the bottom of the frame. It is a disobedient look; he is not playing the game played by the others, who pretend they are unaware of the camera. Instead, he acknowledges the camera, breaking the taboo of the production still (after that of much Hollywood cinema), puncturing the diegetic space the fictional film seeks to seal off. When we isolate that face, the status of the image as snapshot is very clear. But even within the space of the full image, the boy's look encourages a new reading of the odd glances of the figures above him. The tableau is akin to those staged family portraits where everyone labours mightily to look not at the camera, but at one another. All of the family on the right side of the frame therefore stares at the figure on the left, none too easy a task for the girl at the bottom who risks a wrenched neck, while the figure on the left holds his own look within himself. The boy however simply stares the camera down. The editor could have cropped this unsubmissive figure from the bottom of the frame (along with the money). Instead the boy is included, I suspect for the sensation of candidness the youngster supplies. Moreover, the excision of the broader community from the right side of this tableau isolates and intensifies the familiar imagery, and re-balances the photograph so that the mother now occupies the centre point of the shot.

Now clearly there is too much star voltage in this image for the reader to interpret it simply as an anonymous veteran's homecoming as recorded by a photojournalist. But keeping in mind the notion of superimposed readings, let us return for a moment to the celebrity drama *Newsweek* has outlined. The feature article in this instance does not ask the reader to savour gossip concerning the fortunes of an exotic star. Instead an effort is made to link Stewart's return to a prewar profession with the return of veterans to prewar professions everywhere. 'It is like an obstetrician's first delivery after duty on a destroyer', we are told, 'or like a violinist's first solo after a stretch in the field artillery'. Changes in the profession, and importantly changes in the veterans themselves, have left both Stewart and director Frank Capra anxious about their attempts to pick up where they left off before the war. 'On the set', *Newsweek* reports, 'Capra and Stewart worked out their specialised rehabilitation problems together, lending each other comfort and support, and smothering their worries with hard work.' Capra was enough of a name for his 'rehabilitation' to be of journalistic interest, but Stewart was the visible star, cast as the ideal representative of a veteran-hero whose insecurities have surfaced upon returning home.[6] The boyishness Stewart projected as a personality before the war, *Newsweek* notes, has 'vanished with his return from the B-24s, which left him with a few unboyish gray hairs'. His performance is praised as an 'adult, appealing, postwar impersonation'.

The figure of James Stewart thus stands in not only for 'George Bailey', but also for the anxious veteran, whose return informs this cover story as well. The alignment of George Bailey's return with that of Stewart (as actor) and the veteran (as spectator) is by no means perfect however. George Bailey's return is not from the war. Indeed, the fact that he has not gone off to war, but has instead resigned himself to working on the homefront, is part of his problem, or at least a symptom of it. Throughout the narrative, George represses his own desire to conquer the world in favour of his younger brother Harry, who by the end has been awarded the Congressional Medal of Honor for his valour overseas. Thus in contrast, say, to *The Best Years of Our Lives* – with which *It's a Wonderful Life* competed at the box office over the holidays, and at the Academy Awards ceremony the following spring – the question of veteran readjustment is at best marginal to the narrative. Harry's homecoming is purely celebratory, and provides an emotional 'topper' to the general euphoria surrounding George's revival. Yet, George's nightmare vision of dissociation, of the rupture of the family and of small-town values, can also be read as operating within the spirit of postwar *noir*, where the representation of veteran anguish is frequently not literal. That this is not overt in *It's a Wonderful Life* makes the 'mis-reading' suggested by *Newsweek*'s coverage of the film all the more useful.

The effort of the media to situate the film within the news events of the day, to find a context within which to make it legible for its readers, opens up an historical axis which the narrative of the film intersects but does not retrace. Likewise, it allows us to work with a notion of an *historical* spectator, a figure which the narratological construct, the spectator-in-the-text, at some point meets but does not wholly define.

News magazines are a particularly rich medium to focus on here, for the very purpose of these weekly periodicals is to bring unity to a flow of disparate events, to juxtapose fragments in such a way that they are given coherent social meaning in a familiar package. Their general practice of not specifying sources – where and how images were obtained, who or what is transmitting the news – aims at a homogeneous style whereby potentially cacophonous 'voices' are flattened out into a single 'voice' which speaks with authority. Motion pictures are one of the 'voices' to be tamed, and one of the many contexts within which magazine images must be read.

What we are speaking of then is a media network in which text and context interlock; the text itself shifts in and out of view, like the oscillation between figure and ground in an unstable optical illusion. Before we will be able to discuss the notion of an historical spectator with any precision, we must have a clearer sense of the evolving structural relations between the film industry and the various channels defining this image network. Images from Hollywood, and from Hollywood movies, did not proliferate like dandelion seeds blown in the wind; systems grew up around their dissemination. What specific channels interconnect in this system? How is a unified message transmitted across a variety of formats? Also: where are the points of resistance, of transformation, of subversion of meaning? Tracing individual films and film stars is one way to illuminate this circuitry. It may also be an important step in establishing a discourse about film images and imagery which is both critical and historical.

105

NOTES

First published in *Wide Angle*, 6, 4 (1985).

Figures 1, 3, 4, 5, 6 and 7 are reprinted courtesy of *Newsweek* magazine.

1 Russell Merritt has touched on this point with respect to the different procedures employed by the critics to 'read' the famous publicity still of Walter Hall's set for *Intolerance*. See 'On first looking into Griffith's Babylon: a reading of a publicity still', *Wide Angle*, 3, 1 (1979), 22–7.

2 For a history of the national magazine during this period, see Theodore Peterson's *Magazines in the Twentieth Century* (Urbana: The University of Illinois Press, 1956). The relationship between the motion picture and the pictorial magazine industries during their parallel years of development needs to be researched.

3 See 'Marxist Mayor' (Hoan), *Time*, 6 April 1936, cover and 18–20; 'Plan v. plan v. plan' (Hitler), *Time*, 13 April 1936, cover and 24–6; 'Peewee's progress' (Temple), *Time*, 27 April 1936, cover and 36–44.

4 Moreover, the awe with which Uncle Billy is being watched would perhaps make more sense if he were an extraterrestrial figure like Clarence, the angel who visits George on Christmas Eve and vanishes when George recovers. In a recent discussion of the film, Kaja Silverman has proposed that Uncle Billy is in certain respects a worldly twin of Clarence: both possess limited intelligence, modest aspirations, good-heartedness and buffoonery. If so, Billy is perhaps an appropriate surrogate for the absent angel, at least for the purposes of the production still. See 'Male subjectivity and the celestial suture: *It's a Wonderful Life*', *Framework*, 14 (1981), 16–22.

5 'The Stewart touch', *Newsweek*, 30 December 1946, 72–3. Stewart's return in *It's a Wonderful Life* was also featured on the cover of *This Week*, a Sunday newspaper supplement. See Nord Riley, 'Stewart's story', *This Week*, 15 December 1946, 18–19. Also see 'Jimmy Stewart comes back in new film', *Cue*, 12 December 1946, 16–17; Howard Barnes, 'On the screen', *New York Herald Tribune*, 21 December 1946; 'New pictures', *Time*, 23 December 1946, 54; Bert [Bert Briller], '*It's a Wonderful Life*', *Variety*, 25 December 1946; Eliot Norton, 'Jimmy Stewart and Capra in Hub', *The Boston Post*, 29 January 1947; 'Liberty picks a movie eligible for top honors', *Liberty*, 15 February 1947.

6 Capra had made the cover of *Time* on 8 August 1938, so he was no newcomer to magazine publicity. A good deal of the coverage concerning his and Stewart's return to Hollywood also involved their efforts to work free of studio contracts: Stewart had decided not to return to MGM, and Capra was attempting to launch Liberty Films, Inc., along with fellow veterans William Wyler, George Stevens and Samuel Briskin. Liberty Films was considered a bellwether company for independent production after the war, and the trade press especially covered *It's a Wonderful Life* in this context. The somewhat disappointing performance of the film at the box office was subsequently considered a significant factor in the dissolution of Liberty Films in 1947. See Fred Stanley, 'Out of Hollywood', *The New York Times*, 10 February 1946, Sec. 9, p. 1; 'New Pictures', *Time*, 23 December 1946, 54; and 'The price of liberty', *Time*, 26 May 1947, 88.

10

THREE INDIAN FILM STARS

Behroze Gandhy and Rosie Thomas

THE STAR SYSTEM IN INDIA

Early each morning a saffron-robed figure appears on the balcony of a suburban house in Hyderabad. A small crowd gathers to receive the blessings of N.T. Rama Rao, top star of the Telugu cinema, best known over the years for playing the god Krishna. That he was also elected Chief Minister of Andhra Pradesh in 1983 points to the complex way in which the relationship between divinity, film and politics is lived – and exploited – in India. While top Bombay stars no longer act in mythological films,[1] as the genre has been in decline there since the 1960s, the parallels between Indian stars and the gods of the Hindu pantheon are frequently remarked upon: both are colourfully larger than life, their lives and loves, including moral lapses, the subject of voyeuristic fascination and extraordinary tolerance, and stars accept, on the whole graciously, an adoration close to veneration.

As in Hollywood, the power of the Indian star developed gradually but the position stars command today – both economically and in the popular imagination – is the result of an idiosyncratic economic system that has accorded them more absolute power than even their Hollywood contemporaries. Not only is it firmly believed in the industry that stars are a crucial ingredient in the success of any mainstream Indian film (the other key ingredients usually cited being songs and dialogue) but also a vast subsidiary industry has grown up, particularly since the 1960s, around the publication of magazines in all languages, including English, which peddle a veritable torrent of salacious gossip about film stars. While every regional language film industry in India has its own stars, it is those of the Bombay-based Hindi cinema who are particularly powerful, known throughout India (and much of the Third World), and are the focus of the greatest popular attention.

Obviously film stars are valued in India for many of the same reasons as in other cultures: they offer audiences whose lives are limited in various ways – materially and emotionally – the vicarious pleasure of identification with and exploration of the realm of the extraordinary. Interestingly, however, while the stars are enthusiastically followed and adored, their star personae, both on and off screen, frequently encompass behaviours that are decidedly subversive of the strict social mores of Indian society and would be considered 'scandalous' in any other context, even by many of their most dedicated fans. Of course they do not simply transgress: stars are represented as finely balancing their transgressions with personifications of ideal behaviour especially in the domains of kinship and sexuality. Both the films and the sub-text of gossip about stars are most usefully seen as debates around morality, in particular as negotiations about the role of 'tradition' in a modernising India.

Stardom in India developed in parallel with – and with awareness of – the Hollywood star system. Film itself came to India within months of the Lumieres' premières in Paris and London, and the first all-Indian film, *Raja Harischandra* (King Harischandra, D. Phalke), was released in 1913. By the 1920s a large number of Indian entrepreneurs had set up in film production, and, in addition to palatial theatres and purpose-built cinema-houses, exhibition networks had been established throughout the country in the form of touring tents or open-air cinemas. In the 1920s and 1930s production became organised around studios which operated more or less like extended families and stars were primarily studio employees, subject to strict discipline and rigorous contracts. The studio system began to break down in the mid-1940s. War profiteering and illicit arms deals had produced an influx of wealthy independent producers who lured the major marketable asset, stars, away from studios with enormous fees. Throughout the 1950s the trend to diffusion was controlled through the domination of a number of major independent producer/directors, who were so frequently successful at the box-office that they were able to build up regular teams around themselves and in some cases their own facilities bases.

Stars gradually learned that they could call the tune while the industry was run by private financiers who believed that the safest way to minimise their risk on a film was to back films with a well-known star cast. A pernicious star system developed which reached its peak in the mid-1970s with the so-called 'multi-starrers' – films crammed with stars to increase the apparent market value which simply intensified the stranglehold of the top stars who sometimes worked in up to fifty productions at the same time. When these dinosaurean films began to crash at the box-office in the early 1980s, industry finance was severely depleted. However, stars still sign large numbers of contracts simultaneously, command large fees and spend their time racing between studios, working on a dozen or so films simultaneously. Largely because the industry is so extraordinarily fragmented, comprising hundreds of small producers, distributors and exhibitors, regular attempts at regulation have been invariably frustrated by the short-term interests of producers and stars at the top. An added complication has been the fact that contracts are more or less unenforceable (given the slowness of the Indian legal machinery and the degree to which any deal is 'off the record' and depends on personal favours and 'trust') and most producers spend large amounts of their time and energy in chasing and cajoling wayward stars. It was in this context that the so-called 'new cinema' was developed in the 1970s and 1980s, eschewing the familiar stars and high budgets and offering a challenge to this extraordinarily unwieldy system.

The position of female stars in the system, however, must be qualified. Male stars have by far the highest 'value', commanding at least double what comparable female stars earn, and a female star's value is determined largely by which male stars are prepared to work with her. The position of women in the Indian film industry is fraught with ambivalence: in the early years few women would agree to something so demeaning as allowing their photographed image to appear on screen to the gaze of thousands of unknown men across the country. Even prostitutes refused and the early female stars were primarily Anglo-Indian women, such as Sulochana (Ruby Meyers), who did not carry the cultural baggage of strict Hindu and Muslim taboos against women displaying their bodies to the public view. While such taboos gradually broke down and a few 'respectable' girls of middle-class families began to enter films from the 1930s onwards, contradictions remain. For not only is the industry unremittingly male-dominated and considered 'dirty' by many, but female stars are inevitably positioned both as object of veneration and as sex object, as supremely powerful and as passive pawns of a male industry.

While this might be true of female stars in any industry, it is underpinned by a set of ideas about femininity that are unique to the Indian context and undoubtedly fuel the ambivalence. At first sight many female Indian stars might seem a travesty of the stereotype of Indian female docility. However, popular representation of womanhood in India is complexly split. On the one hand one finds the picture of a 'pure' and dutiful woman, whose total identity is structured by a hierarchical authoritarian patriarchal culture. She appears as virginal daughter given as *dan* (sacred gift) to her husband's family, as long-suffering slave who labours for this family and provides it with male heirs, as self-sacrificing mother, or as chaste and modest wife, whose *raison d'être* is to worship her husband as a god and whose life is a succession of prayers, rituals and fasts to ensure his well-being. However, co-existing, apparently contradictorily, with this is a long tradition of images of female strength and authority: woman who is feared, obeyed or worshipped by men, woman who is aggressive to or punishes men, woman who is either independent or a leader of men and whose sexuality is manifest and powerful. While the former might be conventionally recognised as a picture of 'oppressed' womanhood, the latter has sometimes tempted both Indian traditionalists and some (western) feminists to celebrate such apparently strong images as 'positive' and evidence of women's real power. The situation is not, of course, so simple.

This chapter will trace a tradition of representation of potent femininity through fifty years of Indian cinema by focusing on three female stars at three key moments in its history: 'Fearless Nadia', stunt queen of the 1930s and 1940s; Nargis Dutt, famous for *Mother India* in the 1950s; and Smita Patil, who came to stand for the 'modern feminist' in the 1970s and 1980s. It is important to stress that we are not arguing that they are 'typical' of their era, nor that they were necessarily the 'top' stars, but that they each raise interesting questions around female stardom in the Indian cultural and historical context(s). The chapter will attempt to throw light on the ways in which potent femininity has been negotiated in each era, the relationship between each star and her historical (political and economic) context and the range of other cultural representations which are drawn on to 'legitimise' the star persona. We will argue that around each star persona apparently contradictory images of controlled femininity co-exist with each image of strength, as if to diffuse or undermine its threat. We will further suggest that through fifty years of Indian cinema history one can trace an increasing complexity, from the comparatively one-dimensional screen-image of Fearless Nadia to the complex intertwining of on- and off-screen personae of both Nargis and Smita.

FEARLESS NADIA

The single most memorable sound of my childhood is the clarion call of Hey-y-y as Fearless Nadia, regal upon her horse, her hand raised defiantly in the air, rode down upon the bad guys. To us schoolkids of the mid-forties Fearless Nadia meant courage, strength, idealism.

One of Nadia's numerous fans from the pre-Independence generation continues his reminiscences with a description of a typical Nadia film:

The good king was imprisoned by the scheming minister. The righteous among the subjects were tortured or locked up. The helpless princess, driven to despair, unable to find succour, finally decided to act on her own and set things right. And in a moment, the large fair woman, whose discomfort seemed to arise more from the sari she was wrapped in than from the political situation, transformed herself into a masked woman in tight black costume, who could ride, swim, fight, wrestle, fence and take a reverse jump from ground to balcony. It was a moment breathlessly awaited and when it arrived the entire 3-anna[2] contingent stood up on the benches and cheered, to the accompaniment of 'Sit Down' and 'Down You Swine' from the 4-anna chairs . . . [3]

110

Nadia's screen role was that of an avenging angel, who rescued men and society from both natural perils and human tyrants. As such Nadia clearly subverted the predominant cinema stereotype of Indian woman as glamorous object for male desire, or docile suffering victim, although her physical presence was undeniably erotically charged. She rarely wore saris when riding or fighting – they were too constricting – and her favourite outfits, shorts or tight trousers, low-cut shirts and big boots, often exposed plump thighs and a large bosom. Nadia was however clearly coded as a 'good girl': only in one film, *Muqabala* (Confrontation, B. Bhatt and B. Mistry, 1942), did she play the 'vamp' as part of a double role and here the overtly sexualised 'bad sister', flirtatiously smoking, drinking and dancing was emphatically contrasted with the 'good sister', Nadia. Although she was not usually allowed to sing and dance, Nadia was always accompanied by a male hero for romantic interest. However, it is noticeable that, in comparison with her Hollywood counterparts (such as Pearl White of *The Perils of Pauline* who provided the original inspiration for the Nadia series), the Nadia image is tougher (she is a fighter, not simply a stunt woman) and less compromised by a romantic ending: Nadia is as likely to be the final saviour of her male co-star as vice versa. The film-makers invariably complemented Nadia with a second heroine whose role was to provide romantic song, dance and helpless tears.

Nadia was a thundering success from her first starring role as *Hunterwali* (Woman with the Whip, 1934), where, disguised as a masked man and wielding a whip, she roamed the countryside, robbing the rich to feed the poor. Throughout the long series of Nadia films (which only dwindled out in the 1950s – although their heyday was 1935–45) a number of motifs regularly recurred, from her performing dogs and faithful horses, Rajput, Punjab and Punjab ka Beta (Son of the Punjab) to her car, a baby Austin, christened 'Rolls Royce ki Beti' (Daughter of Rolls Royce). Adventures included cliff-top rescues, runaway trains and encounters with ferocious wild animals. Particularly favourite scenes were her gym sessions, which apparently inspired something of a keep-fit craze at the time. Nadia thought nothing of lifting up burly henchmen, throwing them across a room or carrying them on her back. Her tough, capable, omnipotent image also had a distinct message of inspiration for women of the time and her films frequently exhorted women to fight for themselves: in *Diamond Queen* (1940), for example, there is a long scene in which Nadia calls on Hindustani women to educate themselves and shake off their oppressors. She was never allowed to show weakness:

I did have an emotional scene in *Mouj* (Fun, 1943), I had to deliver a long dialogue crying. I really worked for that last scene – I even managed real tears without glycerine. But when the film was finished

111

Figure 10.1 Nadia in *Diamond Queen* (1940)

the distributor insisted to Homi that the scene be cut. And it was. 'Nadia cannot cry' they said.[4]

Nadia was born Mary Evans in Perth in 1910. Her father was a soldier from Wales, her Greek mother a one-time circus artiste. Nadia was brought to India aged one and her mother settled in Bombay when her husband was killed in the First World War. As a girl Nadia learnt horse-riding from her uncle, an army vet in Peshawar, and became an enthusiastic film fan, enviously enjoying the exploits of Pearl White and Ruth Roland, whose films were widely distributed in India at that time, alongside Douglas Fairbanks and, perennial favourite, Charlie Chaplin. Nadia first worked as a shorthand typist in Bombay and began taking dancing lessons as part of a long-standing battle with her weight. Encouraged by her dance teacher she threw up office work and, after a brief debut with Zacko's Russian circus, soon established a reputation as singer and dancer in a troupe that toured throughout the north and south of India, playing in army and civilian clubs as well as in cinemas as a live act to accompany a film. It was the manager of Regal Theatres, Lahore, who insisted on taking her to meet his friend, the Bombay film producer, J. B. H. Wadia.

112

After an initial reluctance on her part – the salary was a meagre Rs150 per month and she was worried about having to speak Hindi – she accepted a three-year contract with him and was immediately at home with the demanding and dangerous stunts which she was required to perform. Despite many hazardous moments, stunt men were hardly ever used at any point in her career.

Wadia Movietone was one of a number of studios that established themselves successfully in Bombay in the 1930s. The Wadia brothers, Jamshed and Homi, made a remarkable team. J. B. H. Wadia was a writer and intellectual, interested in literature and politics, who had ambitions to make his mark on Indian cinema. His younger brother Homi was the more pragmatic partner, a successful director with a hard-headed under-standing of box-office appeal. Scandalising their 'respectable' Parsee family they had initially set up a film laboratory in Kohinoor Studios in the Dadar district of Bombay and they made the first of their eight silent films in 1928. Quick to adapt to the potential of sound by introducing a singer, Firoz Dastur, as hero in *Lal-e-Yaman* (1933), they had an immedi-ate box-office success, on the profits of which they were able to build their own studio, Wadia Movietone, in Dadar. Together the brothers developed a successful business producing cheap sure-fire hits in the mythological and stunt genres, with occasional forays into socials and Arabian Nights style fantasies. Later such films would finance more ambitious projects but disaster at the box-office forced the sale of Wadia Movietone in 1942. Homi managed to set up again shortly after this with Basant Studios on the outskirts of Bombay, at Chembur, and continued to make cheap successful genre pictures, including the Nadia films.

In all the early studios stars were no more than employees of the studio and were expected to attend each day for regular hours. They were paid monthly salaries that were far from excessive: even at her height Nadia earned no more than Rs1,500 per month (£60). Homi describes the disci-pline of the early Wadia Movietone as 'like a school'. At ten each morning a bell would be rung, a register of attendance called and the day's shooting plans announced. Actors not needed on set would either spend the day in rehearsal or might go home. Nadia describes how, on such occasions, she would spend her days diligently rehearsing her stunts in the studio gym with 'my gangsters' as she liked to refer to the dozen or so men she worked with:

Azimbhoy our stunt man taught me sword fighting and used to give us all little hints . . . Homi used to come and tell us the scene he wanted for the day. We would rehearse that in the gym, or on the terrace upstairs, so that when we went on the sets there would be no retakes. We were ready and steady – any retakes were the camera's fault. I had such a lot of fun there.

There was clearly a great deal of camaraderie in the studio, with much laughing and joking, 'like a big happy family' according to both Homi and Nadia. All studio employees, including the stars and the Wadias themselves, would eat lunch at the same table and many of them socialised together after hours.

There was no developed 'marketing' of the stars of these early studios beyond appearances at glamorous functions and some press photographs alongside cozy interviews. Nadia received vast quantities of fan mail, particularly from northern India, would be mobbed if she was recognised in the streets and had a wide following amongst both males and females, and especially young audiences. However, Nadia's popularity was firmly on the back of her film roles and little was publicly known about her personal life: she managed to keep the fact that she was an unmarried mother a secret throughout her screen career. She used to joke however: 'These Wadia boys have ruined my chances of marriage: what man will dare to marry a woman as tough as the screen Nadia?' In the end it was her boss and favourite director, Homi Wadia, whom she eventually married in 1960 – after a twenty-five year romance, allegedly kept under wraps because his traditional Parsee family was opposed to his marrying a film star – and European to boot. She retired from films after this and now spends her time with friends or enjoying her race-horses, largely ignored as a former star.

Like many in the Indian film industry, the Wadias were active supporters of the Independence movement. Although strict British censorship precluded overt references to the Congress Party or its leaders, many Indian film-makers in the 1930s and 1940s experimented with covert allusions to the struggle, through allegory or apparently casual intrusions of pro-Independence symbols or songs. Thus films in which Nadia, for example, rescued an oppressed people from a wicked foreign tyrant who had usurped the kingdom, were clearly read by audiences at the time as anti-British allegories. Nadia saw her role – on screen and off – as supporting the Congress Party and states explicitly: 'in all the pictures there was a propaganda message, something to fight for, for example, for people to educate themselves or to become a strong nation'.

The phenomenon of Nadia's success is intriguing in a number of ways. There is a fine irony in the fact that a 'white' woman starred in Indian films that were patently anti-British and frequently played the role of liberator of an oppressed people, implicitly India. On hiring her, J. B. H. Wadia had in fact suggested that she dye her hair (or people will call you 'Buddhi' (old person)) and change her name from the 'European-sounding' Nadia (a stage name adopted during her dancing days on the advice of an Armenian fortune teller) to the more authentically Hindu 'Devi' (goddess). She had vehemently refused: 'That's not part of my contract. Nadia rhymes with Wadia and besides . . . I'm no "devi".' In talking with her early fans today it is clear that she was in no simple way equated with the British and the films themselves introduce her not as a foreigner but as a 'Bombaywali' (a woman from Bombay) which has the looser connotations of exotic westernised sophistication. She did however have considerable difficulty with her Hindi lines. Although she was able to learn them by heart, she was invariably teased about her pronunciation. She reminisces about one memorable occasion when the whole unit burst into guffaws when she screamed *mujhe chot do* as she landed in the villain's arms. The director had to take her aside and explain the distinction between *chhod* and *chot* – the meaning of one was 'let me go', of the other 'fuck me'.

Although her European origins were apparently disavowed on one level by her audiences, one must speculate that they may have contributed on another level to the legitimation of her strength, eminently physical presence and freedom of movement in the context of colonial India, as well as underpinning the ambivalent frisson of her erotic appeal. British censorship throughout the 1920s had been primarily concerned to protect the image of white women in colonial societies. A report of the Indian Cinematograph Committee of 1925 stated: 'much harm is being done in India by the widespread exhibition of western films. . . . The majority of films, which are chiefly from America, are of sensational and daring murders, crimes, and divorces and, on the whole, degrade the white woman in the eyes of the Indians.'[5] Nadia's 'whiteness' may well have added to the credibility of her power in the colonial context as may the fact that she was, through the films, associated with a gamut of symbols of western technology: trains, planes, cars etc. The very first scene she shot was on the roof of a train and titles of the Wadia films range from *Miss Frontier Mail*, to *Toofan Mail*, *Toofan Express*, *Flying Ranee*, *Hurricane Special* or *Son of Toofan Mail*.

Wadia workers used to refer to mythologicals as 'simply stunt films starring gods and goddesses' and, arguably, these genres represent two ends of a continuum in an ongoing debate/dialogue about tradition and westernisation. Mythologicals offer the audience a reverie about power in arch-traditional forms; stunt films a reverie about power integrally bound up with western technology – and open references to the terms of a western genre. Perhaps Nadia's western origins accounted for her success as heroine of such films, for although several other studios attempted to compete with their own stunt queen heroines, none caught the public imagination in the way that Nadia did.

However, the image of a woman possessed of exceptional physical strength and prowess has a long history that runs throughout traditional Indian popular culture and mythology. On the one hand there is a strong tradition of fearsome mother goddesses, most notably Durga and Kali who, as prime embodiments of the supremely potent female cosmic energy *shakti*, can aggress, maim and kill men if angered. Kali not only demands blood sacrifice of her followers but is usually depicted with a black angry face, wielding an array of terrifying weapons in her four hands, wearing a garland of skulls and dancing on a corpse. The theme is also elaborated in historical legend, with a particular fascination for female warriors such as Jhansi ki Rani, a princess of Madhya Pradesh who, incensed by the British administration's 'doctrine of lapse',[6] joined the Mutiny in 1857, rode into battle disguised as a man and whose brilliant fighting skills flabbergasted her male co-fighters when her identity was discovered. Images of this equestrian empress are common in the popular calendar art, often appearing alongside portraits of Mrs Gandhi in her heyday. A similar, but more contemporary folk heroine has captured the public and media imagination in recent years, the female dacoit (outlaw), of whom Phoolan Devi is the most notorious. Phoolan Devi was a tough ruthless attractive young woman who, fuelled with desire for revenge following a gang rape, led her own gang of male bandits on rampages which terrorised the wealthier landowners in villages of the Chambal Valley throughout the late 1970s. Arguably, Nadia's potency resulted from the way she straddled both traditional and western references. Nevertheless, the radical strength of her image was compromised by her construction as eroticised spectacle.

Nadia's was a comparatively one-dimensional persona and any conflict or contradiction was syphoned off either (rarely) into a double role as 'vamp' or, usually, into a second heroine, who provided the soft, dependent, emotional and devoted side of archetypes of femininity. With Nargis the star persona becomes a more complex construction.

NARGIS

Popularly known as the 'First Lady of the Indian Screen' in the 1940s and 1950s, Nargis stands out as a key star of the 'golden age' of early post-Independence Indian cinema. Her screen persona encompassed a far wider span of models of femininity than Fearless Nadia's: in the course of her career she played roles that ranged from coy coquette to sweet village damsel, from westernised society girl or independent, educated career woman to resilient earth mother and champion of the oppressed peasantry. The constant factor that runs through this diversity is her fundamental 'purity' and moral soundness – she was unequivocally a *heroine* – although Nargis brought to all her roles her own unique combination of dignity, intelligence and rebellious *joie de vivre*.

By the 1940s and 1950s there was a far wider circulation of stories about the off-screen lives of the stars than in the time of earlier stars such as Fearless Nadia, and the star persona of Nargis is a much more complex blend of screen roles and stories from a colourful life. In order to see

Figure 10.2 Mother India (1957)

how this cross-over operates, this section will examine the off-screen persona in the context of her role in a single film, *Mother India* (Mehboob Khan, 1957).[7] While no claims can be made for it as a 'typical' Nargis role, it is probably the role with which she is most strongly identified. Not only was it effectively her final film before retirement – and considered by many to be her most remarkable performance – but *Mother India* itself is the all-time box-office hit of Indian cinema which still guarantees full houses today, allegedly playing in some part of India every day of every year.

The story of *Mother India* concerns a poor peasant woman, Radha, who, left alone with her children, defends her self-respect and an ideal of virtuous womanhood against tremendous odds – famine, flood and a corrupt and lecherous money-lender. She is finally forced to kill her own beloved son, Birjoo, who has turned outlaw, in a single-handed fight

117

against the money-lender and the oppression he represents. On the face of it, this is the story of a strong courageous woman who fends for herself without dependence on men and who – in solidarity with the women of her village – overcomes maternal love to kill her own son when he transgresses the social codes. However, there are a number of, at times contradictory, facets to the character represented here which refer to a spectrum of archetypes of ideal femininity in Indian culture. The range of images which erupt in the course of the film vary from her heroic call to the villagers not to desert their motherland to her being trampled under-foot by them; from being rescued in her son's arms, to stuffing chapatis into her sons' mouths as they pull a plough through their fields; from shots which look down on her blushing coyly behind a wedding veil or as *sindoor* (vermillion) is placed in her parting, to shots which look up at her heroically striding forward, harnessed to her plough; from her crying on her son's shoulder and pleading with him as a lover might, to her wielding a heavy stick, axe and finally gun. The most powerful image – and most horrifying in the Indian context – is of her levelling a shotgun at her son's head. In fact, the two men who are closest to her are both destroyed by association with her: not only does she kill her favourite son but her husband loses both arms following her insistence that they plough some barren land.

Most Indian audiences would, on some level, recognise within this Radha allusions to a variety of figures of Hindu mythology: to the god-desses Sita, Savitri, Radha herself, Lakshmi, as well as the more fearsome mother goddesses, Durga and Kali, referred to in the previous section as powerful symbols of female sacred authority. That there is a degree of contradiction between such images reflects the fact that, in the Hindu tradition, femaleness embodies a fundamental duality, woman as bestower and destroyer. However, female sexual energy is believed to be always potentially dangerous, although it can become beneficent (to men) if con-trolled through marriage, or otherwise subjugated to male authority.[8]

Radha/Nargis is clearly the central figure of the narrative and the main-spring of its action and through the logic of the narrative the Nargis persona becomes in many ways a picture of potent femininity. However, it is important to recognise that, throughout the film, Radha's 'power' or 'strength' is integrally bound up with her respect for 'traditional values', especially 'chastity' or the control of female sexuality. While she appears to be the saviour of the village, it is as a paragon of wifely devotion and chastity, who will even kill her own son to protect the village 'izzat' (ensuring that young girls given to other villages in marriage will be chaste virgins for their husbands' families), that she is accorded respect and authority.

Nargis became a star in the late 1940s. Although she retired from films in 1957, she remained very much in the public eye until her death in 1981.

Her arrival on the scene coincided with a major shift in the production base of the film industry. The Second World War had had a devastating effect on the film industry. War profiteering and illicit arms deals had produced much black-market money, which needed laundering, and this prompted an influx of wealthy independent producers who lured the major marketable asset, stars, away from the studios with enormous fees. Payment to stars began to be made in white and 'black' (off the record, hence untaxed) money and star salaries, which had been controlled to a ceiling of Rs3,000 per month in most of the big studios of the 1930s, rose from Rs20,000 per film in the early forties to around Rs200,000 by 1950, often up to half the total budget of the film.[9] By the mid-fifties they had doubled yet again to around Rs400,000 per film. Studios, faced with such competition from *nouveau riche* free-lance producers, were forced to restructure or die. Most dissolved their permanent staffs and extravagant facilities (that in some cases included zoos, libraries and schools for employees' children) and became no more than a stage facility to be hired by the day by any of the hundreds of small production units. These teams were usually put together on a free-lance basis for a single production at a time. However, the system did allow room for the growth/development of a number of important producer/directors who did build up teams that invariably worked together. Men like Raj Kapoor, Mehboob Khan, V. Shantaram put money earned in their successful films into building their own studios, primarily facilities bases, which did give them some control. However, they had to negotiate for stars along with everyone else, although Raj Kapoor, Guru Dutt and V. Shantaram short-circuited this problem by playing male lead in their own productions. However, all such film-makers were at the mercy of financiers and distributors to raise money for their productions, film by film.

Nargis's star potential was discovered at the age of thirteen by a family friend, Mehboob Khan, and she was gradually recognised as a major marketable asset, particularly when co-starring with Raj Kapoor. While she worked with a number of independent producers in the course of her career, she showed particular loyalties to these two men, with whom she made most of her significant films. Nargis is undoubtedly a central legendary figure of Indian cinema, and most Indian audiences are familiar with – and still discuss – details of her story. Although a number of film publications constructing star images for fans had begun to spring up in the 1950s, they were comparatively bland and sycophantic and most of the salacious material was told through innuendo or by word of mouth as rumour. What follows is as close to the rumours as we are able to get today, but does reflect the ways in which the legend was being retold and reworked up to the early eighties.

It is important to stress that our concern here is with the persona of Nargis as publicly constructed rumour rather than with an 'accurate' biography. The story runs that Nargis was an unfortunate girl, born in Lucknow in 1929 of a famous Muslim courtesan and young Hindu doctor later ostracised from his 'respectable' family for this association. Even as a child she had dreamed of redeeming herself by becoming a doctor, and her mother had sent her to a 'good' Bombay school and disciplined her strictly, keeping her largely away from the film industry throughout her childhood. However, at adolescence, Nargis's mother not only tricked her into (most unwillingly) starring in a film for her friend Mehboob Khan, but allegedly put her daughter's *nath* (virginity) on the market and allowed a wealthy Muslim prince to pay handsomely for her. (Whether or not this is true is irrelevant to this recounting of the myth.)

By the late 1940s Nargis had become a top star, but it was with her professional and personal partnership with Raj Kapoor, handsome young star, producer and director, that she shot to superstardom and notoriety. The couple's 'bold' and very open love affair captured the prurient imagination of the nation: on the one hand it was enviously celebrated, they were young, glamorous, beautiful, rich and said to be passionately in love. They epitomised a 'modern' freedom and lack of inhibition. They flew around the world, were seen photographed with Truman at the White House in 1952, found as pin-ups in bazaars throughout the Arab world and were household names in Russia following the unprecedented success there of *Awaara* (The Vagabond, Raj Kapoor, 1951). The affair was both celebrated and denounced. While she was applauded for her courage in being open about her love and for showing total devotion to 'her' man (for example, she wore only white saris in deference to his whims and slaved with exemplary dedication at his studios for minimal pay), Raj Kapoor was a married man with children. When the affair ended in 1955/6 she was alternately a 'ruined woman' who had her just deserts or a figure of sympathy for being deceived by a lover for whom she had sacrificed all. At that point she was 'rescued' by another man, Sunil Dutt (her screen son in *Mother India*), married him, left the 'dirty' world of the film industry and subsequently gave birth to a son, the first of three children. In the public imagination she then continued to redeem herself by devoting her energies to caring for her husband and son. She also gave dedicated service to community charities, notably spastics, and began to be referred to respectfully as *bhabhi-ji* (lit. elder brother's wife) by the film industry, becoming their public spokesperson and president of the Producers' Association IMPPA. More significantly, she is said to have built up a close friendship with Indira Gandhi over the years and in 1980 was rewarded with a seat in the Rajya Sabha (House of Lords). She was, by then, a national symbol of dignified glamour and respectability, the other 'First Lady' of India – Indira Gandhi's glamorous *alter ego*. Nargis's first parliamentary intervention was stoutly patriotic and wildly controversial: she denounced Satyajit Ray's films for showing India's poverty to the west, rather than 'modern India . . . [for example] dams' and a national debate ensued.

At the age of 51, just as she appeared to have consolidated her public 'Mother India' persona, cancer was discovered and she was rushed to an American hospital. After an extraordinarily long and melodramatic struggle for her life, she died three days before her 'dream' was realised – her beloved son made his public debut as a film star.

Of particular interest is the way in which stories spun around Nargis's life show parallels and tensions with the film she starred in: on the one hand, her public persona became closely identified with the figure of Mother India in later years, on the other, it was very far from it at the time she played the role.[10] While *Mother India* can be seen to be negotiating a number of contradictory images of womanhood, tying them together through a story which emphasises the necessary constraint on female sexuality, the gossip stories tie together a similar diversity of apparently contradictory facets of modern Indian womanhood: the Muslim courtesan, the passionate goddess Radha, the 'westernised' free lover, the devoted Hindu wife, the adoring mother, the powerful politician etc. This is effected through a story of redemption: through Nargis's unflinching dedication to her husband and son (and sacrifice of her career), her original 'bad' uncontrolled sexuality becomes harnessed to the social good, and she becomes a powerful and respectable member of society.

While the diversity of representations of femininity in traditional Indian mythology has been encompassed within the Nargis persona, both on and off-screen, a key concern is with woman deified and idealised as 'mother', an image which attributes to her moral and emotional, as opposed to physical, strength. The moral strength of the 'mother' image requires that the woman's sexuality is firmly controlled – that her purity and honour (*izzat*) be unquestionable. While the physical strength of Fearless Nadia was to some extent undermined by being an erotic spectacle, the moral strength of the Nargis persona in the 1940s and 1950s was interestingly undercut – as well as complemented – by the off-screen stories, although the star legend as it survives today, as a life's trajectory, emphasises potency through a form of redemption symbolised by motherhood.

In Indian society the mother–son relationship is a particularly highly charged dynamic, and it has often been argued that an Indian man's relationship with his mother is a more crucial bond than that with his wife.[11] Moreover, it is through her role as mother of a son that woman effectively acquires a social identity and worth in traditional Indian society. The respective roles are well defined: the ideal son makes a continual show of deference and respect to his mother who stands as paragon of moral virtue, nurturing support and ultimate authority. It is in this relationship that, traditionally, an Indian woman has one of her few real areas of power. Female politicians and professional women invariably

Figure 10.3

derive authority by exploiting the symbol, most notably Mrs Gandhi, whose 1980 election campaign included the slogan: 'The hand that rocks the cradle rules the world.'

One of the most interesting aspects of the mother phenomenon is the way in which it has been turned to nationalist concerns. 'Mother India' was a highly emotive slogan in the Independence context and the concept

122

of the ideal mother's 'purity' is often used as a metaphor for the 'mother-land', with woman represented as the locus of traditional values, culture and mores. The films of the post-Independence decade were on the whole concerned less with overt anti-British sentiment than with constructing visions of a new India. It was an age of great hopes and romantic idealism. *Mother India* describes the emergence of a new India free from both feudal and colonial oppression and a key concern of many of the films of the era was to negotiate a 'modern' India which is neither 'traditional' nor 'western'. The defence of Radha's – and the village women's – chastity is the defence of the 'purity' of a modernising India and the film opens with Radha – as a mud-stained old woman – being entreated by a delegation of deferential village men to open a new irrigation dam. The obsessions of the narrative of the off-screen Nargis manifest a similar concern: how to live femininity in a modernising India. While much of Nargis's fascination obviously lies in her gorgeous sensuality, spirited rebelliousness and unusual beauty, the persona of Nargis, in all its contradictions provides an (ongoing) forum for working through difficult questions of a society in change. In moving to Smita Patil we see these crises of social identity even more clearly developed and we also find a persona within which the on- and off-screen roles gradually become increasingly difficult to extricate from one another.

SMITA PATIL

> I would like to do roles that will project today's woman with all her complexities, dilemmas and problems . . . to show how she's fighting with herself, with society, and with her family structure, to reach somewhere. And in doing so, not be called a bad woman by men or society, but be called a strong individual who's looking for an identity. (Smita Patil, May 1985)

These are the words of a 30-year-old actress, a year before she died tragically, soon after giving birth to her first child. Smita Patil was bred from the New Cinema movement in India, and became one of its most luminous stars, enjoying a career that spanned more than a decade in both the art and commercial cinemas. She was showered with national awards for her acting, given a Padmabhushan – the highest honour awarded to a citizen – and a season of her films was showcased at the Cinémathèque in Paris.

She developed a reputation for being socially conscious and politically committed in her screen roles at a time in the seventies when roles for women were limited to playing decorative romantic partners of male stars. She never held back from using her star image to fund-raise for the Women's Centre in India, which had been initially set up following a

Figure 10.4 Smita Patil in *Bhumika* (1977)

crisis surrounding a notorious case of rape, but was now more active in various aspects of women's politics.

Smita's potential as an actress was discovered by director Shyam Benegal whilst she was a news presenter on Bombay television. Despite a career that has been far more prolific latterly in the mainstream commercial cinema, she is inscribed in the public memory for her early roles, especially Benegal's *Bhumika* (1977) which made her a major star overnight with her face appearing on every Indian magazine cover. The story is inspired by the life of Hansa Wadkar, the Joan Crawford of the Marathi stage and screen, whose tumultuous career as an actress was fraught with painful love affairs which drove her to drink and loneliness in her search for freedom and equality in her roles as actress, wife, daughter and mother. Whilst *Bhumika* tagged Smita with the identity of the sexually independent actress whose star and screen roles were intertwined in the minds of the spectators, her trademark was the no make-up rural wench, or the urban slum dweller, whose wit, verve and vivacity fought the forces of social oppression. If she was not cast as a member of the oppressed social classes, she found herself playing roles that mirrored her own class background, what one can describe as the agitating social worker, the best example of which is Sulabha in Jabbar Patel's *Umbartha* (1981). Although she could never be described as conventionally beautiful in the tradition of the Indian screen heroines, the charms of her flashing dark eyes, earthy sensuality, lithe body and lack of artifice combined into a magnetic screen presence.

For someone who had never seen more than about eight films including religious classics by the age of sixteen, Smita's meteoric career as an actress, which began at the age of seventeen, can only be explained by a set of historical convergences that created her particular star persona. Her image as the 'emancipated' woman of Indian cinema is inextricably linked with the growth of the New Cinema movement in India in the seventies, which emerged as a challenge to mainstream popular cinema. The New Cinema owed its genesis to the change of policy instituted by the government-sponsored Film Finance Corporation in the late sixties, which favoured low budget, experimental proposals, with no star names, which were usually filmed on location. Although in no sense displacing the popularity of mainstream cinema, its thrust had been to attempt a greater realism of representation, which was a radical departure from the tradition of high artifice through song and dance characteristic of popular cinema. Co-existing with its concern to change the cinema formally, was a preoccupation with more serious social issues, hence a new image for women was high on the agenda. The chance to create these new roles for women, rather than the traditional attractions of money and glamour, was the lure for a woman of Smita's background, who saw the possibilities of celluloid charisma enhancing social causes.

Smita belonged to a tightly knit, lower-middle-class Maharashtrian family who were committed to social change and were active members of the Praja Socialist Party, participating in grass-roots organisation of social welfare programmes for the rural and urban slum-dwellers. Her father later became a minister in the Maharashtrian cabinet, a factor which increased the pressures of public scrutiny endured by any actress, but undoubtedly enhanced her appeal as an actress who did not quite fit the traditional mould. The family ethos always scorned the pursuit of wealth for higher social ideals and the children were sent to summer camps where they participated in social work programmes. Smita, an active participant in these Sevadal camps, saw her roles in the New Cinema as an extension of these programmes. They represented an agitation for social change by signalling the plight of women like Amma in *Chakra* (1980) where she plays the role of a mother with a teenage son and defiant lover of a truck-driver, for which she received the National Award; and Bindu in *Manthan* (1976), the untouchable girl who becomes the focus of resistance in the struggle to set up a milk co-operative. In those early years she only chose films according to the integrity of the director, refusing roles she considered stereotyped and relishing the prospect of low budget films as long as they had a 'social' message. This often meant that the conditions for the unit were extremely primitive, especially in the rural areas, but she enjoyed the camaraderie of the unit, re-living her experiences in the Sevadal camps. When she was awarded a cash prize for the National Award she happily donated the funds to the physically handicapped.

By the late seventies the New Cinema was undergoing its inevitable crisis of funding as the films had not achieved widespread distribution, and did not win the support of wider audiences since they transgressed all the rules of popular taste. Many directors were attempting a cross-over, trying to work with bigger stars from the commercial cinema and tackle less socially instructive projects. Smita was caught in the dilemma of abandoning her principles, while finding herself losing key roles to actresses from the commercial cinema. Persuaded by the man she married, who himself was struggling to find a place as an actor in the industry from a background in theatre, she accepted roles from the mainstream at the moment the New Cinema was reconstituting its own identity. Despite an uneasiness in her new roles, with heavy make-up and gruelling schedules, she still managed to get a firm foothold in the industry, without losing her integrity as an actress, bringing her own persona to the role with an accompanying dignity which at its worst was a trifle stolid. By re-establishing her marketability as a star through the commercial cinema, she could win back the roles she had lost with the 'auteur' directors who were also working with budgets approaching mainstream proportions.

If in those early films, Smita was only seen by a handful of art film enthusiasts at Indian and foreign film festivals, or at limited releases in big cities, the most remarkable aspect of her stardom is how she became a star in the first place. In many ways the circulation of gossip through the film fan magazines, newspapers and journals was responsible for fuelling the initial interest, helped by the exposure on Bombay television as a newsreader, as well as being the daughter of a prominent minister.

Like many of her generation of urban women in India, Smita was partially influenced by a western notion of feminism, and her image was somewhat antithetical to the glamorous image of the Indian film-star. Wearing little or no make-up, she was described as 'natural looking' and always dressed in traditional saris which paradoxically enhanced her unconventional image. At first her look of eschewing star presentations was read as having 'no sex appeal' and she was described as dirty, dark and a trifle homespun, the gossip magazines constantly complaining about her 'crushed saris'. But as her persona evolved through the roles she played, she became known as an intelligent, spontaneous woman, who, if lacking traditional sex appeal, had instead an earthy sensuality and great personal magnetism. Her passionate romantic temperament which involved her in problematic affairs, often with married men, was read as immoral, but not untypical of the 'westernised' film heroine, in its own way enhancing her particular charisma. At the moment of crossing over to join the commercial cinema, there was much public soul-searching about the morality of abandoning her principles, to the extent that her acceptance of the first role became a coup for the producer, with her 'moral dilemma' becoming the foremost feature in her marketability.

Once she was part of the mainstream, the irony was that she was never really successful in the roles where her unease was patently obvious. Her physical charms and natural sensuality were lost in the heavy make-up required, and her determination not to be exploited as a 'sex object' made her stand a trifle awkwardly on her dignity, losing the spark from her old fighting spirit into the bargain. Her fans who felt betrayed by her venture into commercial territory mocked one of her early roles in Ramesh Sippy's *Shakti* (1982), where she is zestlessly singing in the rain, albeit in a plain white sari. Forgotten was her award-winning role in *Chakra* which involves her in a practically nude bathing scene as the slum-dweller Amma, but then much is forgiven in the name of art and the nitty-gritty details of realism.

It was an inevitable situation for Smita to find herself in, as the commercial cinema could never replicate the kind of roles that had become her trademark. The tried and tested formulae of popular cinema demanded a powerful male lead, which could never accommodate the agitating heroine who was his equal, especially when she was cast against Amitabh Bachchan, the most popular male star of all time, a role she foolishly accepted in her first encounters with the industry. Yet the fact that she continued to be successful, acting in more films that ever before, having access to a mass audience for the first time, raises a few questions beyond accusations of 'selling out'.

Whilst the majority of the commercial film-makers were at a loss as to how to handle her persona, a few of the directors from the New Cinema who had also negotiated the cross-over into the industry realised the potential of her image, bringing out the elements which had mythological resonances for the culture at large. Unfortunately her career was curtailed by her untimely death, thus not allowing one prevailing myth to dominate, yet an archetype with variations was emerging depending on the director and the kind of cinema being attempted.

The process of transforming Smita's image from a folk heroine to a semi-mythological character varied according to the film-makers' inflections of the myths, which after all were open to different interpretations. Powerful female deities like Durga and Kali, who were popularly represented as threatening, devouring and destructive, were arguably themselves a gross misrepresentation of the original essence of the myth through centuries of patriarchal culture. Durga was created after a combined plea from the gods to the goddess of the Himalayas to rescue the world from the scourge of terrible demons. Kali had sprung from her brow to assist her in destroying the most vicious and truculent man-beasts and this forceful but vital aspect of Durga has been dubbed horrific by male commentaries. Similarly, looking at three films from this 'mythologising' moment in Smita's career, one can detect different embodiments of her feminine power.

Ketan Mehta's *Mirch Masala* (1986) is an interesting film to begin with as it was released after her death; it is renowned for being her last major role and is one of the first Indian films to be shown publicly in New York with widespread US distribution. Ketan, a product of the New Cinema movement, had in his early film *Bhavni Bhavai* (1980) moulded the character of the untouchable gypsy girl Ujaan out of the temperament and vivacity that Smita brought to the role and was aware that he was recreating a 'folk or grass roots image of resistance'. In *Mirch Masala* he cast her as Sonbai, again in a rural setting in his native Gujarat, where she works in a cottage industry, manufacturing red chilli powder (the title of the film). Her outstanding physical charms draw the attention of the visiting collector, who orders the village headman to procure her for his sexual entertainment. The village elders decide to turn a blind eye on what should be a matter of communal honour, in the interests of placating the forces of oppression. Sonbai takes refuge in the factory compound, where the old gatekeeper promises to safeguard her to the point of death. When the collector's soldiers storm the factory gates, the women overwhelm them with red chilli powder, while Smita stands in anticipation with a scythe, ready to attack her persecutors. What is intriguing about her role at this point in her career is how little she is called upon to act and how little is revealed about her character compared to the wife of the headman who activates the women's revolt. She is framed either as an object which provokes desire in her exotic, revealing, ethnic outfits, or as a simmering angel of vengeance, with fierce flashing eyes, holding up the weapon in the shape of a scythe, which makes her reminiscent of the popular pictorial representations of the goddess Kali. Variations of that image often recur in the genre of the female rape and revenge movie.

A more extreme example of this vengeful persona is apparent in Rajiv Sethi's *Angaaray* (1986) where a director from the commercial cinema obviously exploited this latent potential for revenge, casting her as Aarti Varma, who shoulders the family's financial and emotional burdens, is raped by her reptilian boss, and then refused the possibility of marriage owing to her sullied honour. This was a sub-genre of Indian popular cinema which had peaked in the mid-eighties, where the problem was more often the heinous revenge exacted by the heroine, rather than any depiction of the actual rape. It was certainly the case in this instance, when she shoots her rapist in the leg, swipes him with the butt of her rifle and forces him into a car whose door handles have been removed,

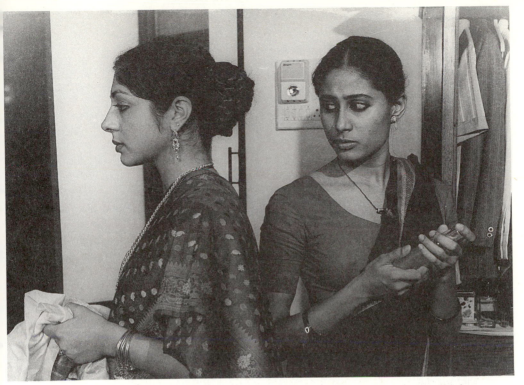

Figure 10.5 Tarang (1984). Smita Patil (right) as Janaki and Kawal Gandhiol as Hansa

then proceeds to puncture the petrol tank and ignite a circle of fuel, whose flames envelope the quarry in a dramatic burst.

In her role as Janaki in Kumar Shahani's *Tarang* (1984) the vengeful archetype is completely turned on its head by Shahani's use of myth and archetype in a cinema which is intent on re-working the feminine tradition and extricating it from centuries of patriarchal culture. Here the two versions of femininity are represented on the one hand by Janaki, played by Smita Patil, the widow of a union organiser who is hired as domestic help by the industrial bosses, and on the other by Hansa, the wife of the boss Rahul. Whilst Janaki contains all the qualities of the strong earth mother, making herself indispensable to the family whilst continuing to support her own proletariat allies in the Union, Hansa, whose name means swan, has all the qualities of precious, delicate, retiring femininity to the point of self-extinction. At the finale which re-enacts a mythological encounter between the goddess Urvashi and the King Pururavas, Smita, who appears in the guise of the goddess Urvashi, rejects one of the most powerful kings of the universe. What is interesting is how the two diver-

129

gent aspects of femininity are combined in the character of Urvashi played by Smita who is dressed like a swan, managing to break down the dichotomy of fertility and frigidity embodied by Janaki and Hansa and transforming it into one of vitality and strength necessary for revolutionary change.

Where Smita was successful in the finely balanced act of keeping her identity alive through the chaotic array of roles in the commercial cinema, the contradiction of her off-screen image remained much harder to negotiate. When she chose to become the 'second wife' of a fellow actor and bear his child, her old loyal fans, who had never minded her past affairs with married men, suddenly put her actions under censorious public scrutiny and condemned her for betraying her feminist principles. She was deemed to have transgressed the morality she was meant to uphold, and ironically punished by the orthodoxy of modernity rather than the society she had touchingly feared would daub her a 'bad' woman. However, her untimely death redeemed her reputation, especially as it was linked with the ultimate feminine duty and sacrifice – giving birth to a son.

Although Smita never occupied the number one position in box-office appeal at any point in that era, her name will be inextricably linked with the decade that marks an increase in images of femininity under threat, as well as images of manifest female strength. This decade, dubbed 'Day of the Villain', was described by a critic as 'the multi-rape phase in the multi-villain film: each villain "gets" to rape at least once'.[12] Against this background, Smita forged her own identity which was neither victim, nor avenging angel. The question remains how far her success in finding an identity remained an isolated phenomenon, confined to her own special persona, or rubbed off on her female screen contemporaries.

The Smita persona embodies the contradictions of an era in which a brand of western feminism came up against a tradition which constructed femininity very differently. While the physical strength of Nadia and the moral strength of Nargis – in all its ambivalence – could ultimately be accommodated within the wide-ranging complex of traditional ideas about potent femininity, the reverberations of Smita's unsettling of these traditional systems have yet to be assimilated.

NOTES

First published in *Wide Angle*, 6, 4 (1985).

1 For more discussion of the evolution of distinctive genres in Indian cinema see Rosie Thomas in *World Cinema Since 1945*, ed. William Luhr, Ungar (New York, 1987).

2 Anna: small coin, 16 annas = 1 rupee.

3 Girish Karnad; 'This one is for Nadia', in *Cinema Vision, India*, 1, 2 (April 1980).

4 All quotes are from an interview with the authors in Bombay (February 1986).

5 Report of the Indian Cinematograph Committee, 1927–8, quoted in E. Barnouw and S. Krishnaswamy, *Indian Film* (New York, OUP, 1980).

6 'Doctrine of lapse'; law passed by the British which disallowed royal inheritance through the female line.

7 This section is abbreviated from 'The mythologisation of Mother India', Rosie Thomas in *Quarterly Review of Film and Video*, 11, 3 (1989).

8 See Susan S. Wadley in D. Jacobson and S. Wadley, *Women in India* (New Delhi, Manohar, 1977).

9 For further details on star salaries see Barnouw and Krishnaswamy (op. cit.).

10 There are a number of bizarre cross-references which are too remarkable to detail here, see *Quarterly Review of Film and Video* (op. cit.).

11 See Ashis Nandy, *At the Edge of Psychology* (New Delhi, OUP, 1980).

12 Madhu Jain, 'Day of the villain', in *India Today* (30 November 1988).

11

A STAR IS BORN AND THE CONSTRUCTION OF AUTHENTICITY

Richard Dyer

This chapter deals with a narrow – but crucial – aspect of the film *A Star is Born*, namely, the notion and construction of 'authenticity'. The processes of authentication discussed are the guarantee of both star 'quality' in general and of the particular image of the star concerned.

It is easy enough to outline the components of Judy Garland's star image in terms of social meanings. I only have to refer the stages in her career to three different stereotypes – the all-American small town girl-next-door; the personification of showbiz good humour and bezazz; the neurotic woman – for you to pick up on the social resonances of her image. If we wanted to understand the specificity of the image and account for its particular appeal and purchase, we could look closer at the precise inflection her image gives to those stereotypes, their place in the wider cultural discourses of the period and the different concerns of the different known Garland audiences. We could begin to see why people paid to go and see her, and to differentiate between the various meanings that could be found in her image.

Yet none of this quite seems to deliver an understanding of the most common-sensical notions attached to the words 'star' and 'charisma' – notions like magic, power, fascination, and also authority, importance and aura. Part of the answer lies in the precise and differentiated relation between the values perceived to be embodied by the star and the perceived status of those values (especially if they are felt to be under threat or in crisis, or to be challenging received values, or else to be values that are a key to understanding and coping with contemporary life). But I also want to suggest that all of this depends on the degree to which stars are accepted as truly being what they appear to be.

There is a whole other way of relating to stars, a way that is essentially deconstructive, that refuses the guarantee that appearances are not deceiving. The most widespread, habitual form of such deconstructive reading practice is camp. Garland's relation to this, a phenomenon deeply rooted in male gay culture, is particularly paradoxical, considering that she is, and precisely in her authenticity, a key icon of traditional gay male culture.[1]

There is a whole litany in the fan literature surrounding stars in which certain adjectives endlessly recur – sincere, immediate, spontaneous, real, direct, genuine and so on. All of these words can be seen as relating to a general notion of 'authenticity'. It is these qualities that we demand of a star if we accept her or him in the spirit in which she or he is offered. Outside of a camp appreciation, it is the star's really seeming to be what she/he is supposed to be that secures his/her star status, 'star quality' or charisma. Authenticity is both a quality necessary to the star phenomenon to make it work, and also the quality that guarantees the authenticity of the other particular values a star embodies (such as girl-next-door-ness, etc.). It is this effect of authenticating authenticity that gives the star charisma, and that is what I want to look at here.

But first we need to consider the peculiarity that authenticity should be so crucial a notion in the whole phenomenon. The vocabulary of immediacy, sincerity, believability and so on is so familiar – since we also use it of people we encounter in life – that its particularity may not necessarily strike us. Yet it seems clear that it is a vocabulary of little more than two or three hundred years existence (or rather, this way of using these words is only that old, the words themselves being much older). The peculiarity of this use of these words is their application to individual persons as the criteria for the truth or validity of social affairs. To put it another way, the truth of social affairs has become rooted not in general criteria governing social behaviour itself but in the performers themselves and, at the same time, the criteria governing performance have shifted from whether the performance is well done to whether it is truthful, that is, true to the 'true' personality of the performer. (I mean performer here in both its theatrical and its sociological usages.) Even truth is a peculiar criterion – we no longer ask if someone performs well or according to certain moral precepts but whether what they perform is truthful, with the referent of truthfulness not being falsifiable statements but the person's 'person'.

This development, charted by Richard Sennett in his book *The Fall of Public Man*, is essential to the development of humanism and individualism. All the major discourses of contemporary western society address themselves to people as individuals, as free and separate human beings who are, in their separateness, the source of all social arrangements. Once individuals, in this sense, become the pivot of the whole ensemble of discourses that make sense of society, it is not surprising that it comes to matter very much whether those individuals are indeed functioning as they appear to be. If the individual is the guarantor of the social order, then he or she must be worthy of that role. Hence – to take one striking example – the enormous moral fervour surrounding lying; taken by the west as an absolute moral wrong, its acceptance as morally useful in many societies baffles us. We are hardly able to think about another's statements without first determining whether the person really does mean what she/he says (and not whether it is right, or expedient, or formally correct, or kind).

Yet just at the point that this way of ordering and understanding human discourse and intercourse establishes itself as the fundament of human affairs, the possibility, and then probability, that what people say is *not* what they mean becomes ever more clear, and disturbing. The major trends within western culture that are hailed as intellectual revolutions have all done their bit to dislodge the security with which the individual holds her/his place as the guarantor of discourse. Marxism (at any rate in its most widely understood form) proposes that the political activity of society, in the form of freely operating spokespeople freely elected by freely constituted (i.e. 'individual') electors, is not the real politics of society at all, which on the contrary resides in the invisible operation and structures of the means and forces of production and reproduction. The behaviourisms propose that what we appear to do freely for reasons of which we are conscious we actually do for reasons that are barely available to consciousness at all, drives and instincts. Psychoanalysis equally proposes that consciousness is not really consciousness, but a surface masking the workings of that consciousness below consciousness that we choose to call unconscious. And some forms of linguistics, and aesthetic modernism associated with them, insist that we do not speak language but that it speaks us, that the individual, far from being the guarantor of discourse, is in fact the product of it. I have sketched in these discourses at the level of their theoretical articulation, but they inform all levels of discourse, to varying degrees and in varying forms. Everyone is familiar with the notions that what we do, say, think and feel, and what happens in the world, are not due to us as we know ourselves but to economic forces, instincts, unconscious motivations, habits and patterns of speech. Two historical developments have further endangered the notion of the individual – the development of the mass media (and in particular advertising, both in itself and as an economic concomitant of commercial radio, television and journalism) and the rise of totalitarianisms (Nazism, Stalinism etc.). The reigning concept behind both of these is that of 'manipulation', of the handling of human discourse and intercourse such as to yield vast profits and despotic power, on the one hand, and a docile populace on the other. (This is not the place to enter into discussion of the validity of notions of mass culture, totalitarianism and manipulation, though we should recognise how deeply problematic they are; what is at issue here is their widespread currency as indicators of the characteristic form of social relations in the 'developed' countries.)

Much of the internal intellectual history of Marxism, behaviourism, psychoanalysis, linguistics and modernism has been the attempt to rec-

oncile their paradigms with those of humanism. I do not propose to go
into that here. What is particularly fascinating about the mass media and
totalitarianism is that, even as they are being identified as destroying the
individual, they are also largely in the business of promoting the individual
and the claims of humanism. To get back to stars, no aspect of the media
can be more obviously attended by hype than the production of stars;
there is nothing sophisticated about knowing they are manufactured and
promoted, it is a sense that is common. Even the media knows it, as films
like *A Star is Born* show. Yet in the very same breath as audiences and
producers alike acknowledge stars as hype, they are declaring this or that
star as the genuine article. Just as the media are construed as the very
antithesis of sincerity and authenticity, they are the source for the presentation of the epitome of those qualities, the true star.

How does the star image pull this off? How is the image authenticated
as something more – truer, more real – than an image? In part, the star
phenomenon is defined by an in-built means of authentication. Stars appear
before us in media texts – films, advertisements, gossip columns, television
interviews and so on – but unlike other forms of representation stars do
not only exist in media texts. To say that stars exist outside of the media
texts in real life would be misleading, but stars are carried in the person
of people who do go on living away from their appearances in the media,
and the point is that we know this. When he got home John Wayne may
have become Marion Morrison again, but there was a real human being
with a continuous existence, that is, who existed in between all the times
he was 'being' John Wayne. But there is no way in which Elizabeth
Bennett can leave the pages of *Pride and Prejudice* (except to be referred
to in other media texts, in parodies, speculative continuations of the story,
adaptations etc.). In the first place then the question of the star's authenticity can be referred back to her/his existence in the real world.

This referral-back is tied up with the fact that stars exist in photographic
media. Stars are a particular instance of the supposed relation between a
photograph and its referent. A photograph is always a photograph *of*
something or somebody who had to have been there in order for the
photograph to be taken. In the light of my remarks above, it is symptomatic that one of the best-known saws about photography is that 'the
camera never lies'. The spread of photography as a casual practice has no
doubt severely dented the confidence with which the camera's truth is
believed: few people are the naive realists that theory refutes. Yet the
residual sense of the subject or person having-been-there remains powerful.
Joan Crawford is not just a representation done in paint or writing – she
is carried in the person née Lucille Le Sueur who went before the cameras
to be captured for us.

And if the existential bond (the indexicality, in C. S. Peirce's terminology) between Crawford and Crawford/Le Sueur in the movie or pin-

up is perceived to be distorted (deauthenticated) by the manipulation of the film-making or photographic process (glamour lighting, clever editing and so on), then we can always go and get photos of her doing the chores at home and cuddling baby Christina. And if we think these activities are a put-up job, then we might get a candid camera shot of her without make-up, or uncover a snapshot of her scowling at Christina. And so on in an infinite regress by means of which one more authentic image displaces another. But then they are all part of the star image, each one anchoring the whole thing in an essential, uncovered authenticity, which can then be read back into the performances, the roles, the pin-ups.

There is no need for what-is-uncovered to corroborate the particular character traits incarnated at the most obvious and familiar level of the star's image. In the development of the star phenomenon in Hollywood the attempt to make the different levels mutually reinforcing was certainly strenuously made – until the manipulations of that became so widely known that sources not apparently identified with Hollywood became the privileged access to the star's 'real' personality. Hence the growth of scandal magazines, unauthorised biographies, candid camera photo-journalism and so on.

The growth of this aspect of the total star text (i.e. as read across all her/his different media manifestations) draws on one possible way of taking the implications of Marxism, linguistics and, most explicitly, psychoanalysis and behaviourism. These displace the individual as the guarantor of discourse, but they do posit – or can be read as positing – a 'real' that is beneath or behind the surface represented by 'the individual' as a discursive category. Indeed, many of the claims of these theoretical discourses on our attention has been in their assertion of revealing a, or the, truth behind appearances, stripping away the veil of bourgeois categories or civilised (repressed) behaviours. The basic paradigm is just this – that what is behind or below the surface is, unquestionably and virtually by definition, the truth. Thus features on stars which tell us that the star is *not* like he or she appears to be on screen serve to reinforce the authenticity of the star image as a whole. And, very often, films made subsequent to a particular exposé will incorporate the truth revealed by the exposé as part of the authentication of the star in her/his next film.

At this point the authentication afforded by the ambivalent star-as-image:star-as-real-person nexus resembles nothing so much as a hall of mirrors. Not every case is so complicated. Many star images were authenticated by showing that the star really was like he or she was on the screen. In other cases, the off-screen reputation is either suppressed (as in the endless word of mouth about which indelibly heterosexual love gods and goddesses were in reality gay) or just does not get widely incorporated into the image's popular currency (e.g. every interview and biography assures us that James Cagney was of a gentle and kindly disposition, but it seems to have had no impact on his image). But the full complexity of the potential inter-relations is illustrated by the career of Judy Garland. For instance, at the end of her career *I Could Go On Singing*, drawing on all the publicity surrounding her problems, offers itself as a guaranteed authentic portrait, and retrospectively, with the knowledge of her experiences as a child and adolescent at MGM, the films of the forties can be re-read for signs of disturbance and neurosis. Thus there is a constant play of authenticating levels in the process of reading the image at different points in time. *A Star is Born* is probably most complex in this regard, since it clearly reworks the MGM Garland image (in notions of innate talent, in various details of dress and performance recalling the innocent girl-next-door of the early films and in the films-within-the-film which, as Wade Jennings points out, resemble nothing so much as the kind of big production number MGM put Garland into in the forties).[2] Yet it seems also to incorporate into it oblique reference to the difficult years immediately preceding it (e.g., as Jennings suggests, in transferring the Garland career to the Mason character) and can also be read, particularly in terms of Garland's performance style, for signs (not hard to find) of what we are pleased to label neurosis.

So far all I have said is still rooted in the basic fact of the star phenomenon, that star images are carried in the person of real people. But it is also clear that this is unstable. Corroboration that a star is really like she/he appears to be *may* work, but may be read as further manipulation; showing that the star is not really like she/he appears to be *may* itself be taken up into the image, its further construction and rereading, but it could shatter the illusion altogether. There is more to authentication – there is a rhetoric of authenticity. This too has its own in-built instability – yesterday's markers of sincerity and authenticity are today's signs of hype and artifice. Nevertheless it is a powerful rhetoric so long as it is not perceived as a rhetoric.

I am not concerned here to try to establish the particular codes of authenticity that were current at given points in time. What interests me here are the reigning notions that inform the shifting rhetorical strategies. Authenticity is established or constructed in media texts by the use of markers that indicate lack of control, lack of premeditation and privacy. These return us to notions of the truth being behind or beneath the surface. The surface is organised and under control, it is worked out in advance, it is public. In terms of performance this would mean that every detail is marked as deliberate and calculated; in terms of narrative it would mean that all the actions that really matter are set in the public domain. This kind of performance and this kind of narrative are, needless to say, just what we don't get when authenticity is at stake.

Much of the effort of a film must be the deployment of markers of authenticity to buoy up the unstable authenticity of the star; and this becomes still more so when the film is about the phenomenon of stardom. Few treatments of stardom are in fact as naive as the title *A Star is Born* suggests. The Cukor–Garland film repeatedly indicates that stars are made by elaborate processes of production and manufacture; the extended 'Born in a Trunk' number is about the fact that being born in a trunk is not being born a star. Yet while it is acknowledging the constructedness of stars, it is also wishing to assert that stars are real, that this star, anyhow (whether we're thinking of her as Esther Blodgett, Vicki Lester or Judy Garland) is authentic. The whole film shifts between acknowledging manufacture as the rule and asserting the authenticity of this particular case.

The crucial moment of this assertion of authenticity is the 'The Man That Got Away' number. We must be convinced by this number that Esther really has 'star quality'; if this does not convince us, everything that follows suggests that her rise to stardom is just hype.

It may establish authenticity just by being Garland's big solo – it may be enough that it is Garland. Done in one long take, it may be accepted as capturing the continuousness of her performance which we may already think of as 'authentic' (the Bazinian notion of the realism of the long take may be pertinent here). But the number is too crucial to the film to rest on that.

The number is located (by what is in fact a false point-of-view) as seen by James Mason (Norman Maine) and followed by his declaration that she has that 'little something extra' that is star quality. He looks at and appraises her, sober (for the first time so far in the film) and without lust (his usual mode of looking, as the previous scene establishes) – his judgement is signalled as unfuddled and disinterested, therefore more authoritative. He is himself a star, as well as a more fully established character in the film than is Esther/Garland at this point. For these reasons, he may be taken as the voice of truth. If he says she's a star, then she is. Still – this is not sure. He is hardly what we would call a reliable witness on the strength of what we have seen so far.

The film has to marshall markers of authenticity. *Lack of control*: several of Garland's gestures and facial (particularly mouth) expressions are redundant in terms of directly expressing or underlining the words or musical phrases of the song; such gestures are habitually read as neurotic (I'm sorry to keep using this word so lightly, but equally endlessly putting inverted commas around it is tedious – I intend neurosis as a socially constructed category) and her off-screen image by 1956 would have made such a reading easy. (For example, she brushes a lock of hair off her forehead after bringing her hand to her throat on the words, 'No more that all time thrill'; but her hair is cropped, there is no lock on it; it is redundant as a practical gesture, but indecipherable as an expressive one, except as a gesture that can be taken to 'betray' neurosis.) *Unpremeditated*: other gestures, together with the opening 'doo doo' and the raised eyebrow on the final piano phrase followed by a satisfied laugh, seem to be called forth by the music, to be improvised. She and the other musicians have already been described as jazz musicians, thus linking them to a music tradition that is assumed to be based on unpremeditated musical expressivity (it is assumed that improvisations in jazz just happen, immediate and spontaneous, unrehearsed); and behind that, there is the link with black culture, which has always functioned as a marker of authenticity and naturalness in white discourses. *Private*: she and the band do not know that they are being observed, that they are on. The dark lighting and the close grouping that the moving camera continually reframes both connote intimacy, not public performance. In all these ways, the number is overdetermined in terms of authenticity.

No number, no scene in a film, can guarantee that it will be read in the way it intends or 'prefers'. The reframing camera which keeps Esther/Garland in the centre *may* remind us that this is a performance for us; that Garland knows we are looking even if Esther doesn't know that Norman is. It is only a step from this to reminding ourselves that this could well be the twentieth take, which scotches the notions of unpremeditated, unrehearsed performance. And so on. But this is to deconstruct the film in the process of viewing, to see the markers of authenticity as markers. It is to go against the grain of the number, and the film.

One of the curious things about this number is that the song does not refer to anything that has happened so far in the film, and it seems to stretch a point to suggest that it refers forward to Norman's suicide. One could see it as referring to Garland's life, her previous marriages and affairs; and this is the resonance the song acquired as she used it in subsequent concert appearances. Yet this was never so insistent a part of her neurotic image as the legacy, in the form of pills and alcohol, of her years as a child star in Hollywood. The authenticity the number is after really has nothing to do with what Esther/Garland is singing about – it is the authenticity of her capacity to sing that is at stake. We must know that her star quality has nothing to do with recording techniques, with mechanical reproduction (even though what we are watching is perforce a recording), but is grounded in her own immediate (= not controlled), spontaneous (= unpremeditated) and essential (= private) self. That guarantees that her stardom is not a con, because an authenticated individual is acting as the guarantor of the truth of the discourse of her stardom. By not having a direct emotional referent, the number reinforces the authenticity of the star quality that can *then* legitimate the authenticity of whatever particular emotions Esther/Vicki will be called upon to express. In this way, the number is an especially interesting indicator of the processes of the authentication of star quality.

NOTES

This paper was given at a Weekend Workshop organised by the British Film Institute Education Department and subsequently published in *Star Signs*, the collected Workshop Papers produced by BFI Education, 1982.

1 See R. Dyer, 'Judy Garland and gay men', in *Heavenly Bodies* (London: Macmillan, 1987), 141–94.
2 Wade Jennings, 'Nova: Garland in *A Star is Born*', *Quarterly Review of Film Studies*, Summer 1979, 321–37.

12

FEMININE FASCINATIONS
Forms of identification in star–audience relations
Jackie Stacey

THE LOST AUDIENCE

Throughout this book – as throughout most film studies – the audience has been conspicuous by its absence. In talking of manipulation . . . consumption . . . ideological work . . . subversion . . . identification . . . reading . . . placing . . . and elsewhere, a concept of audience is clearly crucial, and yet in every case I have had to gesture towards this gap in our knowledge, and then proceed as if this were *merely* a gap. But how to conceptualise the audience – and the empirical adequacy of one's conceptualisations – is fundamental to every assumption one can make about how stars and films work.[1]

My mother obtained a job at the State cinema when I was ten. For me that meant a ticket to Paradise, and regularly I worshipped at the shrine of the gods and goddesses. I couldn't wait for the moment to come when the velvet curtains would sweep apart, the lights dim, and a shared intimacy would settle on the hushed audience. (D. H.)

The first quotation is taken from the conclusion of Richard Dyer's study on stars, the second is written by a film fan remembering the pleasures offered by Hollywood stars in the 1940s and 1950s. Since the publication of *Stars* in 1982 there has been little work to fill the gap referred to in Dyer's conclusion. It is particularly important for feminists to challenge the absence of audiences from film studies, since it has reproduced an assumed passivity on the part of women in the cinema audience. Wanting to find out about female audiences and their relationship to stars, I advertised in two of the leading women's weekly magazines for readers to write to me about their favourite Hollywood star of the forties and the fifties. These decades interested me since much feminist work on Hollywood has looked at the films of this period, which was, as well, a time of changing definitions of femininity in Hollywood and in society generally.

The enthusiastic response of over 300 letters, including some from Canada, the United States and Australia, testifies to the continuing significance of Hollywood stars in women's lives and imaginations. Many letters were several pages long and offered detailed recollections of particular favourite stars, as well as of the cinema generally during this period. Respondents included photos, scrapbooks and original newspaper cuttings about their favourite stars, as well as detailing their appeal in their own words. The letters covered a broad range of topics including how much the cinema, and stars in particular, meant in women's lives; the role of the cinema in wartime Britain; why women stopped being fans of stars; and the particular pleasures of the cinema experience in the context of the 1940s and 1950s. This chapter looks firstly at the reasons for the continued absence of the audience from film studies and then offers some preliminary findings from research in progress into aspects of the relationship between female Hollywood stars and women in the audience.

Within film studies generally, the study of stars has remained predominantly textual. Although Dyer's work challenges some of the existing boundaries of film studies, by linking textual models of semiotic and narrative analysis to a sociological approach to stars, very few studies have succeeded in developing this project in relation to questions about cinema audiences. Analyses of stars have continued to focus on the production of particular significations within the film text, or within other aspects of the cinema industry such as publicity, rather than on how audiences might read them within particular cultural and historical contexts.[2]

There is surprisingly little feminist work on Hollywood stars, and even less on their audiences. Attention to genre (especially melodrama, the woman's film and film noir), to narratives (especially those reproducing the oedipal drama) and to forms of looking (especially voyeurism and fetishism) have tended to dominate the feminist agendas of the 1980s. It is especially puzzling that stars have remained a relatively undeveloped aspect of Hollywood cinema within feminist work since female stars might seem an obvious focus for the analysis of the construction of idealised femininities within patriarchal culture. In the work which has emerged, feminist film theorists have also tended to reproduce a textual analysis of stars. Despite their very different theoretical positions, the two key perspectives within feminist film theory, namely the 'images of women'[3] approach and the 'woman as image'[4] approach, have also shared a common reliance on textual analysis, ignoring the role of the audience in the cinema.

Molly Haskell, for example, discusses the female stars in Hollywood cinema in terms of stereotypes which limit and control definitions of femininity in a male dominated culture. She contrasts, for example, the 'treacherous woman', associated with stars such as Rita Hayworth in *Gilda* and *The Lady from Shanghai* with the 'superfemale', such as Bette Davis in *Jezebel*, who, 'while exceedingly "feminine" and flirtatious, is too ambitious and intelligent for the docile role society has decreed she play', and with the 'superwoman' who 'instead of exploiting her femininity, adopts male characteristics in order to enjoy male prerogatives, or simply to survive'.[5] This latter female type is exemplified by stars such as Katharine Hepburn and Joan Crawford and is different again from the 'sweet and innocent' type, associated with June Allyson, Olivia de Havilland and Judy Garland: 'For every hard-boiled dame there was a soft-boiled sweetheart . . .'[6] Although Haskell's analysis refers outside the film texts to feminine stereotypes in society generally, and to a patriarchal culture in whose interest they are perpetuated, Haskell's discussion of the stars themselves is restricted to the characters portrayed and their narrative treatment in the films.

The other approach to stars within feminist film criticism has been the investigation of female stars as objects of the 'male' gaze. Laura Mulvey, for example, analyses Sternberg's use of Dietrich as the 'ultimate fetish' in her well-known essay 'Visual Pleasure and Narrative Cinema':

> The beauty of the woman as object and the screen space coalesce; she is no longer the bearer of guilt but a perfect product, whose body, stylised and fragmented by close-ups, is the content of the film and the direct recipient of the spectator's look.[7]

This fetishism of the female star within Hollywood cinema is one form of scopophilia (or pleasure in looking) offered to the spectator, the other is the voyeuristic pleasure in the objectification of the female star on the screen. To illustrate this latter process, Mulvey discusses the heroines of Hitchcock's films who are constructed as passive objects of the sadistic controlling voyeurism of the male protagonist, and, by extension, the spectator: 'The power to subject another person to the will sadistically or to the gaze voyeuristically is turned onto the woman as object of both.'[8]

Little attention, then, has been paid to female stars in Hollywood by feminist film theorists outside the ways in which the stars function within the film text.[9] There are, however, a few exceptions which have tried to bring together textual analysis either with ethnographic investigation or with a historical contextualisation of audiences. Helen Taylor's recent book *Scarlett's Women*, for example, analyses audiences' readings of Vivien Leigh in *Gone with the Wind*.[10] Jane Gaines has examined the different definitions of femininity constructed in 1940s fan magazines through which female stars could be read.[11] Angela Partington, whilst maintaining the focus on genre, offers a convincing analysis of the place of female stars in the production of an 'excess' of femininity in melodrama in the 1950s, which can only be understood in relation to other representations and consumer practices, not solely in terms of its own textual operations.[12]

Finally, in *Heavenly Bodies*, Richard Dyer offers a reading of Judy Garland's star image through discourses of gay male subculture. Based on responses to an advert, Richard Dyer's analysis demonstrates the importance of meanings produced outside the film text to the readings audiences make of Hollywood stars. Indeed there could not be better evidence to illustrate the argument against textual determinism, since the readings made by these fans are so clearly based not just outside the film text, or even the cinema, but outside mainstream culture itself, and within a subculture which reverses and parodies dominant meanings.[13]

Investigating audiences

Whilst these studies show that work on audiences is developing,[14] there remain several difficulties in this emerging area of work. One of the particular difficulties with analysing audiences from past decades is that they are not easily accessible. What then are the possible sources for their investigation?[15] First, box-office statistics can give us an indication of which films, and perhaps which stars, were popular and when. Film magazines such as *Cinematograph Weekly*, or *Picturegoer*, ran popularity polls on stars, and these may also indicate in more detail which stars were favoured, when, and for how long. Other surveys done at the time may indicate who went to which films and why, such as the work at the Mass Observation Archive at Sussex University,[16] or the market research produced for commercial reasons, or the sociological research on the 'effects' of films on audiences. Sometimes this information is broken down according to class and gender divisions, which enables conclusions to be drawn about which genres were popular among specific audiences, for example.[17] However, this information, whilst it may give a broad indication of likes or dislikes, offers little insight into the more qualitative dimensions of those preferences.

A richer source of information which offers more details on preferences and audiences' tastes has been what audiences wrote about stars at the time. Letters pages in film magazines contain examples of audience opinion about stars, as well as about other issues. Magazines' and newspapers' letters pages typically include complaints, criticism, appreciation and likes and dislikes letters. They are generally responding to an article or feature on a particular star, film or director, or to controversial questions set up by the editor. The most popular magazine of this kind in the 1940s and 1950s, *Picturegoer*, for example, regularly featured provocative pieces such as 'Charm not Curves' by Vincent Keene, which questioned what constituted desirable femininity.[18] The letters pages in the weeks following were full of differing and wide ranging answers to this question. Letters from readers could be a useful indicator of audiences' preferences and responses to stars, bearing in mind that the topics raised in the letters are shaped by the magazine as a whole and its own editorial criteria. The mode of the magazine thus produces very particular generic conventions through which the readers' letters are channelled.

In addition, the editorial decisions about which letters get published clearly determine what kinds of opinions we can have access to now.[19] Thus letters pages in weekly magazines are interesting in terms of studying the magazine and its role in framing Hollywood in Britain, but less useful in terms of offering detailed sources on audiences.

Fan clubs offer another source of information about audiences in the 1940s and 1950s, but these are often difficult to trace, and much of the fan mail written at this time has been lost or destroyed. The fan clubs which responded to my letters of enquiry said they no longer possessed such old fan mail from Britain.

The final possibility for investigating audiences of the 1940s and 1950s is to analyse people's memories and recollections of the cinema at that time. Yet, as is true of all the sources discussed so far, the rules of enquiry frame the kind of information elicited. Answers to an advertisement asking for recollections of favourite stars inevitably produce a particular set of representations, which are clearly framed by a specific cultural context. First, in my own case, the research concerns women's *memories* of Hollywood stars. The kinds of selections respondents make when remembering what Hollywood stars meant in their lives are therefore mediated in a particular way. Which stars are remembered and how they are remembered must additionally be influenced by the cultural constructions of those stars since that time. For example, audiences may remember stars differently depending on whether the stars are still alive, and if not, how they died (e.g. Marilyn Monroe); whether they still have a fan club (e.g. Deanna Durbin); whether the star continued to have a successful career (e.g. Katharine Hepburn and Bette Davis); whether their films have been shown frequently on television and indeed whether the stars went on to have a television career (e.g. Barbara Stanwyck).

In addition to these factors, memory introduces a particular kind of selection process. What gets remembered and what gets forgotten may depend not only on the star's career since the time period specified, but also upon the identity of the cinema spectator. Having asked women to write about female stars, the kinds of representations offered will be informed by issues such as self-image and self-perception, particularly in relation to gender identity. The different constructions of femininity within Hollywood, such as the power and rebelliousness of Bette Davis or the sexual attractiveness of Marilyn Monroe, or the clean-livingness of Deanna Durbin may have particular appeal in retrospect, and may have come to mean something over the years which it did not in the 1940s and 1950s.[20]

It is this final approach to historical audiences that I am using in this chapter. In particular I want to explore one of the recurring themes of the letters which were sent to me by women in response to my advertisement: the processes of identification at stake in the exchange between female stars and the female spectator. I have chosen to focus on this aspect of the relationship between stars and spectators not only because of its recurrence as a theme in the letters, but also because of its theoretical centrality within feminist criticisms of Hollywood cinema.

A QUESTION OF IDENTIFICATION

The term 'identification' has been central to many debates within psychoanalytic theory and film studies. Within psychoanalytic theory, 'identification' has been seen as the key mechanism for the production of identities. Freud analysed the unconscious mechanisms through which the self is constituted in relation to external objects. In her paper 'Identification and the Star: A Refusal of Difference', Anne Friedberg quotes Freud on identification:

> First, identification is the original form of emotional tie with an object; secondly, in a regressive way it becomes a substitute for a libidinal object-tie, as it were by means of introjection of the object into the ego; and thirdly, it may arise with any new perception of a common quality shared with some other person who is not an object of sexual instinct. The more important this common quality is, the more successful may this partial identification become, and it may thus represent the beginning of a new tie.[21]

The role of vision in identification has always been part of the Freudian formulation (the emphasis on the moment of the sight of sexual difference, for example) but the 'specular role of identification' has taken centre stage in Lacan's theories of the mirror phase, through which subjects are 'constituted through a specular misrecognition of an *other*'.[22]

These models of identification employed within psychoanalysis to explore the developments of unconscious identities have been seen by some film theorists, such as Christian Metz,[23] as analogous to the cinematic experience of spectatorship. As Friedberg outlines:

> Primary identification as Metz describes it (as distinct from Freud's 'original and emotional tie') means a spectator who identifies with both camera and projector, and like the child positioned in front of the mirror, constructs an imaginary notion of wholeness, of a unified body. . . . Secondary identification is with an actor, character or star . . . any body becomes an opportunity for an identificatory investment, a possible suit for the substitution/misrecognition of self.[24]

Psychoanalytic film theorists have thus developed a complex analysis of cinematic identification, based on an analogy between the construction of individual identities in infancy in relation to others, and the process of watching a film on a screen. Whilst this may be an appealing analogy, especially given the centrality of the specular in later psychoanalytic accounts of the development of identity, the question remains as to the validity of such a straightforward transposition: how similar are these processes, and what is being left out of the account of spectatorship by focusing so exclusively on its psychic dimensions? Such a framework offers limited purchase on understanding cinematic identification, with no evidence other than a conceptual analogy of the processes occurring in individual psyches.

In film studies more generally, the term 'identification' has been widely used to suggest a broader set of processes. Drawing on literary analysis, identification has often been used rather loosely to mean sympathising or engaging with a character. It has also been used in relation to the idea of 'point of view', watching and following the film from a character's point of view. This involves not only *visual* point of view, constructed by type of shot, editing sequences and so on, but also *narrative* point of view, produced through the sharing of knowledge, sympathy or moral values with the protagonist. Identification has thus been used as a kind of common-sense term within film and literary studies, referring to a very diverse set of processes, and has yet to be adequately theorised in a manner which provides a satisfactory alternative to the more reductive psychoanalytic models.

Interestingly, feminist writing on the subject of identification in relation to gender identities has developed in two opposing directions. On the one hand, the psychoanalytically informed film criticism following Laura Mulvey's original attack on the visual pleasure of narrative cinema is still marked by a suspicion of any kind of feminine role model, heroine or image of identification. Mulvey's films (such as *Amy!*, 1980), as well as her influential theoretical work, have advocated a rejection of the conventions of popular representations, not simply for the images of femininity constructed, but also for the processes of identification offered to the cinema spectator. 'Identification' itself has been seen as a cultural process complicit with the reproduction of dominant culture by reinforcing patriarchal forms of identity. Anne Freidberg sums up what feminists have seen as the problematic functions of identification thus:

> Identification can only be made through recognition, and all recognition is itself an implicit confirmation of an existing form. The institutional sanction of stars as ego ideals also operates to establish normative figures. Identification enforces a collapse of the subject onto the normative demand for sameness, which, under patriarchy, is always male.[25]

On the other hand, some feminist cultural theorists have attempted to rescue the process of identification from such criticism, and have instead drawn attention to the empowerment through certain forms of identification within the consumption of popular culture. Valerie Walkerdine, for example, offers an analysis of the way the different members of a working-class family read *Rocky II*, which demonstrates the shifting significance of the metaphor of fighting in Rocky's character.[26] Gender differences produce different and conflicting identifications in Walkerdine and the family members; nevertheless identification is reclaimed in Walkerdine's analysis as potentially producing rebellious feelings and a desire to fight the dominant system, as well as being a necessary aspect of cultural consumption.

These two perspectives, then, represent opposite positions on processes of identification in the visual media: the first criticises identification of any kind for reproducing sameness, fixity and the confirmation of existing identities, whilst the second reclaims it as potentially empowering and expressive of resistance. They coincide, however, in taking psychoanalytic accounts of identification as central to their understanding of spectatorship.

Whilst there are detailed psychoanalytic accounts of the psychic processes of identification,[27] however, there has been less investigation of the broader cultural and social dimensions of identification in the cinema. Therefore instead of applying psychoanalytic theory to a film text to investigate identification in the cinema, I shall take the audiences' representations of this process and its meanings as my starting point. This is not to argue that audiences are the source of 'the true meanings' of films or of stars; clearly audiences' recollections are themselves a highly mediated set of cultural representations, as I have discussed above. Instead, the purpose of this investigation is to look at the production of the meaning of stars in the terms of how audiences construct them.

Particularly striking in the letters I received was the diversity of processes represented which could loosely be termed identification. To the extent that identification involves various processes which negotiate the boundaries between self and other,[28] these processes take on a particular significance in the context of popular cinema where women in the audience are offered idealised images of femininity in many different forms. Some of these quite clearly relate back to the psychic processes described by psychoanalysis, and others move into the domain of cultural consumption more generally.

There is a problem finding a term to refer to the women in the audience whose letters are used in this analysis. The term 'female spectator', used so widely within feminist film theory, has been a confusing one; it has been used to refer both to the textual positions constructed by the film, and, often implicitly, to the female members of the cinema audience.[29] At best it is acknowledged that the two processes may, to some extent, be separate, but generally an implicit textual determinism defines assumptions about spectatorship.[30] In addition, the singularity of the reference of the term spectator implies a unified viewing experience, and its usage carries with it a very passive model of how audiences watch films.

I am using 'spectator' here in a rather different way to refer to members of the cinema audience. However, there is a further problem using the term to discuss practices which take place beyond the cinema, since spectator, in this broader sense, refers to a person still in the cinema. This is itself symptomatic of the limited interest in what spectatorship might mean outside or beyond the cinema experience. Spectatorship, when considered as an aspect of cultural consumption, should no longer be seen simply as an extension of a film text replicating infantile misrecognition, nor as an isolated viewing process, but rather as part of a more general cultural construction of identities.

The analysis of the letters which follows is divided into two sections. The first addresses processes of identification which involve fantasies about the relationship between the identity of the star and the identity of the spectator. On the whole these forms of identification relate to the cinematic context. The second section examines forms of identification which involve practice as well as fantasy, in that spectators actually transform some aspect of their identity as a result of their relationship to their favourite star. These practices extend beyond the cinema itself and thus spectatorship is considered in relation to the construction of feminine identities more generally.

Cinematic identificatory fantasies

Devotion and worship

I wanted to write and tell you of my devotion to my favourite star Doris Day. I thought she was fantastic, and joined her fan club, collected all the photos and info I could. I saw *Calamity Jane* 45 times in a fortnight and still watch all her films avidly. My sisters all thought I was mad going silly on a woman, but I just thought she was wonderful, they were mad about Elvis, but my devotion was to Doris Day. (V. M.)

Some letters do not even mention the self, but simply offer evidence of devotion to a female star. However, this is unusual; most letters I received framed their comments on stars in relation to their own identities. In this first group, many of the letters speak of the pleasure produced by some kind of difference from the star, the distance produced by this difference providing a source of fascination. Stars are frequently written about as out of reach, and belonging to a different world or plane of existence:

Film stars . . . seemed very special people, glamorous, handsome and way above us ordinary mortals. (J. T.)

149

I'll never forget the first time I saw her, it was in *My Gal Sal* in 1942, and her name was Rita Hayworth. I couldn't take my eyes off her, she was the most perfect woman I had ever seen. The old cliché 'screen goddess' was used about many stars, but those are truly the only words that define that divine creature. . . . I was stunned and amazed that any human being could be that lovely. (V. H.)

Stars were fabulous creatures to be worshipped from afar, every film of one's favourite gobbled up as soon as it came out. (P. K.)

These statements represent the star as something different and unattainable. Religious signifiers here indicate the special status and meaning of the stars, as well as suggesting the intensity of the devotion felt by the spectator. They also reinforce the 'otherness' of the stars who are not considered part of the mortal world of the spectator. The last example, however, does introduce the star into the mortal world by a metaphor of ingestion reminiscent of the act of communion. Worship of stars as goddesses involves a denial of self found in some forms of religious devotion. The spectator is only present in these quotes as a worshipper, or through their adoration of the star. There is no reference to the identity of the spectator or suggestion of closing the gap between star and fan by becoming more like a star; these are simply declarations of appreciation from afar. The boundaries between self and ideal are quite fixed and stable in these examples, and the emphasis is very strongly on the ideal rather than the spectator. Even in the last statement, where the self is implicit in that the star is to be gobbled up, the star none the less remains the subject of the sentence.

The desire to become

In other examples, the relationship between star and audience is also articulated through the recognition of an immutable difference between star and spectator: 'Bette Davis was the epitome of what we would like to be, but knew we never could!' (N. T.). Yet here the desire to move across that difference and become more like the star is expressed, even if this is accompanied by the impossibility of its fulfilment.[31] The distance between the spectator and her ideal seems to produce a kind of longing which offers fantasies of transformed identities.

These desires to become more like the stars occur on several levels. Many of them are predictably articulated in relation to appearance:

I finally kept with Joan Crawford – every typist's dream of how they'd like to look. (M. R.)

150

And of course her [Betty Grable's] clothes – how could a young girl not want to look like that? (S. W.)

Although I wished to look like a different star each week depending what film I saw, I think my favourite was Rita Hayworth, I always imagined, if I could look like her I could toss my red hair into the wind . . . and meet the man of my dreams . . . (R. A.)

Clearly, stars serve a normative function to the extent that they are often read as role models, contributing to the construction of the ideals of feminine attractiveness circulating in culture at any one time. The age difference between the star and the younger fans is central here: stars provide ideals of femininity for adolescent women in the audience, pre-occupied with attaining adult femininity. Part of this kind of identification involves recognising desirable qualities in the ideal and wanting to move towards it:

Doris Day . . . seemed to epitomise the kind of person who, with luck, I as a child could aspire to be. (B. C.)

I loved to watch Deanna Durbin. I used to put myself in her place. She lived in a typical girl's dream. (J. G.)

These examples demonstrate not simply the desire to overcome the gap between spectator and star, but a fantasy of possible movement between the two identities, from the spectator to the star.

Pleasure in feminine power

However, the difference between the female star and the female spectator is a source of fascination not only with ideals of physical beauty, but also with the stars' personalities and behaviour, which are often admired or envied by spectators. These identifications demonstrate the contradictory pleasures offered by Hollywood stars, on the one hand reproducing normative models of feminine glamour, whilst on the other hand offering women fantasies of resistance. For example, some female stars represented images of power and confidence. These were frequent favourites because they offered spectators fantasies of power outside their own experience.

We liked stars who were most different to ourselves and Katharine Hepburn, with her self-assured romps through any situation was one of them. We were youngsters at the time, and were anything but self confident, and totally lacking in sophistication, so, naturally, Bette Davis took the other pedestal. She who could be a real 'bitch', without turning a hair, and quelled her leading men with a raised eyebrow and sneer at the corners of her mouth . . . (N. T.)

Bette Davis . . . was great, I loved how she walked across the room in her films, she seemed to have a lot of confidence and she had a look of her own, as I think a lot of female stars had at that time . . . (E. M.)

Powerful female stars often play characters in punishing patriarchal narratives, where the woman is either killed off, or married, or both, but these spectators do not seem to select this aspect of their films to write about. Instead, the qualities of confidence and power are remembered as offering pleasure to female spectators in something they lack and desire.

Identification and escapism

This movement from spectator to star is part of the pleasure of escapism articulated in many of the letters. Instead of the difference between the spectator and the star being recognised and maintained, the difference provides the possibility for the spectator to leave her world temporarily and become part of the star's world:[32]

It made no difference to me if the film was ushered in by a spangled globe, the Liberty Lady or that roaring lion, I was no longer in my seat but right up there fleeing for my life from chasing gangsters, skimming effortlessly over silver ice, or singing high and sweet like a lark. (D. H.)

I was only a girl, but I could be transported from the austerity and gloom of that time to that other world on the silver screen. (J. T.)

Joan Crawford – could evoke such pathos, and suffer such martyrdom . . . making you live each part. (M. B.)

In these examples, the movement from self to other is more fluid than in the previous categories, and this fluidity provides the well-known pleasure of the cinema: 'losing oneself' in the film. Here, in contrast to the distinction between self and ideal maintained in the processes of spectatorship discussed above, the spectator's identity merges with the star in the film, or the character she is portraying.

In this first section I have discussed processes of spectatorship which involve negotiating the difference between the star and the spectator in various ways: beginning with the denial of self, in favour of praising the screen goddesses, and moving on to the desire to become like the star, but realising the impossibility of such desires, and ending with the pleasure in overcoming the difference and merging with the ideal on the screen.

Extra-cinematic identificatory practices

Now I want to move on to discuss representations which concern what I shall call 'identificatory practices' of spectatorship. These nearly all relate to forms of identification which take place outside the cinematic context. These practices also involve the audience engaging in some kind of practice of transformation of the self to become more like the star they admire, or to involve others in the recognition of their similarity with the star.

Pretending

... there was a massive open-cast coal site just at the tip of our estate – there were 9 of us girls – and we would go to the site after school, and play on the mounds of soil removed from the site. The mounds were known to us as 'Beverley Hills' and we all had lots of fun there. Each of us had our own spot where the soil was made into a round – and that was our mansion. We played there for hours – visiting one mansion after another and each being our own favourite film star ... (M. W.)

I really loved the pictures, they were my life, I used to pretend I was related to Betty Grable because my name was Betty, and I used to get quite upset when the other children didn't believe me. (B. C.)

Pretending to be particular film stars involves an imaginary practice, but one where the spectator involved knows that it is a game. This is rather different from the processes of escapism in the cinema discussed above whereby the spectator feels completely absorbed in the star's world and which thus involves a temporary collapsing of the self into the star identity. The first example given above is also different in that it involves a physical as well as an imaginary transformation. Furthermore pretending does not simply involve the privatised imagination of the individual spectator, as in the process of escapism, but also involves the participation of other spectators in the collective fantasy games. This kind of representation of the relationship between star and fan is based more on similarity than difference, since the fan takes on the identity of the star in a temporary game of make-believe, and the difference between them is made invisible, despite the recognition of the whole process as one of pretending.

Resembling

Bette Davis – her eyes were fabulous and the way she walked arrogantly ... I have dark eyes, in those days I had very large dark eyebrows ... and my Dad used to say ... 'Don't you roll those

153

Bette Davis eyes at me young lady....'... Now Doris Day, that's
a different thing – we share the same birthday ... (P. O.)

There are numerous points of recognition of similarities between the
spectator and the star. These are not based on pretending to be something
one is not, but rather selecting something which establishes a link between
the star and the self based on a pre-existing part of the spectator's identity
which bears a resemblance to the star. This does not necessarily involve
any kind of transformation, but rather a highlighting of star qualities in
the individual spectator. The significance of particular features, such as
'Bette Davis eyes', seems to exceed physical likeness, to suggest a certain
kind of femininity, in this case a rebellious one which represented a
challenge to the father's authority.

Imitating

Unlike the above process of recognising a resemblance to a star, many
spectators wrote about practices which involved transforming themselves
to be more like the star. This is different from the fantasy of becoming
the star whilst viewing a film, or even expressing the desire to become
more like the star generally, since it involves an actual imitation of a star
or of her particular characteristics in a particular film. In other words this
identificatory practice involves a form of pretending or play-acting, and
yet it is also different from pretending, since pretending is represented as
a process involving the whole star persona, whereas imitation is used here
to indicate a partial taking-on of part of a star's identity.

Several letters gave examples of imitating singing and dancing of favourite stars after the film performance:

> We used to go home and do concerts based on the songs and dances
> we had seen in the films, and one of my friends had an auntie who
> was a mine of information on the words of songs from films ... (B.
> F.)

> The films we saw made us sing and sometimes act our way home
> on the bus ... (J. T.)

> My favourite female star was Betty Grable. The songs she sang in
> the film, I would try to remember, I would sing and dance all the
> way home ... (P. G.)

The imitation of stars was not limited to singing and dancing, but was
clearly a pleasure in terms of replicating gestures, speech and star personalities: 'I had my favourites of course.... One week I would tigerishly
pace about like Joan Crawford, another week I tried speaking in the

staccato tones of Bette Davis and puffing a cigarette at the same time'
(D. H.).

Copying

Although imitation and copying are very closely linked as practices, I
want to use them here differently to distinguish between audiences *imitating* behaviour and activities, and copying appearances. As the attempted
replication of appearance, then, *copying* relates back to the desire to look
like stars discussed above. However it is not simply expressed as an
unfulfillable desire or pleasurable fantasy, as in the earlier examples, it is
also a practice which transforms the spectators' physical appearance.

Copying is the most common form of identificatory practice outside
the cinema. Perhaps this is not surprising given the centrality of physical
appearance to femininity in general in this culture, and to female Hollywood stars in particular. The 'visual pleasure' offered by the glamour and
sexual appeal of Hollywood stars has been thoroughly criticised by feminists elsewhere.[33] Here I am interested in how women audiences related to
these ideals of femininity as presented by Hollywood stars on the screen,
and particularly in how identification extends beyond individualised fantasies into practices aimed at the transformation of identity.

> I was a very keen fan of Bette Davis and can remember seeing her
> in *Dark Victory*. . . . That film had such an impact on me. I can
> remember coming home and looking in the mirror fanatically trying
> to comb my hair so that I could look like her. I idolised her . . .
> thought she was a wonderful actress. (V. C.)

This process involves an intersection of self and other, subject and object.
The impact of the film on the spectator was to produce a desire to
resemble physically the ideal. In front of a reflection of herself, the spectator attempts to close the gap between her image and her ideal image,
by trying to produce a new image, more like her ideal. In this instance,
her hair is the focus of this desired transformation. Indeed hairstyle is one
of the most frequently recurring aspects of the star's appearance which
the spectators try to copy:

> My friends and I would try and copy the hair styles of the stars,
> sometimes we got it right, and other times we just gave up, as we
> hadn't the looks of the stars or the money to dress the way they
> did. (E. M.)

> Now Doris Day. . . . I was told many times around that I looked
> like her, so I had my hair cut in a D.A. style. Jane Wyman was a
> favourite at one stage and I had hair cut like hers, it was called a

tulip. . . . Now Marilyn Monroe was younger and by this time I had changed my image, my hair was almost white blonde and longer and I copied her hairstyle, as people said I looked like her. (P. O.)

These forms of copying involve some kind of self-transformation to produce an appearance more similar to Hollywood stars. Some spectators clearly have a stronger feeling of their success than others; the first example includes a sense of defeat whilst the last seems to be able to achieve several desired likenesses, especially bearing in mind this respondent is the one who had 'Bette Davis eyes'. The difference then between the star and the spectator is transformable into similarity through the typical work of femininity: the production of oneself simultaneously as subject and object in accordance with cultural ideals of femininity.

Copying and consumption

Copying the hairstyles of famous film stars can be seen as a form of cultural production and consumption. It involves the production of a new self-image through the pleasure taken in a star image. In this last section I want to consider an extension of the identificatory practice of copying where it intersects with the consumption of cultural products in addition to the star image. The construction of women as cinema spectators overlaps here with their construction as consumers.

To some extent copying the hairstyles of the stars overlaps with this. However I have separated hairstyles from other aspects of this process, since changing hairstyles does not necessarily involve the actual purchasing of other products to transform the identity of the spectator, although it may do. The purchasing of items such as clothing and cosmetics in relation to particular stars brings into particularly sharp focus the relationship between the cinema industries and other forms of capitalist industry. Stars are consumable feminine images which female spectators then reproduce through other forms of consumption.

and I bought clothes like hers [Doris Day] . . . dresses, soft wool, no sleeves, but short jackets, boxy type little hats, half hats we used to call them and low heeled court shoes to match your outfit, kitten heels they were called . . . as people said I looked like her [Marilyn Monroe] I even bought a suit after seeing her in *Niagara*. (P. O.)

It was fun trying to copy one's favourite stars with their clothes, hats and even make-up, especially the eyebrows. Hats were very much in vogue at that time and shops used to sell models similar to the styles the stars were wearing. I was very much into hats myself and tried in my way (on a low budget) to copy some of them.

Naturally I bought a Deanna Durbin model hat and a Rita Hayworth one. (V. C.)

I'd like to name Deanna Durbin as one of my favourite stars. Her beautiful singing voice, natural personality and sparkling eyes made her films so enjoyable, and one always knew she would wear boleros; in one film she wore six different ones. I still like wearing boleros – so you can tell what a lasting effect the clothes we saw on the screen made on us. (J. D. Member of the Deanna Durbin Society)

Stars are thus identified with particular commodities which are part of the reproduction of feminine identities. The female spectators in these examples produce particular images of femininity which remind them of their favourite stars. In so doing they produce a new feminine identity, one which combines an aspect of the star with their own appearance. This is different from imitation, which is more of a temporary reproduction of a particular kind of behaviour which resembles the star. It transforms the spectators' previous appearance, and in doing so offers the spectator the pleasure of close association with her ideal.

As teenagers and young girls we did not have the vast variety of clothing and choices of make-up that is available today, so hairstyles and make-up were studied with great interest and copied . . . I seem to remember buying a small booklet by Max Factor with pictures of the stars, M.G.M. mostly, with all the details of their make-up and how to apply it . . . (E. H.)

Their make-up was faultless and their fashion of the forties platform shoes, half hats with rows of curls showing at the back under the hat. . . . We used to call the shoes 'Carmen Miranda' shoes . . . I felt like a film star using Lux Toilet soap, advertised as the stars' soap. (V. B.)

Through the use of cosmetic products, then, as well as through the purchasing and use of clothing, spectators take on a part of the stars identity and make it part of their own. The self and the ideal combine to produce another feminine identity, closer to the ideal. This is the direct opposite of the process of identification I began with in the first section, in which the spectator's own identity remained relatively marginal to the description of the pleasure taken in female Hollywood stars. In this final process, the star becomes more marginal and is only relevant in so far as the star identity relates to the spectator's own identity. As has been noted by other commentators, these latter practices demonstrate the importance of understanding Hollywood stars and their audiences in relation to other cultural industries of the 1940s and 1950s.[34]

Figure 12.1 Lux advertisement, from *Picturegoer*, 22 January 1955

158

CONCLUDING COMMENTS

Having outlined some of the different forms of identification in audience–star relationships represented in these letters, it is now important to reconsider some of the earlier models of identification and spectatorship in the light of this research. First, the diversity of processes of identification, including forms of desire, evident in these letters is striking. The idea of a singular process of identification, so often assumed in psychoanalytic film theory, seems unsatisfactory in the light of the range of processes discussed above. In addition, the use of the term 'female spectatorship' to refer to a single positioning by a film text seems equally inappropriate in the light of the diversity of readings of stars by different women in the cinema audiences in the 1940s and 1950s.

As well as categorising the many different kinds of identification in the relationships between audiences and stars, I have also drawn attention to the broad distinction between two different forms of identification: identificatory fantasies (pp. 149–52) and identificatory practices (pp. 153–7). This is not to suggest that the practices do not also involve fantasies, nor that fantasies cannot also be considered as practices. But rather, it is important to extend our understanding of cinematic identification, previously analysed solely at the level of fantasy, to include the practices documented by these spectators, in order to understand the different forms of overlap between stars' and audiences' identities.

Another significant distinction is that between cinematic identification, which refers to the viewing experience, and extra-cinematic identification, referring to the use of stars' identities in a different cultural time and space. So far, film studies has, not surprisingly, been concerned with the former. However, the importance of these extra-cinematic forms of identification to the women who wrote to me came across very forcefully in their letters. Not only was this one of the most written-about aspects of the relationship between stars and audiences, but the pleasure and force of feeling with which they recalled the details of the significance of stars in this context was also striking.

All the above forms of identification relate to a final distinction which I have used to frame the sequence of the quotations: identification based on difference and identification based on similarity. The early categories of identification concern processes where the differences between the star and the spectator produce the sources of pleasure and fascination. The representations of these processes tended to emphasise the presence of the star and de-emphasise the identity of the spectator. The later categories concern processes where the similarity, or at least the possibility of closing the gap produced by the differences between stars and spectators, is the source of pleasure expressed. In these examples the reproduction of the spectators' identities tended to be the focus of the commentary. Thus

159

identifications do not merely involve processes of recognition based on similarity, but also involve the productive recognition of differences between femininities.

Indeed the processes of identification articulated most strongly in terms of difference seem to be those relating more directly to the cinematic context where the image of the star is still present on the screen. The processes, and practices, which involve reproducing similarity seem to be those extra-cinematic identifications which take place more in the spectator's more familiar domestic context, where the star's identity is selectively reworked and incorporated into the spectator's new identity. Even in these cases, identification does not simply involve the passive reproduction of existing femininities, but rather an active engagement and production of changing identities.

The assumption behind much of the psychoanalytic work discussed earlier is that identification fixes identities: 'identification can only be made through recognition, and all recognition is itself an implicit confirmation of existing form'.[35] Many of the examples I have discussed contradict this assumption and demonstrate not only the diversity of existing forms, but also that recognition involves the production of desired identities, rather than simply the confirmation of existing ones. Many forms of identification involve processes of transformation and the production of new identities, combining the spectator's existing identity with her desired identity and her reading of the star's identity.

This research also challenges the assumption that identification is necessarily problematic because it offers the spectator the illusory pleasure of unified subjectivity. The identifications represented in these letters speak as much about partial recognitions and fragmented replications as they do about the misrecognition of a unified subjectivity in an ego ideal on the screen. Thus, cultural consumption does not necessarily fix identities, destroy differences and confirm sameness. If we take audiences as a starting point for understanding the consumption of stars, the active and productive elements of the star–audience relationships begin to emerge.

In challenging previous models of passive female spectatorship, and demonstrating the diversity and complexity of identifications between stars and women in the audience, however, I am not suggesting feminists look at cultural consumption uncritically. Taking audiences as a starting point can present problems for a feminist analysis: how can we remain critical of the dominant meanings of gender produced by Hollywood, whilst at the same time taking seriously the pleasures female spectators articulate about their favourite stars? Perhaps this problem is itself a reason for the reluctance by feminists to analyse female audiences and their relationship to dominant idealised feminine images, such as Hollywood stars.

In asking women to write to me about the appeal of Hollywood stars, it was inevitable I would receive an enthusiastic response. The discrepancy between the passion with which women spectators wrote about their Hollywood favourites and feminist criticisms of the patriarchal constructions of femininity in Hollywood produces a familiar dilemma for feminists working in many areas of cultural analysis. Simply to use what women wrote to me to illustrate the subordinating operations of patriarchal capitalism seems to me to be overwhelmingly patronising, as well as rather pessimistic. But simply to embrace the enthusiastic spirit of the pleasures they describe would be equally problematic, and would reproduce an uncritical populism which leaves behind crucial feminist insights. It therefore remains a challenge to feminists analysing Hollywood cinema to produce critical accounts of dominant cultural representations whilst at the same time developing theories of female cultural consumption as an active and productive process.

NOTES

Acknowledgements
I would very much like to thank Richard Dyer, Sarah Franklin, Anne Gray, Hilary Hinds, Richard Johnson and Celia Lury for their helpful comments on earlier drafts of this paper, and their encouragement and support for this research project. I would also like to thank Christine Gledhill for her interest, enthusiasm and patience.

1   Richard Dyer, *Stars* (London, BFI Publishing, 1979).
2   A notable exception to this is Leo Handel's *Hollywood Looks at its Audience* (Urbana, University of Illinois Press, 1950). Handel's findings are developed further in Andrew Tudor, *Image and Influence: Studies in the Sociology of Film* (London, Allen & Unwin, 1974), chapter 4.
3   Typical of the 'images of women' approach are Molly Haskell, *From Reverence to Rape: The Treatment of Women in the Movies* (Harmondsworth, Penguin, 1974); Marjorie Rosen, *Popcorn Venus* (New York, Coward, McCann and Geoghegan, 1973); and Brandon French, *On The Verge Of Revolt: Women in American Films of the Fifties* (New York, Frederick Ungar Publishing Co., 1978).
4   Typical of the 'woman as image' approach are Laura Mulvey, *Visual and Other Pleasures* (London, Macmillan, 1989); and Constance Penley, ed., *Feminism and Film Theory* (New York, Routledge, and London, BFI Publishing, 1988).
5   Molly Haskell, *From Reverence to Rape*, 214.
6   Ibid., 194.
7   Laura Mulvey, *Visual*, 22.
8   Ibid., 23.
9   Robyn Archer and Diana Simmonds, *A Star Is Torn* (London, Virago, 1986).
10 Helen Taylor, *Scarlett's Women: 'Gone With the Wind' and its Female Fans* (London, Virago, 1989).
11 Jane Gaines, 'War, women and lipstick: fan mags in the forties', in *Heresies*, 18 (1986), 42–7.
12 Angela Partington, 'Melodrama's gendered audience', in Sarah Franklin, Celia Lury and Jackie Stacey, eds, *Off Centre: Feminism and Cultural Studies* (London, Unwin Hyman, forthcoming). See also chapters by Herzog and Gaines, LaPlace and Weiss in this volume.

13 Richard Dyer, *Heavenly Bodies: Film Stars and Society* (London, BFI/Macmillan, 1986), chapter 3. See also Andrew Weiss in this collection.

14 See Bruce A. Austin, *Immediate Seating: A Look at Movie Audiences* (Belmont, California, Wadsworth Publishing Co., 1989).

15 For discussions of historical audiences see Janet Staiger, 'The handmaiden of villainy: methods and problems for studying the historical reception of a film', *Wide Angle*, 8, 1 (1986); Philip Corrigan, 'Film entertainment as ideology and pleasure: towards a history of audiences', in James Curran and Vincent Porter, eds, *British Cinema History* (London, Weidenfeld & Nicolson, 1983); and Sue Harper, 'Popular taste and methodological problems: British historical films in the 1930s', paper given at *Popular European Cinema* conference, University of Warwick, September 1989.

16 See Jeffrey Richards and Dorothy Sheridan, eds, *Mass-Observation at the Movies* (London and New York, Routledge & Kegan Paul, 1987).

17 See Janet Thumin, 'Super special long-run propositions: revenue, culture and popularity in "Cinematograph Weekly"'s annual review', paper at *Popular European Cinema* conference, University of Warwick, September 1989.

18 Vincent Keene, 'Charm not curves', *Picturegoer*, 14 October 1950. Letters responding directly to this article appeared in *Picturegoer*, 9 December 1950.

19 I am grateful to Jane Gaines for pointing out to me that the authenticity of the letters published on film magazine letters' pages remains in question. However the Mass-Observation Archive at Sussex University holds all the original letters written to *Picturegoer* in the year 1940, which would provide a more reliable source for the historical analysis of cinema-goers.

20 See Popular Memory Group, 'On popular memory', in Bill Schwarz *et al.*, eds, *Making Histories: Studies in History, Writing and Theory* (London, Hutchinson, 1982).

21 S. Freud, *Group Psychology and the Analysis of the Ego*, 1921, chapter 7, quoted in Anne Friedberg, 'Identification and the Star: a refusal of difference', in Christine Gledhill, ed., *Star Signs* (London, BFI Publishing, 1982).

22 Ibid., 49.

23 Christian Metz, 'Le Signifiant imaginaire', *Communications*, 23 (1975); tr. Celia Britton, Anwyl Williams, Ben Brewster, Alfred Guzetti, *Psychoanalysis and Cinema: The Imaginary Signifier* (London, Macmillan, 1983).

24 Anne Friedberg, 'Identification and the Star', p. 50.

25 Ibid., 53.

26 Valerie Walkerdine, 'Video replay: families, films and fantasies', in Victor Burgin, James Donald and Cora Kaplan, eds, *Formations of Fantasy* (London, Methuen, 1986).

27 For example, see Jacqueline Rose, *Sexuality in the Field of Vision* (London, Verso, 1986), Mary Anne Doane, *The Desire to Desire: The Woman's Film of the 1940s* (Bloomington and Indianapolis, Indiana University Press, 1987), and Teresa De Lauretis, *Alice Doesn't: Feminism, Semiotics, Cinema* (London, Macmillan, 1984).

28 For a typology of audience–star relations, see Andrew Tudor, *Image and Influence*, 80.

29 See Tania Modleski, 'Introduction: Hitchcock, feminism and the patriarchal unconscious', in *The Woman Who Knew Too Much: Hitchcock and Feminist Theory* (London, Methuen, 1988).

30 This problem is addressed by Annette Kuhn, 'Women's genres', in *Screen*, 25, 1 (1984), 18–28.

31 For a discussion of the representation of desire between women produced by

their differences, see Jackie Stacey, 'Desperately seeking difference', in *Screen*, 28, 1 (1987), 48–61.

32 For a discussion of the pleasurable feelings escapism offers to the cinema audience, see Richard Dyer, 'Entertainment and utopia', *Movie*, 24 (Spring 1977), 2–13.

33 See Laura Mulvey, *Visual*, and E. Ann Kaplan, *Women and Film: Both Sides of the Camera* (London, Methuen, 1983).

34 See Partington, 'Melodrama's gendered audience'.

35 Friedberg, 'Identification and the Star', 53.

Part III

PERFORMERS AND SIGNS

13

ARTICULATING STARDOM

Barry King

Despite the early interest shown by the Prague School, the role of the actor as re-presenter of signs has barely been examined.[1] Thus one of the main purposes of this chapter is to focus attention on the categories and variables that I take to be essential to the semiotics of acting in film and, by extension, television. My second purpose is to develop a means of reconciling a 'political economy' approach to stardom in mainstream (Hollywood) cinema and the theorisation of the star as an interplay of representation and identification. The crux of my argument is that stardom is a strategy of performance that is an adaptive response to the limits and pressures exerted upon acting in the mainstream cinema.

To pursue this argument it is necessary to show how stardom develops as a response to the interaction of three areas of discursive practice or economies – systems of control that mobilise discursive resources in order to achieve specifiable effects. These are: the cultural economy of the human body as a sign; the economy of signification in film; and the economy of the labour market for actors.

But before addressing these points directly, it is necessary to explore the relationship between stage and screen acting, since it is my reading of this relationship that conditions the treatment that follows.

STAGE AND SCREEN

The view that stage acting provides a yardstick against which to evaluate acting on screen is widespread among actors, even among those whose main professional activities have been confined to the screen. A common argument is that the stage is an actor's medium, in the sense that it is on the stage that the actor is best placed to realise his or her 'creative intentions' in character portrayal.[2] While such assertions may be seen as conditioned by the desire to be publicly associated with an elite institution – the 'Stage', its 'Great' tradition etc. – certain empirical features of the work situation of the actor tend to confirm such a judgement.[3]

Two recurrent themes can be identified. First, that 'good' acting is based on some concept of intentionality, or even authorship. It is taken for granted that the participation of the actor(s) in the process of signification should be an outcome of the deployment of a conscious and constitutive control of performance. And it is more or less uniformly held that film (or video) presents a latent and readily actualised threat to this requirement, whereas theatre does not. Second, it is regularly assumed that theatre as a medium, because it entails 'live' performance before an audience and because the duration of the performance is the performance *per se* rather than the provision of materials editable downwards into a performance given elsewhere, requires of the actor a more sustained exercise of skills and commitment than is the case where an editable medium is used.

Preference for the stage, therefore, expresses a reaction and an adaptation to the organisational realities of working in the mainstream theatre and cinema. The discursive practice of acting, in Britain and the USA at least, is deeply implicated in the project of intentionality. The most concrete evidence of this implication relates to the training of actors.[4] The regime of exercises that constitute an actor's training, while certainly increasing his or her adaptability in respect of specialised skills like juggling, dancing and so on, are nevertheless intended to increase the conscious mastery of the actor over verbal, gestural and postural behaviour. In a similar way, versatility of accent, posture, walk and other markers of difference, is *intended* to enable the actor to 'naturalise' such exogenous behaviours (or possibly, some elements of own behaviour to be used consciously in performance) as his or her own for the duration of performance in order to be convincing 'in character'.[5] At its extreme, the prioritisation of intentionality – the intention, in this case, to communicate some 'truth' about the interior reality of the character – has a Cartesian ring about it: the maximisation of conscious control over acquired dispositions, inherited characteristics (the utopia of make-up) and their conventionalised meanings in the culture at large. Taken to its extreme, and to the extent that actors, like any other occupational group, have an interest in excluding untrained entrants, such an extreme has a pragmatic value, such an emphasis requires that: '[the] actor must be able to be true to any conceivable character, making all actions believable and spontaneous.'[6]

More routinely, it leads to the norm of impersonation. This states that in playing any character, the 'real' personality of the actor should disappear into the part or, conversely, that if the range of the actor is limited to parts consonant with his or her personality then this constitutes 'poor' acting. This latter, negatively valued converse, I shall refer to, hereafter, as personification. A number of points can be made about impersonation: for example, it seems to transcend acting styles – Method and Broadway/ repertoire styles tending to propose different strategies of realisation of the same objective – and it serves to grade positively the standing of the actor among peers.[7] But probably the key theoretical issue relates to the concept of authorship implicit in such a project.

As Foucault has argued, the concept of 'Author' can be seen as a principle of coherence, governing the identification, organisation, circulation and reception of texts, rather than as verbal marker denoting a discrete historical identity that unfolds transparently through the text. In this regard, he writes of the 'author function' rather than the 'author'.[8] One of the key thrusts to Foucault's argument is to highlight the various ways in which the romantic conception of the author – as a unified subject purposively unfolding his or her interiority before a reader, a parallel coherence in the sphere of reception – constitutes a denial of inter-textuality. Does the concept of impersonation, in fact, constitute a performance variant of the myth of the author?

My answer to this is, basically, no. To put it bluntly, so long as the contribution of the actor (or for that matter any other functionary in the process of collective production) disappears into character, then the performance text – or more strictly the text created by the ensemble of performances – can be assigned a unitary, global author. Notwithstanding this fact, the romantic myth of the author has readily and voraciously fastened itself to the world of performance by a facile, but plausible extention of the literary conception of the author to that field.[9]

The objective of performance is the re-presentation of a text through the activation of its various parts – in acting usually a narrative realised through its characters or in music the realisation of the score through the execution of its instrumental parts and so on. The relationship between the execution of the 'parts' and the ultimating 'text' may be more or less specified by the nominal author through a system of notation, but the intrinsic relationship between the script or score is intertextual: it is only through the performance – in reality, an ensemble of performances – that the 'text' is fully realised, yet each performance constitutes a specific text in itself, more or less a version or a token of the notated or written text and implicated in the discourse of the past, present and future versions of the text. Thus it is meaningful, if finally misleading, to speak of Shakespeare's Hamlet in relation to Olivier's or Gielgud's Hamlet and so on.[10] The notion of the author as opposed to author-function is clearly, if mistakenly, operative in such formulations in the sense that it is the leading actor's name that is used (especially when he assumes a directorial role) to indicate a specific realisation or re-presentation of the text, but neither the text nor its version constitute a definitive 'work' or vision transhistorically foreclosed around the intentions of the author. For actors, intentionality is doubly articulated: the actor deals with a part which is only a moment of the totality of the performances given by other actors (or other participants, a one-man show is never produced by just one individual) and that totality is itself, as already indicated, intrinsically intertextual. The actor's intention to portray a specific character in a specific way may seem at first sight, and in the case of a leading actor is often so represented, to correspond to authorship conceived as the creative principle of the fixed, delimited text. But the process of character representation through impersonation entails that the actor should strive to obliterate his or her sense of identity in order to become a signifier for the intentionality inscribed in character. Such obliteration returns the project of intentionality to the level of the narrative itself which is usually 'authored' reductively in terms of the director's or playwright's 'vision', rather than as a meaning emergent from a collective art of representation.[11] The full participation of the actor in the narrative as character thereby depends upon the suppression of the literary conception of the author.

The other aspect of intertextuality relates to the fact that the actor as a private individual is already constituted as a sign within the host culture, in so far as his or her behavioural and physical attributes have been read and will be read as cues to personality. The placing of the actor on stage or screen certainly intensifies this inferential process and for the purposes of a single casting may re-enforce characterisation. But overall the range of characters an actor may attempt is limited by the given-ness of her or his physical and behavioural attributes. Once again, impersonation 'frees' the actor for a range of parts in so far as it suppresses what in non-actors would be regarded as the authenticating markers of their personality. These considerations point towards the conclusion that the norm of impersonation serves as the basic instrument of the construction of difference in acting styles.

The impact of the technology of film on impersonation constitutes the final aspect of the situational logic that underpins the preference for stage over screen. Put in its bluntest form, there is a widespread belief among actors and other commentators that film as a medium regularly if not necessarily entails a deskilling process, in the sense of rendering the skills of the actor obsolete or of entailing dilution – the substitution of the untrained actor for the trained. As Edgar Morin put it: 'The cinema does not merely de-theatricalise the actor's performance. It tends to atrophy it.'[12]

While it's absurd to conclude as Morin does that acting in film requires no skills whatsoever, it is important to identify the transformations in the practices of acting that film technology entails. The impact of film on acting rests ultimately on the sheer variety of codes that can be mobilised in order to fabricate the movement of the narrative.[13] The formative capacities of film threaten to disrupt the project of constructing, from actor-located processes of signification, a psychologically consistent character. The construction of character in film is not usually a linear temporal process. The behaviour of the character, a supposedly coherent subject unfolding within the place and time set by the narrative, is very often constituted out of minute quanta of behaviour, repetitiously delivered (takes). Such quanta, necessary because of contractual or locational economies, are dramatically discontinuous in terms of the chronology of character and plot, e.g. the actor as character must play to a character he has never seen or act out the aftermath of an affair that has yet to be enacted. Equally, a given quantum of performance, itself a mere fraction of an action, may be greatly inflected by camera position, omitted altogether, cut and reduced, resited through editing and so on.[14] Alternatively, though interrelatedly, the formative capacity of film, particularly its capacity for sequences in which only inanimate objects appear and their substitution for the actor as a signifier, can readily displace the actor from the action, so that inanimate or non-human animate objects signify states of emotion formally within the capacity of the actor(s) to project.[15]

Thus film technology confronts the actor with an effect which may be broadly identified as de-skilling. This is not to imply that acting in film does not entail the use of skills. A movement from stage to screen in a literal sense involves re-skilling – though conversely the kinds of skills acquired by stage training are not easily mastered by those only experienced in film work.[16] Rather the notion of skill does not rest on some simplistic conception of a fixed technical content so much as the question of whether such content, at whatever level of complexity, is monopolisable by a specific set of workers. And whether in this context the technology is implemented in a way that enhances or undermines the control of the contending parties of employees and employers.[17]

Viewed in this light, it is clear enough that the routinised practices in the mainstream cinema tend to shift the frontier of control away from the actor towards the director or, where this is not the same person, those empowered to render the final cut. Equally it is no small matter for professional standing and employment chances that the formative capacities of film (or video) can be used to compensate for a low level of technical ability as an actor, enabling untrained actors to produce convincing on-screen performances.[18] Under such circumstances a preference for the theatre is not surprising. The requirement of unaided projection and the necessity of repeat performances before a 'live' audience virtually eliminates this threat in the theatre. So, too, it is in the theatre that actors have the greatest degree of direct control over the signifying direction and grain of their performance – even if this control is only unevenly realised in practice.[19]

Again, this preference is materially reinforced by the historical priority of the stage and by the fact that where acting is taught in drama schools and colleges, such teaching has a stage bias, for obvious reasons of cost, but also because the demands of stage acting can be scaled down whereas film acting techniques cannot be readily scaled up.[20]

The drift of these remarks is towards what I would term a qualified technological determinism. Technology always represents a complex of potential uses, but the social relationships of production in which it is embedded tend to prioritise particular forms of use and patterns of techno-logical application over others. Thus the effects of characterisation achiev-able by the cumulative process of the actor's performance on stage are only sustained in film and television if measures are taken to compensate for the atomising effects of normal usage. Where such measures – e.g. rehearsals or collective decision-making – are absent, self-referential com-pensations arise such as playing to the camera, assumption of producer or director's role on the part of leading players and stardom.[21]

I want now to examine stardom as a particular variant of performance in film – a variant that is, I would contend, only comprehensible as an interaction, with varying situational outcomes, of the three economies signalled at the outset of this article.

THE CULTURAL ECONOMY OF THE HUMAN BODY

Performance or representational arts, whether these occur in a theatrical, cinematic or televisual context, necessarily bear a relationship to the diver-sity of signs distributed in the culture at large. The exact nature of the relationship between the representational regime within the theatre and the world outside has been historically variable, but in the West, at least since the late nineteenth century, the theatre and subsequently film and television have been dominated by naturalism. Naturalism may be defined as that mode of theatrical representation which claims that the external aspects of the individual, his or her utterances, behaviour and appearance in everyday settings, gives a privileged access to personal and collective realities.[22]

If we take the familiar contrast between naturalism and more formalistic regimes of theatrical representation in which symbolic as opposed to iconic or indexical signs predominate, such as the Chinese classical or the Japanese Noh theatres, then the implications of naturalism become clear. (C. S. Peirce defines a symbol as signifying by convention, an icon by resem-blance and an index by physical connection.) Under a naturalistic system all signs deployed in performance lay claim (however spurious) to be motivated – to be a mimesis of the extra-theatrical, extra-cinematic and so on. This mimetic relationship can be seen as a constraint on the auton-omy of sign production since the subcoding of resemblance is constantly referred back to the iconic or indexical actuality of the signified – or, rather, what in such a system can be construed as the same, the perception by the audience of verisimilitude. In non-naturalistic theatre, however, the regime of signification creates its own signified(s) by the deployment of highly conventionalised systems and sub-codes of reference – the audience not expecting verisimilitude (in the naturalistic sense) but an internal consistency in the relationship between signifiers and signified. Since even naturalistic regimes have their own specific sub-codes, the difference here is between a covert and overt use of signs and codes of representation and the gearing of the relationship between the signifier(s) and signified(s) as more or less conventional, more or less motivated.[23]

In a theatrical tradition permeated with naturalism, and the American theatre is particularly notable for this development, the actor confronts problems in characterisation that relate to his or her being as a general cultural object rather than a theatrical object.[24] The actor is a re-presenter of signs in that he or she activates or deactivates via impersonation those aspects of the general cultural markers that he or she bears as a private individual for character portrayal.[25] The nub of these problems stems from the fact that if the theatre is to 'mirror' the street, the street is already populated with signs. So that the actor as a member of the host culture – with a given hair colour, body shape, repertoire of gestures, registers of speech, accent, dialect and so on – always pre-signifies meaning. Such a relationship creates difficulties for the process of impersonation which are well known. First, there is the pre-performance selection process of type-casting, which has a persistent tendency towards self-fulfilment – only actors who look the part get the part.[26] This relationship, which ties the actor as it were to biological and social destiny, is compounded by another in performance – the process of semioticisation: the fact that anything appearing in the frame of the proscenium arch or of the camera is by that fact invested with meaning. The difficulty here lies in the suppression of those elements of the actor's appearance and behaviour that are *not intended to mean* at the level of the characterisation.[27]

By contrast, in a theatrical regime where the gearing between offstage codes and onstage coding is low or conventional and is consciously understood to be so by actors and audience alike, the physical qualities of the actor, as supposed characterological markers, provide a weaker constraint on casting. The application of make-up, dress and mannerisms do not require a literal defence, either iconically or indexically. Obviously enough, these differences are only a matter of degree, since as Eco has pointed out, even iconic sign-functions rely on conventions.[28] But it is still the case that naturalism offers a constraint not found in more canonical systems – systems where the distance between stage/screen are formally coded.

THE ECONOMY OF SIGNIFICATION IN FILM

As pointed out above, film (and video) can reduce the actor's control over performance. There remains the question of the features of film as a medium and how these provide, as it were, a semiotic 'conduit' for the implementation of social decisions and objectives related to control. To

understand these features it is necessary to identify the point of engagement of the actor with the narrative through his or her engagement with
character. As Stephen Heath has pointed out, the terms 'character' and
'actor' are ambiguous because they cover what are a whole series of
positionalities in relation to the narrative.[29]

For the purposes of explaining the immediate interaction between actor
and medium, the variables that have a direct pertinence are *character,
person* and *image*. At the same time it is necessary to allow for extension
of the term *image* to cover both filmic and extra-filmic or cinematic
processes of representation and their interaction. In the first place, it has
long been recognised that to any actor's appearance and behaviour before
camera, film adds its own enhancement, producing effects that while originating in the apparatus nevertheless appear to be part of the 'natural'
physical and behavioural properties of the actor.[30] Such a process of
enhancement, whether by omission – the gauzing out of wrinkles in close-
up, 'best side' shots and so on – or by addition, low angle enhancement
of stature, lighting and so on, does not merely affect stars, *but actors in
general*. Second, the image on screen is itself, especially in the case of the
star, usually reinforced by extra-discursive practices, or more exactly the
interaction of filmic and non-filmic discourses.[31] Two of these can be
mentioned here. First, actors tend to develop a 'personality' for purposes
of public interaction, which indicates that they are 'Actors' and suggests
to potential employers that they are interesting and energetic people,
including in this the entire paraphernalia of body maintenance, grooming
and so forth. Second, it is also the case, especially with stars, that the
image on screen is already contextualised by the circulation of biographical
and personal anecdotal materials that frame their appearances on and off
screen. One can go further than this and suggest, as studies of Ingrid
Bergman and Doris Day have shown, that it is the extra-filmic discourse
that has the greatest impact on the public's knowledge of the star, contradicting the evidence of what can be seen at the point(s) of performance.[32]

In this connection, Richard Dyer's term 'star image' is useful, since as
his analysis shows many of the devices used to privilege the presence of
stars in films equally enter into the construction of character. The moment
of the star image is, in fact, the moment of a proprietorial claim to such
effects as though they were a property of the star as a person, a claim
which subsists not primarily in what is represented on screen, but in the
subsidiary literature where the image is rendered as a 'real life' property
of its bearer, the actor as star.

Dyer, on the other hand, in his discussion of stars deploys a global
opposition between character, 'a constructed personage in film', and personality as 'the set of traits and characteristics with which film endows
[characters]'. This definition nevertheless includes audience foreknowledge,
name, appearance and dress, decor and setting – codes which are not

specific to film – alongside codes which are, so that his specification remains ambiguous in respect of the interweaving of the filmic and non-filmic.[33]

In order to preserve what is useful in these specifications for an analysis of acting I suggest the following modifications. The term *character* is adequate as it stands. The term *person* should be taken to include an understanding that the physical presence of the actor is already coded in the general sense of having the socially recognised attributes of an individual in the host culture (however problematic this 'fix' may be), a 'personality', and in the specific sense that this 'personality' is adapted to the exigencies of acting. Likewise, the term *image* should be restricted to the visual impact of the film 'system' on the actor's 'personality' off screen, so that the coherence of the actor's image on screen is clearly identified as a technologically based construction. Finally, I would introduce the term *persona* to cover what Stephen Heath has called 'the conversion of the body, of the person, into the luminous sense of its film image'[34] – an articulation of person and image as I have redefined them. The persona, in other words, is the intersection of cinematic and filmic discursive practices in an effort to realise a coherent subjectivity.

With these background points in mind, I want now to indicate two specifically filmic processes that provide what I referred to earlier as the semiotic conduit through which social decisions affecting the standing of personae or stars are infiltrated into the filmic system. These are: hyper-semioticisation and the displacement of interiority. By the former, I mean to indicate the intensification of the process observed in theatre. The use of close shooting in the cinema invests greater meaning in the actor as a signifying mass, involving in the process of signification parts of the actor's body, such as the eyes, mouth and so forth. This means, in effect, that the actor can signify merely because he or she has automatic or physiologically given qualities, e.g. lip shape and movement, facial mass and habitual expressions.[35] Under such circumstances, impersonation becomes the ever more redefined control of fine as opposed to gross bodily behaviour. The problem here is that as one increases the scale of observation, the range of behaviours approach the uncontrollable or, conversely, mere passivity will signify. The scale of observation has conventional limits. Thus the close-up commonly goes no closer than the face, with more radical variation limited by the canons of naturalism. The face itself, which is posed in point-of-view cutting as the centre of the look and the authenticating moment of the character, is usually presented without make-up. That is to say, make-up is constructed in such a way as to obliterate its own occurrence and where possible the minimally retouched features of the actor provide the basis of the significatory play of depth of shot, focus, lighting and so on.[36] Such a *conventional* system for rendering apparently *motivated* signs seems a logical consequence of naturalism and to a large extent it clearly is. But it comes up against economic criteria, as evidenced by Jack Warner's exasperation at having paid Paul Muni so much for a performance in *Juarez* in which the star is unrecognisable.

For the actor committed to impersonation in such circumstances, the gross details of physical endowment pose severe problems since they are very often unalterable.[37] Generally speaking, the actor cannot be moved out of the naturalistic personality implications of his or her physique, however stereotypical or factually wrong these are. Ernest Borgnine can be made into a better looking Ernest Borgnine, not another Robert Redford.

In fact, the predominant tendency is for the norm of impersonation to be abandoned at the level of casting in favour of a strategy of selection based on personification – let the actor be selected by physical type anyway and let these physical attributes mean in and of themselves. In other words, the actor becomes the most rudimentary form of the sign, the ostensive sign in which the substance of the signifier is the substance of the signified: the actor is the person, has the personality, his or her appearance suggests she/he is, notwithstanding the fact that this construction relies on a first order conventionally in the culture which the actor represents and, sometimes, redefines.[38] Such a form of type-casting is to be found in its most pronounced and literal form in the film (and television) industry and, to a lesser degree, in the theatre.

Thus, the ideal leading man should be aged between 19 and 25 years, at least 5 feet 10 inches tall but not over 6 feet 2 inches, well proportioned physically, handsome, rugged or interesting looking, have all his own teeth and hair. The ideal ingenue should be aged between 18 and 22, 5 feet 3 inches to 5 feet 7 inches tall, possess a well-proportioned body and an exceptionally beautiful and interesting face.[39] Obviously enough, few if any actors meet all these requirements, but this does not remove their pertinence as the criteria of selection. Casting directors may not be able to articulate 'ruggedness' with any precision, but they know it when they see it. Again, it is certainly the case that types change in the long term, but this does not eliminate their effectiveness in the short term. For the majority of actors the short term is all there is.

Given the selection of actors by type, there follows the fact of type-casting as a serial phenomenon: actors are limited to a particular kind of character for their working life – what might be called the Elisha Cook Jr syndrome – or, at least, will be so unless vigorous efforts are made to overcome type. Just as importantly, though, actors become committed in their on- and off-screen life to personification in the hope that by stabilising the relationship between person and image on screen they may seem to be the proprietors of a marketable persona. Robert De Niro is an interesting case in this regard, since he appears, paradoxically, to combine to a stunning level of virtuosity the capacity for impersonation with a drive, role by role, to transform himself physically into the substance of the signified, e.g. Jake La Motta in *Raging Bull*. In fact, De Niro's approach to acting is entirely consistent with an effort to adapt impersonation to the control relationships and techniques implied in film work. On the one hand:

> With a play you've got that one performance that night, but if you're doing a movie it's piece by piece. You can do maybe ten takes – one or two could be exceptional – you've got the chance to get it right. I never tire of doing takes.

On the other:

> The main thing is the script. . . . Then I have to get to know the director . . . because it's so much work – you can be stuck with someone for six months and it's an absolute nightmare. You've got to know that you're on the same track: you can disagree, you can try it your way, their way, ultimately they edit it and it's their film. . . .[40]

In other words, the advantages of takes are premised on the social relations of production. De Niro's commitment to Method acting – his efforts to research the background and seek out real-life models for the characters he portrays – is consistent with the atomising effects of film on character portrayal. Such a radicalising displacement towards the 'real' seeks an authenticating sense of character outside the process of filming. The emphasis on the script points towards a similar form of monitoring device to control portrayal of character 'in pieces' and the physical transformation of the self seems the last step in the mimetic grasp of the extra-cinematic real.

The tendency for film to transform the actor into an ostensive sign, its problematic insertion into the norm of impersonation, is enhanced by the second process, the displacement of interiority. It is generally accepted that film poses limits on the representation of interiority, inclining towards behaviourism, showing the 'surface of things'. The mainstream cinema has developed a range of devices that reconstitute the interior space of the character, but the basic point remains: films tend to re-site the signification of interiority, away from the actor and onto the mechanism. Richard Dyer has ably catalogued these effects elsewhere[41] and I do not intend to pursue them here, but this process of displacement underlies and produces the image. This means that the process of character portrayal in film, whether angled towards impersonation or personification, takes on a quasi-automatic form in which the actor's performance in part originates in his or her behaviour and in part in the action of the filmic apparatus, including in the latter lighting and camera deployment. In other words, the projection of interiority becomes less and less the provenance of the actor and more and more a property emerging from directorial or editorial decision.

177

Under such circumstances, a potential politics of the persona emerges in so far as the bargaining power of the actor, or more emphatically, the star, is materially affected by the *degree* of his or her reliance on the apparatus (the image), as opposed to self-located resources (the person) in the construction of persona. Consequently it is plausible to speak of high and low autonomy stars to compare, for instance, Bette Davis's use of acting skills to broaden her range of characterisations, with Joan Crawford's singular pre-*Mildred Pierce* persona.[42] Similarly, the established policy of building stars from inexperienced players under the studio system, can be seen to contain an element of fabricating subordination among potential stars.

The twinned processes of hyper-semioticisation and displacement of interiority lead to a paradoxical situation: while film increases the centrality of the actor in the process of signification, the formative capacity of the medium can equally confine the actor more and more to being a bearer of effects that he or she does not or cannot originate.

THE ECONOMY OF THE LABOUR MARKET FOR ACTORS

The effects so far identified at the level of film have a latent status, or rather would have were it not for the effects of the labour market on actors seeking continuous and stable employment. The broad features of the labour market for actors in film and television are well known and have remained unchanged for decades. Wherever and whenever we look there is a large oversupply of actors, as measured by membership in the appropriate union. Thus in 1979 roughly 90 per cent of Hollywood's Screen Actors Guild membership of 23,000 earned less than a living wage and among the membership of Equity in the UK, 70 per cent of members are unemployed in any one year.[43] Again, of those actors who do find work, there is a marked disparity between the earnings of leading players and stars, who are able to negotiate personal contracts and the majority of actors who earn at or slightly above the basic rate set by collective agreements; the magnitude of difference being in excess of fifty times, sometimes a hundred. As a result, competition for parts, *given the operation of naturalistic conventions*, lead to an emphasis on what is unique to the actor, displacing emphasis from what an actor can do *qua* actor onto what the actor *qua* person or biographical entity is. In this manner, what Robert Brady calls a personal monopoly is constructed.[44]

In film, the construction of a personal monopoly rests on shifting the emphasis in performance towards personification, but such a shift takes the radical form of carrying the implications of the actor's persona into everyday life. Thus actors seeking to obtain stardom will begin to conduct themselves in public as though there is an unmediated existential connection between their person and their image. Another way to put this is to say that the persona is in itself a character, but one that transcends placement or containment in a particular narrative (or in the case of the vehicle subordinates the narrative to the spectacle of the persona) and exists in cinematic rather than filmic time and space.[45] Indeed, the persona, buttressed by the discursive practices of publicity, hagiography and by regimes of cosmetic alteration and treatment, is relatively durable and if sedimented in public awareness will tend to survive discrepant casting and performances.

For actors of limited or average ability, investing their energies in the cultivation of a persona represents something within their control and a means of competing with actors who have ability in impersonation. Indeed, in the studio system impersonatory skills were assigned a lower value compared to the cultivation of personae.[46] In contemporary times, the tendency towards personification may have increased with the advent of advertising as a field of employment, which combines naturalism with the sedulous cultivation of personal charm as an ingredient in the sales pitch.[47] On the other hand, the self-referentiality of Method acting – the so-called personal expressive realism of Brando, for example – rather than representing the triumph of the actor as impersonator can be seen as a successful adaptation of impersonation to the pressures of personification, deploying impersonation to refer back to the person of the actor, the consistent entity underlying each of his or her roles.[48]

The tendency towards the formation of personae as a monopoly strategy should not be taken as unproblematic, however. The norm of impersonation maintains a powerful presence for a number of reasons. It is an integral value central to the practice of acting itself. Again, even under the most automatised conditions of production, there remains a need for actors who can 'effortlessly' produce performances in character – hence the remark that character actors are a 'brassiere for the star, literally holding him or her up'.[49] Nor is the adhesion to such a norm surprising, given that it provides an avenue of accomplishment for actors who do not fit into prevailing stereotypes. Accordingly, alongside the star system, the realm of the ostensive sign *par excellence*, one finds the operation of a hierarchy of character actors, whose professional reputation, length of careers and durability of earnings may outpace that of the more transitory stars. Such a hierarchy provides, as it were, its own counterstars, individuals like Robert Duvall, for example, whose claims to eminence rest squarely on their impersonatory skills and character playing. On the other hand, one of the decisive and recurrent effects of casting is that a given character type will sediment itself into the actor's personality so that the line between character and persona becomes blurred or, at least, requires extreme vigilance:

I find that the character of JR keeps taking me over in real life. Not

that I get that mean, I hope, but I do find the Texas accent drifting in and out. People I meet really want me to be JR, so it's hard to disappoint them.
(Larry Hagman).[50]

Finally, it is necessary to qualify the view that personification arises *solely* out of the actor's adaptation to his or her conditions of employment. Such conditions are products in turn of the interests of monopoly capital operating in the sphere of cultural production. The ramifications are complex, but basically personification serves the purposes of containing competition amongst the tele-film cartel companies by representing the star's contribution as resting on his or her private properties as a person. In such a manner, a specific production can be valorised by 'values' that are not distributed throughout the field of production as a whole – such as technical expertise, for example. The exploitation of the latter, as the latest wave of special effects pictures show, tends to escalate costs enormously. Equally, the centrality of personae (stars) as an index of value provides a form of control over the detail of performance in favour of those who have control over the text. The readiness of actors to function as ostensive signs can be seen as a defensive strategy: by accepting the loss of autonomy (either real or merely latent) entailed in the transfer of signification from the actor to the camera, with its off-screen constraints arising from stardom as a way of life, the actor paradoxically increases the reliance of the apparatus on his or her presence as a unique object or, more precisely, a behavioural commodity. The contradictory pressures, the paradoxes of identification that are induced by the shifts between personification and impersonation rather than some diffuse notion of a fit between stardom and capitalism provide the basic configuration of stardom in mainstream cinema.

NOTES

This is an abridged version of an article first published in *Screen*, 26, 5 (September/October 1985).

1 A recent discussion can be found in Kier Elam, *The Semiotics of Theatre and Drama* (London, Methuen, 1980). In what follows I will assume for purposes of simplification the perspective of a single film actor (male or female). I wish to acknowledge the useful criticisms of the *Screen* editorial collective, particularly Andrew Higson, of an earlier draft of this paper.

2 See the accounts in Lillian and Helen Ross, *The Player: The Profile of an Art* (New York, Simon and Schuster, 1962) and Ivan Butler, *The Making of Feature Films: a Guide* (London, Penguin, 1961). For a recent statement see Tony Booth's remarks in 'All actors should be working class', *Marxism Today*, October, 1984.

3 Pierre Bourdieu, 'Intellectual field and creative project', in M. F. D. Young (ed.), *Knowledge and Control* (London, Collier-Macmillan, 1971).

4 cf. J. Bensman and R. Lillenfield, *Craft and Consciousness* (Wiley Interscience, 1973).

5   Peter Barkworth, *About Acting* (London, Secker and Warburg, 1980), 13.
6   D. Mixon, 'A theory of actors', *Journal for the Theory of Social Behaviour*, 13, 1 (March 1983).
7   cf. Richard Dyer, *Stars* (London, British Film Institute, 1979), 158. By psychological identification or behavioural imitation, respectively.
8   Michel Foucault, 'What is an author?', *Screen*, 20, 1 (Spring 1979), 13–33.
9   For a recent example of this incursion see Hall Hinson, 'Some notes on method actors', *Sight and Sound*, Summer 1984, 200 ff.
10 cf. Richard Woolheim, *Art and its Objects* (London, Pelican, 1978), 90 ff.
11 The complaint that actors attempt to make any role convincing, regardless of the consequences of making e.g. Eva Peron, loveable, has its origins in this displacement of intentionality.
12 Edgar Morin, *The Stars* (New York, Grove Press, 1960), 144; and on skill, on 152.
13 cf. Bill Nichols, *Ideology and Image* (Bloomington, Indiana University Press, 1981), 82.
14 Bruce Dern has suggested, implausibly, that the actor may overcome the problem of arbitrary editorial control, given the centrality of the character he plays, by making each take the same. See J. Kalter, ed., *Actors on Acting* (Oaktree Press, 1979), 192, and James Mason's remarks in Ivan Butler, op. cit.
15 The classic statement is A. Knox, 'Acting and behaving', in R. Dyer MacCann (ed.), *Film: a Montage of Theories* (E. P. Dutton, New York, 1966).
16 cf. Jack Lemmon's remarks on Tony Curtis in W. Hyland and R. Hatnes, *How to Make It in Hollywood* (Nelson-Hall, 1975).
17 See David Harvey, *The Limits to Capital* (Blackwell, 1982), 109 and 119. For a general discussion, see Paul Thompson, *The Nature of Work* (London, Macmillan, 1983).
18 Rod Steiger makes this point in Ross and Ross, op. cit., 278.
19 The use of 'live' audiences on television would have to be assessed carefully in this regard. Such performances are usually edited for transmission.
20 See P. K. Manning and H. L. Hearn, 'Student actresses and their artistry', *Social Forces*, 47, 1969 and A. K. Peters, 'Acting and aspiring actresses in Hollywood', Ph. D. thesis, UCLA, 1971.
21 V. I. Pudovkin, *Film Technique and Film Acting* (Mayflower edition, 1958), was one of the first to recognise the impact of editing on the actor's motivation and to propose the necessity of involving the actor in the total process of production.
22 See Raymond Williams, *The Long Revolution* (London, Penguin, 1971), 271–99 and M. Gorelik, op. cit., 47 ff.
23 For these reasons Brecht admired the Chinese theatre and saw it as enshrining the 'A-effect'. See John Willett (ed.), *Brecht on Theatre* (London, Eyre Methuen, 1977), 136 ff.
24 On the dominance of naturalism in the US theatre, see G. B. Wilson, *A History of American Acting* (Bloomington, Indiana University Press, 1966).
25 See Richard Sennett, *The Fall of Public Man* (Cambridge University Press, 1974), especially chapter 6, for the history of the relationship between the theatre and the street.
26 J. Turow, 'Casting for TV parts: the anatomy of social typing', *Journal of Communication*, 28 (1978), 19–24.
27 cf. Jonathan Miller cited in Elam, op. cit., 77. Erving Goffman's distinction between signs given and signs given off is important here. See his *The Presentation of the Self in Everyday Life* (London, Penguin, 1971), 14.

28 See Umberto Eco, *A Theory of Semiotics* (Bloomington, Indiana University Press, 1976), 199.

29 Stephen Heath, 'Film and system: terms of analysis', Part II, *Screen*, 16, 2 (Summer 1975), especially 101–7.

30 cf. I. Pichel, 'Character, personality and image: a note on screen acting', *Hollywood Quarterly* (1946), 25–9.

31 'In other words, a film is significant only in so far as it mobilises one discourse to produce effects in another' – Sue Clayton and Jonathan Curling, 'On authorship', *Screen*, Spring 20, 1 (1979), 41. A more extensive treatment of the occupational determinants of stardom, from the side of the cinematic as opposed to the filmic, can be found in Barry King, 'The Hollywood Star System', Ph.D. thesis, University of London, 1984.

32 Richard Dyer, 'Four films of Lana Turner', *Movie*, 25 (1977/8), 30–52; J. Damico, 'Ingrid from Lorraine to Stromboli', *Journal of Popular Film*, 4, 1 (1975), 2–19; and Jane Clarke, M. Merck, Diana Simmonds (eds), *Move Over Misconceptions* (London, British Film Institute Dossier no. 4, 1980).

33 Richard Dyer, *Stars*, op. cit., 100 ff.

34 Stephen Heath, op. cit., 105.

35 cf. D. Thomson, 'The look on the actor's face', *Sight and Sound*, 46, 4 (1976). Bela Balazs' *Theory of Film* is the *locus classicus* of this view.

36 See P. Stallings and H. Mandelbaum, *Flesh and Fantasy* (St Martin's Press, 1978).

37 Though there are examples of anticipatory cosmetic alteration. Joan Crawford's career provides some classic examples.

38 See Umberto Eco, 'Semiotics of theatrical performance', *The Drama Review*, 21 (1976), 111.

39 See N. Blanchard, *How to Break into Movies* (New York, Doubleday, 1978), 41 ff; J. Sleznick, 'The talent hunters', *American Film* (Dec.–Jan. 1979), 60; and L. G. Yoaken, 'Casting', *Film Quarterly* (1958), 36.

40 Transcript of Guardian Lecture, reprinted in *Three Sixty°: British Film Institute News* (May 1985), 10–11.

41 Richard Dyer, *Stars*, op. cit.

42 See Barry King, op. cit.

43 See Jeremy Tunstall and David Walker, *Media Made in California* (Oxford University Press, 1981), 78. If only actors, as opposed to other performers, are taken into account employment is at 80 per cent. See John Lahr, *New Society* (20 December, 1984), 468–9.

44 Robert Brady, 'The problem of monopoly', in Gordon Watkins (ed.), *The Motion Picture Industry*, Annals of the American Academy of Political and Social Science 254 (November 1947), 125–36.

45 cf. Christian Metz, *Psychoanalysis and Cinema* (London, Macmillan, 1982), 67.

46 H. Powdermaker, *Hollywood: The Dream Factory* (New York, Little, Brown and Co., 1950), 206.

47 Employment in advertising is not only an alternative to 'straight' acting but can be very lucrative if syndicated.

48 Roland Barthes, *Image-Music-Text* (Stephen Heath (ed.), London, Fontana, 1977), 75.

49 H. Powdermaker, op. cit., 210.

50 Quoted in *The Sunday Times Magazine* (26 August 1984).

14

SCREEN ACTING AND THE COMMUTATION TEST

John O. Thompson

At the moment, only those who oppose the semiotic study of the cinema seem to want to talk about screen acting. Since a good deal of the meaning of the fiction film is borne by its actors and their performances, this amounts to leaving an important territory in the hands of the enemy (to put it over-belligerently). And some of the standard doctrines and endlessly rediscovered 'truths' about actor and role, screen vs. stage and so on may be inhibiting not only critical but also creative practice in the cinema. Yet it is understandable why this gap in the semiotic programme remains. Performances seem ineffable, and thinking about them induces reverie rather than analysis.

In this chapter I want to propose the controlled extension to screen actors of the semiotic technique called the *commutation test* as a means of prompting a more methodical and reflexive discourse in this area.

I

To begin with, here is a quotation from a recent essay by David Thomson. The point the quotation first makes is a familiar one. Brecht, summing up a conversation with Adorno in his diary in 1942, asserted that 'the theatre's first advantage over the film is . . . in the division between play and performance', and continued 'the mechanical reproduction gives everything the character of a result: unfree and inalterable'.[1] Thomson says the same thing, and then manoeuvres around this apparent blockage at the heart of the cinema's 'nature':

> Stage parts are like concertos – they are supple, lofty and impersonal enough to take on all comers. But parts in films live only briefly: like virginity, once taken, they are not there to be inhabited again. Before shooting, all manner of choices may perplex the film-makers and keep the part blurred: Kim Novak's part(s) in *Vertigo* were designed for Vera Miles; Shirley Temple was first choice to play Dorothy in *The Wizard of Oz* – imagine how 'Over the Rainbow'

183

might have been cosy and wistful instead of the epitome of heart-breaking dreams.... Once a film is made no one else can play the part ... the text in movies is the appearance.

All credit then to Andrew Sarris ... for indicating the waste in arguing over Vivien Leigh or Merle Oberon in Wyler's *Wuthering Heights*. And yet ... the critic can usefully learn things about film through such speculations.... If *Vertigo* had had Vera Miles then the girl might have been as near to breakdown as the wife in *The Wrong Man*, and not the numb pawn of the plot that makes Novak pathetic and touching.... Or – think how sentimental *Kane* might be if Spencer Tracy had been the tycoon. That is useful if only to show how little conventional feeling the film has.[2]

What I am struck by is an analogy between 'such speculations' and an 'operative concept ... already found in Trubetzkoy, but ... established under its present name by Hjelmslev and Udall, at the Fifth Congress of Phonetics in 1936'.[3] The name given it was *commutation*. Roland Barthes discusses the commutation test in *Elements of Semiology*, but in a very compressed manner:

> The commutation test consists of artificially introducing a change in the plane of expression (signifiers) and in observing whether this change brings about a correlative modification on the plane of contents (signifieds) ... if the commutation of two signifiers produces a commutation of the signifieds one is assured of having got hold, in the fragment of syntagm submitted to the test, of a syntagmatic unit: the first sign has been cut off from the mass.[4]

What does this formulation mean? Some differences in language make a difference semantically; others do not, though they are perceptible and may bear information about the speaker's region, social class, sex and so forth; still others are imperceptible save by means of sophisticated measuring instruments. The difference between *p* and *b* is of the first sort (*path* and *bath* are different words), while that between a higher *a* as pronounced in the north of England and the lower *a* of the south is of the second sort (*bath* is the same word with either *a*). The commutation test strictly speaking simply involves trying out a sound change and observing whether a meaning change is produced or not. *Which* meaning change may be irrelevant, because of the arbitrary, unmotivated linkage in language between sound and meaning.[5] How does this compare with what Thomson is doing? He is proposing the substitution in thought of one actor for another, in order to observe not merely *if* a difference in meaning results but *which* difference results. And he is doing so in a context in which we naturally feel that motivation of the sign is important: our sense of whether X is 'right for the part'[6] depends upon canons of suitability governing the signifier (actor)–signified (role) link which we generally assume to be non-arbitrary. One useful effect of thinking about commutation with the phonological analogy in mind is that it encourages us to query these assumptions about suitability, which turn out to be suffused with ideology and to shift with history. But there is no reason to believe that somehow with analysis all motivation should be shown to be illusory (reduction of cinema to language): ideology is not illusion.

II

It might seem that testing for whether substituting one actor for another makes any difference to a film's meaning would be pointless: 'Of course it must!' But this is not so. The stuntman, for instance, or the nude-scene stand-in both supply presences to the screen which have to seem indistinguishable from those of the actor or actress who is being stood in for: here much trouble is taken to ensure that the actual substitution of one body for another makes no difference to the text. Extras may generally be commuted with little if any change of meaning resulting. It is interesting to find that Equity's agreement with Thames Television explicitly defines an extra as 'a performer who is not required to give individual characteris-ations'[7] – that is, a performer who need not, indeed should not, *distinguish* himself or herself. It is not surprising that one un-distinguished figure can be indistinguishably replaced by another. What constraints there are on meaning-preserving replacements seem to operate on the level of the crowd (or a more abstract unit such as the set of passers-by through the whole film): we would notice if *everyone* on the streets happened to be female, or to be bald and so forth. There is an intermediate range of quite minor characters where the situation is blurred, but since the more films one has seen the more subtle individuations one picks up in the minor roles, it might be safest to treat them as functioning distinctively for the 'ideal viewer'. But occasionally indistinguishability is sought deliberately for the sake of the narrative. In Hitchcock's *Strangers on a Train* the promiscuity and vulgar fun-lovingness of Guy's wife Miriam is in part established by having her taken to the amusement park by *two* bland young men – who remain indistinguishable from one another over repeated viewings.

III

Commutation is a device which is designed to allow us consciously to grasp units which were previously invisible, submerged in the smooth operation of the sign system in question. This is why it can work introspec-tively: one *asks oneself* if a change in the signifier would make a difference, and the answer can surprise one. But if all that the commutation of actors reveals is that Cary Grant is not Gary Cooper, it certainly is not worth the trouble: our existing grasp of that gross difference is adequate enough already. If commutation is to justify itself in screen acting analysis, it must reveal something more delicate and less obvious. Why should we not think of a screen performance as composed of 'finer' elements, *features* in the linguistic sense?

The obvious answer is that John Wayne is more complex than a phoneme: whereas a phoneme can be characterised exhaustively in terms of a restricted number of features (Jakobson and Halle manage with twelve),[8] such an analysis is out of the question for the actor's rich and shifting screen presence. But if we move from phonological features to semantic features, the suggestion may not seem so wild. While no one could claim that we are even near to a generally acceptable account of natural language semantics, it can at least be said that: 'most current semantic theories, and many traditional ones too, analyse meaning into "smaller" component meanings, and assign to a lexical item a semantic representation consisting of a complex of semantically primitive elements.'[9] Here a typical feature would be not ±*voiced* or ±*nasal* but ±*abstract* or ±*animate* or ±*male*. How far decomposition into semantic features can be taken is currently a highly controversial question,[10] but it seems undeniable that componential analysis captures many necessary generalisations about the meaning relations between a word and the rest of the lexicon.

IV

Let us see how far the notion of a film performance as a bundle of distinctive features can take us. Each feature functions as a potential distinguisher both within the film itself and in the indefinitely extending space established by viewers' familiarity with cinema in general. For instance, John Wayne's features contrast not only with James Stewart's in the films they both appear in but with Jean-Paul Belmondo's, even if the two actors have never in fact been textually juxtaposed. Texts leave some features and feature-contrasts wholly unthematised and others only implicitly thematised in order to concentrate explicitly on comparatively few. Unthematised features could be altered or redistributed without any change in the meaning of the film resulting. Members of a chain-gang or a chorus-line are distinguished from one another, like the rest of us, by the colour of their eyes; but switching eye-colours around would generally make no difference to the text. Perhaps most feature-contrasts are only lightly or implicitly thematised: switching features turns out, when one thinks about it, to make some difference – perhaps a great deal: a woman in the chain-gang? – but the film operates in such a way as not to encourage one to think about this. Here the commutation test has a useful de-naturalising function. The canons of verisimilitude, plausibility, referentiality and so on that are operating suddenly become visible: *of course* there aren't co-ed chain-gangs, the athletic hero can not be a dwarf, the western hero can not have a Liverpool accent. In every film certain contrasts become highly thematised, presenting themselves as 'what the film is about'. Two or more characters are set up as rivals, as alternative love- or hate-objects (for other characters or the audience or both), as debaters, as couples etc. *The Good, the Bad and the Ugly*; Wayne and Stewart in *The Man Who Shot Liberty Valance*; Bogart and Bacall *passim*; Ava Gardner and Grace Kelly in *Mogambo*; the cousins in *Les Cousins*: here and everywhere in the cinema the audience is explicitly called upon to compare and contrast.

So far we have been talking about features as they pertain to actors as 'nouns', but there is no reason in principle not to extend the programme to the analysis of characters' actions (to the enacted equivalents of 'verb' or 'adjective' predicates) and to the manner in which the actions are performed ('adverbial' features). For critical and pedagogical purposes it is sometimes helpful to restrict oneself to, or at least to set out from, contrasts explicitly thematised in a particular film; this guarantees the pertinence of the features scrutinised and keeps the set of possibilities to be commuted finite. Since, for example, we have no satisfactory finite list of types of smile (although we can assign smiles to categories fairly precisely – thin-lipped, crazy, timid etc.), running through smile-types at random can seem pointless. But the contrast between the smiles of Ava Gardner and Grace Kelly in *Mogambo* is part of the system of that film. Imagining switching the smiles around, so that the young, inexperienced blonde has the sensual, shrewd, good-humoured smile while the older, experienced brunette has the repressed, seldom-used smile, teaches us a good deal about the system of assumptions about types of women which Ford is working within here.[11] Yet it would be wrong always to limit commutation to contrasts embodied in the text. Commuting smiles in *Mogambo* with smile-types wholly foreign to the film (a crazy smile or a cruel smile, say) might or might not be unprofitable depending on the investigation in hand. Such a commutation might be pertinent to an examination of the bounds of decorum within which women in a film like *Mogambo* must keep if the overall good humour of the action is to be sustained and the audience remain unthreatened. When the feature in question is part of a clearly limited paradigmatic set, we need worry even less about applying commutation independently of the film's own thematised contrasts. Perhaps the most obvious example of such a set is the male–female opposition: commutation here almost always has dramatic effects which get us to the heart of 'ordinary sexism' very quickly.

Figure 14.1 Mogambo (1953). Repressed, seldom-used smile

V

Does one test by commuting whole actors or just features? This will depend. Commuting actors may be wasteful and lead to blurry intuitions: if it is already clear which feature is pertinent, manipulating it on its own may be indicated. And what presents itself as a whole-actor commutation may really be a single-feature commutation in disguise. Take the following sharp comment by Marjorie Bilbow, reviewing *Looking for Mr Goodbar*:

A woman seeking the release of sex without love will still attract moral judgements when films about men doing exactly the same thing are taken for granted. In fact, it makes a salutary mental exercise to transpose the lead characters in *Mr Goodbar* and Truffaut's *The Man Who Loved Women*, which is primarily a light

188

Figure 14.2 Mogambo (1953). Sensual, shrewd, good-humoured smile

comedy. Both die sudden and violent deaths at the end; which of the two would you then say is being punished for sinning?[12]

Clearly Marjorie Bilbow is not actually proposing that we check the differences between Diane Keaton and Charles Denner (or between the roles they play) feature by feature as we transpose them. The relevant feature – gender – is already obvious. The use of speaking of the whole roles here is that it points up that not only sexual behaviour but ultimate fate stays constant under transposition; what varies as gender varies is the moral evaluation of that fate. Thus the *unexpected* 'unit' that the commutation isolates lies on the plane of the film's ethical signifieds. In general, whole-actor commutation is useful when it is not yet clear which feature(s) will turn out to be pertinently differential, or how one feature aligns itself

189

with others to effect a single thematised contrast. One feature of Diane Keaton as Teresa in *Mr Goodbar* is her hair colour; but how this operates as a signifier in the film comes into focus less when we commute just hair colours – can she be a red-head? – than when we commute Keaton with Tuesday Weld as the blonde older sister, whose *dyed*-blondeness goes with *only-apparent* innocence in her father's eyes but with *real* dumbness, contrasting with Teresa's educatedness, sincerity, guilt in her father's eyes.

VI

The sort of 'units' that commuting actors isolates – features or traits – are themselves clearly not unanalysable primitives: a tempting but very ambitious programme would be to aim at a decomposition of physiog- nomies, smiles, gaits and similar behaviours into distinctive features speci- fied in physiological terms in the same way that phonological features are specified in terms of the mechanisms of the mouth, throat and tongue. Someone with a penchant for rigour might claim that characterisations such as 'nervous smile' or 'crazy smile' are hopelessly imprecise and impressionistic ('tight-lipped smile' being closer to a satisfactory descrip- tion). However, there are good reasons for not taking the rigorist too seriously, though students of the cinema probably should pay more atten- tion to recent advances in the study of non-verbal communication than we usually do.[13] One trouble with the rigorist's programme is that for many inquiries it would be diversionary: the level of codedness one is interested in is more 'macro', more capable of being related to economic, political and ideological structures. But there is also a problem in principle about the search for primitive elements of behaviour: we have no guarantee that concepts such as 'suave, sophisticated manners', 'crazy smile', 'dizzi- ness' (as in 'dizzy blonde') group together behaviours which are physio- logically unitary. That is, there are almost certainly a number of muscularly distinct smiles which in this culture we would group together as 'crazy', and this would be even more true of what 'sophistication' or 'ruggedness' collect; yet it is at the level of these cultural groupings that we need to operate. Too 'micro' an analysis can destroy the object we are concerned with.

Commutation does respond to one element in the rigorist's reproach, in that its effect is to keep before our attention how problematic the terms we use to characterise differences among performances are. There seem to be differences without terms to capture them,[14] and terms which bundle together an indefinite range of differences. (But in this respect our dis- course about performance is like our discourse about everything else: it is how natural language operates.) This allows for considerable mobility over time in the conceptualising of performances and their details: to recapture the terms that would have been used to characterise features of a silent film performance, for instance, often requires a considerable effort of historical imagination.

VII

Analysing an advertisement for Chanel No. 5 perfume consisting of a close-up of Catherine Deneuve, a picture of a bottle of the perfume, the brand-name in large letters at the bottom of the page and 'Catherine Deneuve for Chanel' in small letters just above this, Judith Williamson sees Chanel as using 'what Catherine Deneuve's face *means to us*' already to establish 'what Chanel No. 5 is trying to mean to us, too':

> It is only because Catherine Deneuve has an 'image', a significance in one sign system, that she can be used to create a new system of significance relating to perfumes. If she were not a film star and famous for her chic type of French beauty, if she did not *mean* something to us, the link made between her face and the perfume would be meaningless. So it is not her face as such, but its position in a system of signs where it signifies flawless French beauty, which makes it useful as a piece of linguistic currency to sell Chanel.[15]

Meaning in a sign system depends on difference; Williamson chooses as a differing woman-sign a model who appears in the ad campaign for Fabergé's *Babe* perfume:

> Catherine Deneuve has significance only in that she is not, for example, Margaux Hemingway. . . . The significance of [the latter's] novelty, youth and 'Tomboy' style, which has value only *in relation* to the more typically 'feminine' style usually connected with modelling, is carried over to the perfume: which is thus signified as new and 'fresh', in relation to other established perfumes. There would be no significance at all in the fact that Margaux Hemingway is wearing a karate outfit and has her hair tied back to look almost like a man's, were it not that *other* perfume ads show women wearing pretty dresses and with elaborately styled hair.[16]

I think Williamson's discussion may overstate the ultimate reducibility to difference of this whole realm of signification, but this is not to say that difference is not immensely important. I want to use Deneuve as an example of the operation of 'the formal relations of pre-existing systems of differences', because these systems are not only what 'advertisements appropriate'[17] but are in the cinema important determinants of *casting*.

Williamson's argument is that we have a much more secure grasp of the difference between Deneuve and Hemingway than we have, or could ever have ('perfumes *can* have no particular significance')[18] with respect to the product; so that transferring the former difference to the latter realm has a persuasive, because cognitive, effect.[19] The question is, in what sense do those firm Deneuve–Hemingway differences exist before one makes that specific comparison? It arises for me with special force in this particular case because it was possible for me fully to follow Williamson's discussion although I knew nothing whatsoever of Margaux Hemingway before reading it. In effect, Williamson has performed a Deneuve–Hemingway commutation, and my prior ignorance of one element in the commutation has not prevented it from 'working'. How can this be? Actually, the significances which Williamson ascribes to Deneuve – '*famous* for her *chic* type of *French* beauty . . . *flawless*' – are not in an uncomplicatedly differential relationship to those of the Hemingway 'image'. Logically enough, but also as if to compensate for Deneuve's +*fame*, Hemingway has +*novelty* whereas Deneuve has −*novelty* (the link between her and Chanel has been maintained for an unusually long time). But one would hardly assign −*chic* to Hemingway (although the *type* of chic shifts); her −*French* trait is not unequivocal ('Margaux' vs. 'Margo',[20] and perhaps a whiff of 'American-in-Paris'-ness left over from another Hemingway); and while someone engaged in karate seems unlikely to maintain 'flawless beauty', one clearly could not speak of a 'flawed beauty'. The underlying contrast seems to involve something like ±*mobility*: Hemingway can retain her sort of beauty in motion, whereas one cannot imagine the Chanel Deneuve being able to move much without her beauty becoming flawed.

What seems to happen is that such individual images as Deneuve's or Hemingway's find or make their place(s) within a network of differences already provided for *by the language*; it is within language that the contrast 'feminine'/'Tomboy' is kept 'in place', and this is a necessary condition for that contrast's embodiment both in the real and in image-deployment within specialised discourses like advertising. At this level, the same contrast ±*feminine* could be embodied by an indefinite number of different figures. But conversely each individual figure is a composite of an indefinite number of determinations, and while only a subset of these will be highlighted by any given commutation, it will still put into play contrasts involving more than a single feature. This means that a contrast on ±*mobility* will always involve more than *just* that once the specific feature-bundle 'Margaux Hemingway' is chosen to embody one pole, even when the other pole is left general ('other perfume ads show women wearing pretty dresses and with elaborately styled hair'); and it will become even richer once the specific feature-bundle 'Catherine Deneuve' is installed at the other pole. This detailed richness is what could not have existed before I knew about Margaux Hemingway, and each new bit of data I acquire about the image enriches the contrast further. But the concepts to illustrate which Williamson posed the contrast of the two images are not dependent upon this richness: many models and actresses could have been chosen who would have embodied any one feature contrast just as well.

The main difference between choosing a model for an advertisement and casting for a film is that the requirements of narrative structure in film, however constraining on their own level, put the features of the actor into play more actively than advertisements do. If there is a single image of Deneuve at work in the Chanel ads and in her films, it is presented and developed more unpredictably where narrative brings out its potential ambiguities.

When Burt Reynolds asked Robert Aldrich to direct him in *Hustle*, Aldrich said:

> 'I'll do this picture on one condition: that you help me get Miss Chanel.' Because the woman's part had been written for an American, and I didn't think it worked that way. I think our middle-class mores just don't make it credible that a policeman can have a love relationship with a prostitute. Because of some strange quirk in our backgrounds, the mass audience doesn't believe it. It's perfectly all right as long as she's not American. So Burt accepted this as a condition, and we put up our money and went to Paris, and waited on the great lady for a week, and she agreed to do the picture.[21]

Here the role in the script included the feature +*American*, and the director modified this to −*American* on credibility grounds. Whether or not Aldrich's unacceptability intuition about the cluster +*American* +*prostitute* +*loved by policeman* was idiosyncratic[22] (the casting of Deneuve seems to me to be splendid, but I wouldn't have thought credibility was its strong point), it certainly underdetermines the choice of Deneuve from the very large set of un-American actresses. The associative leap to 'Miss Chanel' shows that more of the 'Deneuve' feature-bundle was involved, and the tone of the remark about 'waiting on the great lady'[23] might suggest that part of this might be a certain wish to flaw the 'unflawed', to exploit the possibilities of the Miss-Chanel-as-prostitute twist. But there must be something about the bundle which facilitates this twist anyway, since any specification of Deneuve's image in terms of film roles would have to take Bunuel's *Belle du Jour* as a central text. While it and *Hustle* draw on the features that make Deneuve an appropriate signifier for Chanel, both films in different ways put these features at the service of narratives which draw out their darker implications – in *Belle du Jour* the −*mobility* feature is used to connote both frigidity and corpse-likeness; in *Hustle* the 'flawlessness' is made to begin to crack around the edges.

A Catherine Deneuve ad and a Catherine Deneuve film clearly both operate as closed texts to a greater or lesser degree (both *Belle du Jour* and *Hustle* being more open than many, as it happens, whereas a more conventional film such as Terence Young's *Mayerling* might even exceed Chanel ads in closure): but the mechanisms by which they achieve their closure are different, and are themselves made visible by the commutation we achieve by holding Deneuve constant while changing the textual practices which serve as the context of her presentation. The ever-open possibility of doing this leaves the Chanel advertisements open to a certain subversion. So does the way that the Deneuve image is built up from appearances of which some are so narratively charged: Chanel cannot prevent us from thinking of the parts Deneuve has played for Bunuel and Aldrich, with their unwanted, unsettling features.

VIII

There is room for a great deal of detailed research on the history of casting. The breathless run-through of casts once contemplated for well-known films given in a recent article by Linda Rosencrantz[24] illustrates the sort of material which could be of great use in determining which star images were contemplatable for which roles at a given time. It would be good to have accounts of actual casting practice detailed enough to serve as a control on the intuitions commutation affords us about possible and impossible matchings of actor to role. Clearly, casting is subject to powerful ideological constraints. A given role must be filled by someone who possesses or can assume the features felt necessary to sustain it, and both the determination of the features in the script and the organisation of their textualisation in the course of filming will be governed by ideological assumptions about what is 'natural' and 'goes without saying'.

In Don Siegel's *The Shootist*, John Wayne plays an aging gun-fighter dying of cancer and James Stewart plays the doctor who diagnoses the disease. I have never met anyone who could imagine the casting reversed, yet it's hard to see why. Most people, after some thought, say that they can imagine Stewart in the Wayne role (it helps to think back to Stewart's unmannered performances in Anthony Mann Westerns). What seems 'ungrammatical' is Wayne as a doctor. But what is it that we think we know about doctors that makes Wayne's bundle of traits incompatible with his being one? An adjective which sometimes get used to describe Wayne is 'rugged': this is not incompatible with delicacy, as any reviewing of *Rio Bravo* reminds us, but it does seem incompatible with the sort of *indoor* and *studied* (the product of study) delicacy of movement that a doctor, especially a surgeon, is felt to need. Of course the frontier doctor in Westerns isn't exactly a Dr Kildare, but his lack of polish is generally presented as a *decline*, however good-natured, from an earlier level of competence reached 'back East'. The frontier doctor can thus deviate in the direction of a certain ruggedness (often on account of drink), but he generally retains such unrugged features as −*tall* and −*athletic*. A counter-example in terms of these specific features, Victor Mature's Doc Holliday in Ford's *My Darling Clementine*, is tall and athletic but consumptive, alcoholic and bookish; commuting Wayne with Mature here would be unthinkable.

This would seem to suggest that, outside the specific generic context of the Hospital drama, the medical profession is somehow not seen as *macho* enough to sustain a central position within the Hollywood narrative. (Think how impossible it is that *The Shootist* be *about* James Stewart.) Yet this is puzzling, because the medical profession clearly does not lack prestige in America. Why should the role of gunman be worth so much more narratively? This is the sort of question that the facts revealed by commutation force us to ask. They are not easily dealt with by any 'reflection' or 'inverted reflection' model of ideology in fiction – whether what is thought to be reflected is the real or the producing culture's ideal.

IX

I want to conclude briefly by returning to Brecht's 'fundamental reproach', which was that because in the cinema the role and the performer are one, there is no possibility of introducing the sort of gap between them that promotes reflection. There is a problem here, but it does not seem to be insuperable if we are prepared to take as our unit of experience not just the film in front of us at a particular moment but the cinema as a whole (and, beyond that, representational culture generally): a larger system of possibilities and impossibilities which as a system is like, just as it to a large extent depends upon, our language. Like language, the sign systems of the cinema are never textually embodied all at once: to restrict analysis to the 'text itself', to rule out counterfactual statements on methodological grounds, would be a surrender to dogmatic empiricism.

A limited gap *is* opened between actor and role, I think, by the star system itself, with its encouragement to the viewer to see a single figure on the screen as both role and star. What is needed to exploit that gap and open it wider is an awareness, which teaching can promote, of the dependence of both role-meaning and star-meaning upon a network of differences correlated with one another in seemingly naturalised, hence suspect, ways. My practical claim for the commutation test is that it promotes in the viewer the right sort of suspicion.

NOTES

This is a slightly shortened and revised version of an article first published in *Screen*, 19, 2 (Summer 1978). John O. Thompson followed it up with a second article, 'Beyond commutation – a reconsideration of screen acting', in *Screen*, 26, 5 (September/October 1985).

1 Ben Brewster, 'The fundamental reproach (Brecht)', *Cine-tracts*, 2 (Summer 1977), 44–53.

2 David Thomson, 'The look on an actor's face', *Sight and Sound*, 46, 4 (Autumn 1977), 240–4.

3 Roland Barthes, *Elements of Semiology* (London 1967), 65.

4 Ibid.

5 Ibid., 66, quotes a machine-translation expert to just this effect: ' "The difference between the significations [is] of use, the significations themselves being without importance" (Belevitch).'

6 Note that, if 'the text in movies is the appearance' and the 'result' is really 'unfree and inalterable' absolutely – i.e. if for Thomson the medium intrinsically forces actor and role to coalesce utterly for the spectator – it is hard to see how our question of 'rightness for the part' could even be raised.

7 Quoted in Manuel Alvarado and Edward Buscombe, *Hazell: The Making of a TV Series* (London 1978), 20.

8 See Roman Jakobson and Morris Halle, *Fundamentals of Language* (The Hague 1971).

9 Janet Dean Fodor, *Semantics: Theories of Meaning in Generative Grammar* (Hassocks 1977), 144.

10 See ibid., 143–214 for an up-to-date and detailed account of recent argument in the field.

11 The system in question is clearly rather widespread; exactly the same distribution of smile-types, correlated in the same way to hair-colour, turns up in Rohmer's *Ma nuit chez Maud*.

12 *Screen International*, 129 (11 March 1978), 30.

13 An especially heroic research project in this area is that of Ekman and Friesen, who are endeavouring to specify a Facial Action code by isolating minimal units of muscular activity in the face: 'we spent the better part of a year with a mirror, anatomy texts, and cameras. We learned to fire separately the muscles in our own faces.' So far the minimum units isolated number about forty-five, and the researchers have performed and photographed 'between four and five thousand facial combinations' of these units. 'If we wish to learn all the facial actions which signal emotion and those that do not . . . such a method . . . is needed.' See Paul Ekman and Wallace V. Friesen, 'Measuring facial movement', *Environmental Psychology and Nonverbal Behaviour*, 1 (Fall 1976), 56–75.

14 Cf. Eugene A. Nida, *Componential Analysis of Meaning* (The Hague 1975), 19: 'It would be a mistake to think that one can always describe easily the relations between related meanings. For some sets of meanings there may be no readily available terms with which one can talk about the differences. This is true, for example, of colours. We readily recognise that the colours *violet, blue, green, yellow, red*, etc., differ from one another, but we do not have the kind of metalanguage with which we can easily speak about the differences. One could employ technical terminology based on the wavelengths of different colours, but this does not represent the manner in which we normally conceive of colour differences.' It would take us too far afield to go into the matter here, but it should be mentioned that both Wittgenstein and Lacan deny that there could be a true metalanguage for describing human action.

15 Judith Williamson, *Decoding Advertisements: Ideology and Meaning in Advertising* (London 1978), 25.

16 Ibid., 26.

17 Ibid., 27.

18 Ibid., 25. Smells may be meaningless but they are certainly evocative. For a very interesting discussion of why evocativeness may be raised by the fact that

'there is no semantic field of smells', see Dan Sperber, *Rethinking Symbolism* (Cambridge 1975), 115–19.

19 'This seems like the reverse of "totemism", where *things* are used to differentiate groups of people', Williamson, op. cit., 27.

20 An interesting problem: is there anything 'French' about the image of Catherine Deneuve if her name is taken away? (What happens if the Chanel ad remains just as it is save for the substitution of, say, 'Shirley Saunders for Chanel'?)

21 Stuart Byron (interviewing Robert Aldrich), 'I can't get Jimmy Carter to see my movie!', *Film Comment*, 13 (March–April 1977), 52.

22 In *The Choirboys* the cluster reappears, but its 'unacceptability' is now inscribed within the text itself in the form of the violence of a 'bad' sado-masochistic relationship leading to the policeman's shame and suicide.

23 The phrase helps clarify a second Deneuve Chanel ad reproduced by Williamson, op. cit., 28, in which a head-and-shoulders photograph of Deneuve with Chanel bottles bears the text 'It's one of the pleasures of being a woman.' The image might be puzzling because Deneuve is unsmiling, stern-looking, not obviously enjoying any 'pleasure' – save, perhaps, that of being 'the great lady'.

24 'The role that got away', *Film Comment*, 14 (Jan.–Feb. 1978), 42–8.

15

STARS AND GENRE

Andrew Britton

One of the major limitations of Richard Dyer's monograph *Stars* (London, British Film Institute, 1979) arises from his discussion of the relation between stars and genre. Consider, for example, his account of the star 'vehicle'.

> The vehicle might provide (a) a character of the type associated with the star (e.g. Monroe's 'dumb blonde' roles, Garbo's melancholic romantic roles), (b) a situation, setting or generic context associated with the star (e.g. Garbo in relationships with married men, Wayne in Westerns . . .); or (c) opportunities for the star to do her/his thing (most obviously in the case of musical stars . . . but also, for instance, opportunities to display Monroe's body and wiggle walk, scenes of action in Wayne's films). Vehicles are important as much for what conventions they set up as for how they develop them, for their ingredients as for their realisation. In certain respects a set of star vehicles is rather like a film genre such as the Western, the musical, the gangster film. As with genres proper, one can discern across a star's vehicles continuities of iconography . . . visual style . . . and structure. Of course, not all films made by the star are vehicles, but looking at their films in terms of vehicles draws attention to those films that do not fit, that constitute inflections, exceptions to, subversions of the vehicle pattern and the star image. (Dyer, *Stars*, 70–1)

The fundamental error here is the proposition that 'a set of star vehicles' is in any way 'like' a genre. On the contrary, the existence of a genre, *and of a relation between the genres*, is a prior condition of the vehicle: vehicles constitute a distinct sub-set, more or less highly individuated, of conventional relations which always precede the star. It is thus extremely misleading to reduce 'generic context' to something as loose and vague as a 'situation or setting', for 'generic contexts' are inseparable from narrative determinations. Quite apart from the fact that Garbo is *not* primarily associated with 'relationships with married men', but with the 'Anna

Karenina' structure (elderly, post-sexual husband/passionate younger wife/romantic lover), Dyer's suggestion that 'vehicles are important as much for what conventions they set up as for how they develop them', encourages us to forget that the possibilities of development are entailed in (or at least circumscribed by) conventions, and that a film's being a vehicle for a particular star is by no means the major fact in that development. The 'Anna Karenina' narrative implies a dramatic trajectory which is not in the least contingent on the casting of Garbo. While it is clearly crucial to ask why it was that Garbo should have been consigned so often to a structure which channels transgressive female desire into adultery and then leaves it with a 'choice' between renunciation and death, it is equally clear that the vehicle pertains in this case to a generic form with particular limits and parameters.

The 'Anna Karenina' story is an archetypal bourgeois narrative which, in one sense, Garbo cannot effect: the available outcomes (her films enact every conceivable variant), and even the complex pattern of sympathies which problematise our attitude to the heroine's 'crime', are pre-given. In another sense, of course, her effect is crucial, but it is precisely because her films are not 'like' a genre but embedded in one that we can specify what that effect is.

Dyer's discussion of genre implicitly endorses the tendency, in Robin Wood's phrase, 'to treat the genres as discrete' (Wood, 'Ideology, genre, auteur', *Film Comment* (January/February 1977), 47), from which so much genre theory has derived its characteristically solipsistic quality. For if we take as our starting-point the isolation of 'continuities of iconography, visual style and structure' within a single genre, we are condemned to reproduce in our analytical categories the divisions and distinctions implicit in the material itself. The genres *present* themselves as discrete, and a formalist analysis of them is inevitably tautological.

The essential theoretical point here is classically formulated by Marx in the 1857 'Introduction' to *A Critique of Political Economy*, apropos 'the method of political economy':

It would seem to be the proper thing to start with the real and concrete elements, with the actual preconditions, e.g. to start in the sphere of economy with population, which forms the basis and the subject of the whole social process of production. Closer consideration shows, however, that this is wrong. Population is an abstraction, if for instance, one disregards the classes of which it is composed. These classes in turn remain empty terms if one does not know the factors on which they depend, e.g. wage-labour, capital and so on. These presuppose exchange, division of labour, prices, etc. . . . If one were to take population as the point of departure, it would be a very vague notion of a complex whole and through

199

closer definition one would arrive analytically at increasingly simple concepts; from imaginary concrete terms one would move to more and more tenuous abstractions until one reached the most simple definitions. From there it would be necessary to make the journey again in the opposite direction until one arrived once more at the concept of population, which is this time not a vague notion of a whole, but a totality comprising many determinations and relations. (*The German Ideology*, ed. C. J. Arthur (Lawrence and Wishart 1978), 140)

The 'real and concrete elements' of, say, the melodrama 'remain empty terms if one does not know the factors on which they depend'; and it follows at once that one of these factors is the existence of the Western and the small-town comedy – that is, the production and reassertion of a division of labour, as it were, between the genres within the institution of Hollywood. The condition of the irreducibility of the genres is precisely their historical reciprocity: in an apparently paradoxical but very real sense, they are different *because* of what they have in common, not in spite of it. The common ground is that profound conflict of interpretations within the culture – ineliminable because germane *to* the culture – which assigns conflicting meanings to a single term or set of terms. Each genre seeks to regulate this conflict by organising particular 'forms and keepings', and appropriate expectations, whereby specific manifestations and resolutions of contradiction appear as properties of the generic world. The definitions and evaluations of middle America in *Margie* and *Beyond the Forest*, for example, are diametrically opposed to one another, but each is appropriate to the context which the genre creates, and they do not seem, therefore, to be contradictory. While each genre has means and methods of its own both for the enactment and the harmonisation of conflicting values and allegiances, it also exists in a complementary relation to other genres – a relation which *in itself* subserves the negotiation of contradiction by controlling its possible dramatic presence.

Popular American movies presuppose an enormously sophisticated intimacy with the conventions of genre – an intense awareness of the logic of *this* dramatic world as distinct from *that* one – and Hollywood works by encouraging a kind of instinctual formalism which freezes a film as an instance of the categories it employs. The spectacle is naturalised not because its conventions are invisible, but because they are referred to themselves.

If we approach genre from the point of view of its intrinsic thematic relationship to reality and the generation of reality, we must say that every genre has its methods and means of seeing and conceptualising reality, which are accessible to it alone. . . . Every significant genre is a complex system of means and methods for the conscious control

200

and finalisation of reality. (M. M. Bakhtin/P. N. Medvedev, *The Formal Method in Poetics* (Johns Hopkins University Press 1978), 133)

In that the Hollywood genres appear as autonomous units which are only related to one another in as much as they differ – in other words, in that the 'intrinsic thematic relationship to reality and the generation of reality' which the genres, at any historical moment, have in common is suppressed – the reading which a Hollywood film demands seems to have been exhausted at the point at which it is located in the 'means and methods' of the genre to which it pertains. The conventions which the film employs and in relation to which it is readable appear to form the horizon of its reference. It is not that the film does not present itself as a text, but that certain kinds of reading of the text appear to be irrelevant and inappropriate: the text does not generate and finalise reality, it is 'just a horror movie'. In this sense, genre is the film's commodity form, and its status as commodity is underwritten by the entertainment syndrome, which at once encourages the purchase of a film as an object of prospective pleasure and trivialises the pleasure.

Conversely, every Hollywood movie of whatever genre must at least allow for a conservative reading. No film can explicitly authorise the transgression, or assert the bankruptcy, of the ideological absolutes without adopting, as protective camouflage, the ostensible affirmation of them which many Hollywood films offer *without* irony. Indeed, the very condition of the ironic happy ending is a happy ending which is *not* ironic. The effect of these two facts – the apparent autonomy and self-reference of the genres; the obligation of any film apparently to endorse, whatever its real intention, the norms which are massively reproduced within the culture as a whole – is to discourage any process of generalisation from the dramatic world to the reality inhabited by the spectator which fails to conduce to intimations of the rightness of the status quo.

One can say, in effect, that Hollywood both enables and contains a *Beyond the Forest*. Vidor's film is possible because it is 'just' a Bette Davis picture, and we all know the kind of thing that Bette Davis gets up to: the structural assimilation of the subversive product is given in advance. At the same time, this very guarantee creates a space for *Beyond the Forest*; and it has been my fundamental proposition that even films whose *intention* is conservative can leave room, in the very pursuit of their project, for unauthorised use. If genre, and that sub-section of genre the 'vehicle', assign Hollywood movies their commodity form, they also assign them a language of enormous density and complexity, the innovative and transgressive use of which can actually be facilitated by the film's status as commodity. It is because *Beyond the Forest* is just another Bette Davis melodrama that it can do the things that it does.

This thesis has a number of important implications for the study of stars.

(1) The contradictions enacted by stars *in their films* are always at least latent in a particular genre. *Now, Voyager* is a Bette Davis movie, but 'Bette Davis' is a sub-section or inflection of melodrama in its relation to sophisticated comedy. The personae of John Wayne, Gary Cooper, James Stewart, Henry Fonda and Clint Eastwood are all quite distinct, but none of them can be discussed significantly without reference to the concept of the Western hero which they have at various times embodied, or to the tensions within the myth of white American history, refracted through a specific contemporary moment, which the genre articulates.

(2) It follows that the function of stars as embodiments/mediators of contradiction *in their films* must be rigorously distinguished from their other functions and meanings. Dyer argues, correctly, that Garbo's retirement is as crucial a component of the Garbo myth as any of her films, but this is to say no more than that the Garbo myth mystifies the significance of Garbo movies, which are highly particularised variants of a generic preoccupation with women's oppression and self-assertion. The Garbo myth is autonomous, homogeneous and self-sufficient: Garbo films are only readable in relation to, say, the films of Hepburn, Davis and Dietrich, which are embedded in turn in the historical situation of genre. The phrase '*Queen Christina* is a Garbo movie' may posit either the film's commodity form or an analytic category, and it is genre which will determine the significance the phrase is to have. Clearly, the myth, its ramifications and its retroactive effect on the films are of fundamental importance. The last shot of *Queen Christina* is, as extractable fetish, a crux of the myth, but it also has a dramatic function, and describes the *terminus ad quem* of romantic passion for women – exclusion from history and petrifaction as an icon (Christina has just told her dying lover that she will never leave him). The shot embodies a tension between these two meanings, the second of which the myth subsumes in a plangent romantic melancholy which is supposed to represent 'essence of Garbo'. The tension, and the more radical tendency of the Garbo persona, can only be recovered if we see the film's ending as a term in a generic repertoire which is frequently invoked to contain the problems which Garbo raises. The essentialising tendency of myth is, in fact, a part of the process of containment, and obscures the significance which Garbo acquires as an actor in melodramas.

(3) Many stars repeatedly cross genres. In some cases, a star is associated with a particular genre at a particular stage of his/her career – Garbo, for example, who was cast exclusively in melodramas until her last two films. Some stars, too, are virtually genre-specific: most musical stars, by virtue of particular skills, some Western stars (Roy Rogers, Gene Autry), or stars like Karloff and Lugosi who are enveloped in the ethos of a specific

character. It is most often the case, however, that major stars are associated simultaneously with several genres. Thus, for instance, during the 1940s and 1950s Hepburn was cast both in comedies and melodramas, and Stewart's fifties action-movies and domestic melodramas with Anthony Mann are interspersed with his thriller-melodramas for Hitchcock.

This does not mean that the star's work constitutes a new generic entity, but demonstrates again the historical interpenetration of the genres. The historical conditions which produce the possibilities of the kind of action-hero created in the Stewart/Mann Westerns are also such as to create a space within the Western for concerns and thematics which it has previously marginalised, and tilt it towards melodrama and the Gothic. The impulses behind, and the rationale of, male action, traditionally taken for granted, have become crucially problematic (the process can be specified in detail in the great Westerns of the late forties and their complement, film noir), and the function of genre as a regulator of contradiction is disturbed by the genre's own historical trajectory. The heroic adventurer, creator and guarantor of a law of which he is the conscious spokesman, becomes compulsive, divided and inarticulate – that is, 'melodramatic'.

If the Stewart case is exemplary of the tendency of the genres to inherit each other and reassert the terms which their conventions have sought to marginalise or exclude, Hepburn's oscillation between melodrama and comedy draws our attention at once to the differences and the parallels between the strategies which different genres adopt in order to settle similar problems. The fact that the careers of, say, Davis, Stanwyck and Russell reveal an analogous pattern should warn us that it is as dangerous to compartmentalise the stars as it is to hive off the genres. Let us juxtapose, by way of example, *The Philadelphia Story*, *Ninotchka* and *Destry Rides Again* – three films belonging to different genres (sophisticated comedy, romantic comedy and the Western respectively) and all made in the same year (1939). The three stars for whom the films are 'vehicles' – Hepburn, Garbo and Dietrich – had all been labelled 'box-office poison' by *Variety* in 1937, and each work aspired (successfully) to re-establish the star's commercial viability by modifying her image.

It should not be necessary at this stage to reiterate the nature of the overlap between the three star personae: while each is highly specific it is scarcely surprising, given the problematic nature of their sexual identities, that each should have become contentious at the same time. The specificity is reflected in the genre chosen for the come-back: the preservation of a continuity with previous roles is a condition for the appropriate resolution of their intractable elements. Thus the selection of romantic comedy for Garbo bespeaks an attempt to maintain her association with all-consuming romantic love while averting an outcome of tragedy and defeat: the conventions of the genre allow the romantic impulse to be secured within the bourgeois-capitalist status quo, and legitimate the theme of romanticism as rebellion which is so crucial a component of Garbo's melodramas. Similarly, the type of the saloon entertainer allows *Destry* to reiterate the Dietrich image of vamp *chanteuse* while detaching it from the ethos of the exotic foreign cabaret and invoking a generic language which guarantees its suppression; and the 'world' of sophisticated comedy is clearly indicated as the requisite medium for the foregrounding, and amelioration, of Hepburn's rebarbative 'upper-classness'.

The very possibility of using genre in this way is, of course, already suggestive. The condition, in each case, of deploying one genre in order to resolve or soften tensions exacerbated by another is the fact that the genres 'represent different strategies for dealing with the same ideological tensions' (Wood, ibid.). Analogously, the diverse generic *strategies* of the three films embody a common ideological *tactic:* the narrative movements are remarkably similar.

(a) Each star/character is located, at the outset, in a position of social power. Frenchy/Dietrich is the 'real boss' of Bottleneck; Ninotchka/Garbo is a Soviet commissar; Tracy Lord/Hepburn is both a wealthy New England heiress and the *primum mobile* in her family.

(b) This power is seen to be fundamentally un-democratic and un-American. Frenchy's authority is inimical to the 'law and order' of the organic frontier community, Ninotchka is a Bolshevik and Tracy is a walking affront to every article of the populist faith.

(c) The women's power is associated, moreover, with their resistance to sexual regulation by men. Frenchy deprives Callaghan (Mischa Auer), *Destry*'s comic emasculated male, of his trousers, holds the men of Bottleneck in thrall by her sexual charisma and insists on having 'what the boys in the back-room will have'. Ninotchka objects to 'the arrogant male in capitalistic society', and regards romantic love as a mystification of desire which serves to subordinate women. Tracy is a 'virgin goddess' who is unpossessable by men, and an astringent critic of the complementary male vices of sexual dependency and sexual opportunism.

(d) A male educator reclaims the woman for capitalism and 'femininity'. Destry wipes off Frenchy's make-up, and commends her to 'live up to the lovely face' which it conceals: subsequently, Frenchy's commitment to Destry is signalled by her surrender to him of her equivalent of what the boys in the back-room have got, her lucky rabbit's foot (Destry remarks that he hopes it was 'a big strong rabbit'.) Ninotchka discovers, through love, that the revolution must be postponed: 'Give us our moment!' Tracy learns that she has been unfair to all the men in the film and that her strength is the source of their weakness, and re-marries the husband she had contemptuously rejected.

Some such project could no doubt be identified in many American films, with or without the complexities, ambiguities, disharmonies occasioned, in these cases, by the three stars themselves. The point to be made is that we have here a very striking and concrete case of the complementary relation between star personae and between the genres, and of the dialectical interaction between genre and vehicle. To cast Dietrich as a saloon entertainer is to assign to her a character with a particular place in the generic world (analogous to that of related types in other genres), a corresponding evaluation and a possible dramatic life which is severely curtailed by the conventions. While Dietrich's presence cannot avert the generic destiny of the character, the necessity of which is a determinant of the casting in the first place, by the same token the casting (it is, after all, Dietrich and not Virginia Mayo) has its implication for the obligatory reinforcement of the generic judgement on the character-type. The upshot is a radical crisis of value and allegiance within the film, whereby the relative evaluation of 'law' and 'disorder', and indeed, the internal coherence of the categories themselves, is profoundly disturbed. One need only compare Frenchy/Dietrich with Chihuahua/Linda Darnell in *My Darling Clementine* to realise that while such a crisis is implicit in the genre, its *enactment* is not: the casting of a specific actor, clearly, is one possible catalyst of it (another might be the intervention of a specific director). The star in his/her films must always be read as a dramatic presence which is predicated by, and which intervenes in, enormously complex and elaborate themes and motifs, and thereby refers us to a particular state of the social reality of genre, and of the relation between the genres. It is, for example, symptomatic of Dietrich's effect on *Destry Rides Again* that in the final scene, after Frenchy's death, the film registers a sense of regret for her loss: as the triumphant patriarch walks down the street of the newly civilised town, a boy disciple at his side imitating his every movement, a wagon passes in the opposite direction filled with young girls singing Frenchy's first song, 'Little Joe'. Dietrich brings to the film the theme of song/dance as a positive return of the repressed characteristic of the musical, and in so doing generates an ambivalence within the film's definition of the old town from which it never recovers.

(4) Any set of star vehicles reveals recurrent thematic and stylistic features whose particular operation and development are indeed determined by the presence of the star. There are, however, crucial distinctions and discriminations to be made. As Charles Affron points out (*Star Acting* (E. P. Dutton, New York 1977), 95), the production of a *coup de théâtre* around the first appearance of the star's face is a characteristic rhetorical strophe in many Garbo movies, and this draws our attention to the particular value and significance of the face for that star persona. At the same time, this device is a specific inflection of the convention of the star entrance – consider, for example, the introduction of Hepburn in *Morning Glory*, Dietrich in *Shanghai Express*, Wayne in *Stagecoach*, Bogart in *Casablanca*. The potency of this convention allows for such remarkable effects as that produced at the beginning of *Now, Voyager*, the film

elaborately creating the expectation of an 'entrance' by Bette Davis which is then abruptly undermined. Conversely, some Garbo motifs – an emphasis, for instance, on the touching of and sensual communion with inanimate objects – are specific to Garbo. Father/daughter relationships are as central to Hepburn movies as they are rare in Garbo's (*Anna Christie* and *Queen Christina* are the key exceptions), and young wife/elderly husband relationships as characteristic of Garbo as they are foreign to Hepburn. Neither of these thematics makes much sense if we extrapolate it from the language of melodrama, or ignore the fact that such differences are a function of distinct, but reciprocal, interventions of the star vehicle *in* melodrama.

A shortened extract from chapter 6 of Andrew Britton's *Katharine Hepburn: the Thirties and After* (Newcastle upon Tyne, Tyneside Cinema, 1984).

16

SIGNS OF MELODRAMA
Christine Gledhill

It is perhaps no coincidence that critical interest in stars and in melodrama emerged at roughly the same time in the late seventies. A few intriguing suggestions have been offered as to their relationship – most notably Jean Loup Bourget's essay on Joan Crawford as a 'face of melodrama' and Andrew Britton's comments on Katharine Hepburn's tears[1] – but no sustained examination. This chapter starts from the hypothesis that stars function as signs in a rhetorical system which works as melodrama. It proceeds to explore this proposition by investigating the similarity of terms used in recent work on the two phenomena.

Melodrama most commonly refers either to a type of popular Victorian theatre long since superseded, or to Hollywood family melodrama which in its focus on the domestic and personal sphere is considered the province of women. If, however, we want to consider how stars relate to melodrama, the term is better conceived as a mode which embraces a range of Hollywood genres. There is ample precedent for this; nineteenth-century western melodrama, while most sharply codified on the stage, nevertheless produced not only widely divergent theatrical genres, ranging from the military to the domestic, but also a way of viewing the world which informed many areas of artistic and intellectual production. The relative invisibility of melodrama today is due to the rise of realism as a touchstone of cultural worth and to its ghettoisation as a women's form.[2] A major issue, then, for any attempt to understand the operation of the melodramatic mode in contemporary popular culture is its passage from the Victorian period into modern forms of film and television fiction. Arguably stars constitute an important mechanism in this process of transformation.

THE PERSON AND THE MELODRAMATIC PROJECT

'The Hollywood star system', Andrew Britton states, 'is an enormously sophisticated development of . . . [the] tradition of [melodramatic] character and performance, and is inconceivable without reference to it.'[3] In this respect a major conceptual link between melodrama and stardom is the centrality to both systems of the 'person'. Richard Dyer, for example, argues that stars appeal because they exemplify what it is like to be particular kinds of person,[4] while Thomas Elsaesser highlights the process of personalisation which is central to melodrama's treatment of social and ideological conflicts: 'The persistence of the melodrama might indicate the ways in which popular culture has ... resolutely refused to understand social change in other than private contexts and emotional terms.'[5]

Not surprisingly, writers on melodrama and on stars link this focus on the person to bourgeois ideology and its conceptual linch-pin, the individual. The ideology of individualism is also traditionally identified as the source of the novel. The novel, however, has largely been associated with realism as the mode through which a secular fictional world, constructed from the individual's point of view, sustains the imagination of bourgeois society. In many respects stars appear, as Richard Dyer notes, to epitomise the triumph of the novelistic bourgeois hero.[6] However, his comparison of novelistic character with both filmic character and star image suggests that neither are capable of rendering the full interiority and individuation demanded by realist standards. The element of typage remains too marked. Andrew Britton's provocative remarks invite us to look in a different direction to melodrama.

In tracing the genealogy of melodrama Thomas Elsaesser identifies two apparently contradictory tendencies. From the tradition that stems from the medieval morality play and folk ballad derives a 'non-psychological conception of the *dramatis personae*, who figure less as autonomous individuals than to transmit the action and link the various locales within a total constellation'. From the tradition derived from French post-Revolution romantic drama, Elsaesser notes 'the emphasis put on private feelings and interiorised (puritan, pietist) codes of morality and conscience'.[7] Thus a tension is posed between emblematic typage which is public and personalisation which stresses the private.

Peter Brooks's account of melodrama in *The Melodramatic Imagination* suggests that such tension arises from a contradictory demand for a mythic significance grounded in the real world.[8] Melodrama operates on the same terrain as realism – i.e. the secular world of bourgeois capitalism – but offers compensation for what realism displaces. According to Brooks the bourgeois revolution undermined the legitimacy of a sacred world order reflected in the hierarchy of church, monarch and state by a process of secularisation through which the individual became the centre of political and social arrangements. This shift has two consequences. It raises the political question of social control in an order based on the primacy of the individual. And it opens an existential gap in terms of meaning and personal motivation. From this perspective, legitimation of the social order is not simply a political issue, but a psychic one: the newly emerging category of the individual has to incorporate within itself a motivating rationale capable of answering questions to do with commitment, justification and ultimate significance.

Thus the rise of melodrama is a response to the loss of credibility by the cultural forms which hitherto had performed this function, for example, allegory or tragedy. Its immediate historical task, Brooks argues, was to make present what he terms the 'moral occult . . . the repository of the fragmentary and desacralised remnants of sacred myth . . . the realm of meaning and value'.[9] Tied to the conventions of realism, but distrusting the adequacy of social codes and the conventions of representation elaborated during the Enlightenment, melodrama sets out to demonstrate within the transactions of everyday life the continuing operation of a Manichean battle between good and evil which infuses human actions with ethical consequences and therefore with significance.

In terms that describe the ground on which the star phenomenon will arise, Brooks argues that the only remaining source of moral value resides within the human personality itself:

> mythmaking could now only be individual, personal . . . the entity making the strongest claim to sacred status tends more and more to be the personality itself. From amid the collapse of other principles and criteria, the individual ego declares its central and overriding value, its demand to be the measure of all things.[10]

Here the 'person' as the source of desire and motivation is also in the post-sacred world the source of morality and ethics. This reading of morality in nineteenth-century melodrama prepares the way for the psychologisation of character and performance of twentieth-century popular culture: 'Ethical imperatives in the post-sacred universe have been sentimentalised, have come to be identified with emotional states and psychic relationships, so that the expression of emotional and moral integers is indistinguishable.'[11]

The person also, as Andrew Britton notes, holds a social position defined by the 'isolation of certain class and sexual features in a cryptic and compacted form'.[12] Age, race and ethnicity contribute equally emblematic features. However, as Britton's formulation suggests, the personae of melodrama are typed in a different way and to a different end from the social typage of the classic realist novel. In the latter, the accumulation of social detail around individualised characters serves to lead the reader from the individual outwards to the social network within which they take up their position as types. In melodrama this process is reversed. The emblematic types of melodrama lead not outward to society but inward to where social and ideological pressures impact on the psychic: as Brooks argues, in the melodramatic world view 'personality alone is the effective vehicle of transindividual messages'.[13]

Internalisation, however, does not imply the interiority and complexity of the rounded character. Peter Brooks amplifies this apparent paradox:

> There is no 'psychology' in melodrama in this sense; the characters have no interior depth. . . . It is delusive to seek an interior conflict, the 'psychology of melodrama'; because melodrama exteriorizes conflict and psychic structure, producing instead what we might call the 'melodrama of psychology'.[14]

Internalisation of the social is accompanied by a process of exteriorisation in which emotional states or moral conditions are expressed as the actions of melodramatic types. As Robert Heilman notes, dramatic conflict is not enacted *within* such characters, but *between* them and external forces, whether these be 'persons, groups, events, nature'.[15] This double movement of internalisation and exteriorisation explains the paradoxical conjunction in melodramatic character of the emblematic and the personal, of the public and the private, implied by Thomas Elsaesser's two traditions.

MELODRAMATIC PERSONIFICATION AND STARS

The construction of stars exhibits many features found in the dramatis personae of melodrama. Melodramatic characterisation is performed through a process of personification whereby actors – and fictional characters conceived as actors in their diegetic world – *embody* ethical forces. 'Melodramatic good and evil are highly personalised. . . . Most notably, evil is villainy; it is a swarthy, cape-enveloped man with a deep voice.'[16] Here moral forces are expressions of personality, externalised in a character's physical being, in gesture, dress and above all in action. This resort to the body coincides with eighteenth-century theories of expressivity which saw in the spontaneities of movement, gesture, facial expression and inarticulate vocal sounds a 'natural', and therefore more authentic language which could bypass the constraints of socio-linguistic convention. Gesture reveals what words conceal. Thus, since in the melodramatic regime, 'good and evil are moral feelings',[17] gesture becomes a major link between ethical forces and personal desires. Such theories influenced painters and performance modes and in the nineteenth century were popularised in a range of acting manuals, published throughout the decade, which, paradoxically perhaps, attempted to codify a repertoire of gesture and movement according to different emotional states and moral conditions as they intersected with gender and social class.[18]

Star personae are constructed in very similar ways. Stars reach their audiences primarily through their bodies. Photography, and especially the close-up, offers audiences a gaze at the bodies of stars closer and more sustained than the majority of real-life encounters.[19] Bela Balázs, in particular, theorises the close-up on the actor's face as a 'window on the soul' which 'can find a tongue more candid and uninhibited than in any spoken soliloquy, for it speaks instinctively, subconsciously. The languages of the face cannot be suppressed or controlled.'[20]

Colin McArthur argues that the meanings of stars are offered through 'qualities that are almost entirely physical: the way the actor is built, what his [sic] face and body say about the way experience has treated him, the way he walks and talks'.[21] As with melodramatic character, these qualities are selected and heightened to produce an emblematic effect. Lawrence Alloway writes of stars as 'maximised types'. 'In the movies we are faced with figures that embody in terms of contemporary references maximum states of age, beauty, strength, revenge, or whatever.'[22]

Melodrama's mode of personification is not only a question of facial expression and gesture. Nicholas Vardac's examination of nineteenth-century prompt books reveals how melodrama subordinates character to narrative action, staging devices, lighting effects and theatrical *mise en scène* – in other words, to visual rather than to verbal effects. As an example, he describes Henry Irving's 'spectacular entrances into spectacular pictures' as a mode of pictorial characterisation essentially cinematic in nature.[23] Star personae offer similar pictorial beings, staged for the camera both off- and on-screen, with appropriate settings, dress and accoutrements. The entrance of a star into a filmic fiction is frequently subject to a build up on both narrative and pictorial levels, playing on audience expectation and catering to a similar pictorial pleasure.

MELODRAMATIC IDENTITIES AND STARS

In Peter Brooks's account of melodramatic aesthetics, the goal of personification is the production of clear psychic and moral identities: 'the play's outcome turns less on the triumph of virtue than on making the world morally legible.'[24] In this respect, melodrama is a drama of misrecognition and clarification, the climax of which is an act of 'nomination' in which characters finally declaim their true identities, demanding a public recognition till then thwarted by deliberate deceptions, hidden secrets, binding vows and loyalties. For example, at the end of the American melodrama, *The Drunkard* (1844), Cribbs, a corrupt lawyer who is finally exposed, announces his overriding motives:

> CRIBBS. Revenge and avarice, the master-passions of my nature! With my heart's deepest, blackest feelings, I hated the father of Edward Middleton . . .
> RENCELAW. Repentance may yet avail you –
> CRIBBS. Nothing. I have lived a villain; a villain let me die![25]

Thus melodramatic character offers emblematic and at the same time intimate personifications of psychic states and moral identities. Robert

Heilman describes such characters as monopathic, exhibiting 'singleness of feeling' as opposed to the divided self of the tragic hero. The melodramatic persona is totally committed to living out his or her dominant desires, despite moral and social taboo or inter-personal conflict.

These features of melodramatic identity are replicated in the personae of film stars which promise expression of and access to clearly articulated personal identities. Colin McArthur, for example, speaks of Kirk Douglas and Richard Widmark's 'compulsively modern sensibilities and physical presence which best fit them for neurotic or even psychotic roles'.[26] Hollywood films frequently exploit such knowledge in order to replay the melodrama of misrecognition and revelation. In the organ-transplant thriller, *Coma*, the suppressed menace contained within Widmark's silver-haired, paternalistic Chief of Surgery is finally revealed when, his conspiracy to auction human organs uncovered, he declaims the logic of capitalist medicine and, like Cribbs in *The Drunkard*, espouses his identity as villain.

The star vehicle frequently places its star in a role which initially withholds the full persona. In many Clint Eastwood films, for example, the film opens on a downtrodden, apparently defeated figure. The audience waits for the frisson of the character becoming Clint Eastwood.[27] A notorious example of this strategy occurs in *Now, Voyager* which opens with Bette Davis as a repressed, dowdy spinster in the throes of a nervous breakdown. Later in the film, she undergoes a butterfly-like transformation, and ends by assuming the full power of the Davis persona. In such cases the star structure contains within it the drama of recognition. This is illustrated in the star biography which focuses on the persona before stardom and the gradual emergence of the identity which will bring a public following: from Norma Jean Baker to Marilyn Monroe.

EXCESS

Notoriously, the production of melodramatic identities involves excess of expression: hyperbolic emotions, extravagant gesture, high-flown sentiments, declamatory speech, spectacular settings and so on. Star personae produce similar excesses in the filmic realisation of starring roles, in their high living off-screen life styles and in fans' and critics' responses:

> Charlton Heston is an axiom. He constitutes a tragedy in himself, his presence in any film being enough to instil beauty. The pent-up violence expressed by the sombre phosphorescence of his eyes, his eagle's profile, the imperious arch of his eyebrows, his prominent cheekbones, the hard, bitter curve of his lips, the stupendous strength of his torso: this is what he has been given, and what not even the worst of directors can debase.[28]

Peter Brooks explains such excess as the product of the conflict between melodramatic desire and repression which is a central feature of the secular, post-Enlightenment and protestant world.[29] Since there is no empirical evidence for the moral occult, it must be asserted in the face of linguistic, social, psychic and institutional constraint, and consequently often through non-verbal means. Ethical imperatives emerge at the point that human desires engage in the struggle for expression, producing an excess of the signifier – through visual metaphor, gesture or emblematic speech – and making 'large but unsubstantiable claims on meaning'.[30] Michel Mourlet defends the violence of such an aesthetic in Hollywood which 'represents the pursuit of happiness through the drama of the body'.[31] The process of exteriorisation involved in melodramatic and star personification supports this aesthetic by short-circuiting the constraints of linguistic coding and social decorum attendant on verbal language and psychological character construction.

Melodramatic excess exists in paradoxical relation to the form's commitment to the real world. The star system works with similar paradoxes. If the excessive moment in melodrama infuses ordinary characters and relationships with excitement and significance, stars represent ordinary people whose ordinary joys and sorrows become extraordinary in the intensity stardom imparts to them. If melodrama, while confirming the boundaries of social convention, derives its energy through the villain's willingness to break them, the star system promotes model domestic lives irradiated by exciting hints of scandal.

STARDOM FROM STAGE TO SCREEN

Richard Dyer locates the beginning of the star phenomenon in the eighteenth century in an age of emerging individualism when well-known actors began to promote their own personalities and skills as performers along with their roles, arguing that the sense of personality at work in the performance increased the realism of the characterisation.[32] However, it is as performer that the personality of the actor gains renown, making it possible to name character performances after the actor: Garrick's Hamlet, Kean's Richard III and so on. Stardom proper arises when the off-stage or off-screen life of the actor becomes as important as the performed role in the production of a semi-autonomous persona or image, a development which depends on mass circulation journalism and photography.

This slippage between the player's performance of a role and the player's private life suggests an intensification of the process of personalisation in which the relation between the emblematic, moral schemae of melodrama and social reality is recast. In the first instance, the star's attachment to a living, historical person provides an authentication – to use Richard Dyer's term – of what is proposed in the melodramatic persona. Naturalism, realism, authenticity became key terms at the turn of the century, when the theatre sought to reclaim literary and critical respectability and melodrama was denigrated as amusement fit only for children and women. However, as I have noted, realist and melodramatic aesthetics are not antithetical. Rather, they represent different approaches to shared ideological and cultural conditions. During the nineteenth century they developed in tandem in what Nicholas Vardac describes as a 'romantic-realist' aesthetic. He argues that cinema offered superior technological means of achieving the realist representation of romantic fantasy.[33] However, once established, cinema looked to develop the cultural prestige that would attract higher price middle-class audiences, and this entailed the transformation and modernisation of melodramatic practices and themes in line with the prestige of the New Drama and naturalism, changing social mores and new criteria of verisimilitude. The star was a key figure in this process.[34]

For, if, as Peter Brooks contends, a major goal of the melodramatic imagination is the location of signs of a 'moral occult', this must be an on-going process in which new terms are elaborated for new audiences. Arguably, the major technological, social and political changes of the last decades of the nineteenth century made such a shift urgent. Benjamin McArthur's account of the rise of American theatrical stardom suggests how stars contributed to this readjustment. Given the puritan proscription on drama as a deceiving and immoral activity, actors had lived on the margins of American society. This changed at the end of the century, when increasing journalistic attention was paid to theatrical stars. McArthur links this to 'the fin-de-siècle defiance of Victorian norms [which] meant a questioning not only of traditional pieties and social amenities, but more fundamentally of authority itself'.[35] This parallels a similar rejection of nineteenth-century melodramatic personifications which enshrined the sedimented values of a now ossified bourgeois morality. But as this happened, the rising mass media found a new mode of contemporary personification in the figure of the star who embodies social values and identities under reconstruction. Thus, McArthur argues, actors took over the functions of the church and establishment as 'exemplars of morality and lifestyle'.[36] The notorious paradoxes of acting and stardom discussed above (p. 213) gave scope to the desires and taboos of the ethical imagination.

Formally, the star as a composite structure is able to manage the tension between melodrama's emblematic, non-psychological personae and its drive to realise in personal terms social and ethical forces – a drive intensified by the increasing concern with realism towards the end of the nineteenth century. The components I am concerned with here include the 'real person', the 'characters' or 'roles' played by the star in films and the star's 'persona' which exists independently of real person or film character, combining elements of each in a public 'presence'. The real person is the site of amorphous and shifting bodily attributes, instincts, psychic drives and experiences. In contrast, the film character or role is relatively formed and fixed by fictional and stereotypical conventions. The persona, on the other hand, forms the private life into a public and emblematic shape, drawing on general social types and film roles, while deriving authenticity from the unpredictability of the real person. The persona's attachment to a living person who is submitted to intense interrogation by the electronic media bypasses the need for novelistic psychologisation of character while hanging on to the emblematic dimension necessary to melodramatic identity.

Genre is crucial to these exchanges between real person, star persona and melodramatic character. As Paul Willemen notes, genre elaborates a second order reality, in which verisimilitude depends on the internal rules of the particular genre in question.[37] Like melodramatic personae, the characters of genre are governed by the forces that control their particular generic world. They 'personify' its values and imperatives. Generic roles and star personae are produced through similar processes of repetition, differentiation, sedimentation and interchange. Colin McArthur argues that:

> Men such as Cagney, Robinson and Bogart seem to gather within themselves the qualities of the genres they appear in so that the violence, suffering and *angst* of the films is restated in their faces, physical presence, movement and speech ... each successive appearance in the genre further solidifies the actor's screen persona until he no longer plays a role but assimilates it to the collective entity made up of his own body and personality and his past screen roles. For instance, the beat-up face, tired eyes and rasping voice by which we identify Humphrey Bogart are, in part, selections we have made from his roles as Sam Spade, Philip Marlowe and others.[38]

THE MORAL OCCULT AND IDEOLOGY

Richard Dyer states that 'although stars and films are commodities, their only "value" (i.e. what people *use* them *for*) resides in what meanings and affects they have. Stars/films sell meanings and affects.'[39] As representations of persons, stars 'relate to ideas about what people are (or are supposed to be) like'.[40] In his argument, the emblematic dimension of the star condenses less moral than social and ideological values. This stems in part from association through 'type-casting' with particular social or generic types – James Dean, rebel; Marilyn Monroe, dumb-blonde – and in part from the process of embodiment derived from melodramatic personification. 'Stars', Richard Dyer suggests, 'seem actually to possess or even to be the values in question.'[41] For example, Colin McArthur describes 'the kicked-around, lived-in face, the slender, rather puny body, the rasping voice, the gritty humour' of Humphrey Bogart as embodying 'a decidedly modern, urbanised presence and sensibility'.[42]

To what degree do such personifications represent the working of a contemporary 'moral occult'?

> Good and evil can be named as persons are named – and melodramas tend in fact to move toward a clear nomination of the moral universe. The ritual of melodrama involves the confrontation of clearly identified antagonists and the expulsion of one of them.[43]

The significations offered by stars may not represent such bald moral tokens and simple polarities. But in personalising contemporary values, stars are frequently cast in terms of ideological oppositions. For example, the roles of Burt Lancaster and Kirk Douglas in *I Walk Alone* as described by Lawrence Alloway:

> Burt Lancaster is an ex-convict but a loyal friend with a code of honour; by contrast Kirk Douglas is socially acceptable but faithless and corrupt. The two men are maximised symbols, one . . . for old-fashioned entrepreneurial elan (Lancaster as the good boot-legger), and one for modern executive skills (Douglas as corrupt behind a corporate shield).[44]

Here not only do star personae oppose each other; they are played off against film roles. In this way the composite star structure embodies the contradictions of capitalism. This strategy both offers the frisson of moral conflict and permits a more complex ethical articulation.

The difficulty of assigning absolute moral value under the regime of contemporary psychological realism is reflected in the ambiguities condensed in a single star persona. For instance, Colin McArthur's description of Bogart's 'kicked-around, lived-in face' suggests the shift from Victorian Biblical to post-Freudian psychoanalytic and sociological sources of characterisation and ethical value. The Bogart persona, however, makes ambivalence itself an emblem, retaining the clarifying function of melodrama. As Peter Brooks argues of modern film and television genres:

> It is not that melodramatic conflict has been interiorized and refined to the vanishing point, but on the contrary that psychology has been externalized, made accessible and immediate through a full realization of its melodramatic possibilities.[45]

Star personae in their capacity to make emblematic aspects of the lived, contradictory, ambiguous and ultimately unknowable person – which the logic of realism pushes towards a modernist stream of consciousness – facilitate this externalisation of psychological ethics.

Richard Dyer suggests, 'that stars are representations of persons which reinforce, legitimate or occasionally alter the prevalent conceptions of what it is to be a human being in this society'.[46] Thus far I have discussed the role of such personae in films. However, major sites for elaborating star personae exist outside films in studio promotion departments, publicity agencies, newspaper and broadcast journalism, TV chat shows, film criticism, fan magazines and so on.[47] The circulation of subsidiary star texts provides opportunity for gossip and speculation, serving, in John Ellis's words, as a kind of 'moral barometer'.[48]

Through this subsidiary circulation, a fourth component of the star structure, the 'image' is spun off from the persona and film roles, both condensing and dispersing desires, meanings, values and styles that are current in the culture. However, this range of meaning-producing agencies and the internally composite structure of the star mean that the image itself is fragmented and open to contradiction. Thomas Elsaesser suggests that the melodramatic imagination becomes particularly active during periods of intense ideological crisis.[49] In parallel terms Richard Dyer argues that the intensity of star–audience relations – their charisma – lies in their embodiment of ideological contradiction, suggesting that the rise of particular stars can be traced to their condensation of values felt to be under threat or in flux at a particular moment in time. Thus the Monroe image enacts the contradictions between sex and innocence during a period of male-led permissiveness. Dyer deploys notions such as reinforcement, negotiation, contradiction or resistance to analyse the ideological relations between different aspects of the star's image.[50] Such terms grasp stars in their contradictoriness and ambiguity while acknowledging their drive as melodramatic personae towards emblematic monopathy. Stars in this perspective are figures whose fragmentation can make them sites of ideological contestation – of struggle to redefine the 'moral occult' for different social groups.

THE MYTH OF IDENTITY

'The melodramatic utterance breaks through everything that constitutes the "reality principle", all its censorships, accommodations, tonings-down. Desire cries aloud its language in identification with full states of being.'[51] Peter Brooks's description of the identities offered by melodrama as 'full states of being' belongs to an aesthetics committed to 'plenitude' and 'presence'. Robert Heilman describes the pleasures of such representations as 'the sensation of wholeness that is created when one responds with a single impulse or potential which functions as if it were his [sic] whole personality'.[52] 'Presence' is a term used frequently of stars – for example the title of Colin McArthur's article, 'The Real Presence'.[53] Such terms figure pejoratively in cine-psychoanalytic evaluations of the classic narrative cinema as an evasion of the illusions of language and self. Peter Brooks describes melodrama's response to this problem:

We might, finally, do well to recognise the melodramatic mode as a central fact of the modern sensibility . . . in that modern art has typically felt itself to be constructed on, and over, the void, postulating meanings and symbolic systems which have no certain justification because they are backed by no theology and no universally accepted social code.[54]

If realism presumes the adequacy of given linguistic and cultural codes for understanding and representing reality, and modernism embraces the infinite regress of meaning in the self-reflexive play of the signifier, melodrama's rootedness in the real world, its urgent ideological mission to motivate ordinary lives, leads it into an opposing stance. Faced with the decentred self, the evasiveness of language, melodrama answers with excessive personalisation, excessive expression.

Richard Dyer's discussion of authenticity in this volume (pp. 132–40) suggests that stardom is similarly a response to the decentred self of modernism, offering an outlet for melodramatic 'presence' in contemporary terms. Dyer notes a shift in the basis of morality from 'general criteria governing social behaviour' to 'the performers themselves' and that 'the criteria governing performance have shifted from whether the performance is well done to whether it is truthful, that is, true to the "true" personality of the performer'.[55] Truthfulness, Dyer notes, is now referred not to moral precepts but to the 'person's "person"'. In other words the melodramatic demand for clearly defined identity has shifted from fictional to star personae who offer the advantage of authenticating the moral drama in reference to a real person outside the fiction. As in melodrama, expression of star identity is impeded by social constraints – in this case, media manufacture and hype.

> The basic paradigm is just this – that what is behind or below the surface is, unquestionably and virtually by definition, the truth. Thus features of stars which tell us that the star is *not* like he or she appears to be on screen serve to reinforce the authenticity of the star image as a whole.[56]

In this respect, the star represents a maximised type of the person itself, authenticating personality in a culture which at many levels undercuts the power or validity of the person as either theoretical concept or political subject. Star authentication refers less to a generally available reality than to a melodramatic demand that the person make him or herself materially present.

However, the fragmentation of the image arising from its circulation through disparate image-making industries leads John Ellis to question whether stars produce coherent identities at all.[57] Stars represent 'gestures' at identity, engineered largely to entice audiences to consume narratives for the price of a cinema seat in the hope of access to the image in its illusory wholeness and coherence. At the heart of this cine-psychoanalytic argument is the delusion of the 'photo-effect' reduplicated in the star. For, paradoxically, the star, more overwhelmingly present than any actor can be to a theatre audience, is also not, and never can be, there for the audience to cinema. This poignant 'presence in absence' lies at the heart of the desires stimulated by stardom. But it is a genuine paradox in which presence can be understood not as simple mystification but as an assertion by the melodramatic imagination in the face of absence. To argue that star images have no substance outside of film fiction is to ignore the function of social typage, of the cumulative and extra-filmic work of genre discussed above (p. 217) and the process of reiteration in the star-creating media themselves. For in the endlessly circulated 'facts', dicta and gossip of feature articles, studio publicity and interviews can be discerned a drive to produce neither the subtle, differentiated, multilayered character of the realist novel, nor random jottings on famous people, but specified, monopathic presences, who hold up to their audiences magnified yet deeply personalised identities and states of – frequently contradictory – being.

PRESENCE AND PERFORMANCE: FROM MELODRAMA TO METHOD

Presence in film arises from a combination of two aesthetic factors: the indexical nature of photography discussed by John Ellis, which provides images on the basis of the photographed object 'once having really been there'; and the art of performance.

Melodramatic acting constituted a performance mode adapted to the work of internalisation and externalisation. Informed, as I have noted, by eighteenth-century theories of gestural language, and drawing on traditions of pantomime, harlequinade and acrobatics, melodramatic performance sought objectification of internal emotions and motivations in bodily action and vocal declamation, incorporating personal emotion in public gesture. By the late nineteenth century, however, the rise of the New Drama, with its more literary, analytical and naturalist bent and the influential growth of psychology and related disciplines, all of which catered to the tastes of a growing middle-class audience, defined a shift in character construction and performance mode.[58] Characters referred less to pre-existing types; their particularity strove for the illusion of random individuality. A new set of techniques based on psychology and observation from life, valued restraint, underplaying and subtlety and sought to displace what seemed now the limitations of pantomimic ritual and rhetorical dialogue in order to convey the inner life and private personality of the characters. This shift in realist values brought changes in the style of

PRACTICAL ILLUSTRATIONS

OF

𝕽𝖍𝖊𝖙𝖔𝖗𝖎𝖈𝖆𝖑 𝕲𝖊𝖘𝖙𝖚𝖗𝖊 𝖆𝖓𝖉 𝕬𝖈𝖙𝖎𝖔𝖓;

ADAPTED TO

THE ENGLISH DRAMA:

FROM A WORK ON THE SUBJECT BY M. ENGEL,

MEMBER OF THE ROYAL ACADEMY OF BERLIN.

BY HENRY SIDDONS.

𝕰𝖒𝖇𝖊𝖑𝖑𝖎𝖘𝖍𝖊𝖉 𝖜𝖎𝖙𝖍 𝕾𝖎𝖝𝖙𝖞=𝖓𝖎𝖓𝖊 𝕰𝖓𝖌𝖗𝖆𝖛𝖎𝖓𝖌𝖘,

EXPRESSIVE OF THE VARIOUS PASSIONS, AND REPRESENTING THE MODERN
COSTUME OF THE LONDON THEATRES.

𝕾𝖊𝖈𝖔𝖓𝖉 𝕰𝖉𝖎𝖙𝖎𝖔𝖓, 𝕴𝖒𝖕𝖗𝖔𝖛𝖊𝖉.

LONDON:

PRINTED FOR SHERWOOD, NEELY, AND JONES,

PATERNOSTER ROW.

1822.

Figure 16.1

American melodramatic production which were crucial to the transfer of the melodramatic imagination from stage to screen.

Key figures in this process were the American actor-playwright-producers, Steele MacKaye and David Belasco. Both were masters of 'intricate and spectacular staging of popular romantic and melodramatic plays',[59] yet responded to demands for increased psychological realism with a scaled-down performance style employing itemised stage business and small detailed gestures. Steele MacKaye, who was involved in establishing the first American acting schools, made a highly influential adaptation of an acting system codified by the Frenchman, François Delsarte (1811–71), which, according to James Naremore and Susan Roberts, was to have a lasting effect on American film performance. Delsarte's system offered an elaborate analysis of facial and bodily gesture defining 'minute changes in expression for the voice and every major expressive part of the body'.[60] This system, combined with character and life study, aimed to enable actors to attain complete 'spontaneity', 'liberating inner feelings'.[61] Although still stressing the actor's skill and control over emotional depiction in what remained largely a pictorial approach to performance, the emphasis on intimate detail provided considerable opportunity for the insertion of the actor's personality into character production.[62] And access to a recognisable personality, who reappeared in different roles, fed the journalism that produced stardom.

By the early twenties, however, the work of Constantin Stanislavski was known in America. Under the influence of his ideas, the emphasis on the external pictorial details of stage business began to wane in favour of the goal of 'inner life', achieved by psychological analysis of character in a given dramatic structure. It is by now well documented that only a part of the Stanislavski system was taken into American acting ideology, principally his ideas concerning 'affective memory' whereby actors were trained to use their own emotions and experience to plumb the depths of dramatic character. Notoriously, Lee Strasberg's extension of this technique as 'the Method', which was promulgated at the Group Theatre and later in modified form at The Actors' Studio, virtually dissolved the boundary between acting and psychotherapy. Although known as a means of increasing realism, the declared aims and techniques of the Method once more drew realism towards melodramatic concerns.

James Naremore quotes Lee Strasberg's belief that 'the actor need not imitate a human being. The actor is himself a human being and can create out of himself.'[63] This notion draws on the popularisation of Freudian psychoanalysis in America in the forties and fifties and participates in the

Figure 16.2 Sir Martin-Harvey as Sydney Carton in *The Only Way* (1899)

search for authenticity described by Richard Dyer. Richard Blum contrasts the Method to the Stanislavski system in the following terms: 'Stanislavski stressed imagination as the core of acting, and sought emotional truth from the text of the play. Strasberg sought emotional truth from the unconscious of the actor.'[64] In order to achieve this, actors must break with their own inhibitions in relation not only to what is demanded by the play but in terms of their private lives. Strasberg developed the use

Figure 16.3 Marlon Brando in *A Streetcar Named Desire* (1951)

of affective memory – 'probing into the unconscious life of the actor'[65] – and improvisation as techniques for reaching the ultimate goal of the Method: the merging of self and character. Since in this perspective, the unconscious and emotion constitute the essence of the personal self, Method actors were trained to rely 'more on the devices of gesture, expression and stance, and less upon memorised dialogue and props to communicate the point of the action'.[66] Such techniques suggest a return

223

to the primal and ineffable gesture that underpins melodramatic acting for the access it offers to hidden moral drives and desires. Like the melodramatic persona, the Method actor *embodies* conflicts, if not in terms of public rhetoric, then through an equally codifiable set of personal mannerisms, nervous ticks, inarticulate mumblings and so on.

'The Method' proved highly adaptable to characterisation and acting in film. If the character analysis and inner complexity which depends on restrained performance, introspective dialogue and dramatic structure is difficult to achieve in Hollywood cinema, this lack of interiority is offset by the paradoxically intimate relations with the actor's body afforded by cinematography. The ideology of camera as observer and the face as window to the soul opened up new significatory possibilities in terms of the inwardness and personality of the performer. Barry King speaks of the 'hypersemiotic' increase of gestural meaning whereby everything an actor is or does is, when recorded by the camera, potentially meaningful.[67] In this respect, the Method is the contemporary performance mode most able to deliver 'presence', the goal at the heart of both melodrama and stardom. Richard Blum has documented the work of disciples of the Stanislavski system in Hollywood during the thirties and forties and later the influence of the Method via the Actors' Studio which in the fifties supplied directors such as Elia Kazan and Nicholas Ray and trained or influenced a wide range of actors who were to become Hollywood stars, notably Montgomery Clift, Marlon Brando and James Dean.[68]

In contrast to the Stanislavski approach which stressed ensemble playing, the Method clearly supports star performances which as James Naremore points out are regarded as 'little more than fictional extensions of the actors' true personalities'.[69] The intense focus on the personal psychology of the actor fostered the larger-than-life dimension of stardom and brought with it accusations of self-indulgence and elitism. Richard Blum, quoting Walter Kerr, describes the consequent evolution of the Method from the ' "low-keyed naturalism" of the Group Theatre in the thirties to the "open fire" of the Actors' Studio in the fifties, from "prosy accuracy" to "rhythmic power" '.[70] The Method also, in contradistinction to the Stanislavski system, supported type-casting which Strasberg maintained 'eased the merger process of self with character'.[71] Blum quotes Strasberg's admiration of actors such as Gary Cooper, John Wayne and Spencer Tracy who 'try not to act but to be themselves, to respond or react. They refuse to do or say anything they feel not to be consonant with their own characters.'[72] Proclaiming its source in the actor's real self, the Method naturalises the personifying function of melodrama and the star.

The psychoanalytic dimension of the Method coalesced with Hollywood Freud to provide intimations of unseen, unconscious forces that activate the psyche and give rise to conflicting desires and emotions. Richard Blum quotes Kazan as saying: 'The key word, if I had to pick one, is "to want".

We used to say in the theatre, "What are you on stage *for*? What do you walk on stage to get? What do you want?" [73] Getting at such wants means, as for melodrama, penetrating the surface of psychic constraint, social convention and linguistic limitation. In describing the 'rhetoric of authenticity', Richard Dyer defines three founding elements: lack of control, lack of premeditation and privacy. These are common to the ideology of both Method acting and melodrama. They derive from 'notions of the truth being behind or beneath the surface. The surface is organised and under control, it is worked out in advance, it is public . . . just what we don't get when authenticity is at stake.' [74] Thus the Method provides both modern outlet and renewed authentication for the primacy and ethical reach of melodramatic emotion through the techniques which permit access to the workings of unconscious conflicts and desires. At the same time a new inflection is given to the internalisation of social forces characteristic of the melodramatic and star persona:

> Brando, Montgomery Clift, Julie Harris, Eli Wallach, Patricia Neal, Kim Hunter, Anthony Perkins, Rod Steiger, and the other Method performers who emerged in the fifties are best in divided parts based on the unresolved tension between an outer social mask and an inner reality of frustration. [75]

The rationalisations of the rising social and psychological therapies which popularised notions of delinquency, maternal deprivation and social inadequacy provide the melodramatic imagination with a new articulation of the moral occult, recasting the terms of the struggle: it is now the existence of an individual self that is at stake. To this inflection of melodramatic conflict, the Method provided star actors in whose persona the social threatens the self not so much with violent destruction as with nonentity, meaninglessness.

THE MELODRAMATIC AUDIENCE AND STARDOM

If melodrama sentimentalises ethics, at the same time it constructs a new form of audience participation with an appeal to its sympathetic emotions in the working out of poetic justice. As Andrew Britton comments: 'melodrama appeals very directly to our affiliation to, or rejection of, its actants on the basis of the objective social conflicts to which they refer and of which they represent a particular resolution.' [76] In analysing the structure of melodramatic pathos, Thomas Elsaesser suggests that it permits both identification and critical distance. In this structure social and economic contradictions are internalised as the dilemmas of non-psychological, non-introspective, monopathic victims and externalised as inarticulate gesture, overdetermined declamation and expressionist *mise en scène*. Such signs, though not part of the characters' consciousness, are available to the audience who is thereby possessed of more knowledge than the melo-drama's struggling victims. Pathos, then, unlike pity, both draws the audi-ence into the character's dilemma in an act of recognition and empathy and distances the audience in the act of criticising the circumstances which produce that dilemma.

Arguably the star produces a similar pathos. The first promise of the star is access to the personality itself. At the same time the visibility of the star system and the operation of fictional and generic structures empha-sise the economic, social and cultural forces that make such access an illusion. The excess of stardom represents a melodramatic response in the face of this dilemma:

> Like the acting of classical theatrical melodrama, Hollywood star acting is inclined to excess. Obviously, the principle of 'typage' persists – Cagney, Robinson and Bogart all manifest 'gangstericity' – but accompanied by a principle of particularisation, the constant re-inscription of the persona: besides 'gangstericity', Cagney displays 'Cagneyness'.[77]

Excess is produced by the insistence on an identity, a personal monopathy.

Second, the star in condensing select social values becomes him or herself a theatre for the enactment of conflicting forces much in the manner of the melodramatic persona described by Peter Brooks: 'Man [sic] is seen to be, and must recognise himself to be, playing on a theatre that is the point of juncture, and of clash, of imperatives beyond himself that are non-mediated and irreducible.'[78] If in melodrama the theatre is a public space, and its conflicting forces embodied in opposing personae, in the star the personality itself is theatricalised, with conflict taking place within and around the persona. Richard Dyer argues that the particularity of the star may introduce into the type he or she embodies elements which take the type in a new direction, bring out repressed elements or introduce and expose contradictions. The public debates over the Clint Eastwood persona, which, Dyer suggests, exposes contradictions through 'the male fascist, isolate pitch to which . . . [he] . . . has taken the tough guy image',[79] exemplify the way the star theatricalises moral identities, redefining the terms of the moral occult.

However, given the continuous process of renewal and modernisation which must be undergone by cultural forms, Eastwood belongs to the emblematic end of the spectrum of melodramatic/star personae. In terms of the shifts effected by the Method and the greater psychologisation of star personae, melodrama's 'large but insubstantiable claims on meaning'[80] are asserted against the very absence of social imperatives. James Dean's parents in *Rebel Without A Cause* have done little but tiresomely bicker when he thumps the table and yells, 'They're tearing me apart.' The claim, carried in the nervous energy and expressionism of performance, star

226

persona and *mise en scène*, is posed against the inadequacy of the opposition. The film itself represents a search for a means of personalising the polar clash through which ethical commitments can be made. Nicholas Ray's settings – the planetarium, the car floodlit cliff-top for the chickie run and Plato's gothic mansion – seek to provide the theatrical spaces in which limited beings can become stars, personifications of overriding imperatives. Today, when the highly publicised conditions of stardom dramatise the opposition of self and public role, it is, perhaps, stardom itself as a source of identity and meaning which is the goal of authentication.[81]

NOTES

1   J. Bourget, 'Faces of the American melodrama: Joan Crawford', *Film Reader*, 3 (1978), and A. Britton, *Katharine Hepburn: The Thirties and After* (Newcastle upon Tyne: Tyneside Cinema, 1984), an extract from which appears as chapter 15 in this volume.

2   I have discussed these issues more fully in 'The melodramatic field: an investigation', in C. Gledhill (ed.), *Home Is Where the Heart Is* (London: British Film Institute, 1987).

3   Britton, op. cit., 102.

4   R. Dyer, *Stars* (London: British Film Institute, 1979).

5   T. Elsaesser, 'Tales of sound and fury', in Gledhill, op. cit., 47.

6   Dyer, op. cit., 102.

7   Elsaesser, op. cit., 44, 45.

8   P. Brooks, *The Melodramatic Imagination* (New Haven: Yale University Press, 1976).

9   Brooks, op. cit., 4.

10   Brooks, op. cit., 16.

11   Brooks, op. cit., 42.

12   Britton, op. cit., 102.

13   Brooks, op. cit., 33.

14   Brooks, op. cit., 35–6.

15   R. Heilman, *Tragedy and Melodrama* (Seattle: University of Washington Press, 1968).

16   Brooks, op. cit., 16–17.

17   Brooks, op. cit., 54.

18   See L. James, 'Is Jerrold's Black-Eyed Susan more important than Wordsworth's Lucy?', in D. Bradby, L. James and B. Sharrat (eds), *Performance and Politics in Popular Drama* (Cambridge: Cambridge University Press, 1981).

19   See S. McKnight, *Star Dossier 3: Robert Redford* (London: BFI Education, 1989), for a discussion of the close-up in relation to Robert Redford.

20   Quoted in Dyer, op. cit., 17.

21   C. McArthur, 'The real presence', in R. Dyer, *Teachers' Study Guide 1: The Stars* (London: BFI Education, 1979), 99.

22   L. Alloway, *Violent America* (New York: Museum of Modern Art, 1971), 12.

23   N. Vardac, *Stage to Screen* (Cambridge, Mass.: Harvard University Press, 1949), 93–107.

24   Brooks, op. cit., 42.

25   J. L. Smith (ed.), *Victorian Melodramas* (London: Dent, 1976), 136–7.

26 McArthur, op. cit., 101.
27 I am indebted to Angela Martin for her comments on Clint Eastwood.
28 M. Mourlet, 'In defence of violence', in this volume, chapter 17, 233–6.
29 Brooks, op. cit., 41.
30 Brooks, op. cit., 199.
31 Mourlet, chapter 17.
32 Dyer, *Stars*, op. cit., 102.
33 Vardac, op. cit. For a discussion of the relationship between melodrama and realism see also R. Altman, 'Dickens, Griffith, and film theory', *The South Atlantic Quarterly*, 88, 2 (Spring 1989), and J. Stratton, 'Watching the detectives: television melodrama and its genres', *Australasian Drama Studies*, 10 (April 1987).
34 See also R. deCordova in this volume, 17–29.
35 B. McArthur, *Actors and American Culture, 1880–1920* (Philadelphia: Temple University Press, 1984), 141.
36 Ibid.
37 P. Willemen, 'On realisms in the cinema', *Screen*, 13, 1 (Spring 1972).
38 C. McArthur, *Underworld USA* (London: Secker & Warburg, 1972), 24.
39 Dyer, *Teachers' Study Guide 1: The Stars*, op. cit., 18.
40 Dyer, *Stars*, op. cit., 22.
41 Dyer, *Teachers' Study Guide 1: The Stars*, op. cit., 19.
42 C. McArthur, 'The real presence', op. cit., 100.
43 Brooks, op. cit., 16–17.
44 Alloway, op. cit., 12.
45 Brooks, op. cit., 204.
46 Dyer, *Teachers' Study Guide 1: The Stars*, op. cit., 31.
47 Dyer, *Stars*, op. cit. See also Star Dossiers 1, 2, 3 on Marilyn Monroe, John Wayne and Robert Redford, published by the British Film Institute Education Department which contain packs of subsidiary textual and visual material.
48 J. Ellis, 'Stars as a cinematic phenomenon', in *Visible Fictions: Cinema, Television, Video* (London: Routledge & Kegan Paul, 1982).
49 Elsaesser, op. cit.
50 See R. Dyer, 'Charisma', in this volume, 57–9.
51 Brooks, op. cit., 41.
52 Heilman, op. cit., 84.
53 C. McArthur, 'The real presence', op. cit.
54 Brooks, op. cit., 21.
55 R. Dyer, '*A Star Is Born* and the construction of authenticity', in this volume, 132–40.
56 See above, 136.
57 Ellis, op. cit.
58 B. McArthur, op. cit., 183.
59 R. Blum, *American Film Acting: The Stanislavski Heritage* (Ann Arbor, Michigan: UMI Research Press, 1984), 7.
60 S. Roberts, 'Melodramatic performance signs', *Framework*, 32/3 (1986), 69.
61 B. McArthur, op. cit., 100, 102.
62 Ibid., 183–5.
63 J. Naremore, *Acting in the Cinema* (Berkeley: University of California Press, 1988), 18.
64 Blum, op. cit., 52.
65 Ibid.

66 T. Pauly, *An American Odyssey* (Philadelphia: Temple University Press, 1983), 23–4.
67 B. King, 'Articulating stardom', in this volume, 167–82.
68 Blum, op. cit.
69 Naremore, op. cit., 18.
70 Blum, op. cit., 60.
71 Ibid., 52.
72 Ibid.
73 Ibid., 63.
74 Dyer, '*A Star is Born* and the construction of authenticity', in this volume, 137.
75 T. R. Atkins quoted in Blum, op. cit., 65.
76 Britton, op. cit., 102.
77 Ibid., 103.
78 Brooks, op. cit., 13.
79 Dyer, *Stars*, 113.
80 Brooks, op. cit., 199.
81 For enthusiastic exchanges on this subject, I am indebted to Ian Hoare, who I hope will one day write much more on the link between stars and melodrama in general and on James Dean in particular.

Part IV

DESIRE, MEANING AND POLITICS

17

IN DEFENCE OF VIOLENCE

Michel Mourlet

Violence is a major theme in aesthetics. Past or present, latent or active, it is of its nature at the heart of every creative act, even at the very moment it is being denied. To deny that violence exists in a peaceable work is to acknowledge its presence in the deepest level, in the twisted limbs of the work's gestation and in the exercise of will which with fierce determination moulds the material into shape. Violence is decompression: arising out of a tension between the individual and the world, it explodes as the tension reaches its pitch, like an abscess bursting. It has to be gone through before there can be any repose. This is what makes it possible for me to say that every work of art contains violence, or at least postulates it, if art is a way of appeasing violence through its awareness of the terms of the conflict, and the power to resolve it which this knowledge confers.

Sometimes, cinema is talked about in these pages. Cinema is the art most attuned to violence, given that violence springs from man's actions, that moment when a pent-up force overflows and breaches the dam, an angry torrent smashing into anything that stands in its way. This moment, which the other art forms can only suggest or simulate, the camera catches naturally, taking up the torch which literature hands on. Stendhal is superior to Losey up to the point where in what he is describing the intention, the mental undercurrent, can pass to its incarnation in the material and objective world. It is precisely at this point that Losey becomes immeasurably superior to Stendhal.

Elevating the actor, *mise en scène* finds in violence a constant source of beauty. The hero breaks the spell, introducing into the malign order of the world his personal disorder, in his search for a harmony which is both more real and more elevated. What we are defining here is a particular kind of hero, and his name is Charlton Heston or Fernando Lamas, Robert Wagner or Jack Palance. A hero both cruel and noble, elegant and manly, a hero who reconciles strength with beauty (or, in Palance's case, a splendidly animal ugliness) and who represents the perfection of a lordly race, a hero made to conquer, made to portend or to experience the joys of the world. As an exercise in violence, conquest, pride, *mise en scène* in

233

its purest form comes near to what is sometimes called 'fascism', in so far as this word, through a doubtless interesting confusion, has overtones of the Nietzschean concept of a genuine morality as opposed to the conscience of idealists, hypocrites and slaves. To reject this search for a natural order, this zest for effective action, the radiance of victory, is to condemn oneself to understanding nothing of an art that represents the pursuit of happiness through the drama of the body. It takes the innocence of certain theological minds to find a political meaning in an entity which they see as replacing the devil, everywhere to be found with his pot of black paint.

Charlton Heston is an axiom. He constitutes a tragedy in himself, his presence in any film being enough to instil beauty. The pent-up violence expressed by the sombre phosphoresence of his eyes, his eagle's profile, the imperious arch of his eyebrows, the hard, bitter curve of his lips, the stupendous strength of his torso – this is what he has been given, and what not even the worst of directors can debase. It is in this sense that one can say that Charlton Heston, by his very existence and regardless of the film he is in, provides a more accurate definition of the cinema than films like *Hiroshima mon amour* or *Citizen Kane*, films whose aesthetic either ignores or repudiates Charlton Heston. Through him, *mise en scène* can confront the most intense of conflicts and settle them with the contempt of a god imprisoned, quivering with muted rage. In this sense, Heston is more a Langian than a Walshian hero.

For cinema offers us several kinds of violence. At the lowest level, that of Kazan, a frenziedly drunken puppet show whose consummate expression is the contemptible Karl Malden. This is the dominion of the fake, the adulterated, the artificial, the ludicrous nervous twitch. The puerility of intention vies with the ugliness of its expression, and one has no real sense of an actor among all this gratuitous excess, the experiences of a neurotic aesthete glued on to a puppet on a string who makes a noise when you press his belly-button.

The violence in Welles is more honest, even appears to be purely autobiographical; but it is cut back, niggardly, blocked, with no reverberations beyond the noisy commotion it likes making. It is like a child kicking the furniture when he bumps into it: a state of mind exemplified by the scene in which Citizen Kane applies himself to wrecking furniture. Blinded by his own personality, Welles can only make cardboard cut-outs to parade before us as he howls into the loudspeakers.

Let us pass over the violence of Buñuel, whose every expression, every passionate impulse has been at the service of ideas which since adolescence we have been unable to shake off. (How many of us discovered cinema because of him, or because of Welles, when we were sixteen or eighteen? But our ingratitude to ourselves, as well, knows no limit.)

A notch higher, Nicholas Ray offers an image of violence which is fuller, more sensual, more real, but alas unbridled:[1] not the immense pressure of a mass of water turning into a torrent when it is released, but a permanent flood, a swamp, James Mason forever on the edge of tears. A critic wrote some years ago that in a Ray film 'violence burns freely, a kind of aura surrounding the hero's actions; it is a violence that declaims rather than a violence that kills'. What this critic did not appreciate was that in what he intended as praise he had hit on the method of a *mise en scène* whose fuse is blown by constant overloading. Any genuine intensity becomes impossible; passion is unravelled into endless bits and pieces.

It is with Raoul Walsh that we encounter for the first time the true beauty of violence, an illumination of the passage of the hero, a manifestation of his power and his nobility, a moment of challenge. This clean, straight violence does not mark a defeat; it charts a road to victory. It is the violence of war or of the lone conqueror, and what it expresses is the courage to live, an awareness of the struggle between man and the elements, man against man, and an unleashing of the will to win. Walsh's *oeuvre* is an illustration of Zarathustra's aphorism: 'Man is made for war, woman is made for the warrior's repose, and the rest is madness.' All true films of conflict and adventure aspire to this view, but only those of Walsh rise to the level of epic or tragedy.

The suffocating world of Fritz Lang is particularly favourable to generating and sustaining violence, but in a very different sense. Constrained, held back, explicit and latent in every act and every look, and in no way diluted by weakness as in Ray, it is in fact like a tiger about to spring. If Walsh's violence is out in the open, Lang's is subterranean, more enduring in its tragedy. Only terror releases it; the earth crumbles around it and the hero is swallowed up.

But the film-maker who strikes deepest into violence and demonstrates it better than anyone is clearly Losey, of whom Aldrich is a mere uncomprehending disciple, a bombastic caricature. Losey, rather than the maker of *The Big Knife*, merits comparison with some of those astonishing reflexes one sees in actors in the work of Ida Lupino or Mizoguchi. Violence in Losey is just beneath the skin, catching that moment when the pulse frantically quickens as with every magnified heartbeat a man flexes himself to face what is in his way. And as it does so, it discovers a calm, a detumescence. This is a violence that opens a door on to peace and announces an unaccustomed surfeit of happiness.

NOTES

Translated by David Wilson.
First published in *Cahiers du Cinema*, 107 (May 1960) and translated by David Wilson in J. Hillier, 1986, *Cahiers du Cinema*, vol. 2, *The 1960s: New Wave, New Cinema, Re-evaluating Hollywood* (London, Routledge & Kegan Paul in association with the British Film Institute).
1   Mourlet's choice of Nicholas Ray here refers back explicitly to the enormously

important place Ray occupied for *Cahiers* in the 1950s (and continued to hold at this time); see particularly Jacques Rivette, 'Notes sur une révolution', *Cahiers*, 54 (Christmas 1955), translated as 'Notes on a revolution', in vol. 1, ch. 8, and the Dossier on Nicholas Ray in vol. 1, chs 10–15.

18

THE POLITICS OF 'JANE FONDA'

Tessa Perkins

In this chapter I do not intend to write about the actual political beliefs or practice of the woman called Jane Fonda – whatever they may be. I am interested in examining another aspect of the politics of star-images: namely the process by which star-images come to mean something to particular groups. In placing 'Jane Fonda and her politics' inside inverted commas I want to emphasise that 'Jane Fonda' functions as a sign whose meanings have been, and continue to be, the subject of contestation – and it is this contestation that constitutes the politics of 'Jane Fonda'. I am concerned, in particular, to investigate what Jane Fonda meant to feminists in the seventies when the image was radicalised.[1] I will argue that although the ways in which Fonda was written about in the press seemed both to undermine her particular political activities and to attack feminism, feminists in the seventies could use this attack as the basis of a sympathetic identification with the Fonda image. Jane Fonda functioned as a rebellious role model not so much *in spite of* the press reports as *because of them*. The media made use of 'Jane Fonda and her politics' as a means of defining what should constitute 'normal' gender activity. Fonda's significance for feminists was to some extent reinforced by her later films in so far as these circulated feminist ways of thinking and structures of feelings to mass audiences. However, in other ways the films seemed to detract from Fonda's significance.

Jane Fonda is probably best known today as a radical, or some would say 'once-radical', actress. To some she is most closely associated with her controversial involvement in a number of left-wing 'causes' in the late sixties and seventies and to others with more recent and more hard to categorise involvement in body-politics. A smaller, but still significant portion of people will recall a period in the mid-sixties in which she was associated with sexual liberation, her most famous film role of the period being the eponymous heroine of *Barbarella* – a time when she was often referred to as the American Brigitte Bardot. Her earlier image and the roles she played either as an *ingénue* or a 'sex kitten', mainly in the light sex comedies, such as *Sunday in New York* (1964), which were popular in the early sixties (and are more usually associated with such 'unpolitical' stars as Doris Day), are probably remembered by relatively few people. Jane Fonda is also of course known as the daughter of Henry Fonda, who was one of America's leading male film stars for most of Jane's life, and whose image retains powerful connotations of American liberalism even after his death; and as the sister of Peter Fonda, probably still best known for his part in *Easy Rider*. 'Jane Fonda's relationship to men' has been a central theme around which her image has been organised at certain times. This description of Fonda's changing star-image is hardly contentious, nor is the fact that it has changed; star-images are by their nature fluid and polysemic.[2] However, 'changeability' has in fact been one of the ingredients of Jane Fonda's image; but how this changeability has been interpreted and evaluated by different groups, and the sorts of connotations it has for them, has varied enormously; and it is over such interpretations and evaluations that the struggle to restrict what 'Jane Fonda' means occurs.

I first became conscious of the extent to which Jane Fonda held special significance for other feminists ten years ago when I was doing work on Doris Day. Incredulous that a self-respecting feminist thought Doris Day was worth writing about, people invariably asked me why I didn't do something on Jane Fonda. I found it remarkable that Jane Fonda's name came up so consistently. Some waxed lyrical over her physical attributes perhaps confirming Dyer's argument about the homo-erotic attractions of same-sex stars in general and Jane Fonda in particular, while others identified one or two of her films as having been particularly affecting and significant to them personally – *Klute*, *Coming Home* and *They Shoot Horses Don't They?* being referred to most frequently or referred explicitly to her radical politics.

Jane Fonda was, it seemed, the Hollywood star who, in the seventies at least, came closest to being a feminist heroine. Questioned further, many revealed a certain ambivalence about Fonda, an ambivalence which is I suspect even more pronounced today; but it seems to me now that this ambivalence is an important part of her significance. Being 'aware of the contradictions' (i.e. ambivalent) has, after all, become one of the key threads of the women's movement in the seventies. Jane Fonda has been the film star who has herself been most explicitly conscious of those contradictions and most public in her attempts to resolve them. Stars like Jane Fonda who are what Dyer calls 'rebel types' are particularly likely to generate contradictory feelings (for example, of admiration for their rebelliousness and contempt for the complicity with the system against which they (we) are supposedly rebelling) but this does not reduce their significance.

The set of meanings which Jane Fonda came to represent for feminists was produced in two areas (or perhaps I should say 'arenas' since the combative connotations of this term are particularly appropriate here).[3]

First, I will discuss how journalistic representation, such as magazine or newspaper articles about her latest film or accounts of her politics or details about her private life, made available a range of meanings to which feminists could relate in a particular, mainly positive, way. Second, I will suggest what her films, especially those from 1968 onwards, contributed to this image. Media representations could, on the one hand, provide information about Jane Fonda's activities or opinions (e.g. Jane Fonda lived in a small three-bedroomed house rather than a mansion, or Jane Fonda didn't believe in marriage); at this level feminists were likely to find that they frequently approved of her activities or agreed with the political positions she was reported as holding; on the other hand the ways in which Fonda was being written about constituted another source of meaning: for example the 'tone' of many of the articles was frequently belittling if not downright contemptuous. This 'tone' would also produce reactions from feminists which would contribute to what Fonda meant to them.

'THE SWEETIE WHO CAN ACT' – JANE FONDA PRE-1968

Although it is the post-1968 Fonda (and her films) who has seemed to acquire a special meaning for feminists we cannot ignore the pre-1968 Fonda altogether. The reason for this is that many of the feminists who admired her were themselves around before 1968 and had some knowledge of what she represented and a certain relationship to her image. Many had been through a similar range of experiences and changes in the late fifties and/or early sixties. Fonda's political rite of passage paralleled that of many feminists. This shared experience constituted an important element in feminists' identification with Fonda. Furthermore this early period of Fonda's career is frequently alluded to later on in much the same way that feminists found their own 'earlier' phases (as romantic teenagers or hopeful housewives) being constantly called up for analysis. After 1968 Fonda's early career is frequently referred to in the press as if there were some ideal 'pre-political' past when Fonda was an uncomplaining sex kitten.[4]

In fact to reduce Fonda's early career to a single stereotype – such as sex kitten – is to vastly oversimplify and compress it. Fonda's early career was interestingly, and perhaps unusually, varied especially as far as her sexuality was concerned. In her first four films, for example, she went from healthy schoolgirl virgin, a 'bubbly co-ed' as one reviewer of *Tall Story* (1960) described her, representative of ideal American girlhood, to tough and scheming street girl in *Walk on the Wild Side* (1962) – the absolute opposite of ideal American girlhood; from virgin to whore and from a whore to whom sexuality was apparently no problem but something to be used to a widow whose sexuality was *the* problem in *The*

Chapman Report (1962); and then from frigid widow to a dumb southern blonde on her wedding night in *Period of Adjustment* (1962). In the mid-sixties Fonda's roles were similarly varied, a mixture of mildly ironic social comedy (*Any Wednesday* and *Barefoot in the Park*) to the slightly sharper near satire (*Cat Ballou* and *Barbarella*), to tough social-political drama (*The Chase* and *Hurry Sundown*).

While *Cat Ballou*, *Hurry Sundown* and *The Chase* can all be seen as films with a political point to them, Fonda's involvement in them tends to be defined purely in terms of their offering her good parts. Although information about Fonda's opinions is sought and given, Fonda is not described as 'political' at this point. It is Fonda's sexuality, her opinions about sex and her father's opinions about her that are the dominant feature of the media representations of her. In 1964 there is a sense of shock (if also a taste of things to come) when an American magazine editor reacts to Jane Fonda's comments on her recent trip to Russia, 'Who cares?' and remarks that the 'American people want to know about her sex life, not how noble she thinks the Russians are.'[5] In the mid-sixties Fonda lived mainly in France where she had met and fallen in love with Roger Vadim, described by David Lewin in the *Daily Mail* (13 August 1966) as 'the Frenchman of Russian origin who single-handedly created (and married) Brigitte Bardot'. The newspapers insistently drew a parallel between Vadim's relationship with his former wives, Bardot and Stroyberg, and his relationship with Fonda. All of the women were referred to as if they were putty in his hands, and of course the fact that Vadim directed them in films lent added legitimacy to this way of talking. The opening paragraphs of an article in the *Sunday Express* (22 March 1964) entitled 'How Jane Fonda came to acquire the Bardot look' gives some of the flavour of how Fonda's relationship with Vadim was talked about at this time:

> 'Really, you know, this fellow Roger Vadim has simply got to go.
>
> 'Over the years I have been slowly losing patience with him as he has systematically wooed and won some of the most delectable chicks in show business.
>
> 'First Brigitte Bardot. Then Annette Stroyberg. More recently that dark-eyed charmer Catherine Deneuve.
>
> 'All this was bad enough but now he has finally gone too far. For he has stolen the affections of the stunning girl who for months has been the toast of this girl-jaded town (i.e. Paris), 26-year-old Jane Fonda, daughter of actor Henry.'

However, despite the fact that the newspaper reports make it sound as if Fonda is just one more 'delectable' bit for Vadim to acquire and subject to his Svengali will there is another version of Jane Fonda which also manages to surface. For example, Fonda is referred to as 'the woman who won't marry Vadim'. Fonda's cynicism about marriage was widely reported. In what was to become a familiarly belittling way, *The Sun* (4 November 1964) announced that Jane Fonda '*has set herself* up as the new-style star who refuses to be trapped into marriage' (emphasis added). What is particularly worth noting about these accounts is that she expresses her antipathy to marriage on precisely those grounds which feminists would identify in the coming years. 'What I fear about marriage' she was reported as saying in 1964 'is being possessed. Nobody belongs to anybody – why can't we learn that, and why should people expect to get along on all levels?' (*Sunday Express*, 22 March 1964). Time and time again interviews with Fonda suggest that she has a much more intimate understanding of the issues than most film stars which makes it seem as if her involvement must be genuine rather than a fashionable fad. Indeed to a 'knowing' reader (for example a feminist versed in feminist arguments) Fonda generally reveals in her answers that she has more knowledge than the interviewer.

By the mid-sixties then, Fonda was identifiably associated with the 'permissive society' – indeed she was one of its leading voices. Although 1968 is often referred to as if it was the year in which Jane Fonda became political, it is clear that the opinions and feelings Fonda had been reported as expressing in interviews during the sixties were already very much in line with the thinking of many of the young liberals/radicals of the time. By 1968 she was already identifiable as something of a rebel, and many of her film roles would have lent support to the sense of Fonda as being progressive and angry.

This is not to deny that 1968 did represent a radical change in the meanings which were attached to Fonda but part of this change came of course from changes which were quite independent of Fonda. The mid-sixties was a time of major social and political upheaval in both America and Europe which came to a head in 1968. For our purposes the most significant political movement at this time was the newly developing women's liberation movement which was arguably 'born' in the aftermath of 1968. For a time at least after 1968 everything was looked at from a new perspective – and this included film stars. None the less it is true that Fonda herself underwent enormous changes and both the films she was in and the opinions she was reported as holding changed; and consequently the ways in which she was talked about in the press were transformed. From talking about her as some prize piece, a delectable chick to be wooed and won, something that men could compete over, as in the *Sunday Express* extract discussed above, the tone of the articles change, as we will see below. *Barbarella*, made in 1967, is probably the most famous and notorious of Fonda's 'sex symbol' films; *They Shoot Horses Don't They?*, made in 1969, is the first of the more serious, and socially conscious films which are the ones feminists tended to admire. Before examining how the post-1968 films contribute to Jane Fonda's image we should look at the other arena which produced and circulated 'meanings' about her at this time, namely the press, since this press coverage so often constituted the context in which the films were viewed.

'HANOI JANE – A MOUTHY TWERP'

In the late sixties and early seventies press coverage of Fonda emphasised her association with a number of left-wing causes. She was shown supporting the Indians in Alcatraz and was a well-known supporter of the Black Panther movement (although Fonda later sued the FBI for sending the newspapers false information about the extent of her involvement in an attempt to discredit and therefore neutralise her).[6] She was a founding member of the Indo-China peace campaign, which worked to bring an end to America's war with Vietnam. The press reported Fonda's involvement in this campaign and her travels round the country talking to GIs, and published photos of her being arrested at an army base. Fonda's involvement with the anti-war movement, and especially the trips to North Vietnam, were at the time treated by most of the press with varying degrees of scarcely veiled contempt. In an article entitled 'Hanoi Jane – the star who makes America's women see red', *The Sun* (11 August 1972) reported that pressure was mounting for 'Jane Fonda to be tried for treason over her Vietnam war broadcasts' and went on to claim that 'much of America seems already convinced that . . . Jane Fonda betrayed the nation during her Hanoi haunt'. This article is characteristic of many in so far as its rhetoric damns her politics as much by rendering her harmless and ridiculous as by anything else. Underneath the photograph which accompanies the article is the caption 'Jane . . . "a mouthy twerp" ', while above the article runs the slogan ' "Treason" howl over Fonda girl's Vietnam broadcasts'. (Fonda was at this time 34 years old. She was to respond angrily to being referred to as a 'girl'.) Within the article the author, Ray Kerrison, made such comments as:

> She must be the prettiest threat ever posed to American national security. . . . There is no doubt about her sincerity, her naïveté was something else. . . . Jane's trip to Hanoi . . . climaxes nearly three years of 'doing her Thing' – which is trotting around the globe, pushing her causes. Her first big Thing was the American Indian . . .

and so on.

An article in the *Sunday Mirror* (24 September 1972) used a similar strategy. Although not as openly hostile as many articles it none the less manages to ridicule Fonda's politics and suggests that her involvement is faddish. The first and most notable thing about this article is that there is a prominent photograph of a naked Jane Fonda sitting on a beach. The caption reads 'Jane Fonda in the days when Roger Vadim designed her image'. One reading of this would be (a) that the positions Jane Fonda takes (whether physical as in the photo or political as in the article) are merely a function of an 'image' which has been 'designed' – to that extent they are not 'hers', nor are they genuine; and (b) that someone else is designing her image. An alternative but less likely reading would be that Jane Fonda has now wrested control from Vadim. The article's opening paragraphs are also open to alternative readings:

> When Roger Vadim persuaded Jane Fonda, his third wife, to start stripping for success he little dreamt what he was starting. . . . But along with her clothes, Jane also shed just about every feminine inhibition.
>
> And now, while with burning zeal she startles the world with outrageous women's lib, Vadim, her former lord and master from whom she is parted, says of their past life: 'It was like living with Joan of Arc . . . no fun at all . . .'

However a combination of elements suggests that the alternative reading is not the intended one: the use of the nude photograph, the references to Vadim and his control of her image and the references to 'burning zeal' and 'outrageous women's lib' all serve to undermine the feminist opinions Fonda is reported as holding as does a reference in the final paragraph to her being on a ' "cause" kick'. Vadim's comment on their past life as being 'no fun at all' also implies that the breakdown of the marriage was her fault (elsewhere he has referred to 'babysitting for Lenin'). But it also serves as a prediction for her future life – 'no fun at all' – and therefore something to be avoided. To be a Joan of Arc (i.e. a political woman) is to be, and to have, 'no fun'. It is also to be rather childish, is it not?

It was not just the tabloid press that found Fonda's politics hard to take. The supposedly liberal *Guardian* (1971) talked about how attractive a personality she had been in 'her earlier incarnation' and went on to say 'The new Jane Fonda is many things, but one thing she is not is "lovable".' To an extent this says it all – this says what every feminist knows in her heart – that to be a feminist, to be a political woman, is to be 'not lovable'. It is hard to read such a comment and not feel an overwhelming identity and sympathy with the woman who has been defined as unlovable particularly when we place that public declaration of her 'unlovability' next to the descriptions of her former lovability.

As Richard Dyer commented, Fonda demonstrated 'what it is like to be political'. In the early seventies the press seemed to find her image extremely disturbing and revealed in the way they wrote about her a sort of desperate need to bring her back into some recognisable, normal feminine role, to undermine not so much her politics as her claims to be a political being. The language they used to describe her activities was saturated with gendered references and connotations and reproduced an ideology which refuses women the right or the capacity to be political, hence the need always to account for her politics in terms of the man she was currently involved with. The claim that 'the basic engine for change' in Jane Fonda's life 'is men' – that she chooses her politics according to the man she is currently involved with – has been repeated time and time again. However, while such claims were clearly designed to undermine her they are also such classic examples of sexism that feminists were likely to be highly sensitive to the ways in which they were being used.

Fonda was not only rejected by the establishment. Some of her erstwhile 'brothers' on the left also rejected her. Jean-Luc Godard and Jean Pierre Gorin, the radical French film-makers with whom she had made *Tout Va Bien*, went so far as to make a film, *Letter to Jane*, which it is hard not to read as an attack on her politics, while Joseph Losey who had directed her in *The Doll's House* gave interviews which ridiculed her politics and claimed to reveal how difficult she had been.[7] But these criticisms from the male left, spoken with such unerring confidence and authority, could be reinterpreted by feminists. Indeed they could easily work to confirm the authenticity of Fonda's feminism. Even though she was a film star she was still subject to the same dismissive treatment that feminists argued was the lot of all women. Indeed interviews such as the one with Losey suggested strongly that men were ganging up on her; clearly Fonda, like other feminists, was having trouble with the male left.

The 'authenticity' of Fonda's feminism was further demonstrated by the ways in which she responded to the endless questions asking what she thought about the women's movement. Her answers invariably demonstrated much more than a passing sympathy with the movement; she made it clear that she identified with the movement and that it had affected her, changed the way she thought about herself, and the way she understood the world and what she could do in it. It was clear that her politics were affecting her career – during the early seventies she was, as she said, 'greylisted'. She would not accept parts which she felt were demeaning but she was not offered any that were not. It was this sort of understanding and commitment, revealed in press interviews, that was particular about Fonda and that demonstrated her authenticity – it convinced one that whatever the hostile sections of the press said or implied Fonda was more than just a bandwagon feminist.

Fonda's early film roles pre-date the revival of feminism in the late sixties. But one thing in particular is notable: of the sixteen films Fonda made before 1968 *Barbarella* is overwhelmingly the one that is referred to – and almost comes to stand in for all the others. This is important in so far as it becomes part of the 'knowledge' about Fonda which is constantly referred to and has to be 'dealt with'. Certain sections of the media insistently and uncritically foreground particular aspects of the sexuality of earlier roles and seem to take pleasure in holding Fonda responsible for them. Fonda is required to 'answer' an implicit charge from hypothetical feminists, invented by the press, of not having been a feminist, or of having colluded with the enemy. The implication is that if she has played such roles she cannot really be a feminist. Sometimes the interviews do actually ask what Fonda thinks of her 'past', thereby giving her a chance to answer the 'charges' against her. In one such case Fonda is reported as saying that in her view *Barbarella* was less exploitative than many of the other earlier roles; but at other times the charges are simply there in the way the article is written, as in the example from the *Sunday Mirror* quoted above.

This way of writing about Fonda produces contradictory meanings and feeds the ambivalence which I have argued characterises many feminists' feelings about Fonda. On the one hand the 'tone' of the writing invites us to view Fonda with contempt; the 'preferred' reading of this and innumerable other articles is that Fonda, like the feminists/radicals/commies/pinkos she purports to agree with, is not to be taken seriously.

The question for us to consider, however, is what position feminists are likely to take in relation to this? A number of possibilities present themselves but let us consider just two. First, they could agree with the newspaper's implication that Fonda is not to be taken seriously, that she changes her politics to suit the moment; she would be seen as someone who had merely jumped on the feminist bandwagon and would soon jump off again. They may refuse to recognise Fonda as having anything in common with themselves – refuse to acknowledge her as a feminist. Alternatively feminists might well adopt a more oppositional position and object strongly to the article's (implicit or explicit) criticism of Fonda. In this case the article will have provided grounds for sympathetic identification with Fonda. This oppositional reading resists the position offered by the article and demonstrates the way in which a star's image may be a site of struggle. In this case attempts to tie down the meaning of Jane Fonda are refused.

However this is to argue the most optimistic case, as far as resistance is concerned. 'Resistance' is best viewed as one end of a continuum of possible responses. At the other end is presumably complete acceptance of the media's definition of Jane Fonda as, for example, an 'outrageous' woman's libber. But just as Gramsci has argued that hegemonic control was never total, so too we must acknowledge that 'resistance' is neither total nor permanent. Resistant readings may be more or less prone to contamination by the dominant reading. Thus, even though feminists may be quick to identify the media's treatment of Fonda as being anti-feminist and be able to identify the strategies which they are using to attack her politics, none the less some of the mistrust of Fonda which the mainstream (malestream?) press generated could seep into feminists' readings of Fonda, accounting for some of the ambivalence which is characteristic.

'A WEAPON FOR POLITICAL CHANGE'

Fonda's films were equally complex as a source of meanings. The post-1968 films are characterised by a struggle between a distinctively feminist discourse which inflected much of Fonda's performances and aspects of the narrative and a patriarchal discourse which tends to dominate the overall structure of the film – this was particularly noticeable in *Klute*. The films were liable to produce a range of feelings which constituted a complex mixture of responses both to the 'politics' of her decision to make films addressed to mass audiences and to the various roles she played and the intellectual and emotional impact of those roles.[8]

Fonda's decision to use her skills as an actress to make films which might be 'a weapon for political change' could be read by feminists as being either a capitulation to the system or an attempt to use the system. Such alternative meanings are of course familiar oppositions for feminists. For those feminists whose politics did not entail separatism, Fonda could stand as an ideal. Fonda had the power that most women lack – a power which feminism was in a sense attempting to wrest from men. In so far as she already had it, Fonda faced decisions that the success of feminism posed: what do you do once you have power? Can it be used progressively or does power always corrupt? The arguments she put forward about films had their parallels in other sections of the women's movement. Fonda's insistence on the importance of making films which would reach a mass audience reflected the strongly anti-elitist impulses of feminism. Furthermore she challenged what she saw as the conventional wisdom of Hollywood producers 'that people don't want to think . . .' arguing instead that 'people want to be led out of the morass or at least to have a little help in clearing away the confusion' and advocating 'films or any kind of cultural expression that strengthens rather than weakens people'.[9] She lamented the fact that 'people who have a social vision haven't yet found a way to express it in a mass language. There is so much rhetoric and so much sectarianism.' She was not interested in making films which would only be seen or understood by the already converted left-wing elite. In an interview in 1975 she talked about the difficulty of knowing what sort of films to make and whether it was possible to make films as 'a weapon for political change':

> I do have a feeling that, at this stage, in this country anyway, it wouldn't necessarily be a film that offers a solution. I have a feeling that there's a kind of frustration that may be progressive at this point. Perhaps the best we can do now is create in the audience a sense of hopeful frustration.

Fonda's particular political strategy meant that she was not interested in the sort of heroic roles which feminists might have relished seeing her play. Nor was she interested in producing avant-garde movies which would offer little in the way of pleasure. Fonda's films are never obvious feminist or socialist tracts nor did she play characters who were 'radicals' like she was. On the contrary she said: 'I would rather play a fascist, if that exposed something about racism and power, than to play a famous revolutionary.' This seemed a brave and honest decision and the impulse behind it was recognisable as being informed by a feminist politics – a politics of discovery and enablement rather than a politics of the great and the good. Fonda could presumably have justified playing famous feminists or independent women but she chose instead to play characters who 'are full of contradictions'; she wanted to show characters who are 'trying to deal with problems that are real to people'.

However the consequence of the decision not to play specifically feminist or politically conscious women was that the characters Fonda played were frequently hard for feminists to identify with wholeheartedly. On the one hand of course the characters faced problems and contradictions that had been at the centre of feminists' experience and of their discussions about women's experience more generally. For example, Sally Hyde's confused, unseeing but urgent need to resist the control of her patronising and paternalistic husband in *Coming Home*, and tentatively to take a small step towards controlling her own life, was painfully familiar. Lillian's confused but determined commitment to and faith in her friend in *Julia* provided feminists with what must have been one of the first *celebrations* and *affirmations* of friendship between women – and of women as capable of being motivated by politics. But although her films explored what I have referred to above as 'feminist ways of thinking and structures of feelings' these were never allowed their full expression.

In fact the characters Fonda played in the seventies were, at the start of each film at least, very unlike the highly politicised Fonda star-image. In the course of the film the character usually changes and moves closer to the Jane Fonda star-image of an enlightened, independent, radical woman. *Coming Home, Nine to Five, The Electric Horseman, Julia, The China Syndrome, The Doll's House*, all illustrate this. The narrative satisfactions which the films offer us are bound up with the character becoming more like 'Jane Fonda'; being radicalised.[10] However the radicalisation was generally rather minimal which meant that what feminists were likely to take from the film was something akin to a memory of their past, the early days of awakening consciousness, rather than a way forward from where they were at the moment.

A rather more serious problem for feminists was that the character's radicalisation had usually depended on guidance from a man. The role of the male characters in Fonda's films not only operated to weaken or neutralise the character Fonda played, it also functioned to reinforce that problematic part of Fonda's star-image which presented men 'as the engine for change' in her life and dismissed her politics as being merely a function of the man she was currently in love with rather than vice versa, which is how feminists would be inclined to interpret it. Having refused to accept this demeaning explanation which the press give of her politics, feminists must wonder why Fonda did not exercise *more* control over the films she was in during the seventies. Could it be that Fonda did not actually understand the significance of the ways in which the characters she played were dominated by men or was it that even she did not have enough control? This enigma produces something of a crisis in the Fonda image, and specifically in what it could mean to feminists.

On the one hand, one could respect her decision to 'use' the system and to wrest control from Hollywood by setting up her own production company (IPC), admire her performances and refuse the press's reading of her. But all this constructed 'Jane Fonda' as something of an ideally successful and powerful feminist who had actually managed to resolve the contradictions involved in making radical popular movies. The films themselves failed to live up to this ideal; they suggested that either her understanding was at fault or her power was less than total so that she was being forced to compromise her politics. So although in one respect Fonda's films reinforced Fonda's feminist image, in another respect it was the films which made that image problematic and opened up a gap in the oppositional meanings which feminists were giving to 'Jane Fonda'.

In the late seventies and eighties Jane Fonda became a much more 'acceptable' star as far as the media were concerned, and they increasingly constructed her as the mature face of sixties radicalism in general and feminism in particular. Indeed in November 1989 something I once thought inconceivable happened: an article in a colour supplement about aging female stars which included a section on Jane Fonda made no reference whatsoever to her ever having been in any sense 'political'.[11] This does not of course mean that the struggle over what 'Jane Fonda' signifies is over nor that she is no longer important to feminists, nor that the struggle has ceased to be political. On the contrary it demonstrates, as I argued in my opening paragraph, that 'Jane Fonda' functions as a sign whose meanings are still the subject of contestation – and it is in this that the politics of 'Jane Fonda' lies.[12]

NOTES

1 I am not, of course, arguing that this is what she meant for all feminists, let alone for all women. On the contrary it is evident that there is disagreement among feminists around Jane Fonda and/or her films and some of these disagreements are no doubt symptomatic of significant 'political' differences.

2 In *Stars* Richard Dyer argues that star-images are polysemic. That is to say that there may be a multitude of meanings which become attached to a star. These meanings will not necessarily all be consistent with one another – either over

a period of time or at one particular moment in time. But while there may be a number of meanings this does not mean that a star-image can mean anything to anybody; 'polysemy refers to the multiple but finite meanings and effects that a star image signifies'. The analysis of a star-image then involves identifying the different components and elements that make up the image and analysing how they are developed or diminished, stressed or ignored, how they come in to play at different moments in different contexts. The objective of star study, Dyer argues, is not 'to say what (the star's image) meant for the "average person" at various points in her career but rather what the range of things was that she could be read as meaning by different audience members', *Stars*, Richard Dyer (BFI, London, 1979), 72.

3 See Dyer, *Stars*, for discussion of the processes involved in producing star-images. As Dyer argues, contrary to our common-sense assumptions, films are not necessarily an essential source of the meanings of star-images. He cites Zsa Zsa Gabor as a film star whose films few people know, and Marilyn Monroe as a star for whom publicity was probably a more important part of the process.

4 or a 'Sweetie who can really act'. This was the title of an article about Fonda in the *Daily Express*, 10 December 1964. There has not been space in this article to discuss the significance of Fonda's reputation as an actress and what that contributes to her image. However her acting ability is one of the attributes that marks her as different from most other female stars, even this early on, and it remains, with very few exceptions, the one characteristic that is not ridiculed or rubbished by her critics.

5 Quoted in G. Haddad-Garcia, *The Films of Jane Fonda* (New Jersey, Citadel Press, 1981), 110.

6 See *Variety*, 17 December 1975. A full account of Fonda's political involvements, and the way the press covered it is beyond the scope of this article. A useful and sympathetic account can be found in G. Herman and D. Downing, *Jane Fonda: All American Anti-Heroine* (London, Omnibus, 1980) or Dyer, op. cit.

7 'The trouble with Jane Fonda' – Joseph Losey talking to David Lewin in the *Daily Mail*, 10 March 1973.

8 For debate about meanings of Jane Fonda's films for feminists see: D. Giddis, 'The divided woman: Bree Daniels in Klute' in K. Kay and G. Peary, *Women & the Cinema* (New York, Dutton, 1977); C. Gledhill, 'Klute 2: feminism and Klute', in *Women in Film Noir*, ed. E. Ann Kaplan (London, BFI, 1978); and T. Lovell and S. Frith, 'Another look at Klute', in *Screen Education*, 39 (Summer 1981).

9 This, and subsequent quotes in this section are from 'An interview with Jane Fonda', reprinted in K. Kay and G. Peary, op. cit.

10 I am indebted to Victor Perkins for this insight. A similar process is identifiable with another, rather different star – Doris Day. However in the case of Day the character she is playing generally starts off as an independent, rebellious woman who is fighting to keep her autonomy. By the end of the film the Day character has lost the fight, or 'come to realise' that she was wrong to be fighting it, and she happily gives up her independence, and becomes more like the 'sunny, girl-next-door', star-image we associate with Doris Day. In short the characters Day plays are de-radicalised as they move through the film towards the Day star-image. For discussion of the meanings of Doris Day for feminists see J. Clarke and D. Simmonds, *Move over Misconceptions* (London, BFI, 1980) and T. E. Perkins, 'Remembering Doris Day', in *Screen Education*, 39 (Summer 1981).

11 'Famous fading fifties faces', *People* Magazine, 26 November 1989.
12 I am indebted to Christine Gledhill and Jill McKenna for helpful and encourag-
    ing comments on an earlier draft of this article.

19

THE GLUT OF THE PERSONALITY

David Lusted

Jimmy Saville, Tracey Ullman, Denis Waterman, Lenny Henry, Clive James, Jan Leeming . . . Personalities are central to the institution of television. A stock of recognised names acts as an assurance that audiences will return again (and again) to their role as viewers, perpetuating – via advertising or licence revenue – the flow of cash to maintain the institution. There is an economic imperative, then, to television's construction and maintenance of personalities.

The assurance is like an informal contract between production company and audience. Yet, in the same way that promises can be broken, the assurance is no guarantee. It is less a contract than a mythology, for the most part sustained in the face of regular and consistent contrary evidence. The popularity of any personality can rise and fall repetitively. (Yesterday's has-been may be today's discovery and ripe for anonymity tomorrow. Ask Frankies Vaughan and Howerd.) And audiences have been known to refuse the offer of many a personality in particular programmes or series. None the less, as a *system*, like cinema's star system, the mythology has material effects: the production of more personalities in the relentless search for high viewing figures.

The mythology is sustained, of course, by cultural myths beyond television. The cult of the personality is a product of *the myth of the individual*. According to this myth, history is made by extraordinary men (and a few women), irrespective of social movements. The myth has two inflections. One stresses individual achievement through personal effort and competition, and particularly serves the interests of capital. The other is the folk myth (the Cinderella story or the Log-Cabin-to-White-House story) in which the individual succeeds through nature or fate, rather than effort, position or circumstance. The first inflection foregrounds labour, the second denies it and offers genius in its place. The myth of individualism, like all myths, is contradictory.

Nowhere is contradiction more apparent than in television, where the constant need to top up the stock produces a veritable *glut* of personalities,

251

a process which, once acknowledged, exposes the myth of the *rare* individual.

> I knew her for a long, long time. She was a marvellous woman, a one-off, like Tommy Cooper
> (Eric Morecambe, on the death of Diana Dors, *Daily Mail*, 5 May 1984)

Television's personality system dominantly reproduces myths of individualism, then. Yet this statement takes no account of the pleasures sought from or delivered by the system, nor does it allow for different, especially *social*, meanings to appear. If the individualist mythology is contradictory so, too, may be the personality system. Within those contradictions the social groups who make up factions of television's audiences may also find alternative recognitions, affirmations and identifications that are even oppositional to the dominant tendencies of television's personality system.

The coincidence of the deaths of Tommy Cooper (15 April 84), Diana Dors (4 May 84) and Eric Morecambe (27 June 84) offers a convenient (if sad) pretext for a case study to explore these possibilities. Let us see how certain TV personalities may provide pleasure for certain factions of audiences through *social* meanings in opposition to both the personality system and the myth of individualism.

First, recall that the particular biographies of the three reach before and beyond the television institution. They are not just *television* personalities. Cooper and Morecambe were both comedy stars of the variety circuit (music-halls, cabaret, clubs etc.) before and during their television celebrity. Dors was a film star of the sub-species 'sex symbol' and an actress respected for 'difficult' roles (as, for instance, 'Ruth Ellis' in *Yield to the Night*). To this we must add their appearance in television forms that exceeded their origins. Cooper and Morecambe starred in their own light entertainment variety shows on television, as well as guesting (Cooper much more than Morecambe) on the shows of other stars. Dors acted in innumerable fictions, from drama to situation comedy. But also they all appeared in chat shows, game shows, magazines . . . Morecambe, for instance, appeared as himself in an episode of the crime-series *The Sweeney* and, through his connections with Luton Football Club, was frequently sought for interviews on sports programmes. Cooper was as frequent a speaker at televised showbiz functions and a favourite of filmed comedy shows made by another comic, Eric Sykes. Dors appeared in variety shows as a singer and in sketches. She hosted her own chat show for a period and ran a slimming feature for breakfast television shortly before her death. All three, then, whilst identifiable as specialists, were also *icons of intertextuality*. More than personalities, they were television stars, embodying a rich repertoire of reference in popular cultural memory. The point to stress here is that through their many and varied appearances, their names connected with so many factions of audiences, for each of which the meaning of any personality will vary.

What, then, becomes an issue is isolating their *potential* for social meaning in one or many of the types of appearance for particular factions of audience. And, if we are interested in ascribing affirmations, recognitions and identifications they offer to the broadest working-class (but raced, aged and gendered) audiences, it is the *particularities* of the potential meanings they offer those audiences that require attention. My argument will be that each of these personalities connect a specific range of affirmations, recognitions and identifications to specific audience formations, whilst remaining broad and/or complex enough to aggregate majority audiences.

Much of the pleasure of television's light entertainment forms come not only from recognising the skills of personalities (from the physical dexterity of the juggler or magician to the verbal constructions of the raconteur) but also the *risks* at stake. Local failure is always potential and sometimes actual, from the dropped Indian club or transparent illusion to the verbal *faux-pas*. Indeed, Tommy Cooper's comic magician and Eric Morecambe's comic dupe acknowledge and incorporate the pleasure of the risk into their performance personae. These personae admit what the personality system recognises but attempts to efface – the risks of performance. Moreover, the Cooper and Morecambe personalities recognise that audience complicity is central to such an exposure; it becomes a point of negotiation, pleasurable in itself, between personality and audience. For much of light entertainment the recognition is suppressed in the interests of success and the confirmation of talented individuals. In musical variety, for instance, only comedian Les Dawson's off-key piano plays with discord and there is no tradition of *singing* off-key, even in fun. Part of the pleasure of game shows, quizzes and 'talent' contests, for instance, is precisely that they *foreground* the risk of failure; their extraordinary popularity should be no surprise.

The supreme risk, however, is of failure to maintain not just an individual performance but the faith in success and talent underpinning showbiz itself. The risk operates as a neurosis around light entertainment, comparable to that of the myth of individual skill and effort as a guarantor of economic achievement and social status which is at odds with all working-class experience and some working-class consciousness. Diana Dors, pre-eminently, was a personality who declared that risk and threatened that myth in the active manipulation of her own complex persona.

In sum, then, the myths of success and talent routinely risk pleasurable exposure within the *form* of light entertainment, yet the pleasures and meaning of certain personalities derive from their regular de-mystification of that process.

> There have been times that I have known disappointment, even despair. The public never realised because I was laughing on the outside while crying on the inside. Very dangerous – you could easily drown.   (Tommy Cooper, *Daily Star*, 11 November 1982)

There is a simple sense in which all three personalities shared a 'common touch', an expression of collusion with the materiality of working-class life. Unlike personalities such as, say, Michael Parkinson, David Frost or Selina Scott – who represent the cultures of manual and/or domestic labour at one remove, as it were – Cooper, Morecambe and Dors represent a direct and experiential identification with the materiality of working-classness; pub culture over wine bar, soccer over cricket, nappies over nannies. Crudely, it is a matter of class cultural embodiment. Yet there is a more complex sense in which these three personalities can be understood as *social* stars and it exists in their critical distance from the central meanings and functions of the personality system.

All television personalities in non-fiction forms affect connections with their audiences. Through forms of direct address that characteristically punctuate variety (semi-confessionally), chat shows and magazines (familiarly) and news programmes (more formally) alike, appeals to commonality and consensus are supreme. The wit of Cooper, Morecambe and Dors serves as comment on that operation. Cooper employed surreal inanities ('I used to collect dust but I gave it up,' and 'I take my drinks neat – but sometimes I let my shirt tail hang out a bit'); Morecambe parodied, through asides like 'This boy's a fool!' and in a range of exchanges to camera, especially when feigning ignorance of guest stars in his shows with Ernie Wise; Dors could also use a comic mode but, more often, used caustic put-downs on personalities around her whose bonhomie grew excessive ('Calm down, there's a good boy'). These verbal (combined with gestural) devices mark off a distance from the rhetoric of personality, individuating our three personalities as *commentators* upon as well as *collaborators* in the system. These counter-rhetorical devices, colluding with the audience at the expense of the personality system, construct a more social connection to audiences familiar with and attracted by that system.

> For most people life is a bloody awful grind. They do jobs they hate – if they are lucky enough to have a job. So when someone comes along who makes them forget their troubles, it's a relief for them.   (Tommy Cooper, *Daily Star*, 16 Apr. 1984).

All three personalities embody certain characteristics of working-class experience in their performances and, arousingly, in their particular manipulations of the formal strategies and institutional practices of television. In their embodiment of working-class experience, they recognise a sense of 'working-classness' as special and discrete from other class experience. In their manipulation of television they represent a separation from controlling definitions of convention and normality. In the combination of embodiment and manipulation, they affirm the subordinated but, crucially, unbowed and resilient properties of working-class experience.

There is another sense in which the three personalities affirm qualities of class resilience, Cooper most resonantly. His obsessive failure at effecting magic tricks corresponds symbolically to the systematic lack of fit between investment in and rewards of labour. The deployment of humour – in the series of unconnected, surprising and excessive jokes delivered in a bemused, self-deprecating manner – connects precisely with the wit characteristic of groups in manual and domestic labour, effectively a stoical commentary on the absurdity of their class conditions, 'working your end away' to minimal material effect. This quality has its biographical equivalent in Cooper's long history of heart, liver and chest complaints which progressively slurred his speech and slowed his actions. Made visible to his audiences by surrounding publicity but never self-promoted or acknowledged in performance, this biographical recognition adds to that sense of stoicism in the face of personal adversity. Similarly, Morecambe's heart disease and Dors' thyroid complaint (responsible for her size) and, later, cancer, were tragic components of their personal biographies but also recognised sub-texts of their personae. Struggling against debility, the shared knowledge of their frail mortality acts as a recognised, but unspoken, bond of recognition between personality and audience. Undoubtedly, recognition of mortality is classless, but *labouring* through that knowledge has an added frisson for working-class consciousness, in which death through industrial disease and premature ageing has acute meaning. In many ways, the *lifestyle* of showbiz, too, its display of excessive high living, is a symbolic equivalent to the 'live now, pay later' component of working-class culture so deprecated by moralists of the left and centre alike. For the disadvantaged sections of a capitalist economy, at the bottom of the social order, the choice between convention and compliance or refusal and pleasure is not easy. Punishment is the return on both choices but at least, with the latter, there is some fun on the way. Cooper and Dors, especially, can be seen – like Judy Garland or Sid Vicious before them – as exponents of that choice but also as its tragic victims. The tragedy of Cooper and Dors however, had a vivid connection to working-class consciousness. In that context, a buoyant resilience to the physical punishment rendered by the catch-22 of 'the system' has a particular currency.

Recognitions of expressions and forms of resilience are crucial to connecting the popularity of these personalities with their audiences and are not to be denied an importance in sustaining the routine survival tactics of day-to-day oppression.

None the less, resilience alone carries the risk of affirming survival at the expense of transformation. The individualism of these personalities would amount to little more than confirmation of class oppression if it did not also encourage forms of resistance through symbolic calls for social change, models of possibilities and outcomes and strategies to effect them. Morecambe's claim to attention here is specific and conscious. It resides in a particular camera style and address to camera that developed around his manipulation of the stereotype comic fool. The stereotype conventionally takes one of two forms – either the overbearing boor (e.g. Les Dawson, Bruce Forsyth and, earlier, Bob Hope – and, earliest, Punchinello) or the hapless pre-adolescent (e.g. Michael Crawford's Frank Spencer, Frank Crompton and, earlier, Jerry Lewis – and, earliest, Harlequin). Like only W. C. Fields before him – and unique in a double act – Morecambe combines these alternatives, but in a particular way. The Morecambe persona is at once arrogantly self-confident, freely insulting, hyper-active *and* easily (if temporarily) defused, consistently slighted, constantly ignored. Forms of attention seeking such as these are conventionally dismissed as juvenile or lunatic, especially in the social world where deviant characteristics are regularly ascribed to politically oppositional activity in conflict with the status quo. In particular, strikes, demonstrations and picketing can be labelled 'silly' or 'childlike' in order to depoliticise their purpose, deny them rationality and change (consciousness of) their effect. The sophistication of Morecambe's comic persona and the formal differences in its comic context disavows such epithets and puts the lie (for those in the audience socially positioned to recognise it) to similar terms of denunciation in the social world. Instead, Morecambe affirms the appropriateness of forms of opposition and ascribes status to them.

In particular, the formal devices employed by Morecambe – the regular exchange of looks with the audience aside from the sketch or fiction those around him inhabit, his reactions to their attempts to disturb his disruption – affirm a range of *tactical* strategies. They affirm oppositional practices in the face of dominant assurances that they are not necessary; they resist incorporation and demand recognition as right; they are resilient but also resist attempts at modification. In sum, they symbolically affirm subordinated class struggle and evidence not only tactics to survive but strategies to resist.

These particular recognitions connect most clearly with existing forms of organised political opposition, especially within the labour movement, and it is to factions of audiences drawn from such groups that the Morecambe persona and situations offer particular confirmations. For other factions, too, the persona may initiate recognitions and/or inform a developing politicised consciousness.

Where Morecambe *used* the conventions of music-hall and television's direct address, Cooper subverted them. Rehearsals for his shows were notoriously chaotic; refusing scripts, repeatedly missing chalk marks, inserting new routines and one-liners. The shambles of rehearsals were evident to audiences of his performances. A nightmare for programme directors and camera operators, Cooper's performances meant that the camera was invariably in the wrong position at the wrong time. Effectively, gags were lost as punchlines were delivered off-frame, the climaxes of routines were witnessed by a mis-framed camera and longueurs occurred wherein no one seemed sure of intentions. Cooper, in sum, was anarchy to the television institution. The same unpredictability characterised his many 'personal' appearances. A speech for a televised celebrity function comprised breathless nothings as he feigned loss of speech, then a faulty microphone; witness to another's *This Is Your Life*, he affected ignorance of the celebrity he was called to fête: 'Never heard of him', he offered to the teeth-gritting smile of Eamonn Andrews.

Cooper's inability to perform according to any rules affirms a sense of opposition. Yet his iconoclasm is always tempered by control and calm. The form of disruption he represents is an affirmation of a more militant strand of working-class resistance, less regulated, more spontaneous, yet still political. Cooper's logic of no logic is a disruptive tactic, not just in labour politics but also in domestic and other areas of social life.

Finally, Diana Dors. Dors worked centrally, neither on the conventions or forms of television, but transparently on its nature as institution. Publicity conscious from the earliest days of her cinema career, Dors manipulated television's promotional machinery. In a career strewn with personal scandal and professional disputes with managements (in the best showbiz tradition) the distinction between a chaotic lifestyle and self-promotion was rarely clear. Yet, through this, there developed a highly reflexive use of the Dors persona.

Established initially as a sex symbol, she refused the connotations of dumb sexuality. Always self-conscious of the type, she wasted few chances to expose – through exaggerated gestures of female sexuality and a sneering disdain for on-screen predatory males (no-one curled a lip like Dors) – its construction in male voyeurism. Yet, skilfully, the licence of her own sexuality was not lost in the process and the sense of a woman in control, manipulating within the constraints, was paramount. As she aged, she pushed at the connotations of a variant type known as 'the good time girl', retaining its characteristic self-regulating search for pleasure, but denying its characterisation as sin, and crossing the type with another in its celebration of activity in motherhood. Her conversation in chat shows was peppered with *risqué* tales, putting the life into family life, breaking the conventional models of femininity and domesticity. Her challenge to these conventions made her a risk to the institution, hence the short-term irregularity of her appearances, but this merely served to imbue her appearances with critical resonances. Dors offered a challenging model in an antagonistic relation to the meaning of roles customarily allocated to (especially working-class) women and it is likely that the model would connect with the experience and aspirations of that gendered audience. The pleasure she displayed in female company, especially other sexually available mothers like Marti Caine; the negotiated control she exercised over male groups, especially in fictions like *Queenie's Castle*; the assertive-ness at odds with her torch songs; all these offered tactical strategies for changing male-centred discourses about woman's role in heterosexual partnerships and family relations.

Dors disturbed a range of female roles on television. In so doing, she offered connections with women of all ages in a comparable variety of social roles, recognising their experience, demonstrating possibilities for change within that experience and offering models of alternative possibilit-ies. It's also worth asserting – not least to explain the pleasures for *men* in her performances – that Dors held out pleasures in these changes for men troubled by conventional models of male-regulated heterosexual relationships and the unattainable (and undesired) ideals of masculinity those models inscribe.

Finally, whatever the merits or limitations of this particular case-study, I hope it indicates a requirement of cultural criticism to explore structures and strategies of opposition *within* the mythologies of television, especially in the relation of television to its audiences. The requirement is not least in order to avoid breaking faith, not only with the interests of the many factions of the working class who comprise television's audiences, but also with the pleasures and politically oppositional meanings many in those audiences derive from television. This is an area of famine in cultural criticism which would benefit from a sudden glut.

REFERENCES

First published in L. Masterman (ed.), *TV Mythologies* (London, Comedia/Media Press, 1984).
Rick Altman (ed.), *Genre: The Musical* (Routledge, 1981).
Richard Dyer, *Stars* (BFI, 1979). 'Entertainment & Utopia', *Movie*, 24 (Spring, 1977), 2–13, reprinted in Altman (1981). *Light Entertainment*, TV Monograph 2 (BFI, 1973).
John Ellis, 'Star/industry/image', *Star Signs* (BFI, 1981). 'Made in Ealing', *Screen* (Spring, 1975), v, 16, 1 (especially pages 113–18).
Jeff Nuttall, *King Twist: A Biography of Frank Randle* (Routledge, 1978).
With thanks to Jim Cook for supportive criticism.

20

PLEASURE, AMBIVALENCE, IDENTIFICATION
Valentino and female spectatorship

Miriam Hansen

In the context of discussions on cinematic spectatorship, the case of Rudolph Valentino demands attention, on historical as well as theoretical grounds. Increasingly, women spectators were perceived as a socially and economically significant group and films were explicitly addressed to a female spectator, regardless of the actual composition of the audience. As Hollywood manufactured the Valentino legend, promoting the fusion of real life and screen persona that makes a star, Valentino's female admirers in effect became part of that legend. Never before was the discourse on fan behaviour so strongly marked by the terms of sexual difference, and never again was spectatorship so explicitly linked to the discourse on female desire. This conjunction was to inform Valentinian mythology for decades to come – as the cover prose from two biographies illustrates:

> Lean, hot-eyed and Latin, Valentino was every woman's dream. . . . The studio telephones could not handle the thousands of calls from women. They begged for any job that would permit even a momentary glimpse of Valentino. Gladly they offered to work without pay.[1]

While these biographies rarely agree on any facts concerning Valentino's life, they stereotypically relate his personal success and suffering to the ongoing crisis of American cultural and social values.[2] Valentino's body, in more than one sense, became the site of contradictions that had erupted with the First World War. The particular historical constellation that made him as well as destroyed him includes the upheaval of gender relations during the war, such as the massive integration of women into the work force and their emergence as a primary target in the shift to a consumer economy; the partial breakdown of gender-specific divisions of labour and a blurring of traditional delimitations of public and private; the need to redefine notions of femininity in terms other than domesticity and motherhood; the image of the New Woman promoted along with a demonstrative liberalisation of sexual behaviour and lifestyles; the emergence of the companionate marriage.[3]

259

However one may interpret the dialectics of women's so-called emancipation and their integration into a consumer culture, women did gain a considerable degree of public visibility in those years, and the cinema was one of the places in which this increased social and economic significance was acknowledged, in whatever distorted manner. The orientation of the market towards a female spectator/consumer opened up a potential gap between traditional patriarchal ideology on the one hand and the recognition of female experience, needs, fantasies on the other, albeit for the purposes of immediate commercial exploitation and eventual containment.[4] It is in this gap that the Valentino phenomenon deserves to be read, as a significant yet precarious moment in the changing discourse on femininity and sexuality. Precarious, not least, because it sidetracked that discourse to question standards of masculinity, destabilising them with connotations of sexual ambiguity, social marginality and ethnic/racial otherness.

Valentino also presents a challenge to feminist film theory, in particular as it developed during the 1970s within the framework of psychoanalysis and semiology. This debate inescapably returns to Laura Mulvey's essay on 'Visual Pleasure and Narrative Cinema' (1975) which first spelled out the implications of Lacanian-Althusserian models of spectatorship for a critique of patriarchal cinema. Whatever its limitations and blind spots, the significance of Mulvey's argument lies in her description of the ways in which the classical Hollywood film perpetuates sexual imbalance in the very conventions through which it engages its viewer as subject – its modes of organising vision and structuring narratives. These conventions, drawing on psychic mechanisms of voyeurism, fetishism and narcissism, depend upon and reproduce the conventional polarity of the male as the agent of the 'look' and the image of woman as object of both spectacle and narrative. In aligning spectatorial pleasure with a hierarchical system of sexual difference, classical American cinema inevitably entails what Mulvey calls 'a "masculinization" of the spectator position, regardless of the actual sex (or possible deviance) of any real live movie-goer'.[5]

Besides its somewhat monolithic notion of classical cinema and provocatively Manichean stance on visual pleasure, Mulvey's argument has been criticised frequently for the difficulty of conceptualising a female spectator other than in terms of an absence.[6] In the decade since Mulvey's essay was published, however, feminist critics have attempted to rescue female spectatorship from its 'locus of impossibility', in particular in areas elided by the focus on women's systematic exclusion, for example, the 'woman's film' of the 1940s and other variants of melodrama centring on female protagonists and their world.

Another area of feminist investigation, less clearly delineated, is the question of pleasure and attendant processes of identification experienced by women spectators (including feminist critics) in the actual reception of mainstream films, even with genres devoted to male heroes and activities,

260

such as the Western or the gangster film. The female viewer of 'masculine' genres does not fit the mould of the spectator/subject anticipated by these films, and in many of them narcissistic identification with female characters is of marginal interest at best, especially when the spectacle is more dispersed (over landscape and action scenes) than in genres like the musical or romantic comedy which concentrate pleasure around the image of the female body. But neither is reception on the woman's part merely accidental, arbitrary or individual – failing with regard to the meaning-potential of the film. Rather, one might say that the oscillation and instability (which Mulvey and others have observed)[7] in female spectatorship constitutes a meaningful deviation – a deviation that has its historical basis in the spectator's experience of belonging to a socially differentiated group called women. As a subdominant and relatively indeterminate collective formation, female spectatorship is certainly contingent upon dominant subject positions, and thus not outside or above ideology, but it cannot be reduced to an either/or modality.

Ann Kaplan points out the necessity of distinguishing between the historical spectator, the hypothetical spectator constructed through the film's strategies and the contemporary female spectator with a feminist consciousness. But the textually constructed spectator/subject does not have any objective existence apart from our reading of the film, which is always partial and, if we choose, partisan. Therefore, the question of hermeneutics is not only one of measuring historical scopes of reception against each other, but also one of the politics of reading,[8] a question of how to establish a usable past for an alternative film practice. If all the time, desire and money spent by women watching mainstream films should be of any consequence whatsoever for a feminist countertradition, then this activity has to be made available through readings, in full awareness of its complicity and contingency upon the dominant structures of the apparatus, but none the less as a potential of resistance to be reappropriated.[9]

The distinctiveness of the Valentino films lies in focusing spectatorial pleasure on the image of a male hero/performer. If a man is made to occupy the place of erotic object, how does this affect the organisation of vision? If the desiring look is aligned with the position of a female viewer, does this open up a space for female subjectivity and, by the same token, an alternative conception of visual pleasure?

At first sight, Valentino's films seem to rehearse the classical choreography of the look almost to the point of parody, offering point-of-view constructions that affirm the cultural hierarchy of gender in the visual field. Between 1921 (*The Four Horsemen of the Apocalypse*) and 1926, the year of his premature death, Valentino starred in fourteen films, produced by different studios and under different directors.[10] Illustrating the significance of the star as *auteur* as much as the economic viability of vehicles,

Figure 20.1 Blood and Sand (1922)

each of these films reiterates a familiar pattern in staging the exchange of looks between Valentino and the female characters. Whenever Valentino lays eyes on a woman first, we can be sure that she will turn out to be the woman of his dreams, the legitimate partner in the romantic relationship; whenever a woman initiates the look, she is invariably marked as a vamp, to be condemned and defeated in the course of the narrative.

This pattern can be observed in *Blood and Sand* (1922): Doña Sol (Nita Naldi), the president's niece, is shown admiring the victorious torero through binoculars before he looks at her; thus, she is syntactically marked as a vamp. His future wife Carmen (Lila Lee), on the other hand, is singled out by the camera within his point of view. A close-up of his face signals the awakening desire, alternating with an indecipherable long shot of a crowd. The repetition of the desiring look, provoking a dissolve that extricates her from the crowd, resolves the picture puzzle for the spectator and, by the same logic of vision, establishes her as the legitimate companion (further sanctioned by the inclusion of his mother in the point-of-view construction that follows). Thus the legitimate female figure is deprived of the initiative of the erotic look and relegated to the position of scopic object within the diegesis. In relation to the spectator, however, *she shares this position of scopic object with Valentino himself.*

Valentino's appeal depends, to a large degree, on the manner in which he combines masculine control of the look with the feminine quality of 'to-be-looked-at-ness', to use Mulvey's rather awkward term. When Valentino falls in love – usually at first sight – the close-up of his face clearly surpasses that of the female character in its value as spectacle. In a narcissistic doubling, the subject of the look constitutes itself as object, graphically illustrating Freud's formulation of the autoerotic dilemma: 'Too bad that I cannot kiss myself'.[11] Moreover, in their radiant pictorial quality, such shots temporarily arrest the metonymic drive of the narrative, similar in effect to the visual presence of the woman which, as Mulvey observes, tends 'to freeze the flow of action in moments of erotic contemplation'.[12] In Valentino's case, however, erotic contemplation governs an active as well as passive mode, making both spectator and character the subject of a double game of vision.

To the extent that Valentino occupies the position of primary object of spectacle, this entails a systematic feminisation of his persona. Many of the films try to motivate this effect by casting him as a performer (torero, dancer) or by situating him in a historically removed or exotic *mise en scène*; in either case, the connotation of femininity persists through the use of costumes – in particular flared coats and headdresses reminiscent of a bridal wardrobe, as well as a general emphasis on dressing and disguises.

Before considering the possibilities of identification implied in this peculiar choreography of vision, I wish to recapitulate some thoughts on female visual pleasure and its fate under the patriarchal taboo. Particularly interesting in this context are certain aspects of scopophilia that Freud analyses through its development in infantile sexuality, a period in which the child is still far from having a stable sense of gender identity. Stimulated in the process of mutual gazing between mother and child, the female scopic drive is constituted with a *bisexual* as well as an *autoerotic* component. While these components subsequently succumb to cultural hierarchies of looking which tend to fixate the woman in a passive, narcissistic-exhibitionist role, there remains a basic ambivalence in the structure of vision as a component drive. As Freud argues in 'Instincts and their Vicissitudes' (1915), the passive component of a drive represents a reversal of the active drive into its opposite, redirecting itself to the subject. Such a contradictory constitution of libidinal components may account for the co-existence, in their later fixation as perversion, of diametrically opposed drives within one and the same person, even if one tendency usually predominates. Thus a voyeur is always to some degree an exhibitionist and vice versa, just as the sadist shares the pleasures of masochism.[13]

The notion of ambivalence appears crucial to a theory of female spectatorship, precisely because the cinema, while enforcing patriarchal hierarchies in its organisation of the look, also offers women an institutional opportunity to violate the taboo on female scopophilia. The success of a figure like Valentino, himself overdetermined as both object and subject of the look, urges us to insist upon the ambivalent constitution of scopic pleasure. Moreover, as one among a number of the more archaic partial drives whose integration is always and at best precarious, scopophilia could be distinguished from a socially more complicit voyeurism, as defined by the one-sided regime of the keyhole and the norms of genitality.[14]

Equally pertinent to an alternative conception of visual pleasure appears the potential dissociation of sexual and survival instincts, discussed in Freud's analysis of cases of psychogenic disturbance of vision. The eye serves both a practical function for the individual's orientation in the external world and the function of an erotogenic zone. If the latter takes over, if it refuses to accept its subservient role in forepleasure, the balance between sexual and survival instincts is threatened and the ego may react by repressing the dangerous component drive; psychogenic disturbance of vision in turn represents the revenge of the repressed instinct, retrospectively interpreted by the individual as the voice of punishment.

This potentially antithetical relationship of sexual and survival instincts could also be taken to describe the cultural and historical differentiation of male and female forms of vision. Although the neurotic dissociation may occur in patients of both sexes, the balance effected in so-called normal vision appears more typical of the psychic disposition by means of which the male subject controls the practical world as well as the sexual field. Suffice it here to allude to the historical construction of monocular vision in western art since the Renaissance, the instrumental standards imposed upon looking in technical and scientific observation and other disciplines, areas of cultural activity from which women were barred for centuries; on the flip-side of this coin, we find a variety of social codes enforcing the taboo on female scopophilia, ranging from make-up fashions like belladonna through the once popular injunction, parodied by Dorothy Parker, not to 'make passes at girls who wear glasses'.

The construction of femininity within patriarchal society, however, contains the promise of being incomplete. Women's exclusion from the mastery of the visual field may have diminished the pressure of the ego instincts towards the component drives, which are probably insufficiently subordinated to begin with. If such generalisation is at all permissible, women might be more likely to indulge – without immediately repressing – in a sensuality of vision which contrasts with the goal-oriented discipline of the one-eyed masculine look. Christa Karpenstein speaks in this context of 'an unrestrained scopic drive, a swerving and sliding gaze which disregards the meanings and messages of signs and images that socially determine the subject, a gaze that defies the limitations and fixations of the merely visible'.[15]

If I seem to belabour this notion of an undomesticated gaze as a historical aspect of female subjectivity, I certainly don't intend to propose yet another variant of essentialism. To the extent that sexual difference is culturally constructed to begin with, the subversive qualities of a female gaze may just as well be shared by a male character.

The feminine connotation of Valentino's 'to-be-looked-at-ness', however, destabilises his own glance in its very origin, makes him vulnerable to temptations that jeopardise the sovereignty of the male subject. When Valentino's eyes become riveted on the woman of his choice, he seems paralysed rather than aggressive or menacing, occupying the position of the rabbit rather than that of the snake. Struck by the beauty of Carmen, in *Blood and Sand*, his activity seems blocked, suspended; it devolves upon Carmen throwing him a flower to get the narrative back into gear. Later in the film, at the height of his career as a torero, Valentino raises his eyes to the president's box, an individual centred under the benevolent eye of the State, when his gaze is side-tracked, literally decentred, by the sight of Doña Sol in the box to the right. The power of Valentino's gaze depends upon its weakness – enhanced by the fact that he was actually nearsighted and cross-eyed – upon its oscillating between active and passive, between object and ego libido. The erotic appeal of the Valentinian gaze, staged as a look within the look, is one of reciprocity and ambivalence, rather than mastery and objectifications.

The peculiar organisation of the Valentinian gaze corresponds, on the level of narrative, to conflict between the pleasure and the reality principle. Whenever the hero's amorous interests collide with the standards of male social identity – career, family, paternal authority, or a vow of revenge – the spectator can hope that passion will triumph over pragmatism to the point of self-destruction.[16] As the generating vortex of such narratives, the Valentinian gaze far exceeds its formal functions of providing diegetic coherence and continuity; it assumes an almost figural independence. Thus the films advance an identification with the gaze itself; not with either source or object, but with the gaze as erotic medium which promises to transport the spectator out of the world of means and ends into the realm of passion.

The discussion of gendered patterns of vision inevitably opens up into the larger question of identification as the linchpin between film and spectator, the process that organises subjectivity in visual and narrative terms. Most productively, feminist film theorists have taken up the debate by insisting on the centrality of sexual difference, questioning the assumption of a single or neutral spectator position constructed in hierarchically ordered, linear processes of identification. The difficulty of conceptualising a female spectator has led feminists to recast the problem of identification in terms of instability, mobility, multiplicity, and, I would add, temporality. Likewise, a number of feminist critics are trying to complicate the role of sexual difference in identification with the differences of class and race, with cultural and historical specificity. The question of who is the subject of identification is also and not least a question concerning which part of the spectator is engaged and how: which layers of conscious or unconscious memory and fantasy are activated, and how we, both as viewers and as critics, choose to interpret this experience.[17]

It seems useful at this point to invoke Mary Ann Doane's distinction between at least three instances of identification operating in the viewing process: (1) identification *with* the representation of a person (character/-star); (2) recognition of particular objects, persons, or action *as* such (stars, narrative images); (3) identification with the 'look', with oneself as the condition of perception, which Metz, in analogy with Lacan's concept of the mirror phase, has termed 'primary'.[18]

The first form of identification with the integral person filmed engages the female viewer transsexually insofar as it extends to the Valentino character; thus, it raises the problem of spectatorial cross-dressing – unless we consider other possibilities of transsexual identification beside the transvestite one. The alternative option for the woman spectator, passive-narcissistic identification with the female star as erotic object, appears to have been a position primarily advertised by the industry,[19] but it appears rather more problematic in view of the specular organisation of the films.

If we can isolate an instance of 'primary' identification at all – which is dubious on theoretical grounds[20] – the Valentino films challenge the assumption of perceptual mastery implied in such a concept by their foregrounding of the gaze as an erotic medium, a gaze that fascinates precisely because it transcends the socially imposed subject/object hierarchy of sexual difference. Moreover, the contradictions of the female address are located in the very space where the registers of the look and those of narrative and mise-en-scène intersect. In offering the woman spectator a position which is structurally analogous to that of the vamp within the diegesis (looking at Valentino independently of his initiating of the look), identification with the desiring gaze is both granted and incriminated, or, one might say, granted on the condition of its illegitimacy. This may be why the vamp figures in Valentino films (with the exception of *Blood and Sand*) are never totally condemned, inasmuch as they acknowledge a subliminal complicity between Valentino and the actively desiring female gaze.

The least equivocal instance of identification operating in the Valentino films is that which feeds on recognition, the memory-spectacle rehearsed with each appearance of the overvalued erotic object, the star.[21] The

Figure 20.2 The Eagle (1925)

pleasure of recognition involved in the identification of and with a star is dramatised, in many Valentino films, through a recurrent narrative pattern, which in turn revolves around the precarious cultural construction of the persona of the Latin Lover. Often, the Valentino character combines two sides of a melodramatic dualism, which he acts out in a series of disguises and anonymous identities. Thus, in *The Sheik* (1921), the barbaric son of the desert turns out to be of British descent; in *Moran of the Lady Letty* (1922), the San Francisco dandy proves himself a hearty sailor and authentic lover; the Duke of Chartres in exile becomes Monsieur Beaucaire; and the Black Eagle pursues courtship instead of revenge under the assumed identity of Monsieur LeBlanc.[22] The spectator recognises her star in all his masks and disguises – unlike the female protagonist whose trial

267

Figure 20.3 Monsieur Beaucaire (1924)

of love consists of 'knowing' him regardless of narrative misfortune or social status.

Like most star vehicles, Valentino films have notoriously weak narratives and would probably fail to engage any viewer if it weren't for their hero's charisma. Many of his films are adapted from well-known popular novels, preferably costume dramas.[23] While there is some delight in action, in the sense of activity, physical movement, and gesture, there is very little suspense, very little of the game of concealing and revealing, of the dialectic of desire, knowledge, and power that has led theorists like Barthes, Bellour, and Heath to define all narrative as predicated on Oedipus. Identification in terms of narrative movement is likely to fall short of the plot in its totality, while closure tends to reside in smaller units, cutting across visual and narrative registers, defined by the succession of masks, disguises, milieus, and scenarios.

The emphasis on costumes, disguises, on rituals of dressing and undressing, undermines, in tendency, the voyeuristic structure of spectatorship in that it acknowledges the spectator as part of the theatrical display. This is emblematic in the famous dressing scene in *Monsieur Beaucaire*, during which Valentino punctuates the exercise in procrastination with occasional asides in the direction of the camera.[24] Such mutual recognition, in conjunction with the viewer's epistemological superiority over the female protagonist, encourages identification via a fantasy in which the spectator herself authorises the masquerade; the publication, as late as 1979, of a Valentino paper-doll book would testify to the persistence of this phantasy in popular iconography.

But this is not the only type of scenario which organises identification in the Valentino films. Pervasively, in these films, spectatorial pleasure is imbricated with self-consciously sadomasochistic rituals[25] The more interesting instances of sadomasochistic role-playing take place in the context of the legitimate, romantic relationship. In *The Eagle*, Mascha turns out to be the daughter of the odious landowner against whom Valentino, in his persona as the Black Eagle, has pledged revenge on his father's deathbed. At one point, his men kidnap her and proudly present the catch to their leader. As he gets off his horse and steps toward her with a whip ready to lash out, the genre seems to slide into porn: the masks, the whip, phallic hats – insignia of anonymous lust, traces of the search for nonidentity in eros.[26] That Valentino actually directs the whip against his own men is the alibi the narrative provides for a kinky shot, the *défilement* into propriety; yet it does not diminish the subliminal effect. Valentino recognises Mascha and, protected by his unilateral anonymity, continues the game in a more or less playful manner. This game is accomplished within the legitimate relationship only by means of the mask which temporarily suspends the mutuality of the romantic gaze in Valentino's favour.

The emphasis on the sadistic aspects of the Valentino persona echoes the publicity pitch advertising him to female audiences as the 'he-man', the 'menace', reiterated, as late as 1977, by one of his biographers: 'Women were to find in *The Sheik* a symbol of the omnipotent male who could dominate them as the men in their own lives could not.'[27] And, when in the film of that title the son of the desert forces the blue-eyed Lady Diana on his horse, ostensibly for her own pleasure ('lie still you little fool'), millions of women's hearts were said to have quivered at the prospect of being humiliated by the British-bred barbarian. Despite the display of virility in *The Sheik* (1922; based on the novel by Edith Maude Hull), however, this film initiated the much publicised rejection of Valentino by male moviegoers, which had more to do with the threat he presented to traditional norms of masculinity than with the actual composition of audience.[28] Not only the stigma of effeminacy but also, equally threatening, a masochistic aura was to haunt Valentino to his death and beyond. There were widespread rumours about his private life – homosexuality, impotence, unconsummated marriages with lesbians, dependency on domineering women, the platinum 'slave bracelet' given to him by his second wife, Natasha Rambova. More systematically, the masochistic elements in the Valentino persona were enforced by the sadistic placement of the spectator in the films themselves. There is hardly a Valentino film that does not display a whip, in whatever marginal function, and most of them feature seemingly insignificant subplots in which the spectator is offered a position that entails enjoying the tortures inflicted on Valentino or others.[29]

The oscillation of the Valentino persona between sadistic and masochistic positions is yet another expression of the ambivalence that governs the specular organisation of the films. I wish to return to Freud's essay, 'A child is being beaten' (1919), not only for its focus on female instances of sadomasochistic fantasy, but also because it elucidates a particular aspect of the Valentino figure as fantasmatic object.[30] The formula, 'a child is being beaten', which, regardless of any actually experienced corporal punishment, may dominate masturbation fantasies of the latency period, is remarkable in that it stereotypically reiterates the mere description of the event, while subject, object and the role of the person fantasising remain indeterminate. On the basis of jealousy feelings aroused by the Oedipal constellation, Freud proceeds to reconstruct three different phases with explicit reference to female adolescents: (1) 'My father is beating the child that I hate' (presumably a younger sibling); therefore, 'he loves only me'; (2) 'I am being beaten [therefore loved] by my father' (the regressive substitute for the incestuous relationship); (3) 'a child is being beaten.' While the second, sexually most threatening phase succumbs to repression, the first phase is reduced to its merely descriptive part and thus results in the third, in which the father is usually replaced by a more distant male authority figure. Thus the fantasy is sadistic only in its form – but grants masochistic gratification by way of identification with the anonymous children who are being beaten. This series of transformations reduces the sexual participation of the girl to the status of spectator, desexualising both content and bearer of the fantasy (which, as Freud remarks, is not the case in male variants of the beating fantasy). Just as important in the present context, however, is the observation that in both male and female versions of the sadomasochistic fantasy the children who are being beaten generally turn out to be male. In the case of the female fantasy, Freud employs the concept of the 'masculinity complex', which makes the girl imagine herself as male and thus allows her to be represented, in her daydreams, by these anonymous whipping boys.

The deepest, most effective layer of the Valentino persona is that of the whipping boy – in which he resembles so many other heroes of popular fiction devoured by adolescent girls (one of the examples Freud cites is *Uncle Tom's Cabin*). Freud's analysis of the sadomasochistic fantasy suggests that we distinguish between the sadistic appeal articulated in point-of-view structures on the one hand, and the masochistic pleasure in the identification with the object on the other. Transsexual identification,

270

instead of being confined to simple cross-dressing, relies here as much on the feminine qualities of the male protagonist as it does on residual ambiguity in the female spectator. This simultaneity of identificatory positions is enabled by an interactional structure, a scenario whose libidinal force, protected by a series of repressive/rhetorical transformations, can be traced back to the nursery.

Unlike the one-sided masochistic identification with a female protagonist encouraged by the 'woman's film', female identification in Valentino films could be construed to entail the full range of transformations proposed by Freud. As Valentino slips into and out of the part of the whipping boy, intermittently relegating the woman to the position of both victim and perpetrator, he may succeed in recuperating the middle phase of the female fantasy from repression ('I am being beaten – and therefore loved – by my father') and thus in resexualising it. This possibility is suggested above all by the unmistakable incestuous aura surrounding the Valentino persona; however, the appeal here is less that of a relationship between father and daughter than one between brother and sister, which turns on the desire of both for an inaccessible mother.[31]

In making sadomasochistic rituals an explicit component of the erotic relationship, Valentino's films subvert the socially imposed dominance/submission hierarchy of gender roles, dissolving subject/object dichotomies into erotic reciprocity. The vulnerability Valentino displays in his films, the traces of feminine masochism in his persona, may partly account for the threat he posed to prevalent standards of masculinity – the sublimation of masochistic inclinations after all being the token of the male subject's sexual mastery, his control over pleasure.

Sadomasochistic role-playing most strikingly intersects with the choreography of vision in *The Son of the Sheik* (1926; based on another novel by E. M. Hull), Valentino's last and probably most perverse film. Due to a misunderstanding that propels the narrative, Yasmin (Vilma Banky) represents a combination of both female types, vamp and romantic companion. Although transparent to the spectator, the misunderstanding on Ahmed/Valentino's part – that Yasmin lured him into a trap, thus causing him to be captured and whipped by her father's gang – has carefully been planted early on in the film by means of an editing device. The film's first close-up shows the face of Yasmin, lost in erotic yearning, which dissolves into a matching close-up of Valentino; a somewhat mismatched cut in turn reveals him to be looking at her legs as she is dancing for a crowd. A dissolve back to Yasmin's face eventually confirms the status of the sequence as a flashback which stages the usual discovery of the woman through Valentino's look; the objectification here is compounded by the demeaning situation, the fragmentation of Yasmin's body as well as the emphasis on money in the deployment of the romantic gaze. The potential misreading of the flashback as a point-of-view shot on the part of the woman falsely implicates Yasmin as a transgressor, thus supporting her double inscription as victim later on in the film, as both scopic and masochistic object. Herself ignorant of her lover's misunderstanding, Yasmin is kidnapped by him and imprisoned in his tent. His revenge accordingly consists in refusing her the mutuality of the erotic look and culminates in a veritable one-eyed stare with which he transfixes her to the point of rape. Valentino's unilateral transgression of the romantic pact is supposedly vindicated by the powerful image of him crucified, humiliated and whipped earlier on in the film. This image of Valentino as victim, however, erroneously ascribed to Yasmin's authorship and not even witnessed by her, is primarily designed for the benefit of the spectator. No doubt there remains an asymmetry in the sadomasochistic role reversal on the diegetic level: a female character can assume an active part only at the price of being marked as a vamp; sadistic pleasure is specularised, reserved for the woman in front of the screen.

The multiple ambiguities articulated on the specular level of *The Son of the Sheik* contrast with the more flatly patriarchal discourse of the narrative, not to mention the simple-minded sexist and racist title prose. As if to conceal – and thus unofficially to acknowledge and exploit – this gap between narrative and visual pleasure, the Oedipal scenario is overinscribed to the point of parody. Valentino's private love/revenge affair meets with strong resistance on the part of his father who bends an iron rod with his mere hands in order to demonstrate his paternal power; Valentino, a chip off the old block, responds by straightening it out again. Only when his understanding mother, Lady Diana (Agnes Ayres), invokes a flashback to her own kidnapping in *The Sheik* does the father recognise and accept his successor. They reconcile in the course of yet another kidnapping scene, this time rescuing Yasmin from her father's gang: in the midst of tumultuous swashbuckling father and son shake hands, temporarily losing sight of the woman, the object of their endeavour.

Beneath this Oedipal pretext, as it were, the film offers a connotative wealth of deviations which radiate in a dialectic of repression and excess from the Valentino character to all levels of *mise en scène* and cinematography. Exotic costumes, oriental decor and desert landscape provoke a sensuality of vision which constantly undermines the interest in the development of the narrative. Extreme long shots show Valentino riding through a sea of sand shaped like breasts and buttocks; he prefers the skin-folds of his tent to the parental palace, and he experiences in the allegorical moonlit ruin the pitfalls of adult sexuality, the threat of castration. Though concealing dangerous abysses, the eroticised landscape becomes a playground of polymorphous desire, in which the signs of virility – sables, pistols, cigarettes – remain phallic toys at best. The screen itself becomes a maternal body, inviting the component drives to revolt against their subordination. These textured surfaces do not project a realistic space which the hero,

272

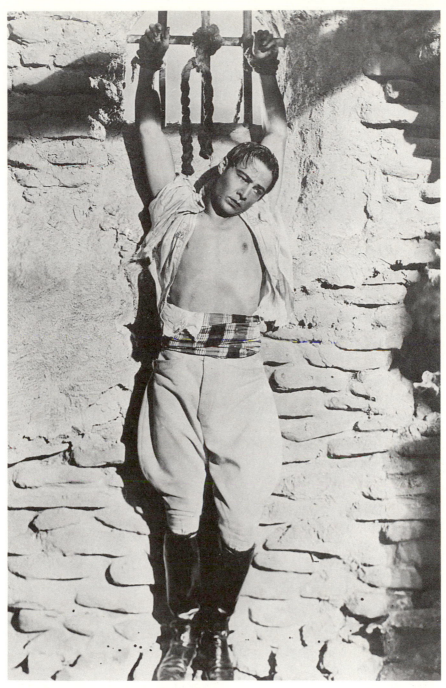

Figure 20.4 The Son of the Sheik (1926)

273

traversing it, would be obligated to subject. Rather, they construct an oneiric stage which cannot be bothered with perspective and verisimilitude. With a degree of unreality of which the silent screen was yet capable, Valentino's last film admits to the reality of a fantasy that assimilates the Oedipal scenario for its own purposes. Not only does it force the father to identify with the phallic caprices of his youth, but it even more thoroughly subverts the Oedipal script in its casting: Valentino himself plays the role of the father in whose mirror image the son achieves a presumably adult male identity which inevitably – and barely masked – reveals itself as both narcissistic and incestuous.

The appeal of the Valentino fantasy is certainly regressive, beckoning the female spectator (to revise Mulvey) beyond the devil of phallic identification into the deep blue sea of polymorphous perversity. Such an appeal cannot but provoke the connotation of monstrosity which the films displace on to figures like the vamp or the sadomasochistic dwarf in *The Son of the Sheik*, a vicious caricature of Orientalism. The threat posed by Valentino's complicity with the woman who looks, like the affinity of monster and woman in Linda Williams's reading of the horror film, is not a threat merely of sexual difference but of a different *kind* of sexuality, different from the norm of heterosexual, genital sexuality.[32] While playing along with narrative conventions that assert the latter (e.g. the figure of couple formation), the Valentino films allow their spectators to repeat and acknowledge the more archaic component drives, reminders of the precarious constructedness of sexual identity. Moreover, in locating pleasure in the tension – if not excess – of partial libido in relation to genitality, they project a realm of the erotic as distinct from the socially cultivated ideal of a 'healthy sex life'.[33]

To claim a subversive function for polymorphous perversity as such is highly problematic, as Foucault asserts, given the degree to which disparate sexualities themselves have been appropriated by a discourse binding pleasure and power. It is therefore all the more important to reconsider the historical moment at which Valentino enters that discourse, marking its conjunction with other discourses, in particular those of social mobility and racial otherness. In a liberal gesture, Alexander Walker ponders the paradox of the Valentino craze; that is, that it took place alongside the progressive liberation of American women from traditional roles: 'It was a perverse way of celebrating your sex's emancipation.'[34] Perverse, yes, but not so paradoxical. As revisionist historians have argued, the New Woman was usually not as emancipated as her image suggested, and her access to consumer culture often entailed an underpaid job, loneliness and social insecurity or, in the case of married women, the multiple burdens of wage labour, housework and childrearing.[35] The period's demonstrative obsession with sexual reform may well confirm Foucault's argument on sexuality as discourse at large; still, this discourse must have had different implications for women than for men, or for single working women as compared, for instance, to upper-middle-class housewives.

However complicit and recuperable in the long run, the Valentino films articulated the possibility of female desire outside of motherhood and family, absolving it from Victorian double standards;[36] instead, they offered a morality of passion, an ideal of erotic reciprocity. Moreover, unlike the feminine reaction of sexual liberation in the shape of Elinor Glyn (the Edwardian novelist who invented the 'it' girl), Valentino did not render the erotic a matter of social etiquette to be rehearsed by the aspiring female subject.[37] Rather, in focusing pleasure on a male protagonist of ambiguous and deviant identity, he appealed to those who most strongly felt the effects – freedom as well as frustration – of transition and liminality, the precariousness of a social mobility predicated on consumerist ideology.

If the Valentino films had no other critical function, they did present, by way of negation, a powerful challenge to myths of masculinity in American culture between the wars. The heroes of the American screen were men of action, like Douglas Fairbanks or William S. Hart, whose energy and determination was only enhanced by a certain lack of social graces, especially toward women. Even the more romantic stars, like Richard Barthelmess or John Barrymore, seemed to owe their good looks to a transcendent spirituality rather than anything related to their bodies and sexuality. Valentino not only inaugurated an explicitly sexual discourse on male beauty, but he also undercut standards of instrumental rationality that were culturally associated with masculine behaviour; his resistance to expectations of everyday pragmatism, his swerving from the matter-of-fact and reasonable, may after all account for his subterranean popularity with male movie-goers, whether homosexual or heterosexual.

But Valentino's otherness cannot be explained exclusively in terms of masculinity and its discontents. Beyond the feminine connotations of his persona, his appeal was that of a 'stranger'. Whatever distinguished previous and contemporary male stars from each other, they were all Americans; that is, they did not display any distinct ethnic features other than those that were already naturalised as American. Valentino, however, bore the stigma of the first-generation, non-Anglo-Saxon immigrant – and was cast accordingly. He began his career as a seducer/villain of dark complexion, male counterpart of the figure of the vamp. When female audiences adopted him, despite the moral/racist injunction, he developed the persona of the Latin Lover, marketed as a blend of sexual vitality and romantic courtship. It is not surprising, then, that the paragons of virility responded to the threat he posed in a strongly nativist tone.[38] Yet more systematically, the films themselves both thematised and contained the scandal of his otherness through a recurrent pattern of the double identity mentioned earlier – a pattern which has to be read as a textual symptom of the repression of racial difference.

Valentino's darker self is ostensibly southern European, somewhat redeemed by a veneer of French manners; in the context of American cinema and American culture, however, he could not have escaped the discursive economy of race and sex, encapsulated in the fear and repressed desire of miscegenation.[39] Sexual paranoia towards black men, rampant since the mid-1890s, reached a new pitch during the 1920s, precipitated by the imagined effects of women's sexual liberation. In terms of this economy, Valentino would have thrived on the fascination with the mulatto, a figure notoriously inscribed with sexual excess (cf. *The Birth of a Nation*), while historically inseparable from the white masters' abuse of black women. Whether or not Valentino touched upon that particular nerve, the connotation of racial otherness was masked by a discourse of exoticism – the Arab sheik, the Indian rajah, the Latin-American gaucho – allowing the female spectator to indulge in the fantasy at a safe distance. Sure enough, the respective narratives reveal the passionate Arab to be of British descent, like Tarzan, just as the lascivious gaucho in *The Four Horsemen* proves himself worthy of his French blood by dying on the field of honour. In such operations of fascination and disavowal, the Valentino films illustrate the ambivalence and fetishism characteristic of all racial stereotypes, the interdependence of racial and sexual difference.[40] At the same time, they mark a historical shift – if not, considering the force of repression provoked, an accidental leap or lapse – which enforced a transvaluation of the taboo and thus its partial recognition, albeit under the guise of the exotic.

Some afterthoughts on the psycho-social enigma posed by the cult of Valentino seem appropriate here. While we may speculate on the appeal of the Valentino persona for both a textually and historically constructed female spectator, the massive impact of this appeal and the social forms it assumed remain quite mysterious. Roland Barthes speaks of the cult of the Valentinian face: 'truly feminine Bacchanalia which all over the world were dedicated to the memory of a collectively revealed beauty'.[41] Inevitably, however, such Dionysian rites are contaminated by the mechanisms of the mass media; the voyeuristic and fetishistic aspects of the Valentino excesses cannot be explained away. How could millions of women have indulged in such specifically male perversions? Barthes may ascribe the cult of Valentino to the aura of his face ('*visage*' vs. '*figure*'); yet for Valentino himself and his female admirers it was certainly no less a cult of his body. In scores of publicity stills Valentino poses working out semi-nude, and in *Blood and Sand* and *Monsieur Beaucaire* he insisted on including dressing scenes that would display individual parts of his body (note the close-up of his foot in *Blood and Sand*). Such exhibitionism, given the mechanisms of the apparatus, cannot escape fetishisation: the male body, in its entire beauty, assumes the function of a phallic substitute. The more desperately Valentino himself emphasised attributes of physical prowess and virility, the more perfectly he played the part of the male impersonator, brilliant counterpart to the female 'female' impersonators of the American screen such as Mae West or the vamps of his own films.

For the history of American cinema, on the threshold of its classical period, Valentino represents a unique instance of subversive irony – in that the commodity marketed as an idol of virility should have proven its success in the shape of a phallic fetish, a symbol of the missing penis. Valentino's miraculous career as a male impersonator illuminates the basic discrepancy between the penis and its symbolic representation, the phallus, thus revealing the male subject's position within the symbolic order as based upon a misreading of anatomy.[42] If women's fascination with Valentino, on whatever level of consciousness, expressed a recognition of that discrepancy, their massive and collective identification with this peculiar fetish also, and not least, asserted the claim to share in the reputation and representation of phallic power.

In the interaction with female audiences, however, the fetishisation of Valentino's body assumed forms of theatricality which tended to subvert the mechanisms of separation intrinsic to cinematic voyeurism and fetishism. His female fans actively assailed the barriers that classical cinema was engaged in reaffirming, taking the star system more literally than the institution might have intended, while the media on their part short-circuited the dialectics of public and private for the narrative of Valentino's life. Once women had found a fetish of their own, they were not content with merely gazing at it, but strove actually to touch it. Moreover, they expected him to reciprocate their fetishistic devotion: Valentino received intimate garments in the mail with the request to kiss and return them (which he did). The cult of Valentino's body finally extended to his corpse and led to the notorious necrophilic excesses: Valentino's last will specifying that his body be exhibited to his fans provoked a fetishistic run for buttons of his suit, or at least candles and flowers from the funeral home.[43] The collective *mise en scène* of fainting spells, hysterical grief and, to be accurate, a few suicides, cannot be reduced to a mere spectacle of mass-cultural manipulation. It may be read, among other things, as a kind of rebellion, a desperate protest against the passivity and one-sidedness with which patriarchal cinema supports the subordinate position of women in the gender hierarchy. In such a reading, even the commercially distorted manifestation of female desire might articulate a utopian claim – to have the hollow promises of screen happiness be released into the mutuality of erotic practice.

NOTES

This is an abridged version of an article published in *Cinema Journal*, 25, 4 (Summer 1986), c. 1986 by the Board of Trustees of the University of Illinois. This essay appears in revised and expanded form in Miriam Hansen's *Babel and Babylon: Spectatorship in American Silent Film*, Harvard University Press, 1991.

1 Brad Steiger and Chaw Mank, *Valentino: An Intimate and Shocking Expose* (New York: MacFadden, 1966) and Irving Shulman, *Valentino* (1967; New York: Pocket Books, 1968). Also see Vincent Tajiri, *Valentino: The True Life Story* (New York: Bantam, 1977); Noel Botham and Peter Donnelly, *Valentino: The Love God* (New York: Ace Books, 1977); Edouard Ramond, *La Vie amoureuse de Rudolph Valentino* (Paris: Librarie Baudiniere, n.d.). For a filmography and bibliography, compiled by Diane Kaiser Koszarski, see Eva Orbanz, ed., *There Is A New Star in Heaven . . . :Valentino* (Berlin: Volker Spiess, 1979) and Alexander Walker, *Rudolph Valentino* (Harmondsworth: Penguin, 1976).

2 Valentino came to symbolise the failure of the American Dream, especially to more highbrow critics of culture like H. L. Mencken (*Prejudices, Sixth Series*, 1927) and John Dos Passos (*The Big Money*, 1936). Ken Russell's film, *Valentino* (1977), based on the Steiger/Mank biography and starring Rudolf Nureyev in the title role, articulates this theme through its pervasive references to *Citizen Kane*, such as the use of *post mortem* multiple flashback narration and other corny allusions.

3 Among the many reassessments of the period, see Estelle B. Freedman, 'The New Woman: Changing views of women in the 1920s', *Journal of American History*, 56, 2 (September 1974), 372–93; Mary P. Ryan, *Womanhood in America*, second edn (New York: New Viewpoints, 1979), ch. 5; Julie Matthaei, *An Economic History of Women in America* (New York: Schocken, 1982), especially chps 7–9.

4 This hypothesis implies a concept of the public sphere, in particular that of an alternative or counter public sphere as developed by Oskar Negt and Alexander Kluge in *Öffentlichkeit und Erfahrung/Public Sphere and Experience* (Frankfurt: Suhrkamp, 1972). For a review in English, see Eberhard Knödler-Bunte, 'The proletarian public sphere and political organization', *New German Critique*, 4 (Winter 1975), 51–75; and my own paraphrase of Negt and Kluge in 'Early silent cinema: whose public sphere?' *New German Critique*, 29 (Spring/Summer 1983), 155–9. The role of the cinema for women during this period of transition is discussed in Judith Mayne, 'Immigrants and spectators', *Wide Angle*, 5, 2 (1982), 32–41; Elizabeth Ewen, 'City lights: immigrant women and the rise of the movies', *Signs*, 5, 3 (1980), S45–S65; Mary Ryan, 'The projection of a new womanhood: the movie moderns in the 1920s', in *Our American Sisters: Women in American Life and Thought*, second edn, Jean E. Friedman and William G. Shade, (eds) (Boston: Allyn and Bacon, 1976), 366–84.

5 Laura Mulvey, 'Afterthoughts . . . inspired by *Duel in the Sun*', *Framework*, 15–17 (1981), 12; 'Visual pleasure and narrative cinema' originally appeared in *Screen*, 16, 3 (Autumn 1977), 6–18.

6 For a still useful discussion of Mulvey in a larger context of directions of recent theory, see Christine Gledhill, 'Developments in feminist film criticism' (1978), rpt in *Re-Vision: Essays in Feminist Film Criticism*, Mary Ann Doane, Patricia Mellencamp, Linda Williams (eds) (Los Angeles: AFI Monograph Series, 1983), 18–48. Among articles devoted primarily to a critique of Mulvey, see David Rodowick, 'The difficulty of difference', *Wide Angle*, 5, 1 (1982), 4–15; Janet Walker, 'Psychoanalysis and feminist film theory', *Wide Angle*, 6, 3 (1984),

16–23. For discussions challenging the Metzian/Mulveyan paradigm of spectatorship altogether, see Gaylyn Studlar, 'Masochism and the perverse pleasures of the cinema', *Quarterly Review of Film Studies*, 9, 4 (Fall 1984), 267–82; Gertrud Koch, 'Exchanging the gaze: re-visioning feminist film theory', *New German Critique*, 34 (Winter 1985), 139–53.

7   Mulvey, 'Afterthoughts', 12.

8   See Jürgen Habermas's critique of Gadamer, *Zur Logik der Sozialwissenschaften* (Frankfurt: Suhrkamp, 1970), 174ff; 'Der Universalitätsanspruch der Hermeneutik', *Kultur und Kritik* (Frankfurt: Suhrkamp, 1973), 264–301.

9   This project obviously involves some 'reading against the grain' but ultimately has a different objective: rather than merely to expose, from film to film, the textual contradictions symptomatic of the repression of female subjectivity under patriarchy, a rewriting of film history in a feminist sense seeks to discover traces of female subjectivity even in the most repressive and alienated form of consumer culture. The paradigm I have in mind is Benjamin's huge work on the Paris Arcades which Susan Buck-Morss (in a forthcoming book) reads as a dialectical *Ur*-history of mass culture. Also see Habermas, 'Consciousness-raising or redemptive criticism: the contemporaneity of Walter Benjamin' (1972), *New German Critique*, 17 (Spring 1979), 30–59.

10 A more consistent trait in Valentino's history with the industry is the high number of women in the production of his films, although this was generally more often the case before 1930. His most important films had scripts written by women, in particular June Mathis who 'discovered' him, but also Frances Marion; *Blood and Sand* was brilliantly edited by Dorothy Arzner; Alla Nazimova and Natacha Rambova, a designer and also his second wife, exerted their artistic and spiritual(ist) influence on many productions, with or without credit.

11 Sigmund Freud, 'Three essays on the theory of sexuality' (1905), *Standard Edition* (hereafter *SE*), 7: 182.

12 Mulvey, 'Visual pleasure', 11.

13 Sigmund Freud, 'Instincts and their vicissitudes', *SE*, 14: 128ff; 'Three essays', *SE*, 7: 156ff., 199f. and passim.

14 I am much indebted here to the work of Gertrud Koch; for essays available in translation, see 'Why women go to the movies', *Jump Cut*, 27 (July 1982); and 'Female sensuality: past joys and future hopes', *Jump Cut*, 30 (March 1985). Also see Christian Metz's distinction between cinematic and theatrical voyeurism in *The Imaginary Signifier* (Bloomington: Indiana University Press, 1982), 64–6, 91–8.

15 Christa Karpenstein, 'Bald führt der Blick das Wort ein, bald leitet das Wort den Blick', *Kursbuch*, 49 (1977), 62. Also see Jutta Brückner's important essay on pornography, 'Der Blutfleck im Auge der Kamera', *Frauen und Film*, 30 (December 1981), 13–23; Brückner links the historical 'underdevelopment' of women's vision with the modality of dreams, as a more archaic form of consciousness: 'This female gaze, which is so precise precisely because it is not too precise, because it also has this inward turn, opening itself to fantasy images which it melts with the more literal images on the screen, this gaze is the basis for a kind of identification which women in particular tend to seek in the cinema' (19).

16 Two of Valentino's most popular films, *The Four Horsemen* and *Blood and Sand*, actually culminate in the protagonist's death, bringing into play the deep affinity of eros and death drive which Freud observes in his fascinating paper on 'The theme of the three caskets' (1913), *SE*, 12: 289–301. According to Enno Patalas, Valentino himself identified much more strongly with these two roles

than with the superficial heroism of the Sheik, *Sozialgeschichte der Stars* (Hamburg: Marion von Schröder Verlag, 1963), 96f.

17 See Janet Walker, 'Psychoanalysis and feminist film theory' (note 6), 20ff.; de Lauretis, 'Aesthetic and feminist theory', *New German Critique*, 34 (Winter 1985), 164ff.

18 Doane, 'Misrecognition and identity', *Ciné-Tracts*, 3, 3 (Fall 1980), 25; Metz, *The Imaginary Signifier*, 46ff., 56ff. and passim.

19 This option actually prevails in contemporary statements of female spectators; see Herbert Blumer, *Movies and Conduct* (New York: Macmillan, 1933), 69–70. In retrospect, however, as I frequently found in conversations with women who were in their teens at the time, the female star has faded into oblivion as much as the narrative, whereas Valentino himself is rememberd with great enthusiasm and vividness of detail.

20 Doane, 'Misrecognition and identity', 28ff.; Doane's major objection to Metz's concept of primary identification is that, based as it is on the analogy with the Lacanian mirror stage and thus the hypothetical constitution of the male subject, the concept perpetuates, on a theoretical level, the patriarchal exclusion of female spectatorship.

21 See Richard Dyer, *Stars* (London: BFI, 1979).

22 This pattern of combining dark and light oppositions in one and the same character must have been perceived as typical of the Valentino text; see the change of Dubrovsky's alias in *The Eagle* from Pushkin's Monsieur Deforge to Valentino's Monsieur LeBlanc.

23 Alexander Walker, *Rudolph Valentino* (Harmondsworth: Penguin, 1977), 54f.

24 As Tom Gunning points out, such instances of direct address were rather common in erotic films before 1908, but thereafter persist only in the pornographic tradition – 'the seeming acknowledgment of the presence of the spectator-voyeur gives these films much of their erotic power'. 'An unseen energy swallows space: the space in early film and its relation to American avant-garde film', in *Film Before Griffith*, John Fell (ed.) (Berkeley: University of California Press, 1983), 359.

25 A number of critics have recently commented upon the role of sadomasochistic structures in cinematic identification: Rodowick, 'The difficulty of difference' (note 6, above); Doane, 'The woman's film', *Re-vision*; 67–82; Kaja Silverman, 'Masochism and subjectivity' (on Cavani's *Portiere di Notte), Framework*, 12 (1980), 2–9. Also see Jessica Benjamin, 'Master and slave: the fantasy of erotic domination', in *Powers of Desire: The Politics of Sexuality*, ed. Ann Snitow *et al.* (New York: Monthly Review Press, 1983), 280–99.

26 Koch, 'Schattenreich der Körper: Zum pornographischen Kino', in *Lust und Elend: Das erotische Kino* (Munich: Bucher, 1981), 35; 'The Body's Shadow Realm' in *October*, 50 (Fall 1989), 3–29. The investment in eros as a negation of the principle of social identity is, of course, a topos of the Frankfurt School, especially in the work of Adorno; see his and Horkheimer's critique of the subject under patriarchy and monopoly capitalism in *Dialectic of Enlightenment* (Amsterdam: Querido, 1947), his aphorisms and fragments, dating back to the period of exile, in *Minima Moralia* (Frankfurt: Suhrkamp, 1951), as well as later essays in cultural criticism such as 'Sexualtabus und Recht heute', *Eingriffe* (Frankfurt: Suhrkamp, 1963), 104.

27 Tajiri (note 1), 63.

28 The male contingent among Valentino fans is not to be underestimated, including Elvis Presley, Kenneth Anger and other luminaries; see Kenneth Anger, 'Rudy's rep', in *Hollywood Babylon* (London: Straight Arrow Books, 1975;

New York: Dell, 1981); and his contribution to a catalogue of the Berlin Film Festival retrospective of Valentino's work, 'Sich an Valentino erinnern heisst Valentino entdecken', discussed by Karsten Witte, in 'Fetisch-Messen', *Frauen und Film*, 38 (May 1985), 72–8. Ken Russell's film (see note 2) both exploits and disavows Valentino's place in the homosexual tradition. More important than biographical fact is the question of how Valentino challenged dominant standards of masculinity, which is also a question of their social and historical variability and changeability.

29 The sadistic spicing of cinematic pleasure (far from being the exclusive domain of Von Stroheim) is still rather common in pre-Code films, though seldom with such strong effects on the sexual persona of the protagonist. Consider, for instance, a sequence early on in the Pickford vehicle *Sparrows* (1926) in which the villain (Gustav von Seyffertitz) crushes a doll sent, by an absent mother, to one of the children he keeps as slaves; the camera lingers, close-up, on the remnants of the doll as it slowly disappears in the swamp. The fascination deployed in such a shot far exceeds narrative motivation; i.e. its function for establishing Mr Grimes as irredeemably evil.

30 Freud, 'A child is being beaten', *SE*, 17, 186. The essay has been much discussed in recent film theory; for example, Rodowick, 'The difficulty of difference' (see n.6), and Doane, 'The woman's film' (see n. 25).

31 This incestuous-narcissistic aura is encapsulated in a portrait showing Valentino and Rambova in profile and, obviously, in the nude; rpt in Walker, 73; and Anger, *Hollywood Babylon*, 160–1.

32 Williams, 'When the woman looks', *Re-Vision*, 83–96. The point Williams makes with regard to a number of classic horror films also elucidates the function of the dark/light split in the Valentino character: 'the power and potency of the monster body . . . should not be interpreted as an eruption of the normally repressed animal sexuality of the civilized male (the monster as double for the male viewer and characters in the film), but as feared power and potency of a different kind of sexuality (the monster as double for the woman)' (87).

33 Adorno, 'Sexualtabus' (note 26), 104–5; the phrase is used in English and without quotation marks; also see 'This side of the pleasure principle', *Minima Moralia: Reflections from Damaged Life* (London: New Left Books, 1974). Marcuse's plea for polymorphous perversity in *Eros and Civilization* (1955; Boston: Beacon Press, 1966) is more problematic, especially in light of the Foucaultian analysis of the 'perverse implantation' (*The History of Sexuality*, 1), but Marcuse himself takes a more pessimistic view in his 'Political Preface 1966', while maintaining a utopian distinction between sexual liberty and erotic/political freedom (xiv–xv). Already during the 1920s, the prophets of a 'healthy sex life' were numerous, drawing on the essentialist sexual psychology of Havelock Ellis, on the newly discovered 'doctrine' of psychoanalysis, as well as libertarian positions developed among the Greenwich Village boheme, although not necessarily all that liberating for women; see writings by Hutchins Hapgood, Max Eastman, V. F. Calverton and – probably the single most repressive instance of sexual hygiene – Floyd Dell, *Love in the Machine Age: A Psychological Study of the Transition from Patriarchal Society* (New York: Farrar & Rinehart, 1930).

34 Walker, *Rudolph Valentino*, 8, 47 and passim.

35 See works cited above, note 3.

36 *Blood and Sand*, closest to the melodramatic matrix, is the only film that makes Valentino's mate a mother; by contrast, most other female characters

opposite Valentino have tomboyish qualities (especially Moran in *Moran of the Lady Letty*), an air of independence, owing to either a superior social status or work and, above all, a certain 'mischievous vivacity' (Ryan, see n. 4) that was associated with the New Woman.

37 Glyn actually endorsed Valentino's sex appeal, and he starred in *Beyond the Rocks* (1922), based on one of her novels. Still, the focus on a male star distinguishes the Valentino films from films that more immediately functioned to train their audiences in 'fashionable femininity'; Ryan, 'Projection' (note 4), 370f.

38 See the notorious 'Pink powder puff' attack in the *Chicago Tribune*, 18 July 1926, reported in *Hollywood Babylon*, 156–8.

39 For this aspect of the Valentino persona I am indebted to Virginia Wright Wexman as well as to Richard Dyer's work on Paul Robeson; Winifred Stewart and Jean Hady, who remember the Valentino cult during their teenage years in Martinsburg, West Virginia, further encouraged the following speculations. Also see Jacqueline Hall, ' "The mind that burns in each body": women, rape, and racial violence', in *Powers of Desire* (note 25), 337.

40 Homi K. Bhabha, 'The other question: the stereotype and colonial discourse', *Screen*, 24, 6 (November–December 1983), 18–36.

41 Roland Barthes, 'Visages et figures', *Esprit*, 204 (July 1953), 6.

42 Richard Dyer suggests that all representations of the male body, especially however, of male nudity, share this fate, since the actual sight of the penis, whether limp or erect, is bound to be awkward, thus revealing the discrepancy between it and the symbolic claims made in its name, the hopeless assertion of phallic mastery; 'Don't look now: The male pin-up', *Screen*, 23, 3–4 (Sept.–Oct. 1982).

43 Any Valentino biography will elaborate on these events with great gusto. For the most detailed account, including an astonishing chapter on Valentino's afterlife ('Act V: Cuckooland'), see Shulman's book (note 1).

21

'A QUEER FEELING WHEN I LOOK AT YOU'
Hollywood stars and lesbian spectatorship in the 1930s

Andrea Weiss

Boldly claiming to 'tell the facts and name the names', in July 1955 *Confidential Magazine* embarked on telling 'the untold story of Marlene Dietrich'. The exposé reads, 'Dietrich going for dolls', and goes on to list among her many female lovers the 'blonde Amazon' Claire Waldoff, writer Mercedes d'Acosta (rumoured to be Greta Garbo's lover as well), a notorious Parisian lesbian named Frede, and multi-millionaire Jo Carstairs, whom *Confidential Magazine* dubs a 'mannish maiden' and a 'baritone babe'.[1]

The scandal sheet may have shocked the general public by its disclosures, but for many lesbians it only confirmed what they had long suspected. Rumour and gossip constitute the unrecorded history of the gay subculture. In the introduction to *Jump Cut*'s Lesbian and Film Issue, the editors begin to redeem gossip's lowly status: 'If oral history is the history of those denied control of the printed record, then gossip is the history of those who cannot even speak in their own first-person voice.'[2] Patricia Meyer Spacks in her book *Gossip* pushes this definition further seeing it not only as symptomatic of oppression but actually as a tool which empowers oppressed groups: '[Gossip] embodies an alternative discourse to that of public life, and a discourse potentially challenging to public assumptions; it provides language for an alternative culture.'[3] Spacks argues that through gossip those who are otherwise powerless can assign meanings and assume the power of representation. Her concept of gossip as the reinterpreting of materials from the dominant culture into shared private values could also be a description of the process by which the gay subculture in the United States in the early twentieth century began to take form.

Something that, through gossip, is commonplace knowledge within the gay subculture is often completely unknown on the outside, or if not unknown, at least unspeakable. It is this insistence by the dominant culture

Figures 21.1 – 21.4 Morocco (1930)

284

on making homosexuality invisible and unspeakable that both requires and enables us to locate gay history in rumour, innuendo, fleeting gestures and coded language – signs I will consider as historical sources in order to examine the importance of the cinema, and certain star images in particular, in the formation of lesbian identity in the 1930s.

By the time her 'unspeakable' sexuality was spoken in *Confidential Magazine*, Marlene Dietrich was no longer a major star. She had not yet stopped making movies, but she was not a major box-office draw in the United States, and would soon return to the European cabaret stage on which she began. The appeal of her sophistication, her foreign accent and exotic, elusive manner, had been replaced by a new, very different kind of star image, that of the 1950s all-American hometown girl, exemplified by Doris Day and Judy Holliday. Had the article been published in the 1930s when Dietrich was at her peak, it may well have cut her career short. The studios went to great lengths to keep the star's image open to erotic contemplation by both men and women, not only requiring lesbian and gay male stars to remain in the closet for the sake of their careers, but also desperately creating the impression of heterosexual romance – as MGM did for Greta Garbo in the 1930s.[4]

But the public could be teased with the *possibility* of lesbianism, which provoked both curiosity and titillation. Hollywood marketed the suggestion of lesbianism, not because it intentionally sought to address lesbian audiences, but because it sought to address male voyeuristic interest in lesbianism. The use of innuendo, however, worked for a range of women spectators as well, enabling them to explore their own erotic gaze without giving it a name, and in the safety of their private fantasy in a darkened theatre. Dietrich's rumoured lesbianism had been exploited in this way by Paramount's publicity slogan for the release of *Morocco* (Josef von Sternberg, 1930): 'Dietrich – the woman all women want to see.' This unnaming served to promote intrigue while preventing scandal. Lesbians may well have suspected, for example, that Mercedes d'Acosta and Salka Viertel were the great loves of Greta Garbo's life, but the 'general public' only remembered that she once agreed to marry John Gilbert. (Garbo used to answer Gilbert's many proposals of marriage with 'you don't want to marry one of the fellows'.)

What the public knew, or what the gay subculture knew, about these stars' 'real lives' cannot be separated from their 'star image'. For this reason I am not concerned with whether the actresses considered here were actually lesbian or bisexual, but rather with how their star *personae* were perceived by lesbian audiences. This star persona was often ambiguous and paradoxical. Not only did the Hollywood star system create inconsistent images of femininity, but these images were further contradicted by the intervention of the actress herself into the process of star image production; certain stars such as Katharine Hepburn, Marlene

Dietrich and Greta Garbo often asserted gestures and movements in their films that were inconsistent with and even posed an ideological threat within the narrative. And the use of rumour and gossip about stars, especially by marginalised groups such as lesbians, further enabled different kinds of desire and identification to become focused on particular star images.

In the famous scene from *Morocco*, Amy Jolly (Marlene Dietrich), dressed in top hat and tails, kisses a woman in the cabaret audience, then takes her flower and gives it to a man (Gary Cooper). This flirtation with a woman, only to give the flower to the man, is a flirtation with the lesbian spectator as well, and a microcosm of the film's entire narrative trajectory. The film historian Vito Russo has written of this scene, 'Dietrich's intentions are clearly heterosexual; the brief hint of lesbianism she exhibits serves only to make her more exotic, to whet Gary Cooper's appetite for her and to further challenge his maleness.'[5] But if we bring to the scene the privileged rumour of Dietrich's sexuality, we may read it differently: as Dietrich momentarily stepping out of her role as femme fatale and 'acting out that rumoured sexuality on the screen'.[6]

Not only rumour but also the scene's cinematic structure allowed for lesbian spectators to reject the 'preferred' reading (as described by Vito Russo, above) in favour of a more satisfying homoerotic interpretation. Amy Jolly's performance – her singing a French song in Dietrich's inimitable voice and her slow, suave movements across the stage – is rendered in point-of-view shots intercut with the two contending male characters. Yet when her song is finished and she steps over the railing separating performer and audience, the image becomes a tableau. When Amy Jolly looks at the woman at the table, she quickly lowers her eyes to take in the entire body – to 'look her over'; Amy Jolly then turns away and hesitates before looking at her again. The sexual impulses are strong in this gesture, impulses that are not diffused or choked by point-of-view or audience cutaway shots. Dietrich's gaze remains intact.

Furthermore, in the scene's conclusion, in the giving of the flower to Tom Brown (Gary Cooper), she inverts the proper heterosexual order of seducer and seduced. Her costume, the tuxedo, is invested with power derived both from maleness and social class, a power which surpasses his, as represented by his uniform of a poor French legionnaire. While he is 'fixed' in his class, she is able to transcend momentarily both class and gender. This fluidity and transcendence of limitations can be seductive for all viewers, male and female; for lesbian viewers it was an invitation to read their own desires for transcendence into the image. Richard Dyer has pointed out: 'Audiences cannot make media images mean anything they want to, but they can select from the complexity of the image the meanings and feelings, the variations, inflections and contradictions, that work for them.'[7]

This process of selecting certain qualities from certain stars was especially important for lesbian spectators in the 1930s, who rarely saw their desire given expression on the screen. By providing larger than life cultural models, Hollywood stars exercised a captivating power over the general public; for lesbian spectators struggling to define their sexual identities and with virtually no other models within the ambient culture, this power must have been intensely persuasive and attractive. Aspects of certain star images were appropriated by the growing number of women who began to participate in the emerging urban gay subculture, and played an influential role in defining the distinctive qualities of that subculture.[8]

The early 1930s, of course, were the worst years of the Great Depression, and any discussion of the emergence of the gay subculture in this period must specify that it was largely metropolitan, middle class and white. Antony James' claim in 'Remembering the Thirties' that 'It was a wonderful time to be in New York, to be young and to be gay' clearly did not hold true for everyone.[9] But even individuals scraping by on shoestring budgets often saved for the Saturday matinee. And for those who could not afford the box-office, the marquees, posters and magazine covers still made Hollywood stars into a household image. Stars served as cultural models for a large spectrum of homosexuals across America, not only for those able to participate in the developing urban gay communities.

This fledgling gay subculture of the 1930s consisted of people who as yet lacked enough self-consciousness to see themselves as belonging to a minority group. Unlike racial and ethnic minorities, they grew up in households where their parents not only did not share their lifestyle but actively fought it with the help of the law, psychology, religion and sometimes violence. For a people who were striving toward self-knowledge, Hollywood stars became important models in the formation of gay identity.[10] The sub-texts of films also provided the opportunity to see in certain gestures and movements an affirmation of lesbian experience – something that, however fleeting, was elsewhere rarely to be found, and certainly not in such a popular medium. This affirmation served to give greater validity to women's personal experience as a resource to be trusted and drawn upon in the process of creating a lesbian identity. Richard Dyer summarises this process by claiming that 'gays have had a special relationship to the cinema', because of isolation and an intensified need to use the movies as escapism, because the need to 'pass for straight' elevated illusion to an art form or because the silver screen was often the only place our dreams would ever be fulfilled.[11]

As Vito Russo points out in *The Celluloid Closet*, the film *Queen Christina* (Rouben Mamoulian, 1933) has met in the past some of these needs even though the lesbianism of the real-life queen is not overtly depicted. He writes, 'In *Queen Christina*, Garbo tells Gilbert that "it is possible . . . to feel nostalgia for a place one has never seen". Similarly the film *Queen Christina* created in gay people a nostalgia for something they had never seen on screen.'[12] Greta Garbo herself insisted that the Holly-wood version of Christina was too glamorous and that Swedes who saw the film would expect a more realistic depiction. But despite Swedish audiences' expectations or Garbo's protests, Mamoulian's Christina would be glamorous and fall in love with a man.[13] Through her performance, however, Garbo was able to compensate for what was omitted from the script, giving her portrayal sufficient sexual ambiguity so that her move-ments, voice and manner became codes for lesbian spectators.

The one scene in which Queen Christina kisses Countess Ebba on the lips expresses obvious sexuality, but there are other visual clues in this particular scene that also allow for a lesbian reading. For example, the process of getting dressed into male attire seems to be a daily ritual for Queen Christina and her servant, their movements are so co-ordinated. Because of this the scene does not appear as a transvestite reversal, in which a woman transforms herself into a man, but rather it privileges a different reading: that of remaining a woman while rejecting the dominant codes of femininity, a process 'naturalised' by the ease with which it is done. Within this scene, Christina's little story about Molière, who said that marriage is shocking, reverses the sentiment thus far spoken that the queen's not marrying is shocking. For viewers privy to the gossip about Garbo's relationship with the film's screenwriter, Salka Viertal, the inclusion of Molière's comment about enduring the idea of sleeping with a man in the room can easily be seen as a lesbian joke. Finally, the interaction between Queen Christina and Countess Ebba relies on sexual innuendo within their dialogue and gestures, revealing the desire of the two women for each other and the frustration of having duty and responsibility interfere with that desire.

In another key scene, the chancellor tries to impress upon Christina the importance of marriage as a duty. After she responds by saying, 'I do not wish to marry, and they can't force me', there is a long silent take of her face, and she resumes with, 'The snow is like a wild sea. One can go out and be lost in it, and forget the world, and oneself.' This famous close-up on Garbo's face encourages the viewer to identify with the character's longing, as Andrew Britton points out, 'to make the spectator's experience of Garbo's face the analogue of Christina's experience of the landscape'.[14] In addition to this erotic contemplation of Garbo's face, her romantic choice of desire over duty could have special resonance for lesbians who were struggling to make a similar choice in their own lives. When the chancellor warns her that 'you cannot die an old maid', her response is ironic but serious: 'I have no intention to, Chancellor; I shall die a bachelor.' In this final statement she is no longer pleading to be under-stood, but has closed the debate by appropriating male language in the way she has appropriated male clothing to claim her power.

Such an act had far different meaning in the 1930s than it would have today: appropriating male language or values was not male-identified and hence anti-feminist, but rather the opposite. The historian Carroll Smith-Rosenberg, describing the New Woman/Lesbian of the 1930s, writes: 'They wished to free themselves completely from the considerations of gender, to be autonomous and powerful individuals, to enter the world as if they were men. Hence they spoke with male metaphors and images.'[15] When understood in its historical context, one finds that although Hollywood attempted to purge the story of Queen Christina from the taint of lesbianism, the sub-text left itself wide open to possible lesbian readings.

Film theorist Mary Ann Doane defines the position assigned to the female spectator by the cinema as 'a certain over-presence of the image – she *is* the image'.[16] This female spectator position lacks sufficient distance for either voyeurism or fetishism, the two forms of looking on which visual pleasure is based according to contemporary film theory. The notion of a feminine 'over-presence' draws on the Freudian argument that women do not go through the castration scenario which demands the construction of a distance between men and the female image. To simplify a complex argument, Doane finds that the theoretical female spectator's pleasure in the cinema can take the form of masochism in over-identification with the image, or of narcissism in becoming one's own object of desire, or it may be possible, by re-inserting the necessary distance, for the woman's gaze to master the image. This distance can be achieved through two kinds of transformation which Doane identifies as transvestism and masquerade. Female transvestitism involves adopting the masculine spectatorial position; female masquerade involves an excess of femininity, the use of femininity as a mask, which simulates the distance necessary for the pleasure of looking.[17]

Whether or not one accepts this psychoanalytic model, alone it cannot account for the different cultural positioning of lesbians at once outside of and negotiating within the dominant patriarchal modes of identification. The psychoanalytic approach can only see lesbian desire as a function of assuming a masculine heterosexual position. I believe that other, non-psychoanalytic models of identification must be called upon, which could account for the distance that makes possible the pleasure the female image offers the lesbian spectator.

The Motion Picture Code of 1934 proscribed references to homosexuality in the cinema, resulting in a dearth of images that can be considered 'lesbian'. Lesbian images have been chronically absent from the screen, even prior to the reign of the code, and it is questionable whether a lesbian spectator would enter into the spectatorial position of 'over-presence' in relation to the heterosexual female image, of becoming one with that image. When a star or her character *can* be considered lesbian, she is usually exoticised, made 'extraordinary' either by the star quality

of the actress or by the power given to the character (or in the case of
Queen Christina, both). In this way the star system often served to
distance lesbian spectators from the 'lesbian' star or character, while rules
against the representation of homosexuality in the cinema served to distance lesbian spectators from the prevailing image of femininity. In other
words, identification involves both conscious and unconscious processes
and cannot be reduced to a psychoanalytic model that sees sexual desire
only in terms of the binary opposition of heterosexual masculinity and
femininity; instead it involves varying degrees of subjectivity and distance
depending upon race, class and sexual differences. For working-class lesbians in the 1930s, for example, across huge gulfs of experience, glamorous
upper-class white heterosexual star images often held tremendous sexual
appeal.[18] For a lesbian who perceived herself as 'butch' in the 1930s,
identification most likely did not require what film theorist Laura Mulvey
has called a 'masculinisation of spectatorship' in order to connect with the
male star, he who controls the action and has a power that for two
hours and 35 cents she could appropriate.[19] For a 'femme' the problem of
spectatorship was also complex and remains largely a matter of speculation.

An identification process thus complicated by different cultural and
psychosexual positioning places lesbians outside of conventional gender
definitions, as a gender in-between, which partially explains the attraction
to certain androgynous qualities in the cinema. Lesbians who were fascinated with *Morocco* and *Queen Christina* when these films were first
released spoke endlessly of the allure of their 'ambiguity', a quality that
carries great appeal among people who are forced to live a secret life.[20]

The sexually ambiguous, androgynous qualities that Marlene Dietrich
and Greta Garbo embody found expression in the emerging gay subculture
of the 1930s. Garbo and Dietrich were part of the aristocratic, international
lesbian set which was this subculture's most visible and influential component; as such they played a role in defining the meaning of androgyny for
the small, underground communities of lesbians across the country who
saw their films and heard about them through rumour. Writing about the
use of androgyny in images by lesbian artists and writers of the period,
Flavia Rando has observed: 'In an atmosphere heavy with repressive theories, androgyny offered women struggling to create a lesbian identity a
possible alternative framework for self-definition.'[21] Rando has found that
for lesbians Romaine Brooks and Natalie Barney, androgyny represented
a spiritual transcendence of human limitations. (Katharine Hepburn's
androgynous image in *Sylvia Scarlett* offered this potential, as I will discuss
further.)

But while sexual androgyny was embraced as a liberating image by some
(especially more privileged) lesbians, it came to have a different, less
positive meaning within the dominant culture. Androgyny began to be
associated in the early twentieth century with the 'Mannish Lesbian', a

concept developed by sexologists, particularly the Austrian Richard von Krafft-Ebing, as an expression of sexual and social deviance. As a new generation of women was moving out of the private sphere and into the public, transforming the traditional concepts of femininity, psychoanalysts and sexologists constructed the concept of the pervert, the invert, the outcast, the 'Mannish Lesbian' as a boundary to restrain women's exploration of possible new roles. The 'Mannish Lesbian' was an image taken up by male sex reformers and modernist writers of the 1920s to symbolise social disorder and decay.

It is not, however, as though lesbians held one unified conception of androgyny while the dominant culture constructed an opposite, equally coherent one. Many lesbians in small towns across America had little access to the urban lesbian enclaves, and received whatever knowledge they had by reading medical journals (when they could get hold of them), often internalising what little they could understand of their 'scientific' diagnosis.[22] And these diagnoses varied widely, from Krafft-Ebing's view of homosexuality as a functional sign of degeneration, to Freud's theories of childhood causality, to Havelock Ellis' insistence on 'sexual inversion' as a congenital condition. Studies show that lesbians in the 1920s and 1930s began to adopt some of the language of the sexologists, even though the terms were often at odds with how they felt about themselves.[23] Although lesbians also rejected much of the new sexologic theory, they interacted with and lived economically within the dominant culture, and as such the 'Mannish Lesbian' and other models of deviance had considerable influence on their self-image.

The historian Carroll Smith-Rosenberg has described this 'Mannish Lesbian' image as that of 'a sexually atavistic and ungovernable woman, associated with the 1920s bar culture and with European decadence'.[24] Certainly Dietrich and Garbo on some level evoked this, Dietrich in her films and Garbo in the mystique that surrounded her personal life. Dietrich's image is virtually inseparable from the bar culture setting or from the decadent cabaret stage; even the film *Blonde Venus*, a radical departure for her in that she plays a poor, devoted and selfless mother rather than an independent woman, has her performing some of her most outrageous cabaret acts to support her poor son.

Although as a cabaret singer in *Blonde Venus* Dietrich gives many performances, she appears in male attire – a white tuxedo – for the act only once: immediately after she has been rejected by her husband and has had her son taken away from her. Because she has been portrayed as an unfit mother, and is now without husband or child, her status as an unnatural woman is confirmed by her cross-dressing.

Garbo in *Queen Christina* and Dietrich in *Morocco* and *Blonde Venus* each evoke aspects of Smith-Rosenberg's description of the 'Mannish Lesbian' of the 1920s and 1930s as 'sexually powerful, yet ultimately defeated and impotent'.[25] Yet their androgynous qualities held a sexual appeal that the 'Mannish Lesbian' did not. Although they function within the narrative according to Smith-Rosenberg's model – as a sexual threat that must be contained – their appropriation of male clothing (while retaining female identity), their aloof and inscrutable manners and their aggressive independence provided an alternative model upon which lesbian spectators could draw. This model was an appealing departure both from heterosexual images of femininity and from the images of deviance that pervaded the medical texts. Other Hollywood films of the 1930s also utilised this double-edged image that was at once subversive and confirming of the social order: the 1933 film *Blood Money* features Sandra Shaw in tuxedo with monocle, a contemporary lesbian fashion; Katharine Hepburn dons male attire and assumes the independence and privilege of men in both *Sylvia Scarlett* (1936) and *Christopher Strong* (1933); and the original German film, *Viktor/Viktoria* (1933) was closely followed by its British version, *First a Girl* (1935), both of which featured a woman who 'passed' as a homosexual man while projecting an image with lesbian overtones. Such recurring appearances in the early 1930s of this cross-dressing image are not mere coincidences, but embody crucial historical debates that had begun to move from the pages of scientific journals and women's private diaries into public discourse. The twenties had seen the publication of Radclyffe Hall's novel, *The Well of Loneliness*, which 'caused great upheavals in the American judicial system, spilling out into the newspapers and becoming a topic of conversation for people across America'.[26] The lesbian themed play *The Captive* created a sensation on Broadway. The debates over changing definitions of gender and sexuality in the early twentieth century were now fought out over the terrain of popular culture.

The cinema as the most widespread and powerful form of popular entertainment became an especially important battleground. The films addressed here are those that are stretched and pulled by struggles between images of powerlessness and power, between the dominant cinema's metaphor of sexual deviance and the inverting of this metaphor by female stars (who brought to it a strong sexual appeal that the 'Mannish Lesbian' lacked) and by lesbian spectators (who appropriated cinematic moments and read their own fantasies into them). And particular images generate meanings which are in conflict with their function within the narrative; poignant lesbian moments are constricted by the demands of heterosexual narrative closure. Thus, while the ending of both *Morocco* and *Queen Christina* can be viewed as affirming the heterosexual contract, it is also possible that lesbians found pleasure in these resolutions, partly because the endings are relatively open, permitting a range of interpretations, and partly because the heterosexual relationships they promote are still considered unacceptable (for reasons of class and status); they are not the

293

socially sanctioned relationships that the characters have been encouraged to choose.

The endings of both *Morocco* and *Queen Christina* are complex and ambiguous. The romantic image of Amy Jolly following her man into the desert does not necessarily make for an affirmation of the heterosexual social order. Queen Christina's choice to relinquish the throne in order to marry the Spanish ambassador can be viewed more as an action to escape the narrow confines of her life of duty than as a heterosexual triumph. Moreover, in *Queen Christina*, the Spanish ambassador dies before they are united, leaving Christina alone to search for something she has not yet known. Amy Jolly and Queen Christina actually become more liminal and marginal in the films' conclusions, rejecting their pasts, their nationalities and their social positions. Although each character can be viewed as having made the ultimate sacrifice for a man, in doing so they have moved outside of the culture in which the heterosexual contract is constructed and maintained. In *Morocco*, Amy Jolly moves through the city's gate into the expanse of the desert, leaving her shoes behind in the sand, strong visual symbols for this departure from her culture. Queen Christina leaves on a ship, standing alone as its figurehead, her inscrutable Garbo face contradicting the aims of narrative closure. While heterosexual viewers might have found an affirmation of heterosexuality in the films' resolutions, lesbians could perceive the scenes as moving away from and rejecting the heterosexual social order.

Another example of how different social spectators could have completely different readings is offered by the film *Sylvia Scarlett*, which endeared Katharine Hepburn to lesbians while it discredited her to the general public. At its premiere in New York, the audience booed, yelled and began walking out after twenty minutes; the *New York Sun* called it a 'tragic waste of time and screen talent'.[27] In *Sylvia Scarlett* Hepburn plays a girl who masquerades as a boy in order to help her criminal-father leave the country. But to the knowing audience who has watched her transformation from 'Sylvia Snow' to 'Sylvester Scarlett', she's Katharine Hepburn in drag. In one scene a young male artist (played by Brian Aherne) looks at Sylvester Scarlett to make sense of his attraction to the young 'man', to understand why he gets 'a queer feeling when I look at you'. While gay men are the object of this 'mistaken identity' joke, which acknowledges gay desire only as the expression of misinterpreted heterosexuality, lesbian spectators were able to select from the layers of Hepburn's star image – her rejection of female weakness as Sylvia Snow, her synthesis of masculine and feminine traits – those gestures, expressions, costumes and looks which in the 1920s and 1930s were being selectively embraced by the emerging urban lesbian subculture as signs of lesbianism.

Sylvia Scarlett belongs to the generation of New Women that the sexologists had warned against. She takes on the stance of a man and has replaced

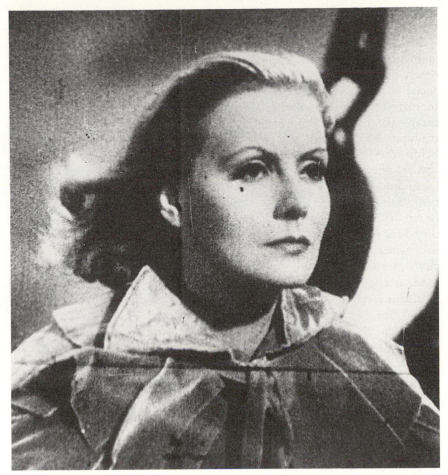

Figure 21.5 Queen Christina (1933)

her father's authority, temporarily at least, with her own. Yet Katharine Hepburn's image is not sexually threatening in the way that Marlene Dietrich's in *Morocco* or Greta Garbo's in *Queen Christina* are. She does not try to appropriate male clothing, language or manner as a woman, as 'Sylvia'; she only borrows from male prerogative when she attempts to pass as 'Sylvester', a boy. That the film is a comedy and she is presented as still a child also contribute to diffusing the danger she represents. Still, within the discourse of the dominant cinema she is a transgressor who is suggestive of the 'Mannish Lesbian': when her femaleness is detected, she will be called a 'freak of nature' and an 'oddity', expressions which reflect the new body of thought that shaped public consciousness in the early

Figure 21.6 Sylvia Scarlett (1936)

twentieth century towards homosexuality as deviance and towards the New Woman as sexual pariah.

But certain qualities undermine this image of deviance, qualities that were embedded in the text through Hepburn's performance, perhaps through director George Cukor's own homosexuality and through the unique positioning of lesbian spectatorship. Sylvia Scarlett can be seen as outside of conventional gender definition, not as a man but as a different kind of woman. In short, she represents the Trickster, a creative force that appears across time in literature and myth. Carroll Smith-Rosenberg defines the Trickster as being 'of indeterminate sex and changeable gender', and as 'a creature who exists to break taboos, violate categories, and defy structure'.[28] In *Sylvia Scarlett* it is the Trickster who suggests that her group should abandon crime and perform in a travelling carnival by the sea. The carnival world represents disorder and illusion, a twilight world closely associated with homosexuality, while the sea, as in *Queen Christina*, symbolises the unknown, a place where identity is not already 'fixed'.

In one crucial scene, Sylvia plays the wise fool; she speaks in riddles and tells disturbing truths. Her defence of another woman reveals elements of her femaleness, retained while in male masquerade – as the film's title, bringing together 'Sylvia Snow' and 'Sylvester Scarlett' into a third identity, confirms. Her crying out of 'I want the sea, I want the sea!' further suggests that she does not completely fit in either a masculine or feminine construction. She momentarily steps out of the scene to address the audience directly, and here she turns the social order upside down (one of the Trickster's primary functions) by addressing, not the standard male viewer who is the intentional, omnipresent subject of most cinematic address, but women instead (as represented by the back of Dennie Moore's head in the lower left frame as a stand-in for the female spectator).

But as Smith-Rosenberg has pointed out in her discussion of the Trickster in Virginia Woolf's *Orlando*:

> its inversion of order is transitory. It suggests but does not effect an alternative order. Woolf uses Orlando to expose the absurdity of rigid gender rules and the pomposity of the male literary canon. But Orlando changes neither England nor literature. She/he merely suggests what might be.[29]

Sadly, so too for Sylvia Scarlett. Her transcendence of human limitations is temporary, and the social order contains and remoulds *her* behaviour more than she can alter it. Similarly, the moments in *Queen Christina*, *Morocco* and *Sylvia Scarlett* that have poignancy for lesbians are fleeting, transitory moments; they too simply suggest what might be and then are snatched from us by their incorporation into, and co-optation by, the discourse of the dominant cinema.

Film theorist E. Ann Kaplan has argued that 'to appropriate Hollywood images to ourselves, taking them out of the context of the total structure in which they appear, will not get us very far'.[30] We need to understand how the discourse of the dominant cinema works to contain the most threatening aspects of women's sexuality by using lesbianism as its boundary, to make what is unspeakable – in the case of *Sylvia Scarlett* – harmlessly laughable. Still, lesbian spectators have been able to appropriate cinematic moments which seem to offer resistance to the dominant patriarchal ideology, and to use these points of resistance and the shared language of gossip and rumour to, in some measure, define and empower themselves. As such, the cinema's contribution towards the formation of lesbian identity in the early twentieth century should not be underestimated.

In *The Celluloid Closet*, Vito Russo quotes the *Herald Tribune* review of *Queen Christina* when it first appeared:

What do facts and theories matter? Christina, to all those who see Garbo's film, will always be the lovely girl who fell in love with the Spanish Ambassador in the snow, and no amount of professional research will ever change her.[31]

For lesbian spectators who saw Garbo's film in the early 1930s, however, Queen Christina will always be the lovely girl who dressed in male attire and refused to marry, and no amount of heterosexual cover will ever change her.

NOTES

This essay is an abbreviated version of a chapter from my book on lesbian representation in the cinema: *Vampires and Violets*, reproduced by kind permission of Pandora Press/HarperCollins Ltd. I'd like to acknowledge the generous help of the following individuals who read drafts of this paper and gave me useful suggestions and criticisms: Jerma Jackson, Christine Gledhill, Harold Poor, Greta Schiller, Janice Welsch, Diane Carson, Linda Dittmar, Miriam Hansen, Judy Walkowitz and Mark Finch.

1 K.G. McClain, 'The untold story of Marlene Dietrich', *Confidential Magazine* (July 1955), 22.
2 E. Becker, M. Citron, J. Lesage and B.R. Rich, Introduction to Lesbians and Film special section, *Jump Cut*, 24/25 (March 1981), 18.
3 P.M. Spacks, *Gossip* (New York, Alfred A. Knopf, 1985), 46.
4 A. Britton, *Katharine Hepburn: The Thirties and After* (Newcastle upon Tyne, Tyneside Cinema, 1984), 16.
5 V. Russo, *The Celluloid Closet* (New York, Harper & Row, 1981), 14.
6 Becker, Citron, Lesage and Rich, op. cit., 18.
7 R. Dyer, *Heavenly Bodies: Film Stars and Society* (New York, St Martin's Press, 1986), 5.
8 Research into the role of the cinema in the formation of the gay subculture has shown its importance among gay men. See essays by Richard Dyer and Jack Babuscio in Dyer's *Gays and Film*, and the chapter on the importance of Judy Garland to the gay male subculture in Dyer's *Heavenly Bodies*. I do not know of any similar study for the lesbian subculture.
9 A. James, 'Remembering the thirties', *The Yellow Book*, on file at the Lesbian Herstory Archives, New York City, 7.
10 The experiences of living a 'double life' in the 1930s, of self-doubt and ignorance about homosexuality and of the oppression encountered at the hands of the family, psychology and the law are common themes expressed in a series of interviews conducted by myself and others for the Before Stonewall Film Project, on file at the Lesbian Herstory Archives, New York City.
11 R. Dyer (ed.) *Gays and Film* (London, British Film Institute, 1977; New York, Zoetrope, 1984), 1.
12 Russo, 1981, op. cit., 65.
13 R.L. Bell-Metereau, *Hollywood Androgyny* (New York, Columbia University Press, 1985).
14 Britton, 1984, op. cit., 11.
15 C. Smith-Rosenberg, 'The new woman as androgyne: social disorder and gender crisis, 1920–1936', in *Disorderly Conduct* (New York, Oxford University Press, 1985), 295.

16 M.A. Doane, 'Film and the masquerade: theorising the female spectator', *Screen*, 23, 3/4 (September/October 1982), 78.

17 Ibid., 82 and 87.

18 A Black lesbian, recalling the movie stars who were important to her growing up in Chicago in the 1950s, looked back to the films of the 1930s, especially *Morocco*: 'I was just enthralled with Dietrich. . . . She has a sustaining quality about her that I know has turned on thousands of women in this world. I can't say I identified with her. I wasn't thinking in terms of black and white in those days . . . [It was just] lust, childhood lust, I'm sure.' Quoted in July Whitaker, 'Hollywood Transformed', *Jump Cut*, 24/5 (March 1981), 35.

19 L. Mulvey, 'Afterthoughts on visual pleasure and narrative cinema in relation to *Duel in the Sun*', *Framework*, 15, 16, 17 (1981).

20 Unpublished interviews with (Ms) Christopher Sitwell and Karl Bissinger, on gay life in the 1930s, May 1988.

21 F. Rando, 'Romaine Brooks: the creation of a lesbian image', unpublished paper.

22 The prevalence of 'looking for clues to the self' in medical texts on homosexuality in the 1930s can be seen in interviews conducted by myself and others for the Before Stonewall Film Project, housed at the Lesbian Herstory Archives, New York City.

23 Katharine B. Davis' 1929 study of *Factors in the Sex Life of Twenty-Two Hundred Women* reveals not only that homosexual relations were common (26 per cent) among the unmarried women surveyed, but that by the 1920s, as same-sex relations were redefined as psychopathic, many women began to describe themselves as 'abnormal', 'unnatural' and 'pervers[e] . . .', even though they claimed that these descriptions did not match their self-image. Katharine B. Davis, *Factors in the Sex Life of Twenty-Two Hundred Women* (New York, Harper and Row, 1929), 290–2.
    Vern and Bonnie Bullough's study of twenty-five lesbian friends in Salt Lake City in the 1920s and 1930s shows that they discussed sexologists' theories on homosexuality in order to understand themselves, yet consistently denied that they were 'perverts' or 'pathological cases'. Still, the Bulloughs' findings indicate 'how much assumptions about a "deviant" group, even when these assumptions are rejected by the group, have considerable influence on the self-image of its members'. Vern and Bonnie Bullough, 'Lesbianism in the 1920s and 1930s: a newfound study', *Signs*, 2, 4 (Summer 1977), 903–4.

24 Smith-Rosenberg, op. cit., 282.

25 Ibid.

26 A. Weiss and G. Schiller, *Before Stonewall: the Making of a Gay and Lesbian Community* (Tallahassee, FL., Naiad Press, 1988), 24.

27 *New York Sun* quoted in James Spada, *Hepburn* (Garden City, NY, Doubleday and Co., 1984), 57.

28 Smith-Rosenberg, op. cit., 291.

29 Ibid., 292.

30 E.A. Kaplan, 'Is the gaze male?', in A. Snitow, C. Stansell and S. Thompson (eds.) *Powers of Desire: The Politics of Sexuality*, New York, Monthly Review Press (1983), 314.

31 Russo, op. cit., 66.

22

MONSTER METAPHORS
Notes on Michael Jackson's *Thriller*

Kobena Mercer

Michael Jackson, megastar. His LP, *Thriller*, made in 1982, has sold over 35 million copies worldwide and is said to be the biggest selling LP in the history of pop. Jackson is reputed to have amassed a personal fortune of some 75 million dollars at the age of 26. Even more remarkably, he's been a star since he was 11 and sang lead with his brothers in the Jackson Five, the biggest selling group on the Tamla Motown label in the 1970s. The Jackson Five practically invented the genre of 'teeny-bopper' pop cashed in upon by white pop idols like Donny Osmond. While such figures have faded from memory, classic Jackson Five tunes like 'I Want You Back' and 'ABC' can still evoke the pride and enthusiasm which marked the assertive mood of the 'Black Pride' cultural movement.

After he and his brothers left Motown in the mid-1970s and took more artistic control over their own productions, Jackson developed as a singer, writer and stage performer. His *Off The Wall* LP of 1979, which established him as a solo star, demonstrates the lithe, sensual texture of his voice and its mastery over a diverse range of musical styles and idioms, from romantic ballad to rock. Just what is it that makes this young, black man so different, so appealing?

Undoubtedly, it is the voice which lies at the heart of his appeal. Rooted in the Afro-American tradition of 'soul', Jackson's vocal performance is characterised by breathy gasps, squeaks, sensual sighs and other wordless sounds which have become his stylistic signature. The way in which this style punctuates the emotional resonance and bodily sensuality of the music corresponds to what Roland Barthes called the 'grain' of the voice – 'the grain is the body in the voice as it sings'.[1] The emotional and erotic expressiveness of the voice is complemented by the sensual grace and sheer excitement of Jackson's dancing style: even as a child, his stage performance provoked comparisons with James Brown and Jackie Wilson.

But there is another element to Jackson's success and popularity – his image. Jackson's individual style fascinates and attracts attention. The ankle-cut jeans, the single-gloved hand and, above all, the wet-look hairstyle which have become his trademarks, have influenced the sartorial repertoires of black and white youth cultures and been incorporated into mainstream fashion.

Most striking is the change in Jackson's looks and physical appearance as he has grown. The cute child dressed in gaudy flower-power gear and sporting a huge 'Afro' hairstyle has become, as a young adult, a paragon of racial and sexual ambiguity. Michael reclines across the gatefold sleeve of the *Thriller* LP, dressed in crisp black and white on a glossy metallic surface against a demure pink background. Look closer – the glossy sheen of his complexion appears lighter in colour than before; the nose seems sharper, more aquiline, less rounded and 'African' and the lips seem tighter, less pronounced. Above all, the large 'Afro' has dissolved into a shock of wet-look permed curls and a new stylistic trademark, the single lock over the forehead, appears.

What makes this reconstruction of Jackson's image more intriguing is the mythology built up around it, in which it is impossible or simply beside the point to distinguish truth from falsehood. It is said that he has undergone cosmetic surgery to adopt a more white, European look, although Jackson denies it.[2] But the definite sense of racial ambiguity writ large in his new image is at the same time, and by the same token, the site of a sexual ambiguity bordering on androgyny. He may sing as sweet as Al Green, dance as hard as James Brown, but he looks more like Diana Ross than any black male soul artist. The media have seized upon these ambiguities and have fabricated a 'persona', a private 'self' behind the image, which has become the subject of speculation and rumour. This mythologisation has culminated in the construction of a Peter Pan figure. We are told that behind the star's image is a lonely 'lost boy', whose life is shadowed by morbid obsessions and anxieties. He lives like a recluse and is said to 'come alive' only when he is on stage in front of his fans. The media's exploitation of public fascination with Jackson the celebrity has even reached the point of 'pathologising' his personality:

> Even Michael Jackson's millions of fans find his lifestyle strange.
> It's just like one of his hit songs, Off The Wall. People in the know say–
> His biggest thrill is taking trips to Disneyland.
> His closest friends are zoo animals.
> He talks to tailor's dummies in his lounge.
> He fasts every Sunday and then dances in his bedroom until he drops of exhaustion. So showbusiness folk keep asking the question: 'Is Jacko Wacko?'
> Two top American psychiatrists have spent hours examining a detailed dossier on Jackson. Here is their on-the-couch report.[3]

Jackson's sexuality and sexual preference in particular have been the focus

301

for such public fascination, as a business associate of his, Shirley Brooks, complains:

> He doesn't and won't make public statements about his sex life, because he believes – and he is right – that is none of anyone else's business. Michael and I had a long conversation about it, and he felt that anytime you're in the public eye and don't talk to the press, they tend to make up these rumours to fill their pages.[4]

Neither child nor man, not clearly either black or white and with an androgynous image that is neither masculine nor feminine, Jackson's star-image is a 'social hieroglyph', as Marx said of the commodity form, which demands, yet defies, decoding. This article offers a reading of the music video *Thriller* from the point of view of the questions raised by the phenomenal popularity of this star, whose image is a spectacle of racial and sexual indeterminacy.

REMAKE, REMODEL: VIDEO IN THE MARKETING OF *THRILLER*

In recent years the 'new', hybrid medium of music video has come to occupy a central importance in the sale and significance of pop music. As 'adverts' to promote records, pop videos are now prerequisites to break singles into the charts. As industrial product, the medium – institutionalised in America's cable network MTV, owned by Warner Communications and American Express – has revitalised the economic profitability of pop by capitalising on new patterns of consumption created by the use, on a mass scale, of video technology.[5] From its inception, however, MTV maintained an unspoken policy of excluding black artists. Jackson's videos for singles from the *Thriller* LP were the first to penetrate this racial boundary.

The videos for two songs from that LP, 'Billy Jean' and 'Beat It', stand out in the way they foreground Jackson's new style. 'Billy Jean', directed by Steve Barron, visualises the 'cinematic' feel of the music track and its narrative of a false paternity claim, by creating through a 'studio-set' scenario, sharp editing and various effects an ambience that complements rather than illustrates the song. Taking its cue from the LP cover, it stresses Jackson's style in his dress and in his dance. Paving stones light up as Jackson twists, kicks and turns through the performance, invoking the 'magic' of the star. 'Beat It', directed by Bob Giraldi (who made TV adverts for MacDonald's hamburgers and Dr Pepper soft drinks) visualises the anti-macho lyric of the song. Shots alternate between 'juvenile delinquent' gangs about to begin a fight, and Michael, fragile and alone in his bedroom. The singer then disarms the gangs with superior charm and grace as he leads the all-male cast through a dance sequence that synthesises the cinematic imagery of *The Warriors* and *West Side Story*.

302

These videos, executed from designs by Jackson himself, and others in which he appears such as 'Say, Say, Say' by Paul McCartney and 'Can You Feel It' by The Jacksons, are important aspects of the commercial success of *Thriller* because they breached the boundaries of race on which the music industry has been based. Unlike stars such as Lionel Richie, Jackson has not 'crossed over' from black to white stations to end up in the middle of the road: his success has popularised black music in white rock and pop markets, by actually playing with imagery and style which have always been central to the marketing of pop. In so doing, Jackson has opened up a space in which new stars like Prince are operating, at the interface between the boundaries defined by 'race'.

'Thriller', the LP title track, was released as the third single from the album. The accompanying video went beyond the then-established conventions and limitations of the medium. According to Dave Laing, these conventions have been tied to the economic imperative of music video:

> first, the visuals were subordinated to the soundtrack, which they were there to sell; second, music video as a medium for marketing immediately inherited an aesthetic and a set of techniques from the pre-existing and highly developed form of television commercials.[6]

Thus one convention, that of fast editing derived from the montage codes of TV advertising, has been overlaid with another: that of an alternation between naturalistic or 'realist' modes of representation (in which the song is performed 'live' or in a studio and mimed to by the singer or group), and 'constructed' or fantastic modes of representation (in which the singer-/group acts out imaginary roles implied by the lyrics or by the 'atmosphere' of the music). 'Thriller' incorporates the montage and alternation conventions, but organises the flow of images by framing it with a powerful *story-telling* or *narrational* direction which provides continuity and closure. Since 'Thriller', this story-telling code has itself become a music video convention: director Julien Temple's 'Undercover of the Night' (Rolling Stones, 1983) and 'Jazzin' for Blue Jean' (David Bowie, 1984) represent two of the more imaginative examples of this narrativisation of the music by the direction of the flow of images. 'Thriller' is distinguished not only by its internal and formal structure, but also by the fact that it is 'detached' from a primary economic imperative or rationale. The LP was already a 'monster' of a commercial success before the title track was released as a single: there was no need for a 'hard sell'. Thus the 'Thriller' video does not so much seek to promote the record as a primary product, but rather *celebrates the success the LP has brought Michael Jackson* by acting as a vehicle to showcase its star. In the absence of a direct economic imperative, the video can indulge Jackson's own interest in acting: its use of cinematic codes and structures provides a framework for Jackson to act

303

as a 'movie-star'. Jackson himself had acted before, in *The Wiz* (1977), an all-black remake of *The Wizard of Oz* in which he played the Scarecrow. He professes a deep fascination with acting:

> I love it so much. It's escape. It's fun. It's just neat to become another thing, another person. Especially when you really believe it and it's not like you're acting. I always hated the word 'acting' – to say, 'I am an actor.' It should be more than that. It should be more like a believer.[7]

In 'Thriller', Jackson acts out a variety of roles as the video engages in a playful parody of the stereotypes, codes and conventions of the 'horror' genre. The intertextual dialogues between film, dance and music which the video articulates also draw us, the spectators, into the *play* of signs and meanings at work in the 'constructedness' of the star's image. The following reading of the music video considers the specificity of the music track, asks how the video 'visualises' the music and then goes on to examine the internal structure of the video as an intertext of sound, image and style.

'THRILLER': A READING

Consider first the specificity of the music track. The title, which gives the LP its title as well, is the name for a particular genre of film – the 'murder-mystery-suspense' film, the detective story, the thriller. But the lyrics of the song are not 'about' film or cinema. The track is a mid-tempo funk number, written by Rod Temperton, and recalls similar numbers written by the author for Michael Jackson such as 'Off the Wall'. The lyrics evoke allusions and references to the cinematic culture of 'terror' and 'horror' movies but only to play on the meaning of the word 'thriller'. The lyrics weave a little story, which could be summarised as 'a night of viewing some . . . gruesome horror movies with a lady friend'.[8] The lyrics narrate such a fictional scene by speaking in the first person:

> Its close to midnight and somethin' evil's lurkin' in the dark
> . . . . You try to scream, but terror takes the sound before you make it
> You start to freeze, as horror looks you right between the eyes
> You're paralysed.

Who is this 'you' being addressed? The answer comes in the semantic turn-around of the third verse and chorus in which the pun on the title is made evident:

> Now is the time for you and I to cuddle close together
> All thru' the night, I'll save you from the terror on the screen

I'll make you see, that [Chorus] This is thriller, thriller-night, 'cause
I could thrill you more than any ghost would dare to try
Girl, this is thriller . . . so let me hold you tight and share a killer,
thriller tonight.[9]

Thus the lyrics play a *double entendre* of the meaning of 'thrill'.

As Iain Chambers has observed: 'Distilled into the metalanguage of soul
and into the clandestine cultural liberation of soul music is the regular
employment of a sexual discourse.'[10] Along with the emotional complexities of intimate relationships, physical sexuality is perhaps *the* central preoccupation of the soul tradition. But, as Chambers suggests, the power of
soul as a cultural form to express sexuality does not so much lie in the
literal meanings of the words but in the passion of the singer's voice and
vocal performance. The explicit meanings of the lyrics are in this sense
secondary to the sensual resonance of the individual character of the voice,
its 'grain'. While the 'grain' of the voice encodes the contradictions of
sexual relationships, their pleasures and pain, the insistence of the rhythm
is an open invitation to the body to dance. Dance, as cultural form and
sexual ritual, is a mode of decoding the sound and meaning articulated in
the music. In its incitement of the listener to dance, to become an active
participant in the texture of voice, words and rhythm, soul music is not
only 'about' sexuality, but is itself a musical means for the eroticisation
of the body.[11] In 'Thriller' it is the 'grain' of Jackson's voice that expresses
and plays with this sexual sub-text and it is this dimension that transgresses
the denotation of the lyrics and escapes analytic reduction. Jackson's
interpretation of Temperton's lyric inflects the allusions to cinema to
thematise a discourse on sexuality, rather than film, and the 'story' created
by the lyrics sets up a reverberation between two semantic poles: the
invocation of macabre movies is offset by the call to 'cuddle close
together'.

The element of irony set in motion by this semantic polarity is the
'literary' aspect of the sense of parody that pervades the song. Special
sound effects – creaking doors and howling dogs – contribute to the pun
on the title. Above all, this play of parody spreads out in Vincent Price's
rap, which closes the record. The idea of a well-established white movie
actor like Price delivering a 'rap', a distinctly black urban cultural form,
is funny enough. But the fruity, gurgling tones of the actor's voice, which
immediately invoke the semi-comic self-parody of 'horror' he has become,
express the affectionate sense of humour that underpins the song:

Darkness falls across the land. The midnight hour is close at hand.
Creatures crawl in search of blood, to terrorise y'awl's neighbourhood. And whosoever shall be found, without the soul for getting
down, must stand and face the hounds of hell, and rot inside a
corpse's shell.

The parody at play here lies in the quotation of soul argot – 'get down', 'midnight hour', 'funk of forty thousand years' – in the completely different context of horror movies. The almost camp quality of refined exaggeration in Price's voice and his 'British' accent is at striking odds with the discourse of black American soul music.

As we 'listen' to the production of meanings in the music track the various 'voices' involved in the production (Temperton, Jackson, Price, Quincy Jones etc.) are audibly combined into parody. One way of approaching the transition from music to video, then, would be to suggest that John Landis, its director, brings aspects of his own 'voice' as an 'author' of Hollywood films into this dialogue. It seems to me that Landis's voice contributes to the puns and play on the meaning of 'thriller' by drawing on conventions of mainstream horror movies.

STORY, PLOT AND PARODY

Landis introduces two important elements from film into the medium of music video: a narrative direction of the flow of images and special-effects techniques associated with the pleasures of the horror film. These effects are used in the two scenes that show the metamorphosis of Michael into, first, a werewolf, and then, a zombie. The use of these cinematic technologies to create the metamorphoses is clearly what distinguishes 'Thriller' from other music video. 'Thriller' gives the video audience *real thrills* – the 'thrill' of tension, anxiety and fear associated with the pleasure offered by the horror genre. The spectacle of the visceral transformation of cute, lovable Michael Jackson into a howlin' wolf of a monster is disturbing, because it seems so convincing, 'real' and fascinating. As Philip Brophy remarks: 'The pleasure of the (horror) text is, in fact, getting the shit scared out of you – and loving it: an exchange mediated by adrenalin.'[12]

Both special effects and narrative return us to the direction of John Landis, who also directed *An American Werewolf in London* (1979). *American Werewolf* is a horror comedy; it retells the traditional werewolf myth, setting its protagonists as tourists in England attacked by a strange animal, into which one of them then turns during the full moon. The film employs pop tunes to exacerbate its underlying parody of this mythology – 'Moondance' (Van Morrison), 'Bad Moon Rising' (Creedence Clearwater Revival) and 'Blue Moon' (Frankie Lymon and the Teenagers). And this humour is combined with special effects and make-up techniques which show the bodily metamorphosis of man to wolf in 'real time', as opposed to less credible 'time-lapse' techniques. The 'Thriller' video not only refers to this film, but to other generic predecessors, including *Night of the Living Dead* (1968) by George Romero and *Halloween* (1978) by John Carpenter. Indeed, the video is strewn with allusions to horror films. As Brophy observes:

It is a genre which mimics itself mercilessly – because its statement is coded in its very mimicry. . . . It is not so much that the modern horror film refutes or ignores the conventions of genre, but it is involved in a violent awareness of itself as a saturated genre.[13]

Thus cinematic horror seems impelled towards parody of its own codes and conventions.[14] With hindsight it is tempting to suggest that 'Thriller's' music track was almost made to be filmed, as it seems to cue these cinematic references. Certain points within the video appear to be straightforward transpositions from the song: 'They're out to get you, there's demons closin' in on ev'ry side/ . . . Night creatures call and the dead start to walk in their masquerade', and so on. But it is at the level of its *narrative structure* that the video engages in an intertextual dialogue with the music track.[15]

Unlike most pop videos, 'Thriller' does not begin with the first notes of the song, but with a long panning shot on a car driving through woods at night and the 'cinematic' sound of recorded silence. This master shot, establishing the all-seeing but invisible 'eye' of the camera, is comparable to the discursive function of third-person narration. The shot/reverse-shot series which frames the dialogue between the two protagonists about the car running out of gas establishes 'point-of-view' camera angles, analogous to 'subjective', first-person modes of enunciation. These specific cinematic codes of narration structure the entire flow of images and give the video a beginning, a middle and an end. 'Thriller' incorporates the pop video convention of switching from 'realist' to 'fantastic' modes of representation, but binds this into continuity and closure through its narrative. The two metamorphosis sequences are of crucial importance to this narrative structure; the first disrupts the 'equilibrium' of the opening sequence, and the second repeats but differs from the first in order to bring the flow of images to its end and re-establish equilibrium. Within the story-telling conventions of the horror genre the very appearance of the monster/werewolf/vampire/alien signals the violation of equilibrium: the presence of the monster activates the narrative dynamic whose goal or end is achieved by an act of counter-violence that eliminates it.[16]

In the opening sequence of 'Thriller' equilibrium is established and then disrupted as the dialogue and exchange of glances between Michael and the girl (as the male and female protagonists of the story) establish 'romance' as the narrative pre-text. The girl's look at Michael as the car stops hints at a question, answered by the expression of bemused incredulity on his face. Did he stop the car on purpose? Was it a romantic ruse, to lure her into a trap? The girl's coquettish response to Michael's defence ('Honestly, we're out of gas') lingers sensually on the syllables, 'So . . . what are we going to do now?' Her question, and his smile in return, hint at and exacerbate the underlying erotic tension of romantic intrigue between the two characters. Michael's dialogue gives a minimal 'character' to his role as the boyfriend: he appears a somewhat shy, very proper and polite 'boy next door'. The girl, on the other hand, is not so much a 'character' as the 'girlfriend' type. At another level, their clothes – a pastiche 1950s retro style – connote youthful innocence, the couple as archetypical teen lovers. But this innocent representation is unsettled by Michael's statement: 'I'm not like other guys.' The statement implies a question posed on the terrain of gender, and masculinity in particular: why is he different from 'other guys'?

The sequence provides an answer in the boyfriend's transformation into a monster. But, although the metamorphosis resolves the question, it is at the cost of disrupting the equilibrium of 'romance' between the two protagonists, which is now converted into a relation of terror between monster and victim. The chase through the woods is the final sequence of this 'beginning' of the narrative. The subsequent scene, returning to Michael and the girl as a couple in a cinema, re-establishes the equation of 'romance' and repositions the protagonists as girlfriend and boyfriend, but at another level of representation.

In structural terms this shift in modes of representation, from a fantastic level (in which the metamorphosis and chase take place) to a realist level (in which the song is performed) is important because it retrospectively implies that the entire opening sequence was a film within a film, or rather, a film within the video. More to the point, the 'beginning' is thus revealed to be *a parody of 1950s B-movie horror*.

> While Hammer were reviving the Universal monsters . . . American International Pictures began a cycle whose appreciation was almost entirely tongue-in-cheek – a perfect example of 'camp' manufacture and reception of the iconography of terror.
>
> The first film in this series bore the (now notorious) title *I Was A Teenage Werewolf* (1957). . . . The absurdity of the plot and acting, and the relentless pop music that filled the soundtrack, gave various kinds of pleasure to young audiences and encouraged the film-makers to follow this pilot movie with *I Was A Teenage Frankenstein* and with *Teenage Monster* and *Teenage Zombie*, creations that were as awful to listen to as they were to see.[17]

Parody depends on an explicit self-consciousness: in 'Thriller' this informs the dialogue, dress style and acting in the opening sequence. In its parody of a parody it also acknowledges that there is no 'plot' as such: the narrative code that structures the video has no story to tell. Rather it crates a simulacrum of a story, a parody of a story, in its stylistic send-up of genre conventions. But it is precisely at the level of its self-consciousness that 'Thriller's' mimicry of the *gender roles* of the horror genre provides an anchor for the way it visualises the sexual discourse, the play on the meaning of the word 'thriller' on the music track.

GENRE AND GENDER. 'THRILLER'S' SEXUAL SUB-TEXT

As the video switches from fantastic to realist modes of representation, the roles played by the two protagonists shift accordingly. The fictional film within the video, with its narrative pretext of 'romance', positions Michael and the girl as boyfriend and girlfriend, and within this the fantastic metamorphosis transforms the relation into one of terror between monster and victim. If we go back to Michael's statement made in this scene, 'I'm not like other guys', we can detect a confusion about the role he is playing.

The girl's initial reply. 'Of course not. That's why I love you,' implies that it is obvious that he is 'different' because he is the real Michael Jackson. When, in her pleasure at his proposal, she calls him by his proper name she interpellates him in two roles at once – as fictional boyfriend and real superstar. This ambiguity of reference acknowledges Jackson's self-conscious acting style: we, the video audience, get the impression he is playing at playing a role and we 'know' that Jackson, the singer, the star, is playing at the role of a 'movie-star'. In 'Thriller', Michael's outfit and its stylistic features – the wet-look hairstyle, the ankle-cut jeans and the letter 'M' emblazoned on his jacket – reinforce this meta-textual superimposition of roles. If Michael, as the male protagonist, is both boyfriend and star, his female counterpart in the equation of 'romance' is both the girlfriend and at this meta-textual level, the fan. The girl is in two places at once: on screen and in the audience. As spectator of the film within the video she is horrified by the image on the screen and gets up to leave. 'Fooled' by the violent spectacle of the metamorphosis, she mistakes the fantastic for the real, she forgets that 'it's only a movie'. The girl's positions in the fictional and realist scenes mirror those of the video spectator – the effects which generate thrills for the audience are the events, in the story world, that generate terror for the girl.

The girl occupies a mediated position between the audience and the image which offers a clue to the way the video visualises the music track. In the middle section, as the couple walk away from the cinema and Michael begins the song, the narrative roles of boyfriend and girlfriend are re-established, but now subordinated to the song's performance. This continuity of narrative function is underlined by the differentiation of costume style: Michael now wears a flashy red and black leather jacket cut in a 'futuristic' style and her ensemble is also contemporary – t-shirt, bomber jacket and head of curls like Michael's own. This imagery echoes publicity images of Jackson the stage performer. As the song gets under way Jackson becomes 'himself', the star. The girl becomes the 'you' in the refrain 'Girl, I could thrill you more than any ghost would dare to try.'

On the music track, the 'you' could be the listener, since the personal and direct mode of enunciation creates a space for the listener to enter and take part in the production of meanings. In the video, it is the girl who takes this place and, as the addressee of the sexual discourse enunciated in the song, her positions in the video-text create possibilities for spectatorial identification. These lines of identification are hinted at in the opening scene in which the girl's response to Michael's wooing enacts the 'fantasy of being a pop star's girlfriend', a fantasy which is realised in this section of the video.[18]

BEAUTY AND THE BEAST – MASKS, MONSTERS AND MASCULINITY

The conventions of horror inscribe a fascination with sexuality, with gender identity codified in terms that revolve around the symbolic presence of the monster. Women are invariably the victims of the acts of terror unleashed by the werewolf/vampire/alien/'thing': the monster as non-human Other. The destruction of the monster establishes male protagonists as heroes, whose object and prize is of course the woman. But as the predatory force against which the hero has to compete, the monster itself occupies a 'masculine' position in relation to the female victim.

'Thriller's' rhetoric of parody presupposes a degree of self-consciousness on the part of the spectator, giving rise to a supplementary commentary on the sexuality and sexual identity of its star, Michael Jackson. Thus, the warning 'I'm not like other guys' can be read by the audience as a reference to Jackson's sexuality. Inasmuch as the video audience is conscious of the gossip which circulates around the star, the statement of difference provokes other meanings: is he homosexual, transsexual or somehow pre-sexual?

In the first metamorphosis Michael becomes a werewolf. As the recent *Company of Wolves* (directed by Neil Jordan, 1984) demonstrates, werewolf mythology – lycanthropy – concerns the representation of male sexuality as 'naturally' bestial, predatory, aggressive, violent – in a word, 'monstrous'. Like 'Thriller', *Company of Wolves* employs similar special effects to show the metamorphosis of man to wolf in 'real time'. And like the Angela Carter story on which it is based, the film can be read as a rewriting of the European folktale of 'Little Red Riding Hood' to reveal its concerns with subjects of menstruation, the moon and the nature of male sexuality. In the fictional opening scene of 'Thriller' the connotation of innocence around the girl likens her to Red Riding Hood. But is Michael a big, bad wolf?

In the culmination of the chase sequence through the woods, the girl takes the role of victim. Here, the disposition of point-of-view angles between the monster's dominant position and the supine position of the victim suggests rape, fusing the underlying sexual relation of 'romance' with terror and violence. As the monster, Michael's transformation might suggest that beneath the boy-next-door image there is a 'real' man waiting to break out, a man whose masculinity is measured by a rapacious sexual appetite, 'hungry like the wolf'. But such an interpretation is undermined and subverted by the final shot of the metamorphosis. Michael-as-were-wolf lets out a blood-curdling howl, but this is in hilarious counterpoint to the collegiate 'M' on his jacket. What does it stand for? Michael? Monster? Macho Man? More like Mickey Mouse. The incongruity between the manifest signifier and the symbolic meaning of the Monster opens up a gap in the text, to be filled with laughter.

Animals are regularly used to signify human attributes, with the wolf, lion, snake and eagle all understood as signs of male sexuality. Jackson's subversion of this symbolism is writ large on the *Thriller* LP cover. Across the star's knee lies a young tiger cub, a brilliant little metaphor for the ambiguity of Jackson's image as a black male pop star. This plays on the star's 'man-child' image and suggests a domesticated animality, hinting at menace beneath the cute and cuddly surface. Jackson's sexual ambiguity makes a mockery out of the menagerie of received images of masculinity.[19]

In the second metamorphosis Michael becomes a zombie. Less dramatic and 'horrifying' than the first, this transformation cues the spectacular dance sequence that frames the chorus of the song. While the dance, choreographed by Michael Peters, makes visual one of the lines from the lyric, 'Night creatures crawl and the dead start to walk in their masquerade', it foregrounds Jackson-the-dancer and his performance breaks loose from the video. As the ghouls begin to dance, the sequence elicits the same kind of parodic humour provoked by Vincent Price's rap on the music track. There humour lay in the incongruity between Price's voice and the argot of black soul culture. Here a visual equivalent of the incongruity is created by the spectacle of the living dead performing with Jackson a funky dance routine. The sense of parody is intensified by the macabre make-up of the ghouls, bile dripping from their mouths. Jackson's make-up, casting a ghostly pallor over his skin and emphasising the contour of the skull, alludes to one of the paradigmatic 'masks' of the horror genre, that of Lon Chaney in *The Phantom of the Opera* (1925).

Unlike the werewolf, the figure of the zombie, the undead corpse, does not represent sexuality so much as asexuality or anti-sexuality, suggesting the sense of *neutral eroticism* in Jackson's style as dancer. As has been observed:

The movie star Michael most resembles is Fred Astaire – that *paragon of sexual vagueness*. Astaire never fit a type, hardly ever played a traditional romantic lead. He created his own niche by the sheer force of his tremendous talent.[20]

The dance sequence can be read as cryptic writing on this 'sexual vagueness' of Jackson's body in movement, in counterpoint to the androgyny of his image. The dance breaks loose from the narrative and Michael's body comes alive in movement, a rave from the grave: the scene can thus be seen as a commentary on the notion that as star Jackson only 'comes alive' when he is on stage performing. The living dead invoke an existential liminality which corresponds to both the sexual indeterminacy of Jackson's dance and the somewhat morbid lifestyle that reportedly governs his off-screen existence. Both meanings are buried in the video 'cryptogram'.[21]

METAPHOR-MORPHOSIS

Finally, I feel compelled to return to the scene of the first metamorphosis. It enthralls and captivates, luring the spectator's gaze and petrifying it in wonder. This sense of both fear and fascination is engineered by the video's special effects. By showing the metamorphosis in 'real time' the spectacle violently distorts the features of Jackson's face. The horror effect of the monster's appearance depends on the 'suspension of disbelief': we know that the monster is a fiction, literally a mask created by mechanical techniques, but repress or disavow this knowledge to participate in the 'thrills', the pleasures expected from the horror text. Yet in this splitting of belief which the horror film presupposes, it is credibility of the techniques themselves that is at stake in making the 'otherness' of the monster believable.[22]

The Making of Michael Jackson's Thriller (1984) demonstrates the special effects used in the video. We see make-up artists in the process of applying the 'mask' that will give Jackson the appearance of the monster. Of particular interest is the make-up artists' explanation of how the werewolf mask was designed and constructed: a series of transparent cells, each with details of the animal features of the mask, are gradually superimposed on a publicity image of Jackson from the cover of *Rolling Stone* magazine. It is this superimposition of fantastic and real upon Jackson's face that offers clues as to why the metamorphosis is so effective. Like the opening parody of the 1950s horror movie and its confusion of roles that Jackson is playing (boyfriend/star), there is a slippage between different levels of belief on the part of the spectator.

The metamorphosis achieves a horrifying effect because the monster does not just mutilate the appearance of the boyfriend, but plays on the audience's awareness of Jackson's double role; thus, the credibility of the special effects violates the image of the star himself. At this meta-textual level, the drama of the transformation is heightened by other performance-signs that foreground Jackson as star. The squeaks, cries and other word-less sounds which emanate from his throat as he grips his stomach grotesquely mimic the sounds which are the stylistic trademark of Jackson's voice and thus reinforce the impression that it is the 'real' Michael Jackson undergoing this mutation. Above all, the very first shots of the video highlight the make-up on the star's face (particularly the eyes and lips), the pallor of his complexion, revealing the eerie sight of his skull beneath the wet-look curls. The very appearance of Jackson draws attention to the artificiality of his own image. As the monstrous mask is, literally, a construction made out of make-up and cosmetic 'work', the fictional world of the horror film merely appropriates what is already an artifice. I suggest that the metamorphosis be seen as *a metaphor for the aesthetic reconstruction of Michael Jackson's face.*

The literal construction of the fantastic monster mask refers to other images of the star: the referent of the mask, as a sign in its own right, is a commonplace publicity image taken from the cover of a magazine. In this sense the mask refers not to the real person or private 'self' but to Michael Jackson-as-an-image. The metamorphosis could thus be seen as an accelerated allegory of the morphological development of Jackson's facial features: from child to adult, from boyfriend to monster, from star to superstar – the sense of wonder generated by the video's special effects forms an allegory for the fascination with which the world beholds this star-as-image.

In 1983, Jackson took part in a two-hour TV special to celebrate Motown's twenty-fifth anniversary, in which vintage footage was intercut with each act's performance; the film was then edited and used as a 'support' act on Motown artists' tours in England. This is how the reception of the film was described:

> The audience almost visibly tensed as Michael's voice . . . took complete control, attacking the songs with that increased repertoire of whoops, hiccups and gasps, with which he punctuates the lyric to such stylish, relaxing effect. And then he danced. The cocky strut of a super-confident child had been replaced by a lithe, menacing grace, and his impossibly lean frame, still boyishly gangly, when galvanised by the music, assumed a hypnotic, androgynous sexuality. Certainly, it was the first time in a long, long time I'd heard girls scream at a film screen.[23]

Amid all the screaming elicited by 'Thriller' it is possible to hear a parody of those fans' response. As a pop idol Michael Jackson has been the object of such screaming since he was eleven years old.

In 'The Face of Garbo' Barthes sought to explore the almost universal appeal of film stars like Chaplin, Hepburn and Garbo by describing their faces as *masks*: aesthetic surfaces on which a society writes large its own preoccupations.[24] Jackson's face can also be seen as such a mask, for his image has attracted and maintained the kind of cultural fascination that makes him more like a movie-star than a modern rhythm and blues artist. The sexual and racial ambiguity of his image can be seen as pointing to a range of questions about images of sex and race in popular culture and popular music. If we regard his face, not as the manifestation of personality traits but as a surface of artistic and social inscription, the ambiguities of Jackson's image call into question received ideas about what black male artists in popular music should look like. Seen from this angle his experimentation with imagery represents a creative incursion upon a terrain in pop culture more visibly mapped out by white male stars like Mick Jagger, David Bowie and Boy George. At best, these stars have used androgyny and sexual ambiguity as part of their 'style' in ways which question prevailing definitions of male sexuality and sexual identity. Key songs on *Thriller* highlight this problematisation of masculinity: on 'Wanna Be Startin' Somethin'' the narrator replies to rumour and speculation about his sexuality, on 'Billy Jean' – a story about a fan who claims he is the father of her son – he refuses the paternal model of masculinity, and on 'Beat It' – 'Don't wanna see no blood, Don't be a macho man' – he explicitly refuses a bellicose model of manliness.

What makes Jackson's use of androgyny more compelling is that his work is located entirely in the Afro-American tradition of popular music and thus must be seen in the context of imagery of black men and black male sexuality. Jackson not only questions dominant stereotypes of black masculinity,[25] but also gracefully steps outside the existing range of 'types' of black men. In so doing his style reminds us how some black men in the soul tradition such as Little Richard used 'camp', in the sense that Susan Sontag calls 'the love of the unnatural: of artifice and exaggeration',[26] long before white pop stars began to exploit its 'shock-value'. Indeed, 'Thriller' is reminiscent of the 'camp' excesses of the originator of the combination of music and horror in pop culture, Screamin' Jay Hawkins. Horror imagery has fascinated the distinctly white male genre of 'heavy metal' in which acts like Alice Cooper and Ozzy Osbourne consume themselves in self-parody. But like Hawkins, whose 'I Put a Spell on You' (1956) borrowed from images of horror to articulate a scream 'that found its way out of my big mouth *directly* through my heart and guts',[27] Jackson expresses another sort of 'screaming', one that articulates the erotic materiality of the human voice, its 'grain'. Writing about a musical tradition radically different from soul, Barthes coined this term to give 'the impossible account of an individual thrill that I constantly experience in listening to singing'.[28] 'Thriller' celebrates the fact that this thrill is shared by millions.

NOTES

This is a slightly shortened version of an article first published in *Screen*, 26, 1 (January/February 1986).

1   Roland Barthes, 'The grain of the voice', in Stephen Heath (ed.) *Image-Music-Text* (London: Fontana, 1977), 188.
2   Robert Johnson, 'The Michael Jackson nobody knows', *Ebony* (USA), December 1984.
3   *The Sun*, 9 April 1984.
4   Quoted in Nelson George, *The Michael Jackson Story* (London: New English Library, 1984), 106.
5   On music video, see Michael Boodro, 'Rock videos: another world', *ZG* ('Breakdown' issue, London 1984); Dessa Fox, 'The video virus', *New Musical Express*, London, 4 May 1985; Dave Laing, 'Music video: industrial product – cultural form', *Screen*, 26, 2 (March/April 1985), and Andy Lipman, 'The world of Salvador Disney', *City Limits*, 24 May 1985.
6   Laing, 'Music video', 81.
7   Quoted in Andy Warhol and Bob Colacello, 'Michael Jackson', *Interview* magazine, October 1982.
8   George, *Michael Jackson Story*, 108.
9   From *The Great Songs of Michael Jackson* (London: Wise Publications, 1984).
10 Iain Chambers, *Urban Rhythms: Pop Music and Popular Culture* (London: Macmillan, 1985), 148.
11 Iain Chambers, *Urban Rhythms*, 143–8, *passim*; see also, Richard Dyer, 'In defence of disco', *Gay Left*, 8 (Summer 1979).
12 Philip Brophy, 'Horrality', reprinted in *Screen*, 27, 1 (1988).
13 Ibid.
14 S. S. Prawer, *Caligari's Children: The Film as Tale of Terror* (Oxford University Press, 1980).
15 The 'Thriller' video is generally available as part of *The Making of Michael Jackson's Thriller*, Warner Home Video, 1984.
16 Stephen Neale, *Genre* (London: British Film Institute, 1980), 21, 56, 62.
17 Prawer, *Caligari's Children*, 15.
18 On personal modes of enunciation in pop discourse, see Alan Durant, *Conditions of Music* (London: Macmillan, 1984), esp. 201–6. The 'fantasy of being a pop star's girlfriend' is examined in Dave Rimmer, *Like Punk Never Happened: Culture Club and the New Pop* (London: Faber, 1985), 112.
19 One of Freud's most famous patients, The Wolf Man, makes connections between animals and sexuality clear. The Wolf Man's dream also reads like a horror film: 'I dreamt that it was night and that I was lying in my bed. Suddenly the window opened of its own accord, and I was terrified to see some white wolves were sitting on the big walnut tree in front of the window.' Cf. Muriel Gardiner, *The Wolf Man and Sigmund Freud* (London: Hogarth Press and Institute of Psychoanalysis, 1973), 173. Freud's reading suggests that the terror in the dream manifests a fear of castration for a repressed homosexual desire.
20 Quoted in Nelson George, *Michael Jackson Story*, 83–4.
21 The notion of 'cryptonymy' as a name for unconscious meanings emerges in Nicholas Abraham and Maria Torok's re-reading of Freud's Wolf Man. See Peggy Kamuf, 'Abraham's wake', *Diacritics* (Spring 1979), 32–43.
22 Neale, *Genre*, 45.
23 Geoff Brown, *Michael Jackson: Body and Soul* (London: Virgin Books, 1984), 10.
24 Roland Barthes, *Mythologies* (London: Paladin, 1973).

25 On stereotypes of black men in pop culture (music, film, entertainment and sport) see Isaac Julien, 'The other look', unpublished BA dissertation, St Martin's School of Art, 1983.
26 Susan Sontag, 'Notes on camp', in *Against Interpretation* (Eyre & Spottiswoode, 1969).
27 Gerry Hirshey, *Nowhere to Run: the Story of Soul* (London, Pan, 1984).
28 Roland Barthes, 'The grain of the voice', op. cit.

SELECT BIBLIOGRAPHY

There is a whole publishing industry devoted to stars and stardom, so any bibliography must be selective. This list offers extensive coverage of articles and books in English on theoretical and critical issues. It includes critical articles or more popular works on individual stars where these are exemplary of general issues or for what they reveal of how stars are constructed and circulate in society. For the same reason it also includes a selection of more general popular and early books on stars. On the whole, review articles on the careers of, or interviews with, individual stars are excluded. The list also includes some general works on the sociology of leisure and celebrity, cultural politics, fashion, the body, sexuality and representation which are central to a study of stars and stardom.

Useful further sources of bibliographic information are the British Film Institute Information Department index cards under the headings: stars, star system (different countries), stars (individual), acting, actors and actresses, homosexuality and cinema, homosexuality and the media, homosexuals and television, racialism in the cinema, racialism in the cinema – negroes, blacks and the cinema (different countries), personalities on television, blacks and television.

Stephen Bourne's dissertation, 'Black and Asian performers in British Films 1930–1949' (London College of Printing, 1988), provides useful biographical, filmographic and bibliographic information. *The Women's Film Bibliography*, newly revised by Sam Cook and published by the British Film Institute Education Department, contains a comprehensive section on women stars. The BFI Education Department also publishes a number of teaching packs on stars which are listed in the following bibliography. The BFI TV Unit is currently working on a project which will record all the appearances of black actors in British television.

Affron, C. (1977) *Star Acting*, New York: E. P. Dutton. On Gish, Garbo and Davis.
—— (1980) 'Performing performing: irony and affect', *Cinema Journal*, 20, 1, Fall. On Lana Turner in *Ziegfeld Girl* (1941) and *Imitation of Life* (1959).

Agan, P. (1984) *The Decline and Fall of the Love Goddesses*, Los Angeles: Pinnacle Books.

Alberoni, F. (1972) 'The powerless elite: theory and sociological research on the phenomenon of the stars', in D. McQuail (ed.) *Sociology of Mass Communications*, London: Penguin.

Allen, J. (1980) 'The film viewer as consumer', *Quarterly Review of Film Studies*, 5, 4, Fall.

Allen, R. C. (1980) *Vaudeville and Film 1895–1915: A Study in Media Interaction*, New York: Arno.

Alloway, L. (1971) *Violent America*, New York: Museum of Modern Art. Discusses stars as conventions in Hollywood films.

—— (1972) 'Iconography of the movies', in I. Cameron (ed.) *Movie Reader*, London: November Books.

Alpert, H. (1971) 'The falling stars', in A. F. McClune (ed.) *The Movies: An American Idiom: Readings in the Social History of the American Motion Picture*, Rutherford: Fairleigh Dickson University Press.

Anger, K. (1975) *Hollywood Babylon*, London: Straight Arrow Books.

—— (1986) *Hollywood Babylon II*, London: Straight Arrow Books; New York: Dell, 1981.

Antonioni, M. (1961) 'Reflections on the film actor', *Film Culture*, 22/3.

Archer, R. and Simmonds, D. (1986) *A Star Is Torn*, London: Virago. Study of women singers who starred in music-hall, cinema and the recording industry, examining the relation between female fame and personal tragedy.

Arvidson, L. (1925) *When the Movies Were Young*, New York: E. P. Dutton. Reprinted under Mrs D. W. Griffith, 1969, New York: Dover Publications.

Auster, A. (1979) 'Mary Pickford (1893–1979) – the star the working class found', *Cineaste*, 9, 4, Summer.

Baker, M. (1978) *Rise of the Victorian Actor*, London: Croom Helm.

Balázs, B. (1970) *Theory of the Film: Character and Growth of a New Art*, New York: Dover. Chapters on 'The close-up', 'The face of man' (reprinted in G. Mast and M. Cohen [1974] *Film Theory and Criticism*, New York: Oxford University Press) and 'Heroes, beauty, stars and the case of Greta Garbo'.

Balio, T. (1975) 'Stars in business: the founding of United Artists', in T. Balio (ed.) *The American Film Industry*, rev. edn 1986, Madison, Wisconsin: University of Wisconsin Press.

Barnouw, E. and Krishnaswamy, S. (1980) *Indian Film*, New York: Oxford University Press.

Barry, I. (1926) 'Acting' and 'Stars', in *Let's Go to the Pictures*, London: Chatto and Windus.

Barthes, R. (1972) 'The face of Garbo', in A. Lavers (trans.) *Mythologies*, London: Jonathan Cape. Reprinted in G. Mast and M. Cohen (1974) *Film Theory and Criticism*, New York: Oxford University Press.

Bathrick, S. K. (1979) 'A beauty and a buddy', *Jump Cut*, 21. Review article of P. Erens, *The Films of Shirley MacLaine*. Reprinted in P. Stevens (ed.) (1985) *Jump Cut: Hollywood, Politics and Counter-Cinema*, New York: Praeger.

Bauml, B. and Bauml, F. (1975) *A Dictionary of Gestures*, Metuchen, New Jersey: Scarecrow.

Baxter, P. (1978) 'On the naked thighs of Miss Dietrich', *Wide Angle*, 2, 2.

Bazin, A. (1967) *What is Cinema?* vol. 1, H. Gray (trans.) Berkeley: University of California Press. Chapter on Chaplin.

—— (1971) *What is Cinema?* vol. 2, H. Gray (trans.) Berkeley: University of

California Press. Chapters on Chaplin in *M. Verdoux* and *Limelight* and on Jean Gabin.

Bell, D. (1976) *The Cultural Contradictions of Capitalism*, New York: Basic Books.

Bell-Metereau, R. (1985) *Hollywood Androgyny*, New York: Columbia University Press.

Benelli, D. (1979) 'Rossellini's *Stromboli* and Ingrid Bergman's face', *Movietone News*, 62/3, 29 December.

Berlin, G. and Bruce, B. (1986) 'The superstar story', *CineAction!*, 7, December. On Warhol and his stars at the 'Factory'.

Bernheim, A. L. (1964) reprint, *The Business of the Theatre: An Economic History of the American Theatre*, New York: Benjamin Blom.

Betterton, R. (ed.) (1987) *Looking On: Images of Femininity in the Visual Arts and Media*, London: Pandora. General issues on sexual politics, feminism and representation.

Betts, E. (1960) *Inside Pictures: With Some Reflections from the Outside*, London: The Cresset Press. Sections on the star system.

Blum, R. (1984) *American Film Acting: The Stanislavski Heritage*, Ann Arbor, Michigan: UMI Research Press.

Bogle, D. (1973) *Toms, Coons, Mulattoes, Mammies and Bucks*, New York: Bantam, Viking.

Boorstin, D. (1962 and 1963) *The Image. A Guide to Pseudo-Events in America*, London: Weidenfeld & Nicolson, and Harmondsworth: Penguin.

Bordwell, D., Staiger, J. and Thompson, K. (1985) *The Classical Hollywood Cinema: Film Style and Mode of Production to 1960*, New York: Columbia University Press.

Bourget, J. (1978) 'Faces of the American melodrama: Joan Crawford', *Film Reader*, 3.

Bourne, Stephen (1983 and 1984) 'Star equality', *Films and Filming*, 351 and 352, December and January.

—— (1988) 'Black and Asian performers in British Films 1930–1949', dissertation, London College of Printing.

Bowers, Ronald (1976) *The Selznick Players*, South Brunswick: A. S. Barnes.

Braudy, L. (1976) *The World in a Frame*, Garden City, New York: Anchor/Doubleday. Chapter 3 on the function of the actor/star in films.

—— (1976) 'Film acting: some critical problems and proposals', *Quarterly Review of Film Studies*, 1, 1, February. Surveys criticism, journalism and biographies for attitudes to actors and acting; includes a bibliography on acting.

—— (1986) *Frenzy of Renown: Fame and Its History*, New York: Oxford University Press.

Britton, A. (1983) *Cary Grant: Comedy and Male Desire*, Newcastle upon Tyne: Tyneside Cinema. Reprinted in *CineAction!*, 7, December 1986.

—— (1984) *Katharine Hepburn: The Thirties and After*, Newcastle upon Tyne: Tyneside Cinema.

Bronski, M. (1978) 'Judy Garland and others: notes on idolisation and derision', in K. Jay and A. Young (eds) *Lavender Culture*, New York: Harcourt Brace Jovanovich.

Brooks, L. (1983) *Lulu in Hollywood*, New York: Knopf.

Brooks, P. (1976) *The Melodramatic Imagination: Balzac, Henry James, and the Mode of Excess*, New Haven: Yale University Press.

Brown, W. R. (1970) *Imagemaker: Will Rogers and the American Dream*, Columbia, Missouri: University of Missouri Press.

Bruno, M. (1970) *Venus in Hollywood: The Continental Enchantress from Garbo to Loren*, New York: Lyle Stuart.

Budge, B. (1988) 'Joan Collins and the wilder side of women – exploring pleasure and representation', in L. Gamman and M. Marshment (eds) *The Female Gaze: Women as Viewers of Popular Culture*, London: The Women's Press.

Burchill, J. (1986) *Girls on Film*, London: Virgin Books.

Burns, E. (1972) *Theatricality*, London: Longman.

Butler, J. (1990) *Star Texts: Image and Performance in Film and Television*, Detroit: Wayne State University Press.

Buxton, D. (1983) 'Rock music, the star system and the rise of consumerism', *Telos*, 57, Fall.

Cagney, J. (1976) *Cagney on Cagney*, Garden City, New Jersey: Doubleday.

Cahiers du Cinema (collective text) (1980) '*Morocco*', translated by Diana Matias, in P. Baxter (ed.) *Sternberg*, London: 1980, British Film Institute. A post-structuralist re-reading of the film which includes the role of the star.

Caillois, (1979) *Man, Play and Games*, New York: Schoken Books.

Cameron, I., and E. (1967) *The Heavies*, London: Studio Vista.

—— (1969) *The Broads*, London: Studio Vista.

Carrol, D. (1972) *The Matinee Idols*, London: Peter Owen.

Carson, B. (1984) 'Romantic perfection: the Torvill & Dean story', in L. Masterman (ed.) *TV Mythologies: Stars, Shows and Signs*, London: Comedia/MK Press.

Cawelti, J. G. (1980) 'Performance and popular culture', *Cinema Journal*, 20, 1, 1980.

Chaplin, C. (1966) *My Autobiography*, Harmondsworth: Penguin.

CineAction! (1986) 7, December. Special issue on stars.

Cinema Journal (1980) 20, 1, Fall. Special issue on film acting.

Clark, J., Merck, M. and Simmonds, D. (1981) *Move Over Misconceptions: Doris Day Reappraised*, BFI Dossier, 5, London: British Film Institute.

—— (1982) 'Doris Day case study: stars and exhibition', in C. Gledhill (ed.) *Star Signs: Papers from a Weekend Workshop*, London: British Film Institute Education Department.

Clurman, H. (1945) *The Fervent Years: The Story of the Group Theatre and the Thirties*, New York: Hill & Wang, rev. edn, 1957.

Cody, D. J. (1977) *The Star Personality: A Study of Four Western Stars*, Ann Arbor, MI: University of Michigan Microfilms. PhD dissertation.

Cole, T. and Krich Chinoy, H. (1970) *Actors on Acting*, New York: Crown.

Commission on Educational and Cultural Films (1932) *The Film in National Life*, London: George Allen & Unwin.

Comolli, J. (1978) 'Historical fiction – a body too much', *Screen*, 19, 2, Summer. The actor and representation of historical persons.

Cook, B. (1976) 'Why TV stars don't become movie stars', *American Film*, 1, 8, June.

Cook, P. (1979/80) 'Star signs', *Screen*, 20, 3/4, Winter.

—— (1982) 'Stars and politics', in C. Gledhill (ed.) *Star Signs: Papers from a Weekend Workshop*, London: British Film Institute Education Department.

Cook, S. (ed.) (1990) *The Women and Film Bibliography*, rev. edn, London: British Film Institute. Includes a comprehensive listing of articles on and interviews with women stars.

Cooke, A. (1970) *Douglas Fairbanks: The Making of a Screen Character*, New York: Museum of Modern Art.

—— (1971) *Garbo and the Night Watchmen*, New York: McGraw-Hill.

Cooke, L. (1986) 'Acting in the cinema: notes on *The Acting Tapes*', London: BFI

Education. Advisory document, including teaching notes and bibliography to support two fifty-four-minute tapes available for hire from the BFI Film & Video Library.

Coward, R. (1985) *Female Desires: How They Are Sought, Bought and Packaged*, London: Paladin.

Cripps, T. (1970) 'Paul Robeson and black identity in American movies', *Massachusetts Review*, 11, 3, Summer.

—— (1977) *Slow Fade to Black*, Oxford: Oxford University Press.

Croce, A. (1972) *The Fred Astaire and Ginger Rogers Book*, New York: Outerbridge and Lazard. Analysis of their star image.

Croy, H. (1959) *Starmaker: The Story of D. W. Griffith*, New York: Duell, Sloan & Pearce.

Cruse, H. (1978) 'The creative and performing arts and the struggle for identity and credibility', in H. A. Johnson (ed.) *Negotiating the Mainstream*, Chicago: American Library Association.

Curtis, A. (ed.) (1974) *The Rise and Fall of the Matinee Idol*, New York: St Martin's.

Damico, J. (1975) 'Ingrid from Lorraine to Stromboli: analyzing the public's perception of a film star', *Journal of Popular Film*, 5, 1.

Dandridge, D. and Conrad, E. (1970) *Everything and Nothing. The Dorothy Dandridge Tragedy*, New York: Abelard & Schuman.

de Beauvoir, S. (1960) *Brigitte Bardot and the Lolita Syndrome*, B. Frechtman (trans.) London: Andre Deutsch and Weidenfeld & Nicolson.

deCordova, R. (1986) 'Genre and performance: an overview', in B. K. Grant (ed.) *Film Genre Reader*, Austin: University of Texas Press.

——(1990) *Picture Personalities: The Emergence of the Star System in America*, University of Illinois Press.

Demaris, O. (1986) 'I didn't want to be who I was', *Parade*, 27 July. Interview with Michael Caine.

De Mille, W. C. (1939) *Hollywood Saga*, New York: E. P. Dutton.

Dempsey M. and Gupta, U. (1982) 'Hollywood's color problem', *American Film*, 7, 6, April.

Diderot, D. (1957) 'The paradox of acting', in W. Archer, *Masks or Faces*, New York: Hill & Wang.

Doll, S. (1989) 'Elvis Presley: all shook up. The effect of ideology and subculture on star image', dissertation, Northwestern University.

Donald, J. (1985) 'Stars', in P. Cook (ed.) *The Cinema Book*, London: British Film Institute.

Durgnat, R. (1965a) 'Getting cinema on the right wavelength', *Films and Filming*, 11, 5, February. On star figures, performance styles and directors' use of them.

—— (1965b) *Greta Garbo*, London: Studio Vista. Analysis of her star image.

—— (1967) *Films and Feelings*, London: Faber and Faber. Chapters 8–12 on stars and the way they embody attitudes and values.

Dyer, R. (1971) 'The meaning of Tom Jones', in Centre for Contemporary Cultural Studies, *Working Papers in Cultural Studies*, 1, Spring.

—— (1973) *BFI Television Monograph 2: Light Entertainment*, London: British Film Institute.

—— (1977) 'Entertainment and utopia', *Movie*, 24, Spring.

—— (1978) 'Resistance through charisma: Rita Hayworth and *Gilda*', in E. A. Kaplan (ed.) *Women in Film Noir*, London: British Film Institute.

—— (1979a) *Stars*, London: British Film Institute, 1979. Includes a comprehensive bibliography.

—— (1979b) *Teachers' Study Guide 1: The Stars*, London: BFI Education.

—— (1979c) *The Dumb Blonde Stereotype*, London: BFI Education. Document-ation to accompany a film study extract compilation, available for hire from the Film & Video Library, British Film Institute.

—— (1980) *Star Dossier I: Marilyn Monroe*, London: BFI Education. Includes slide set and facsimile documents.

—— (1982a) 'Don't look now – the male pin-up', *Screen*, 23, 3/4, September/October.

—— (1982b) 'The Son of the Sheik', *The Movie*, 126.

—— (1987) *Heavenly Bodies: Film Stars and Society*, London: Macmillan. On Monroe, Robeson and Garland.

Dyer, R. (ed.) (1977) *Gays and Film*, London: British Film Institute.

Eco, U. (1976) 'Semiotics of theatrical performance', *The Drama Review*, 21.

Edwards, C. (1965) *The Stanislavski Heritage*, New York: New York University Press.

Eells, G. (1976) *Ginger, Loretta and Irene Who?*, New York: G. P. Putnam's Sons. A comparison of Ginger Rogers, Loretta Young, Miriam Hopkins, Ruth Etting, Kaye Frances and Irene Bentley in Hollywood.

Elam, K. (1980) *The Semiotics of Theatre and Drama*, London: Methuen.

Ellis, J. (1982) 'Stars as a cinematic phenomenon', in *Visible Fictions: Cinema, Televison, Video*, London: Routledge & Kegan Paul. An approach drawing on cine-psychoanalysis.

Erens, P. (1978) *The Films of Shirley MacLaine*, New York: A. S. Barnes.

—— (1979) 'In defense of stars: a response', *Jump Cut*, 21. Reply to S. K. Bathrick (1979) 'A beauty and a buddy'. Reprinted in P. Steven (ed.) (1985) *Jump Cut: Hollywood, Politics and Counter-Cinema*, New York: Praeger.

Ewen, S. and Ewen, E. (1982) *Channels of Desire: Mass Images and the Shaping of American Consciousness*, New York: McGraw-Hill.

Fadiman, W. (1973) *Hollywood Now*, London: Thames & Hudson. Chapter on 'The star'.

Faller, G. (1987) 'The function of star and performance in the Hollywood musical: Eleanor Powell, Sonia Henie, Esther Williams', dissertation, Northwestern University.

Fernandez, R. (1978) 'Designing for the stars: interview with Walter Plunkett', *The Velvet Light Trap*, 18, 27/9.

Film Comment (1985) 'A separate cinema', 21, 5 September/October. 'Midsection' on black stars and genres.

Friedberg, Anne (1982) 'Identification and the star: a refusal of difference', in C. Gledhill (ed.) *Star Signs: Papers from a Weekend Workshop*, London: British Film Institute Education Department.

Fuentes, A. and Schrage, M. (1987) 'Deep inside porn stars: interview with Veronica Hart, Gloria Leonard, Kelly Nichols, Candida Royalle, Annie Sprinkel and Veronica Vera', *Jump Cut*, 32.

Gabor, M. (1973) *The Pin-Up: A Modest History*, London: Pan Books.

Gaines, J. (1980) 'The showgirl and the wolf', *Cinema Journal*, 20, 1, Fall.

—— (1982) 'The popular icon as commodity and sign: the circulation of Betty Grable, 1941–55', dissertation, Northwestern University.

—— (1986) 'War, women and lipstick: fan mags in the forties', *Heresies*, 18.

—— (1989) 'The Queen Christina tie-ups: convergence of show window and screen', *Quarterly Review of Film and Video* 11, 1.

Gaines, J. and Herzog, C. (eds) (1991). *Fabrications: Costume and the Female Body*, New York: Routledge. Includes a comprehensive bibliography on Hollywood costumes, fashion/body/consumer culture, and feminism and cultural studies.

Gam, R. (1986) *Actress to Actress: Memories, Profiles, Conversations*, New York: Nick Lyons Books. An actress and film writer on film and theatre stars, including a chapter on Indian film stars.

Geraghty, C. (1986) 'Diana Dors', in C. Barr (ed.) *All Our Yesterdays: 90 Years of British Cinema*, London: British Film Institute.

Gish, L. (1969) *The Movies, Mr. Griffiths and Me*, Englewood Cliffs, NJ: Prentice-Hall.

Gledhill, C. (ed.) (1983) 'Introduction' to *Star Signs: Papers from a Weekend Workshop*, London: British Film Institute Education Department.

Goffman, Erving (1951) 'Symbols of class status', *British Journal of Sociology*, 2.

—— (1959) *The Presentation of Self in Everyday Life*, Garden City, New York: Doubleday; London: Penguin, 1971.

—— (1976) *Gender Advertisements*, London: Macmillan.

Goldberg, R. L. (1979) *Performance: Live Art 1909 to the Present*, London: Thames and Hudson.

Goldstein, L. (1973) 'Familiarity and contempt: an essay on the star-presence in film', *Centennial Review*, 17, Summer.

Goodman, J. (1981) 'Jane Fonda: banking on message movies', *American Film*, 7, 2, November.

The Greystone Seminar (1976) 'Dialogue on film', *American Film*, 1, 10, September. Interview with Sidney Poitier.

Griffith, R. (1970) *The Movie Stars*, New York: Doubleday.

Guiles, F. L. (1969) *Norma Jean*, New York: McGraw-Hill.

Gupta, C. D. and Hoberman J. (1987) 'Pols of India', *Film Comment*, 23, 3, May/June.

Halsey, S. & Co. (1976) 'The motion picture industry as a basis for bond financing', in T. Balio (ed.) *The American Film Industry*, Madison, Wisconsin: University of Wisconsin Press.

Hampton, B. (1970) *History of the American Film Industry: From Its Beginnings to 1931*, New York: Dover Publications, rev. edn.

Handel, L. A. (1950) *Hollywood Looks At Its Audience*, Urbana, IL: University of Illinois Press.

Hanna, J. L. (1988) *Dance, Sex and Gender: Signs of Identity, Defiance and Desire*, Berkeley: University of California Press.

Hansen, M. (1991) *Babel and Babylon: Spectatorship in American Silent Film*, Cambridge, Mass.: Harvard University Press. Part 3, 'The return of Babylon: Rudolph Valentino and female spectatorship (1921–6)'.

Hanson, S., King Hanson, P. and Broeske, P. H. (1985), 'Ruling stars', *Stills*, 20, June/July. On the independent production companies set up by contemporary stars.

Haskell, M. (1974) *From Reverence to Rape: The Treatment of Women in the Movies*, New York: Holt, Rinehart & Winston, and Harmondsworth: Penguin.

Haskins, J. with Benson, K. (1984) *Lena. A Personal and Professional Biography of Lena Horne*, New York: Day & Stein.

Herman, G. and Downing, D. (1980) *Jane Fonda: All American Anti-Heroine*, London: Omnibus.

Hess, T. B. (1973) 'Pin-up and icon', in T. B. Hess and L. Nochlin (eds) *Woman as Sex Object*, London: Allen Lane.

Hicks, J. (1975) 'Rock Hudson: the film actor as romantic hero', *Films in Review*, 267–89, May.

Higashi, S. (1978) *Virgins, Vamps, and Flappers: The American Silent Movie Heroine*, St Albans, VT: Eden Press Women's Publications.

—— (1979) 'Cinderella vs. statistics: the silent movie heroine as a jazz-age working girl', in M. Kelly (ed.) *Woman's Being, Woman's Place: Female Identity and Vocation in American History*, Boston: G. K. Hall.

Higson, A. (1985) 'Acting taped – an interview with Mark Nash and James Swinson', *Screen*, 26, 5, September/October.

—— (1986) 'Film acting and independent cinema', *Screen*, 27, 3/4, May/August.

Hirsch, F. (1984) *A Method to Their Madness: The History of the Actors' Studio*, New York: Norton.

Holmlund, C. (1986) 'Sexuality and power in male doppelganger cinema: the case of Clint Eastwood's *Tightrope*', *Cinema Journal*, 26, 1, Fall.

Holston, K. (1988) *Starlet: Biographies, Filmographies, TV Credits and Photos of 54 Famous and Not So Famous Leading Ladies in the 60s*, Jefferson, NC: McFarland & Co.

Holt, G. and Quinn, P. (1988) *Star Mothers: The Moms Behind the Celebrities*, New York: Simon & Schuster.

Horrigan, B. (1978) 'An afterword note to Jean-Loup Bourget's article', *Film Reader*, 3.

Hughes, E. (1931) *Famous Stars of Stardom*, Boston: L. C. Page & Co.

Hunt, A. (1984) ' "She laughed at me with my own teeth": Tommy Cooper – television anti-hero', in L. Masterman (ed.) *TV Mythologies: Stars, Shows and Signs*, London: Comedia/MK Press.

Jacobowitz, F. (1986) 'Joan Bennett: images of femininity in conflict', *CineAction!*, 7, December.

Jacobs, L. (1968) *The Rise of the American Film: A Critical History*, New York: Teachers College Press, rev. edn.

Jacobson, L. (1984) *Hollywood Heartbreak: The Tragic and Mysterious Deaths of Its Most Remarkable Legends*, New York: Simon & Schuster.

Jaehne, K. (1986) 'Seeking connections: an interview with Julie Christie', *Cineaste*, 15, 2.

Jarvie, I. C. (1970) *Towards a Sociology of the Cinema*, London: Routledge, 1970.

Jennings, Wade (1979) 'Nova: Garland in *A Star Is Born*', *Quarterly Review of Film Studies*, 4, 3, Summer.

Johnson, C. (1973) 'Women's cinema as counter-cinema', in C. Johnston (ed.) *Notes on Women's Cinema*, London: Society for Education in Film and Television.

—— (1975) 'Feminist politics and film history', *Screen*, 16, 3, Autumn. Review article on Molly Haskell's *From Reverence to Rape* and Marjories Rosen's *Popcorn Venus*.

Kalter, J. (ed.) (1979) *Actors on Acting: Performance in Theatre and Film Today*, New York: Sterling.

Kaplan, A. E. (1974) 'The success and ultimate failure of *Last Tango in Paris*', *Jump Cut*, 4, November/December. Exploration of the relation between Brando's image and the film's *mise en scène*.

Kay, K. and Peary, G. (1975) 'Talking to Pat O'Brien', *The Velvet Light Trap*, 15.

Kehr, D. (1986) 'A star is made', *Film Comment*, 15, 1, January/February. Changes in the mode of star production and the role of television, contrasting the careers of Henry Winkler and John Travolta.

Kemp, P. (1988) 'Degrees of radiance: Astaire, Fosse and Hollywood glamour', *Cinema Papers*, 68, March.

Kindem, G. (ed.) (1982) 'Hollywood's movie star system: a historical overview', in *The American Movie Industry: The Business of Motion Pictures*, Carbondale: Southern Illinois University Press.

King, B. (1986a) 'Stardom as an occupation', in P. Kerr (ed.) *The Hollywood Film*

Industry, London: Routledge & Kegan Paul in association with the British Film Institute.

—— (1986b) 'Screen acting – reflections on the day', *Screen*, 27, 4/5, May/August.

—— (1987) 'The star and the commodity: notes towards a performance theory of stardom', *Cultural Studies*, 1, 2, May.

—— (forthcoming, 1990) *Understanding Stardom* (provisional title), Oxford: Polity Press.

Kirby, E. T. (1972) 'The Delsarte method: three frontiers of actor training', *Drama Review*, 16, 1, March.

Klapp, O. E. (1962) *Heroes, Villains and Fools*, Englewood Cliffs: Prentice-Hall.

Klaprat, C. (1985) 'The star as market strategy: Bette Davis in another light', in T. Balio (ed.) *The American Film Industry*, rev. edn, Madison, Wisconsin: University of Wisconsin Press.

Klumph, I. and Klumph, H. (1922) *Screen Acting: Its Requirements and Rewards*, New York: Falk Library.

Knox, A. (1966) 'Acting and behaving', in R. D. MacCann, *Film: A Montage of Theories*, New York: E. P. Dutton.

Kobal, J. (1980) *The Art of the Great Hollywood Portrait Photographers*, London: Allen Lane, 1980.

Kobbe, G. (1905) *Famous Actresses and Their Homes*, Boston: Little, Brown.

Kracauer, S. (1950) 'Stage vs. screen acting: 1. The theoretical differences are fundamental', *Films in Review*, 1, 9, December.

—— (1961) 'Remarks on the actor', in *Nature of Film: The Redemption of Physical Reality*, London: Dennis Dobson. Published in America as *Theory of Film*.

Kramer, M. (1983) 'Jean Seberg, the FBI, the media', *Jump Cut*, 28, April.

Lakoff, R. T. and Scherr, R. L. (1984) *Face Value: The Politics of Beauty*, Boston: Routledge & Kegan Paul.

Lang, K. and Lang, G. (1965) 'Fashion: identification and differentiation in the mass society', in M. E. Roach and J. Bubolz Eicher (eds) *Dress, Adornment, and the Social Order*, New York: Wiley & Sons.

Langer, J. (1981) 'Television's "Personality system" ', *Media, Culture and Society*, 3, 4, October.

LaPlace, M. (1985) 'Bette Davis and the ideal of consumption: a look at *Now, Voyager*', *Wide Angle*, 6, 4. Revised and expanded as 'Producing and consuming the woman's film: discursive struggle in *Now, Voyager*', in C. Gledhill (ed.) (1987) *Home is Where the Heart Is*, London: British Film Institute.

Leab, D. J. (1975) *From Sambo to Superspade. The Black Experience in Motion Pictures*, London: Secker & Warburg.

Lepper, D. (1980) *Star Dossier 2: John Wayne*, London: BFI Education. Includes slide pack and facsimile documents.

Lewis, L. (ed.) (1990) *The Adoring Audience: Fan Culture and Popular Media*, London: Unwin Hyman. A collection of theoretical and applied essays on fans of popular music, television and film.

Lippe, R. (1986) 'Kim Novak: a resistance to definition', *CineAction!*, 7, December.

—— (1987) 'Rock Hudson: his story', *CineAction!* 10, October. Relates biographer's methods of dealing with Rock Hudson and AIDS to his earlier film image.

Lowenthal, L.(1961) 'The triumph of mass idols', in *Literature, Popular Culture and Society*', Englewood Cliffs: Prentice-Hall.

Lurie, A. (1981) *The Language of Clothes*, New York: Random House.

McArthur, B. (1984) *Actors and American Culture, 1880–1920*, Philadelphia: Temple University Press.

McArthur, C. (1967) 'The real presence', *Sight and Sound*, 36, 3, Summer. Reprinted in R. Dyer (1979) *Teachers' Study Guide 2: The Stars*, London: BFI Education.

McCaffrey, D. (1968) *Four Great Comedians: Chaplin, Lloyd, Keaton, Langdon*, London: A. Zwemmer.

McConathy, D. and Vreeland, D. (1978) *Hollywood Costume*, New York: Harry N. Abrams.

McCreadie, M. (ed.) (1973) *The American Movie Goddess*, New York: John Wiley & Sons.

—— (1982) 'Latter-day Lorekis: new screen heroines', *Cineaste*, 12, 2.

McDonald, A. P. (ed.) (1987) *Shooting Stars: Heroes and Heroines of the Western Film*, Bloomington, Ind.: Indiana University Press.

McDonald, G. D. (1953) 'Origin of the star system', *Films in Review*, 4, November.

McFarlane, B. (1982 and 1983) 'Creatures great and small', *Cinema Papers*, 41, December and March. An analysis of the star biography genre.

McGilligan, P. (1982) *Cagney: The Actor as Auteur*, South Brunswick: A. S. Barnes.

McKnight, S. (1988) *Star Dossier 3: Robert Redford*, London: BFI Education. Includes slide pack and facsimile documents.

McLaughlin, R. (1974) *Broadway and Hollywood*, New York: Arno Press.

Mailer, N. (1973) *Marilyn*, London: Hodder & Stoughton.

Malone, M. (1979) *Heroes of Eros: Male Sexuality in the Movies*, New York: E. P. Dutton.

Maltby, R. (1982) 'The political economy of Hollywood: the studio system', in P. Davies and B. Neve (eds) *Cinema, Politics and Society in America*, Manchester: University of Manchester Press.

—— (1985) *Harmless Entertainment: Hollywood and the Ideology of Consensus*, London: Scarecrow.

Mandelbaum, H. (1979) 'A mannequin's face: Joan Crawford', *Bright Lights*, 8.

—— (1981) 'Bette Davis: a talent for hysteria', *Bright Lights*, 3, 1.

Mann, D. (1989) 'The spectacularization of everyday life: recycling Hollywood stars and fans in early television variety shows', *Camera Obscura*, 16.

Mariani, J. (1977) 'Models turned actresses', *Millimeter*, 5, 7, July/August.

Marsh, M. (n.d.) *Screen Acting*, Los Angeles: Photo-Star Publishing. Mae Marsh's account.

Martin, A. (1988) 'Confessions of a mask', *Cinema Papers*, 68. On glamour.

Martin, M. (1985) 'Leading ladies in B-Westerns, 1921–1954', *Classic Images*, 116, February.

—— (1985) 'Leading ladies of the Western, Part 2', *Classic Images*, 117, March.

Masterman, L. (ed.) (1984) *TV Mythologies: Stars, Shows and Signs*, London: Comedia/MK Press.

Matthews, P. (1988) 'Garbo and phallic motherhood – a "homosexual" visual economy', *Screen*, 29, 3, Summer.

May, L. (1980) *Screening Out the Past: The Birth of Mass Culture and the Motion Picture Industry*, New York: Oxford University Press.

Mayer, J. P. (1948) *British Cinemas and Their Audiences*, London: Dennis Dobson.

Mayersberg, P. (1969) *Hollywood the Haunted House*, London: Allen Lane/Penguin. Chapter 4, 'The wench is dead', on stars.

Medhurst, A. (1986) 'Dirk Bogarde', in C. Barr (ed.) *All Our Yesterdays: 90 Years of British Cinema*, London: British Film Institute.

Mellencamp, P. (1986) 'Situation comedy, feminism and Freud: discourses of Gracie and Lucy', in T. Modleski (ed.) *Studies in Entertainment: Critical Approaches to Mass Culture*, Bloomington, Ind.: Indiana University Press.

Mellon, J. (1978) *Big Bad Wolves: Masculinity in the American Film*, London: Elm Tree Books.

Merton, R. K. (1946) *Mass Persuasion*, New York: Harper & Brothers.

Messel, R. (1928) 'Actor versus producer' and 'The star in Nebula', in *This Film Business*, London: Ernest Benn.

Miller, G. (1984) 'The (sex) symbol: Marilyn, prime time and the Nielsens', *Literature/Film Quarterly*, 12, 4.

Modleski, T. (ed.) (1986) *Studies in Entertainment: Critical Approaches to Mass Culture*, Bloomington and Indianapolis: Indiana University Press.

Monaco, J. (1978) *Celebrity: The Media as Image Makers*, New York: Delta Publishing.

Mordden, E. (1983) *Movie Star: A Look at The Women Who Made Hollywood*, New York: St Martin's Press.

Morella, J. and Epstein, E. Z. (1971) *Rebels: The Rebel Hero in Films*, New York: The Citadel Press.

Morin, E. (1960) *The Stars*, trans. R. Howard, New York: Grove Press.

Morris, C. (1906) *The Life of a Star*, New York: McClure, Phillips.

Morse, M. (1986) 'The television news personality and credibility: reflections on the news in transition', in T. Modeleski (ed.) *Studies in Entertainment: Critical Approaches to Mass Culture*, Bloomington and Indianapolis: Indiana University Press.

Mulvey, L. (1975) 'Visual pleasure and narrative cinema', *Screen*, 16, 3, Autumn. Reprinted in L. Mulvey, *Visual and Other Pleasures*, London: Macmillan, 1989.

—— (1981) 'Afterthoughts on visual pleasure and narrative cinema in relation to *Duel in the Sun*', *Framework*, 15/16/17. Reprinted in C. Gledhill (ed.) *Star Signs: Papers from a Weekend Workshop*, London: British Film Institute Education Department.

Naremore, J. (1988) *Acting in the Cinema*, Berkeley: University of California Press.

Neale, S. (1983) 'Masculinity as spectacle', *Screen*, 24, 6, November/December.

O'Brien, M. E. (1983) *Film Acting: The Techniques and History of Acting for the Camera*, New York: Arno.

Owens, C. (1985) 'Posing', in K. Linker and J. Weinstock, *Difference: On Representation and Sexuality*, New York: The New Museum of Contemporary Art.

Pacteau, F. (1986) 'The impossible referent: representation of the androgyne', in V. Burgin, J. Donald and C. Kaplan (eds) *Formations of Fantasy*, London: Methuen.

Palmer, S. (1988a) *British Film Actors' Credits, 1895–1987*, Jefferson, NC: McFarland & Co.

—— (1988b) *A Who's Who of Australian and New Zealand Film Actors: The Sound Era*, Metuchen, NJ: Scarecrow Press.

Parish, J. R. (1977) *Film Actors' Guide: Western Europe*, Metuchen, NJ: Scarecrow Press.

Parkenson, M. (1988) 'The tragedy of Dorothy Dandridge', *Black Film Review*, 4, 2, Spring.

Perkins, T. E. (1979) 'Rethinking stereotypes', in M. Barrett, P. Corrigan, A. Kuhn and J. Wolff (eds) *Representation and Cultural Production*, London: Croom Helm.

—— (1981) 'Remembering Doris Day: some comments on the subject and the season', *Screen Education*, 39, Summer. Review article on *Move Over Misconceptions* and National Film Theatre season.

Pines, J. (1975) *Blacks in Films*, London: Studio Vista.

Pirie, D. (ed.) (1981) 'The deal', in *The Anatomy of the Movies*, London: Windward.

Poitier, S. (1980) 'Walking the Hollywood color line', *American Film*, 5, 6 April.

Polheumus, T. (ed.) (1978) *The Body Reader: Social Aspects of the Human Body*, New York: Pantheon.

Posner, C. 'Jane Fonda's most important part: role model for young women of the 1980s', *Films in Review*, 38, 3, March.

Powdermaker, H. (1950) *Hollywood: the Dream Factory*, Boston: Little, Brown & Co. Chapters on acting and stars.

Pudovkin, V. I. (1953) 'Stanislavski's system in the cinema', *Sight and Sound*, 22/3, January/March.

—— (1958) *Film Technique and Film Acting*, I. Montagu (trans.) London: Mayflower.

Quinland, D. (1983) 'Those wicked, wicked ladies and their wicked, wicked ways', *Photoplay*, 34, 4, April.

Rajadhyaksha, A. (1986) 'Julie Christie: far from the Hollywood crowd', *American Film*, 8, 7, May.

Richards, J. (1984) *The Age of the Dream Palace: Cinema and Society in Britain 1930–1939*, London: Routledge & Kegan Paul. Part 3, *The Stars*. On Gracie Fields, George Formby and Jessie Matthews.

Richards, J. and Sheridan, D. (eds) (1987) *Mass Observation at the Movies*, London: Routledge & Kegan Paul.

Riesman, D. (1950) *The Lonely Crowd*, New Haven: Yale University Press.

Roach, J. and Felix, P. (1988) 'Black looks', in L. Gamman and M. Marshment (eds) *The Female Gaze*, London: The Woman's Press.

Roberts, S. (1986) 'Melodramatic performance signs', *Framework*, 32/3. Discusses the Delsarte system and its influence on performance in Hollywood melodrama.

Roffman, P. and Simpson, B. (1984) 'Black images on white screens', *Cineaste*, 13, 3.

Rogin, M. (1987) *Ronald Reagan: The Movie and Other Episodes in Political Demonology*, Berkeley: University of California Press.

Rosen, M. (1973) *Popcorn Venus: Women, Movies, and the American Dream*, New York, Avon Books.

Ross, L. and Ross, H. (1962) *The Player: The Profile of an Art*, New York: Simon and Schuster. An autobiographical interview book.

Ross, M. (1941) *Stars and Strikes: Unionization of Hollywood*, New York: Columbia University Press.

Rosten, L. C. (1941) *Hollywood: The Movie Colony, the Movie Makers*, New York: Harcourt, Brace & Co.

Russo, V. (1981) *The Celluloid Closet*, New York: Harper & Row.

Ryan, M. P. (1976) 'The projection of a new womanhood: the movie moderns in the 1920s', in J. E. Friedman and W. G. Shade, *Our American Sisters: Women in American Life and Thought*, 2nd edn, Boston: Allyn & Bacon.

Sarris, A. (1977) 'The actor as auteur', *American Film*, 11, 7, May.

—— (1986) 'Cary Grant's antic elegance', *The Village Voice*, 16, December.

Saxton, M. (1975) *Jayne Mansfield and the American Fifties*, Boston: Houghton Mifflin.

Schickel, R. (1973) *His Picture in the Papers: A Speculation on Celebrity in America, Based on the Life of Douglas Fairbanks, Sr.*, New York: Charterhouse.

—— (1985) *Common Fame: The Culture of Celebrity*, London: Pavilion/Michael Joseph.

—— (1987a) 'No method to his madness', *Film Comment*, 23, 3, May/June. On Ronald Reagan.

—— (1987b) *Striking Poses: Photographs from the Kobal Collection*, London: Pavilion/Michael Joseph.

Scott, J. F. (1975) *Film – the Medium and the Maker*, New York: Holt, Rinehart & Winston.

Screen (1985) 26, 5, September/October. Special issue on screen acting.

Seiter, E. (1986) 'Stereotypes and the media: a re-evaluation', *Journal of Communication*, 36, 2, Spring.

Sennett, R. (1978) *The Fall of Public Man*, New York, Vintage Books.

Seton, M. (1958) *Paul Robeson*, London: Dennis Dobson.

Shaffer, L. (1973) 'Some notes on film acting', *Sight and Sound*, 42, 2, Spring.

—— (1977/8) 'Reflections on the face in film', *Film Quarterly*, 31, 2, Winter.

Shafrensky, R. (1983), 'Jean Seberg: an American dream?', *Jump Cut*, 28, April.

Shah, R. (1981) 'The social significance of film stars', in *The Indian Film*, Westport, Conn: Greenwood Press. Reprint of 1950 publication by Motion Picture Society of India.

Shaver, C. L. (1954) 'Steele MacKaye and the Delsartian tradition', in K. Wallace (ed.) *History of Speech Education*, New York: Appleton-Century-Crofts.

Sheinwold, P. F. (1980) *Too Young to Die*, London: Cathay.

Shipman, D. (1970) *The Great Stars – The Golden Years*, London: Hamlyn.

—— (1972) *The Great Stars – The International Years*, London: Hamlyn.

Shorter, E. (1982) *A History of Women's Bodies*, New York: Basic Books.

Simmonds, D. (1984) *Princess Di The National Dish*, London: Pluto. The making of a media star.

Sinclair, M. (1979) *Those Who Died Young*, London: Plexus.

Singleton, J. (1988) 'Portrait of a survivor', *Black Film Review*, 4, 2, Spring. On Vonetta McGee.

Slide, A. (1973) *The Griffith Actresses*, Cranbury, NJ: A. S. Barnes.

—— (1974) 'The evolution of the film star', *Films in Review*, 25, 10, December.

—— (1976) *The Idols of Silence: Stars of the Cinema Before the Talkies*, Cranbury, NJ: A. S. Barnes.

Staiger, J. (1985) 'The eyes are really the focus: photoplay acting and film form and style', *Wide Angle*, 6, 4.

Stebbins, G. (1902) *The Delsarte System of Expression*, New York: Edgar S. Werner.

Steele, V. (1985) *Fashion and Eroticism: Ideals of Feminine Beauty from the Victorian through the Jazz Age*, New York: Oxford University Press.

Stein, F. (1986) 'Mae West as debunker of sex', *Hollywood Spectator*, 11, 2 May 9.

Stein, R. (1974) *The Pin-Up from 1852 to Now*, London: Hamlyn.

Steinem, G. (1973) 'Marilyn – the woman who died too soon', in *The First Ms Reader*, New York: Warner.

Stevens, T. (1980) 'Signs of life: acting and representation', *Screen Education*.

Strasberg, L. (1987) *A Dream of Passion: The Development of the Method*, ed. E. Morphos, Boston: Little & Brown.

Studlar, G. (1988) *In the Realm of Pleasure: Von Sternberg, Dietrich, and the Masochistic Aesthetic*, Urbana and Chicago: University of Illinois Press.

—— (1989) 'Discourses of gender and ethnicity: the construction and de(con)struction of Rudolph Valentino as other', *Film Criticism*, 13, 2.

—— (1991) 'Masochism, masquerade, and the erotic metamorphoses of Marlene Dietrich', in J. M. Gaines and C. C. Herzog (eds) *Fabrications: Costume and the Female Body*, New York: Routledge.

Susman, W. (1979) ' "Personality" and the making of twentieth century culture', in J. Higham and P. K. Conkin (eds) *New Directions in American Intellectual History*, Baltimore: The Johns Hopkins University Press.

Taylor, R. G. (1984) *Marilyn in Art*, London: Elm Tree Books.

Thomas, R. (1990) 'The mythologisation of Mother India', *Quarterly Review of Film and Video*, 12, 1, Spring.

Thomson, D. (1977) 'The look on an actor's face', *Sight and Sound*, 46, 4, Autumn.

—— (1980) 'Waiting for Garbo', *American Film*, 6, 1, October.

—— (1981/2) 'All our Joan Crawfords', *Sight and Sound*, 51, 1, Winter.

—— (1984) 'Charms and the man', *Film Comment*, 20, 1, February. On Cary Grant.

Thorpe, M. (1939) 'Glamour', in *America at the Movies*, New Haven: Yale University Press.

Thorstein, V. (1899) *The Theory of the Leisure Class: An Economic Study of Institutions*, New York: Macmillan. Reprint 1925, paperback 1970, London: George Allen and Unwin.

Thumim, J. (1986) ' "Miss Hepburn is humanised": the star persona of Katharine Hepburn', *Feminist Review*, 24, Autumn.

Took, B. (1989) *Comedy Greats: A Celebration of Comic Genius Past and Present*, Wellingborough, Northamptonshire: Equation. A reference guide.

Tressider, J. (1974) *Heart-Throbs*, London: Marshall Cavendish. A picture book.

Trilling, D. (1963) 'The death of Marilyn Monroe', in *Claremont Essays*, New York: Harcourt Brace Jovanovich.

Tudor, A. (1974) *Image and Influence*, London: Allen & Unwin.

Tunstall, J. and Walker, D. (1981) *Media Made in California*, Oxford: Oxford University Press.

Turim, M. (1983) 'Fashion shapes: films, the fashion industry and the image of women', *Socialist Review*, 17, September/October.

Tyler, P. (1970) *Hollywood Hallucination*, New York: Simon and Schuster. Reprint of 1940 publication.

Vasnder, A. and Lenglet, P. (eds) (1987) *Indian Cinema Superbazaar*, New Delhi: Vikas.

The Velvet Light Trap 7 (1972). Special issue on the film actor.

Vincendeau, G. (1985) 'Community, nostalgia and the spectacle of masculinity – Jean Gabin', *Screen*, 26, 6, November/December.

Wagenknecht, E. (1962) *Movies in the Age of Innocence*, Norman: University of Oklahoma Press. Chapters on Mary Pickford, Famous Players and Lillian Gish.

Walker, A. (1966) *The Celluloid Sacrifice*, London: Michael Joseph. Reprinted 1968 as *Sex in the Movies*, Harmondsworth: Penguin.

—— (1974) *Stardom, the Hollywood Phenomenon*, Harmondsworth: Penguin.

—— (1978) *The Shattered Silents: How the Talkies Came to Stay*, London: Elm Tree Books/Hamish Hamilton. Considerable information on stars.

Watney, S. (1985) 'Katharine Hepburn and the cinema of chastisement', *Screen*, 26, 5, September/October. Review article of A. Britton, *Katharine Hepburn: The Thirties and After*.

—— (1987) 'Stellar studies', *Screen*, 28, 3, Summer. Review of R. Dyer, *Heavenly Bodies*.

Weis, E. (ed.) (1981a) *The Movie Star*, Harmondsworth: Penguin.

—— (1981b) *The National Society of Film Critics on the Movie Star*, New York: Viking Press.

Weiss, A. (1991) *Vampires and Violets: Lesbians in the Cinema*, London: Unwin Hyman.

Wexman, V. W. (1979) 'Kinesics and film acting: Humphrey Bogart in *The Maltese Falcon* and *The Big Sleep*', *The Journal of Popular Film and Television*, 7, 1.

Whitaker, J. (1981) 'Hollywood transformed: interviews with lesbian viewers', *Jump*

Cut, 24/5. Reprinted in P. Steven (ed.) (1985) *Jump Cut: Hollywood, Politics and Counter-Cinema*, New York: Praeger.

Whitaker, S. (1976) 'The rebel hero', in J. Pascall (ed.) *Hollywood and the Great Movie Stars*, London: Phoebus.

White, A. (1984) 'White on black', *Film Comment*, 20, 6, November/December. On the lack of films about black experiences, starring black actors.

Wilson, G. (1966) *A History of American Acting*, Bloomington, Ind: Indiana University Press.

Winokur, M. (1987) 'Improbable ethnic hero: William Powell and the transformation of ethnic Hollywood', *Cinema Journal*, 27, 1, Fall.

Wlaschin, K. (1979) *The Illustrated Encyclopedia of the World's Great Movie Stars and their Films*, London: Salamander Books.

Wood, R. (1976) 'Acting up', *Film Comment*, 12, 2, March/April.

—— (1978) 'Venus de Marlene', *Film Comment*, 12, 2, March/April.

Woodhouse, B. 'Stars in their courses', in *From Script to Screen*, London: Winchester Publications. On the British film industry.

Yacowar, M. (1979) 'An aesthetic defense of the star system', *Quarterly Review of Film Studies*, 4, 1, Winter.

—— (1980) 'Actors as conventions in the films of Robert Altman', *Cinema Journal*, 20, 1, Fall.

Zolotow, Maurice (1961) *Marilyn Monroe, An Uncensored Biography*, London: W. H. Allen.

INDEX

Note: *Illustrations are shown by bold figures*

Adorno, T.W. 183
Adrian, Gilbert 35, 89, 91; and Crawford 77, 80–1, 83, 86–7, 90
Affron, Charles 205
Alberoni, F. 57
Aldrich, Robert 193–4, 235
Alexander, Karen viii; on black women xiv, 45–54
Allen, Robert C. 9, 20
Alloway, Lawrence 211, 216
Allyson, June 143
Althusser, Louis 260
American Aristocracy 58
American, The 58
American Werewolf in London, An 306–7
Amos and Andy 37
Amy! 147
Andrews, Eamonn 257
Angaaray 128
Angel Heart 52
Anger, Kenneth 280
Anna Christie 206
Anna Karenina 198–9
Any Wednesday 240
Arthur, C.J. 200
Arzner, Dorothy 279
Astaire, Fred 37, 38, 311–12
Auer, Mischa 204
Autry, Gene 202
Awaara 120
Ayres, Agnes 272

Bacall, Lauren 187
Bakhtin, M.M. 201
Balazs, Bela 210–11
Baldwin, James 47, 52
Banky, Vilma 271

Barbarella 237, 240, 241, 244–5
Bardot, Brigitte 240
Barefoot in the Park 240
Barney, Natalie 291
Barron, Steve 302
Barrymore, Ethel 37
Barrymore, John 275
Bartet, Mme 22
Barthelmess, Richard 275
Barthes, Roland: on commutation 184; on faces 276, 313; on Oedipus 268; on singing 300, 314
Baxter, Warner 31–2
Belafonte, Harry **46**, 48
Belasco, David 8, 9, 22, 221
Belle du Jour 193
Belloc-Lowndes, Marie 89
Belmondo, Jean-Paul 186
Benegal (film-maker) 124
Benny, Jack 37
Bergman, Ingrid 40, 174
Bernhardt, Sarah **13**, 14, **23**
Bernheim, Alfred L. 8, 14–15
Berry, John 48
Best Years of Our Lives, The 104
Beyond the Forest 200, 201
Beyond the Rocks 282
Bhatt, B. 111
Bhavni Bhavai 128
Bhumika **124**
Big Knife, The 235
Big Store, The 39
Bilbow, Marjorie 188–9
Binford, Lloyd T. 49
Birth of a Nation 49, 276
Blackton, J. Stuart 5, 11
Blonde Venus 292
Blood Money 293

Blood and Sand **262**, 263, 265, 266, 276–7, 279, 281
Blum, Richard 222, 224
Bogart, Humphrey 187, 205, 215–16, 226
Bonet, Lisa 52, 53
Borgnine, Ernest 176
Bourget, Jean Loup 207
Bowie, David 303, 314
Brady, Robert 178
Brando, Marlon 59, 179, **223**, 224, 225
Brecht, Bertolt 183, 195
Brenninkmeyer, Ingrid 84
Bride Wore Red, The 86, 91
Briscoe, Lottie 26
Britton, Andrew 207, 208, 209, 225, 289; on stars and genre xvi, 198–206
Broken Bath, The 4
Brooks, Peter 208–18 *passim*, 226
Brooks, Romaine 291
Brooks, Shirley 302
Brophy, Philip 306–7
Brückner, Jutta 279
Bunny, John 24
Buñuel, Luis 193–4, 234
Business as Usual 52

Cabin in the Sky 50, **51**
Cagney, James 136–7, 215, 226
Caine, Marti 258
Calamity Jane 149
Camel Thru a Needle's Eye 34
Camille 13, 90–1
Cantor, Eddie 37
Capra, Frank 104, 106
Captive, The 293
Carillo, Leo 31
Carmen Jones **46**, 47, 48
Carpenter, John 306
Carstairs, Jo 283
Carter, Angela 310
Casablanca 205
Cat Ballou 240
Chained 90, 91
Chakra 125, 127
Chambers, Iain 305
Chaney, Lon 311
Chaplin, Charlie 112, 313
Chapman, Tracy 52–3, 54
Chapman Report 240
Chase, The 240
China Syndrome, The 247

Choirboys, The 197
Christopher Strong 75, 293
Citizen Kane 184, 234, 278
Clift, Montgomery 224, 225
Cobbler and the Millionaire, The 21
Colbert, Claudette 35
Coma 212
Coming Home 238, 247
Company of Wolves 310
Coogan, Jackie 62
Cook, David A. 3
Cook Jr, Elisha 176
Cooke, Alistair 58
Coomes, Carol **94–5**, 96
Cooper, Alice 314
Cooper, Gay 185, 202, 224, **284–5**, 287
Cooper, Tommy xvii, 252–5, 257
Cosby Show, The 52
Cousins, Les 187
Crawford, Joan xv, 35, 135–6; autonomy 178; and fashion 74, 77–8, **79**, 80–1, 83–4, **85**, 86, 89; identification with 143, 150, 152, 154; and melodrama 207
Crawford, Michael 256
Cripps, Thomas 49
Crompton, Frank 256
Crosby, Bing 37
Cukor, George 138, 296

d'Acosta, Mercedes 283, 286
Dancing Lady 86, 91
Dandridge, Dorthy **46**, 47–9, 51–2, 53
Dark Victory 155
Darnell, Linda 205
Dastur, Firoz 113
Davis, Bette 31, 35, 38; autonomy 178; and genre 201–2, 203, 206; identification with 143, 145, 150–6 *passim*; and melodrama 212
Davis, Katharine B. 299
Dawson, Les 253, 256
Day, Doris 238, 286; de-radicalising characters 249; identification with 149, 151, 154, 155, 156; image 174
de Havilland, Olivia 143
De Niro, Robert 176–7
Dean, James 59, 215, 224, 226
deCordova, Richard viii, 14; on star system xiv, 17–29
Delsarte, François 221
Demetrius and the Gladiators 158

DeMille, Cecil 33
Deneuve, Catharine 191–4, 197, 240
Denison, Jack 49
Denner, Charles 189
Destry Rides Again 203–4, 205
Devi, Phoolan 116
Diamond Queen 111, **112**
Dietrich, Marlene xvii, 75; and genre
    202, 203–4, 205; and lesbianism 283,
    284–5, 286–7, 291, 292, 295, 299; as
    'ultimate fetish' 143
DiMaggio, Joe 43
Dinner at Eight 36, 39
Doane, Mary Ann 266, 280, 290
Dodd, Claire 31
Doll's House, The 244, 247
Dors, Diana xvii, 252, 253–5, 257–8
Douglas, Kirk 212, 216
Drunkard, The 211–12
Durbin, Deanna 145, 151, 157
Dutt, Guru 119
Dutt, Nargis xv, 110
Dutt, Sunil 120, **122**
Duvall, Robert, 179
Dyer, Richard viii, 142, 177; on
    audience 141; on authenticity xii, xv,
    132–40, 218, 222, 225; on charisma
    xv, 57–9, 217; on genre 198–9, 202;
    on history of stardom 213; on
    homosexuality and lesbianism 144,
    288; on male nudity 282; on
    meanings and values 215–17; on
    melodrama 213, 215–16, 226; on
    novelistic hero 208; on political stars
    243; on polysemic stars 248–9; on
    publicity 249; on 'rebel types' 238;
    on selection of meaning 287; on star
    image 174–5

Eagle, The 267, 269
Eastwood, Clint 60, 202, 212, 226
Easy Rider 238
Eaton, Walter Prichard 22
Eckert, Charles viii, xv; on
    consumerism xiv, 30–9, 88; on Shirley
    Temple xv, 60–73
Einfeld, Charles 31, 32
Einfeld, F.D.R. 32
Eisenstein, Sergei 58, 97
Ekman, Paul 196
Electric Horseman, The 247
Elizabeth II, Queen 43, 75

Elliott, Sam 53
Ellis, Havelock 292
Ellis, John 217, 218–19
Elsaesser, Thomas 208, 210, 217, 225
Evans, Mary *see* Nadia

Fairbanks, Douglas 58, 112, 275
Farrell, Glenda 31, 75
Fatal Beauty 53
Fidler, Jimmie 37
Fields, Sylvia 34
Fields, W.C. 256
First a Girl 293
First Lady 35
Fiske, Mr 8
Fiske, Mrs 6, 8, 9, 14
Flying Ranee 115
Fonda, Henry 202, 238
Fonda, Jane xvii, 237–50
Fonda, Peter 238
Fontaine, Joan 48
Fontaine, Lynne 34
For Better, For Worse 33
Ford, John xii, 187, 194
Forsyth, Bruce 256
42nd Street 31, 32
Foster, Preston 31
Foucault, Michel 169, 274
Four Horsemen of the Apocalyspe, The
    261, 276, 279
Francis (star) 38
Frede 283
Freeman, Wilma 36
Freud, S./Freudianism 73; on animals
    and sexuality 315; on death drive
    279; on drives 263; on identification
    146; on lesbianism 292; and Method
    224; psychoanalysis 221, 224; on
    sadomasochism 270–1
Friedan, Betty 58
Friedburg, Anne 146, 147
Friesen, Wallace V. 196
Frohman, Charles 9
Frost, David 254

Gabor, Zsa Zsa 249
Gaines, Jane Marie viii, 143; on fashion
    xv, 74–91
Gandhi, Indira 116, 120, **122**
Gandhiol, Kawal **129**
Gandhy, Behroze viii; on Indian stars
    xi, xv, 107–31
Garbo, Greta xvii; face as mask 313;

and fashion 77, 78; and genre 198–9, 202, 203–4, 206; and lesbianism 283, 286–92 *passim*, 294, **295**, 298
Gardner, Ava 47, 51, 187, **189**
Garland, Judy; identification with 143, 144; as star 132–3, 137–9; death 255
Gaynor, Janet: lookalikes 34, 35
George, Boy 314
Giannini, A.P. 30
Gielgud, Sir John 169
Gifford, Walter S. 63–4, 66, 67
Gilbert, John 286
Gilda 142
Giraldi, Bob 302
Gledhill, Christine viii; on melodrama 207–29
Glyn, Elinor 275, 282
Go Into Your Dance 36
Godard, Jean-Luc 244
Goddard, Paulette 38
Gold Diggers of 1935 36
Goldberg, Whoopi 52, 53, 54
Gone with the Wind 50, 143
Good, the Bad and the Ugly, The 187
Goodwin (star) 14
Goose and the Gander, The 36
Gorin, Jean Pierre 244
Grable, Betty 151, 153, 154
Gramsci, A. 245
Grand Hotel 86
Grant, Cary 185
Grau, Robert 6
Griffith, D.W. 5
Grimes, Karolyn **94–5**, 96
Gunning, Tom 280

Hackett, James K. 14
Hagman, Larry 179–80
Hall, Radclyffe 293
Halle, M. 186
Hallelujah 50
Halloween 306–7
Hampton, Benjamin B. 3, 6, 8, 14
Jansen, Miriam viii; on Rudolph Valentino xvi, 259–82
Harlequin 256
Harlow, Jean 36, 38
Harris, Julie 225
Harris, Thomas: on Grace Kelly and Marilyn Monroe xiv, 40–4
Hart, William S. 60, 275
Harvey, Sir Martin **222**

Haskell, Molly xiii, 38, 54, 142–3
Haskins, J. 49, 50
Hawkins, Jimmy **94–5**, 96
Hawkins (singer) 314
Hayes, Helen 37
Hayward, Susan **158**
Hayworth, Rita 47; identification with 142, 150–1, 157
Head, Edith 35, 87, 89
Hearts in Dixie 50
Heath, Stephen 174, 175, 268
Heilman, Robert 210, 217
Hemingway, Margaux 191–2
Henry, Lenny 251
Hepburn, Katharine xvii; face as mask 313; and fashion 75; and genre 202, 203–4, 205, 206; identification with 143, 145, 151; and lesbianism and androgyny 286, 291, 293–5, **296**, 297; and melodrama 207
Herzog, Charlotte Cornelia ix; on fashion xv, 74–91
Heston, Charlton xvi, 212, 233–4
Hiroshima mon amour 234
His Picture in the Papers 58
Hitchcock, Alfred 143, 185, 203
Hjelmslev 184
Holland, Mildred 11, **12**
Holliday, Billie 52
Holliday, Judy 286
Hoover, Herbert 62–3, 68, 69, 72
Hope, Bob 256
Hopkins, Miriam 34
Horne, Lena 48, 50, **51**, 52
Howard, Leslie 37
Howerd, Frankie 251
Hulda from Holland 18
Hull, Edith Maude 269, 271
Hunter, Kim 225
Hunter-wali 111
Hurrell, George 89, 90
Hurrican Special 115
Hurry Sundown 240
Hustle 193
Hutton, Betty 85

I Could Go on Singing 137
I Walk Alone 216
I Was a Teenage Frankenstein 308
I Was a Teenage Werewolf 308
In Caliente 36
Innescourt, Frieda 34

Irving, Henry 211
Island in the Sun 48
It's a Wonderful Life 93, **94–5**, 96–7, 104–5, 106

Jackson Five 45, 300
Jackson, Michael xi, xviii, 300–16
Jacobs, Lewis 3, 5, 6
Jagger, Mick 314
Jakobson, R. 186
James, Anthony 288
James, Clive 251
Jennings 137
Jezebel 143
Jhansi ki Rani 116
Johnson, Arthur **25**
Johnson, Grady 43
Jolson, Al 37
Jones, Quincy 306
Jordan, Neil 310
Juarez 176
Julia 247
Jumping Jack Flash 53

Kaplan, E. Ann 261, 297
Kapoor, Raj 119, 120
Karloff, Boris 202
Karpenstein; Christa 264–5
Kazan, Elia 224–5
Keaton, Diane 189–90
Keene, Vincent 144
Kelly, Grace 41, 42, 43–4, 187, **188**
Kerr, Walter 224
Kerrison, Ray 242
Khan, Mehboob 117, 119–20
King, Barry ix, 224; on articulation of stardom xvi, 167–82
Kirkland, Murial 34
Klingender, F.D. 61
Klute 238, 246
Koppelman, Roberta 75, **77**
Krafft-Ebbing, Richard von 292

La Plante, Laura 31
Lacan xiii, 146, 260, 266, 280
Lady for a Day 75
Lady from Shanghai, The 143
Lady Sings the Blues 52
Laemmle, Carl 3, 10, 97
Laing, Dave 303
Lal-e-Yaman 113
Lamarr, Hedy 38
Lamas, Fernando 233

Lambert, Albert 22
Lamour, Dorothy 85
Lancaster, Burt 216
Landis, John 306
Lang, Fritz 234, 235
Lawrence, Florence 3, 5, **25**, 97
Le Sueur, Lucille 135
Lee, Lila 262
Leeming, Jan 251
Legge, S. 61
Leigh, Vivien 143, 184
Lelauney, Monsieur 22
Lemaître, Jules 22
Lessing, Frank 25–6
Letter to Jane 244
Letty Lynton dress 74–5, 78, **79**, 80–1, 83, **85**, 88–90
Lewin, David, 240
Lewis, Jerry 256
Lion and the Mouse, The 14
Lombard, Carole 38
Looking for Mr Goodbar 188–90
Lord, Pauline 34
Losey, Joseph 233, 235, 244
Louise, Anita 35
Lowenthal, Leo 40
Loy, Myrna 38
Lugosi, Bella 202
Lumière, Sidney 108
Lupino, Ida 235
Lusted, David ix; on personality xi, xvii, 251–8
Lymon, Frankie 306

McArthur, Benjamin 214
McArthur, Colin 211, 212, 215–16, 217
McCartney, Paul 303
McDonald, Jeanette 37
Macherey, Pierre 8
MacKaye, Steele 221
Mahogany 52
Making of Michael Jackson's Thriller, The 312
Malaga 48
Malden, Karl 234
Mamoulian, Rouben 288–9
Man who Loved Women, The 188
Man who Shot Liberty Vallance, The 187
Manhattan Madness 58
Mankiewicz, Joseph 86–7
Mann, Anthony 194, 203

Mannequin 86, 90, 91
Mansfield, Richard 9, 26
Manthan 125
Margie 200
Marion, Frances 279
Marlowe, Julia 9
Marx, K./Marxism 73, 134, 136; on genre 199–200; on money, role of 71; on 'social hieroglyph' 302
Mason, James 48, 137, 138, 235
Mathis, June 279
Mature, Victor 194–5
Mayer, J.P. 59
Mayer, Louis B. 61
Mayerling 193
Medvedev, P.N. 201
Mehta, Ketan 128
Menjou, Adolfe 66
Mercer, Kobena ix; on Michael Jackson xi, xviii, 300–16
Metz, Christian 146, 266, 280
Meyers, Ruby 109
Mildred Pierce 178
Miles, Vera 183–4
Miller, Arthur 43
Mills, Earl 47
Miranda, Carmen 157
Mirch Masala 128
Miss Frontier Mail 115
Mistry, B. 111
Mitchell, Thomas **94–5**, 96
Mix, Tom 31
Mizoguchi 235
Mogambo 187, **188–9**
Molière 289
Mona Lisa 52
Monroe, Marilyn: and genre 198; identification with 145, 156; image 41–4, 47, 53, 58, 212, 215, 217, 249
Monsieur Beaucaire **268**, 269, 276
Moore, Dennie 297
Moore, Phil 48
Moran of the Lady Letty 267, 281–2
Morecambe, Eric xvii, 252–7
Morgan, J.P. 61, 69, 71
Morin, Edgar 59, 170
Morin, Pilar 10
Morning Glory 205
Morocco **284–5**, 286–7, 291–5 *passim*, 297, 299
Morrison, Marion *see* Wayne
Morrison, Van 306

Mother India 110, **117**, 118, 120–3
Mouj 111–12
Mounet, Paul 22
Mourlet, Michel 213; on violence xvi, 233–6
Mr Smith Goes to Washington 97
Mulvey, Laura 143, 147, 260–1, 263, 291
Muni, Paul 176
Mugabala 111
My Darling Clementine 194–5, 205
My Gal Sal 150

Nadia xv, 110–11, **112**, 113–16, 121
Naldi, Nita 262
Naremore, James 221, 224
Nargis 116, **117**, 118–23
Nazimova, Alla 279
Neal, Patricia 225
Niagara 156
Nicholas, Harold 47
Nida, Eugene A. 196
Night at the Ritz, A 36
Night of the Living Dead 306–7
Nine to Five 247
Ninotchka 203
No More Ladies 83
Northrup, Harry S. 27
Novak, Kim 183–4
Now, Voyager 202, 205–6, 212
Nureyev, Rudolph 278

Oakie, Jackie 37
Oberon, Merle 184
Olivier, Sir Lawrence 169
O'Neill, James 14
Only Way, The **222**
Orry-Kelly (designer) 35, 75, 89
Osbourne, Ozzy 314
Osmond, Donny 300
Our Blushing Brides 86, 90, 91

Palance, Jack 233
Palcy, Euzhan 54
Parkinson, Michael 254
Partington, Angela 143
Patalas, Enno 279
Patel, Jabbar 125
Patil, Smita xv, 123, **124**, 125–8, **129**, 130
Peirce, C.S. 135, 172
Perils of Pauline, The 111
Period of Adjustment 240

Perkins, Anthony 225
Perkins, Tessa: on Jane Fonda xvii, 237–50
Peters, Michael 311
Phalke, D. 108
Phantom of the Opera, The 311
Philadelphia Story, The 203
Pickford, Mary **5**, 6, 10, **18**, 29, 37, 281
Plunkett, Walter 35
Porgy and Bess 48
Possessed 86
Potemkin 97
Powell, Dick 32
Preminger, Otto 48
Presley, Elvis 59, 280
Price, Vincent 305–6, 311
Prince 303
Punchinello 256

Queen Christina 202, 206; and lesbianism 288–94 *passim*, **295**, 297–8

Raging Bull 177
Rainier, Prince 43
Raja Harischandra 108
Rama Rao, N.T. 107
Rambova, Natasha 270, 279
Rando, Flavia 291
Ray, Nicholas 224, 227, 234–6
Ray, Satyajit 120
Rebel Without a Cause 226–7
Reed, Donna **94–5**, 96
Reggie Mixes In 58
Rehan, Ada 9
Réjane (star) 13, 14
Return of Ulysses, The 22
Reynolds, Burt 193
Rich, Irene 37
Richie, Lionel 303
Rio Bravo 194
Roberts, Susan 221
Robinson, Edward G. 37, 215, 226
Rockefeller family 30, 61, 72
Rocky II 148
Rogers, Buddy 34
Rogers, Roy 202
Roland, Ruth 112
Romero, George 306
Roosevelt, Franklin Delano 31, 64–5, 68, 69
Rose, Helen 77–8
Rosen 38
Rosencratz, Linda 194

Ross, Diana 45, 52, 301
Rourke, Mickey 52
Royer (designer) 35
Russell, Jane 38, 203
Russell, Ken 278, 281
Russo, Vito 287, 288, 297

Sadie McGee 86, 91
Sans-gène 13
Sarris, Andrew 184
Saville, Jimmy 251
Schiaparelli, Elsa 83
Scott, Selina 254
Sennett, Richard 133
Serpent and the Rainbow, The 52
Sethi, Rajiv 128
Seymour (columnist) 83
Shahani, Kumar 129
Shakespeare, William 169
Shakti 127
Shanghai Express 205
Shantaram, V. 119
Shaw, Sandra 293
Shearer, Norma 34, 35, 75, 77, 78
Sheik, The 267, 269–70, 272
Shils, E.A. 57
Shootist, The 194, 195
Showboat 51
Siegel, Don 194
Sippy, Ramesh 127
Skinner, Otis 9
Slide, Anthony, 6, 8
Smith, Madeleine 89
Smith-Rosenberg, Carroll 290, 292–3, 296–7
Smoodin, Eric 19
Son of the Sheik, The 271–2, **273**, 274
Sontag, Susan 314
Sothern, E.S. 9
Spacks, Patricia Meyer 283
Sparrows 281
Speed that Kills, The 39
Stacey, Jackie ix; on identification xiii, xv, 141–63
Stagecoach 205
Stanislavski, Constantin 221–2
Stanwyck, Barbara 38, 145, 202
Star is Born, A 132, 135, 137–9
Steiger, Rod 225
Stendhal 233
Sternberg, Josef von 143, 286
Stevenson, Edward 35

Stewart, James: and genre 202, 203; in pair with Wayne 186–7, 194–5; return of 93, **94–5**, 96–7, 104, 106
Stormy Weather 50
Strange Interlude 75
Strangers on a Train 185
Strasberg, Lee 221–4
Streetcar Named Desire, A **223**
Stroyberg, Annette 240
Sunday in New York 237
Sweeney, The 252
Sykes, Eric 252
Sylvia Scarlett 291, 293, 294, **296**, 297

Talbot, Lyle 31
Taliaferro, Mabel 11
Tall Story 239
Tamango 48
Tarang **129**, 130
Taylor, Elizabeth 47
Taylor, Helen 143
Teenage Monster 308
Teenage Zombie 308
Temperton, Rod 304, 305, 306
Temple, Julien 303
Temple, Shirley xv, 60–73, 92, 183
They Shoot Horses Don't They 238, 241
Thomas, Rosie ix; on Indian stars xi, xv, 107–31
Thompson, John O. ix; on acting and commutation test xvi, 183–97
Thomson, David 183, 184
Thriller xi, xviii, 300–16
Time-Lock Safe, The 4
Toofan Mail films 115
Tout va bien 244
Tracy, Spencer 184, 224
Trubetzkoy, Nikolay 184
Truffaut, François 54, 188
Truman, Harry 120
Tudor, Andrew 59
Turner, Florence 6, 10
Turner, Lana 38, 85
Turpin, Ben 6
Tyson, Cathy 52, 53

Udall (linguist) 184
Ugrin, Tony 66
Ullman, Tracey 251
Umbartha 125

Vadim, Roger 240, 242–3
Valentino, Rudolph xvi, 259–82, **262**, **267–8**, **273**
Valentino 278, 281
Vallee, Rudy 37
Vardac, Nicholas 211, 214
Vaughan, Frankie 251
Vertigo 183, 184
Vicious, Sid 255
Vidor, King 201
Viertel, Salka 286, 289
Viktor/Viktoria 293

Wadia, Homi 113–14
Wadia, Jamshed B.H. 112–13, 114
Wadkar, Hansa 124
Wagner, Robert 233
Waldman, Bernard, 34, 88
Waldoff, Claire 283
Walk on the Wild Side 239
Walker, Alice 54
Walkerdine, Valerie 148
Wallach, Eli 225
Walsh, Raoul 234, 235
Warner, Jack 61, 176
Warriors, The 302
Waterman, Dennis 251
Wayne, John xii, 135; and genre 198, 202, 205; and linguistics 186; and melodrama 224; in pair with Stewart 186–7, 194–5
Weber, Max xv, 57, 58
Weiss, Andrea ix–x; on lesbian spectator xvii, 283–99
Weld, Tuesday 190
Welles, Orson 234
West, Mae 277
West Side Story 302
White, Pearl 6, 111, 112
Why Change Your Wife 33
Widmark, Richard 212
Willemen, Paul 215
Williams, Linda 274, 281
Williamson, Judith 191–2, 197
Winfrey, Oprah 54
Wing, Toby 31
Wise, Ernie 254
Wiz, The 52, 304
Wizard of Oz, The 183; black version of 304
Wolfe, Charles x; on publicity photographs xv, 92–106

Women, The 86, 90
Wood, Robin 199, 204
Woolf, Virginia 297
Wrong Man, The 184
Wuthering Heights 184
Wyler, William 184

Wyman, Jane 155

Yield to the Night 252
Young, Loretta 34, 38
Young, Owen D. 63–4, 66, 67
Young, Terence 193